BACKFIRE

CENTER ON GLOBAL ENERGY POLICY SERIES

BACKFIRE

HOW SANCTIONS RESHAPE THE WORLD AGAINST U.S. INTERESTS

AGATHE DEMARAIS

Columbia University Press
New York

9293

Columbia University Press
Publishers Since 1893
New York   Chichester, West Sussex
cup.columbia.edu

Library of Congress Cataloging-in-Publication Data
are available from the Library of Congress
ISBN 978-0-231-19990-9 (hardback)
ISBN 978-0-231-55333-9 (ebook)

LCCN 2022015745

Columbia University Press books are printed on permanent and
durable acid-free paper.
Printed in the United States of America

Cover design: Milenda Nan Ok Lee
Cover image: welcomeinside / © Shutterstock

TO MY GRANDPARENTS

CONTENTS

PREFACE

I n 2002 a brutal civil war was raging in Sudan. In an attempt to force
Khartoum to start peace talks with the opposition, members of the
U.S. Congress discussed imposing sanctions on energy firms working in the African country. The reasoning of the American lawmakers
was simple: the threat of sanctions might be sufficient to persuade the
Sudanese government, anxious to avoid an exodus of foreign businesses
from Khartoum, to negotiate with the rebels. Congress decided that the
best way to pile the pressure on Sudan's rulers was to impose innovative measures preventing the global oil companies that did business with
Sudan from raising capital on U.S. financial markets.[1]

The U.S. administration fiercely opposed Congress's proposal, fearing that such sanctions would ultimately hurt America. They would
in any case have been largely symbolic; amid the devastation brought
by the conflict, only three companies—from Canada, China, and
Sweden—were still operating in Khartoum. Yet barring foreign businesses from tapping U.S. financial markets appeared to run counter to
Washington's long-held commitment to the free movement of capital,
one of the ingredients of America's economic success. Skeptics pointed
out that to escape American sanctions, multinationals could also be
tempted to raise debt or issue stocks in other financial centers such as

London, Singapore, or Tokyo. It looked like Washington was going to shoot itself in the foot. In the end, Congress shelved its proposal.

The controversy over the Sudan sanctions started a debate about sanctions overreach. Since then, the discussion has never stopped. It has become even more intense in recent years as coercive economic measures, such as trade tariffs, financial sanctions, and export controls, have become the bedrock of U.S. diplomacy. However, trouble is looming. The over-use of sanctions is fueling resentment against Washington around the world, leading U.S. friends and foes alike to rethink their ties to America and find alternative avenues for doing business. This is exactly what critics of the Sudan sanctions had feared.

It is not surprising that sanctions have become so popular over the past two decades: they have many selling points. For one, they are a quick way for the United States to demonstrate resolve and punish bad behavior. After Russia invaded Ukraine in 2022, it took Washington less than two days to impose penalties on Moscow. In addition, sanctions are a low-cost policy. Only a handful of civil servants are needed to draft sanctions. The burden of implementing U.S. sanctions falls on multinationals and banks, which shoulder lost opportunities and compliance costs.[2]

The immediate political and human costs of sanctions also appear to be low, making them more attractive than other forms of coercion, such as military intervention. Sanctions fill the void in the diplomatic space between ineffective declarations and potentially deadly military operations. With sanctions, the U.S. administration can pressure countries to comply with its demands from the safety of Washington. When journalists asked Treasury Secretary Steven Mnuchin what the United States could do to halt Turkey's attack against the Kurds in Syria in 2019, his default response was to invoke sanctions: "We can shut down the Turkish economy."[3]

Finally, U.S. sanctions have proven to be effective in persuading countries to alter their behavior. Iran is a case in point. If sanctions had not put tremendous pressure on the Iranian economy, it is doubtful that Tehran would have ever agreed to sign the 2015 nuclear deal. An added bonus is that sanctions tend to boost the approval ratings of policy makers who impose them.[4] It is therefore not surprising that Congress has long been the most enthusiastic backer of sanctions; politicians have constituents to please, and appearing to act decisively to defend U.S. interests is usually a vote winner.

—————— ☙ ——————

I discovered sanctions while working as a financial attaché for the French Treasury in Moscow in 2014. I had a crash course in sanctions after Russia illegally annexed Crimea and started to back separatist rebels in eastern Ukraine. I continued to develop my knowledge of sanctions in my next posting, at the French embassy in Beirut. From there, I followed economic and financial developments in 15 Middle Eastern countries—including several that were under U.S. sanctions, such as Iran, Iraq, Lebanon, Syria, and Yemen. I spent around half of my time on the ground, having long conversations with government officials, businesspeople, and ordinary citizens about life under sanctions.

I was covering Iran when the nuclear deal was signed in 2015. However, the excitement of seeing this landmark agreement being signed soon gave way to frustration. Despite the lifting of sanctions, European firms remained wary of reentering the Iranian market; they all thought the United States would not stay true to its word and would soon reimpose sanctions on the Islamic republic. This was a problem: getting European companies to return to Iran was the main way of convincing Tehran that it had done the right thing by signing the deal and that it should abide by its terms for the Iranian economy to recover. Yet it proved impossible to persuade most Western firms and banks to start doing business with Iran once again.

The Iranian example shows how the threat—real or perceived—of U.S. sanctions has become a key factor influencing global business strategies. In retrospect, European companies were proved right in their decision not to go back to Tehran; under the Trump presidency, the

United States unilaterally exited the nuclear deal in 2018 and reimposed crippling sanctions on Iran shortly afterward. By then, I had moved to London and joined the Economist Intelligence Unit, where I continue to keep a close eye on sanctions.

Iran's example is not unique. Over the past decade, I have seen first-hand how sanctions have come to play a major role in the lives of millions of people and in companies around the world, both in sanctioned and—importantly—sanctioning countries. This is only part of the story. Sanctions also reshape relations *between* countries and, in turn global geopolitics. Few, if any, foreign policy tools have as big an impact as sanctions. Yet the ripple effects of sanctions remain understudied. In fact, only defense experts appear to have an interest in the side effects of sanctions; they are largely ignored by economists and political scientists.

This book is not for or against sanctions. It does not take a view on whether the United States should resort to sanctions when it feels that its interests are being threatened. However, if it wants to ensure the long-term effectiveness of arguably its most powerful economic weapon, America has to build a clear picture about the side effects of sanctions and of how these shape the strategies of companies, allies, and enemies across the world.

I

SANCTIONS GENESIS

1

FROM EMBARGOES TO SANCTIONS

A Brief History

anctions have become trendy. Newspaper articles regularly discuss the impact of U.S. sanctions on Iran, Russia, or Venezuela. Companies around the world hire teams of lawyers and compliance officers to make sure that their business dealings are sanctions-compliant. Targeted countries boast that they have found inventive ways to circumvent sanctions. Twenty years ago, the man on the street would have been hard pressed to explain the concept of sanctions. Nowadays, most people have a basic understanding of how sanctions work: they inflict economic, financial, and social pain on a country to make it change its behavior.

U.S. sanctions have a global impact. Over the past two decades, America has imposed more sanctions than the European Union, the United Nations, and Canada combined.[1] Nowadays, Washington has around 70 sanctions programs, targeting more than 9,000 individuals, companies, and economic sectors in virtually every country in the world.[2] Some penalties focus on non-state actors, such as Islamist terror groups, Latin American drug cartels, and Syrian warlords. Other programs apply to entire countries, such as Venezuela, Cuba, or North Korea. Iran and Russia are by far the most targeted states, being subjected to thousands of sanctions designations.[3]

The drive to impose coercive economic measures comes from the highest levels of the U.S. government: Treasury Secretary Steven Mnuchin liked to boast that he spent half of his time working on sanctions.[4] Unusually, Mnuchin gave press briefings on the latest sanctions himself, taking dozens of questions from hordes of journalists. Within the Biden administration, the picture is the same; it took Biden only three weeks to sign his first sanctions designations in response to a military coup in Burma.[5] Secretary of State Antony Blinken even wrote a book about sanctions.

The U.S. enthusiasm for sanctions dates back several decades. In the 1990s more than half of the world's population was already under American sanctions.[6] Back then, lobbyists already worried about the "sanctions frenzy,"[7] wondering whether sanctions had become the reflex response for governments confronted with a new problem. In 1998 President Bill Clinton lamented that the United States had become "sanctions happy."[8] He feared that the country was "in danger of looking like we want to sanction everybody who disagrees with us and not help anybody who agrees with us."[9]

The trend has accelerated in recent years. In 2017–2020 the Trump administration put more than 3,900 people and companies under sanctions—reaching an average of almost four sanctions designations every working day.[10] By comparison, President George W. Bush imposed sanctions on 3,484 individuals and entities in eight years.[11] Iran was, by far, Trump's main target; his administration imposed 77 rounds of sanctions on Tehran, or nearly two per month. This was massive, but it pales in comparison with the response of the Biden administration to Russia's invasion of Ukraine in 2022. Only two months after the attack, the United States had imposed penalties on around 1,000 Kremlin-linked individuals, banks and companies.[12]

Sanctions may be in vogue, but they are not new. They date back all the way to the ancient Greek era. In 432 BC Athenian statesman Pericles imposed a blockade against the city of Megaria to protest against the abduction of three women. Fast-forward from ancient Greece, and most historians agree that the first modern-day sanctions were deployed during the Napoleonic Wars of the early nineteenth century. In 1806 French emperor Napoleon imposed an embargo against British trade in an attempt to asphyxiate Britain's economy.

The continental blockade, as it became known, relied on a simple principle. Ships that were coming from Britain could not unload cargo or disembark passengers in French-controlled ports and colonies across the world. Links between Britain and continental Europe were effectively cut, including the mail. Unsurprisingly, the embargo led to a drastic reduction in British trade with Europe. However, this is only part of the story. The British were quick to adapt to the blockade, reorienting trade routes toward the American continent. Britain's efforts to mitigate the impact of the French embargo did not stop here. To circumvent Napoleon's blockade, the British also quietly established smuggling routes to Europe.

British efforts proved successful: despite the French embargo, the total value of British exports rose by more than 20 percent between 1805 and 1810.[13] Amid the economic devastation that the Napoleonic Wars brought across Europe, this was an impressive feat. Unbeknownst to the British, they had just shown that countries under sanctions adapt to evade them or at least to lessen their impact. More than two centuries later, the lesson still holds.

Napoleon's trade embargo against Britain lasted for six years, until the French emperor realized that the blockade was hurting France; customs revenues had dropped, and shopkeepers were left scrambling to find suppliers for products that they used to import from Britain's colonies, such as coffee, cocoa, or sugar. Again, the lesson remains valid. Sanctions do not harm only their intended targets: the measures often cause ripple effects and may incur costs for the country that imposes them, too.

Nowadays, sanctions are a common diplomatic tool for the United States to advance its interests. In their simplest form, modern-day U.S.

sanctions target individuals, freezing the assets that they hold in America. When such people become "designated individuals," their U.S. bank accounts are blocked. Targeted people are also barred from traveling to the United States. Sanctioned individuals often boast about being targeted by American sanctions, as this shows that they are well-connected and powerful at home.

Despite the media hype around a few high-profile cases, such as penalties against Hong Kong's head of state Carrie Lam after a crackdown on free speech or on Russian president Vladimir Putin following Russia's invasion of Ukraine, sanctions against individuals are of limited value. In fact, their purpose is mainly symbolic. The people whom such sanctions target often have a good idea that not all is well in the relations between their home country and the United States. They usually take precautionary measures to hide or move their assets away from America well before they fall under sanctions.

Such preemptive steps are often not needed, anyway. The most common scenario is that targeted individuals have no assets in the United States and no plans to travel to America; they often (rightly) fear that they might encounter serious problems either on U.S. soil or when they return to their home country. For many rogue regimes, travel to the United States is seen as a sure sign that the person in question intends to defect to America and must therefore be "dealt with." This usually does not bode well for the life expectancy of the unfortunate traveler. Thus, these sanctions are theater.

Beyond individual penalties, America's sanctions arsenal includes several other weapons. The most common of them are trade embargoes; financial sanctions (which cut a country's access to the U.S. dollar or to the international banking system); and sectoral penalties (which target specific economic sectors, such as oil production, in a given country). Not all of these tools were available in the 1950s, when the United States started to use sanctions to advance its foreign policy goals. At the time,

Washington's toolkit for economic coercion included only trade embargoes. These represent the best-known and perhaps easiest-to-grasp form of economic sanctions: all trade ties are cut.

The most famous U.S. trade embargo is the one that President Dwight Eisenhower imposed against Cuba in 1960 in response to Cuban leader Fidel Castro's decision to nationalize three American oil refineries. Retaliation against Cuba for the seizure of the plants was not the White House's real objective, however. Eisenhower's main aim was regime change in Havana. The U.S. administration felt uncomfortable about the idea of having a close Soviet ally less than 100 miles from Florida's coastline. For Washington, fostering regime change in Cuba was a top priority before other Latin American nations turned into hotbeds of Communism.

In 1959 the United States represented, by far, Cuba's largest trade partner: American companies absorbed 73 percent of Cuba's exports and provided 70 percent of its imports. The U.S. trade embargo prohibited all commerce across the Florida Strait. In turn, commerce between the United States and Cuba stopped suddenly, leaving the Cuban regime scrambling to find other trade partners to meet its import needs. Given Cuba's reliance on the United States for trade, Washington knew that the embargo would put Havana under tremendous economic pressure. From this perspective, the blockade was a resounding success. According to the United Nations, the embargo has cost Cuba US$130 billion since 1960 (and counting).[14] However, in spite of this tangible economic cost, the U.S. embargo against Cuba has not achieved Washington's desired goal of regime change.

It is hard to assess the effectiveness of sanctions, given that we do not have the counternarrative: no one knows what would have happened if sanctions had not been imposed in the first place. Yet it is hard to find evidence of sanctions-induced changes in Cuba that benefited the United States. The simplest illustration of this: six decades after Castro came to power, Cuba's Communist one-party system remains in place.

The regime's longevity partly reflects Cuba's ability to adapt to the U.S. blockade. After the embargo was imposed, Havana quickly deepened ties with the Soviet Union. Moscow started to buy the sugar that Cuba previously exported to the United States. The Soviets also provided the Cuban regime with much-needed oil after U.S. energy exports to the island stopped. More recently, Cuba started to cultivate relations with China. Nowadays, Beijing is Cuba's largest trade partner, providing Havana with machinery and consumer goods.[15] From this perspective, the Cuban embargo may well have benefited Russia and China. This is ironic, as both countries are among America's main foes.

Havana's enhanced links with Moscow and Beijing are one reason why the Cuban embargo has failed. Another is that America did not manage to persuade its allies to join its blockade of the island; U.S. partners never saw Cuba as a threat to their security. Despite the embargo, Cuba continues to trade freely with other countries; Canada—hardly a U.S. enemy—represents one of Cuba's largest trade partners.[16] The island has commercial links with almost every country around the world, except for the United States, and represents a significant global supplier of nickel and medicines.

Arguably one of the main achievements of the U.S. trade embargo is to have encouraged Cuba to deepen trade ties with nearly every other state across the globe. The American blockade has not succeeded in bringing about any of Washington's stated goals in Cuba. It took the United States several decades to design a more effective form of economic coercion. About 40 years later, North Korea became the testing ground for a new approach to sanctions.

―――― ⸲⸲⸲ ――――

U.S. sanctions against North Korea, which initially took the form of a trade embargo, date back to the Korean War in the early 1950s. Since then, the objective of these penalties—fostering regime change in Pyongyang—has never changed. The U.S. administration has always seen the ruling Kim dynasty as a threat to U.S. national security. The Kims have long been developing missiles that could target American cities. The North Korean regime also sells weapons to terror groups. However, the United States could probably live with all this, given

North Korea's small economic footprint and the country's remoteness from America.

U.S. sanctions against North Korea initially had a mostly symbolic aim: they were a legacy of America's involvement in the Korean conflict. Usefully, they also gave impetus to plans to create a governmental agency in charge of sanctions. In 1950 the newly created, but at the time fairly innocuous, U.S. Treasury's Office of Foreign Assets Control (OFAC) had a single task: administering the embargo against North Korea.

For 50 years, OFAC had little to do in terms of Korea-related work. The embargo was in place, but its day-to-day administration was mostly uneventful. In 2003 that changed abruptly when North Korea withdrew from an international treaty meant to prevent nuclear proliferation. Shortly afterward, the situation became even more alarming: Pyongyang started to conduct nuclear tests. This led the United States to add another, much graver, transgression to the list of North Korea's faults: fostering the proliferation of nuclear weapons. Reflecting a growing aversion to military intervention, the United States and other Western powers chose the sanctions route to pressure Pyongyang to drop its nuclear plans.

Western consensus over the need to keep North Korea in check meant that sanctions against Pyongyang were imposed under the aegis of the United Nations. Their main provisions seek to restrict North Korea's oil imports and coal exports. By curbing the regime's access to energy resources, Western countries hope to slow Pyongyang's ability to develop weapons. Measures that restrict North Korea's ability to export coal—one of the only commodities that the regime produces—follow the same logic. The aim is to squeeze North Korean finances to limit the country's capacity to develop nukes.

The U.S. commitment to a multilateral approach toward North Korea showed that Washington had learned some lessons from the Cuban embargo. Instead of going alone against a rogue regime, as it did with Cuba, the administration worked with allies and the United Nations to implement sanctions against North Korea. This is a key difference. As a result, Pyongyang cannot easily evade U.S. penalties by developing trade ties with other countries. This does not mean that the embargo against

North Korea is working perfectly, however. Even the best-designed trade embargoes can be evaded. This is probably their biggest flaw.

Amid fierce competition, North Korea stands at the top of the global ranking of sanctions busters.[17] In the past 20 years, North Korean smugglers have devised inventive methods to import oil and export coal well above UN-mandated levels. One of the most common techniques involves switching off the real-time tracking devices of ships involved in illegal trade. Vessels whose transponders are turned off do not appear on international tracking systems, allowing them to perform so-called dark voyages.[18] In turn, North Korea's illegal ship-to-ship transfers of oil or coal in the middle of the East China Sea are hard to detect, especially remotely.

If they choose to keep their transponders on to avoid raising suspicions, North Korean smugglers tend to mask the true destination of their ships. They pretend that they are going to African ports, for instance, when they are really sailing to North Korean waters. To arrange where to meet to perform ship-to-ship transfers, crews send each other their coordinates via WeChat, a popular Chinese messaging service. North Korean smugglers do not stop here. They also go as far as changing the aspects of the ships involved in illegal activities. As a result, security agencies struggle to recognize those vessels on satellite images.

In 2018 UN inspectors uncovered a perfect example of a combination of all of these sanctions-busting techniques. They tracked the whereabouts of the *Yuk-Tung*, a ship that had been put under UN sanctions for helping North Korea to import oil illegally.[19] After months of investigation, UN inspectors found that the owners of the *Yuk-Tung* had put in place an elaborate strategy to evade international penalties.

For starters, the smugglers spoofed the ship's identity on international tracking systems. They pretended that the *Yuk-Tung* was a Panama-flagged vessel named *Maika*. The real *Maika* belonged to a legitimate company that had nothing to do with North Korea. On tracking devices, the *Yuk-Tung*'s (illicit) whereabouts became those of the (legitimate)

Maika. Meanwhile, the real *Maika* ship was anchored off Lome, in Africa. Security agencies seeking to track the whereabouts of the *Yuk-Tung* saw the movements of the *Maika* in the Gulf of Guinea.

The smugglers' plans went well beyond spoofing. They forged a false certificate of registry for the *Yuk-Tung* under the name of the *Maika.* The crew of the *Yuk-Tung* also repainted the ship to erase the previous YT logo, replacing the *Yuk-Tung's* international identification number on its stern with that of the *Maika.* The owners of the *Yuk-Tung* had not chosen the *Maika* ship randomly: the *Yuk-Tung* and *Maika* were twin sister ships, built in the same year with similar appearances. Security agencies that detected activity from a ship looking like the *Yuk-Tung*, which UN sanctions barred from sailing, thought that it was the unsanctioned *Maika.*

All of these inventive techniques made it possible for the *Yuk-Tung* to continue to perform illegal ship-to-ship oil transfers off the North Korean coast undetected for several months. The value of these illicit transfers was not trivial: UN inspectors believe that it stood at around US$7.5 million. This may sound like a lot, but the *Yuk-Tung* scheme that the United Nations uncovered only represents the tip of the iceberg. Many other ships have been engaging in similar activities for decades, highlighting how targeted countries adapt to evade trade embargoes.

The ability of the North Korean regime to evade sanctions highlights the flaws of trade embargoes.[20] A first problem is that blockades are extremely difficult to monitor. Sanctioning countries do not have the capacity to inspect all cargo planes and ships sailing around the world. Taking only maritime smuggling into account, there are almost 100,000 cargo ships sailing across international seas.[21] Inspecting all of them once a month would entail 1.2 million inspections per year, that is to say around 3,300 per day across the world's oceans. This would be an impossible feat even if all law enforcement agencies across the world did just that, every day of the year.

Another issue is that most of the time, trade embargoes miss their intended target. They rarely hurt the well-connected elites of rogue regimes. North Korea is a case in point. More than 40 percent of the North Korean population (or more than 10 million people) are undernourished.[22] Nine million North Koreans have no access to basic health facilities. Around 20 percent of North Korean children are stunted as a result of poor nutrition and repeated infections. Meanwhile, the members of the North Korean elite continue to access luxury goods thanks to the networks that Pyongyang has built to evade the UN embargo.

Blockades also impede the activities of humanitarian workers. On paper, embargoes are not meant to complicate the work of aid organizations. However, most international agencies mention sanctions as the first impediment to their activities in rogue countries such as North Korea. A common complaint is that the UN embargo prohibits the export of water-cleaning pumps and food-processing machinery to North Korea, impeding the population's access to clean water and food products.

Faced with this criticism, the United Nations is quick to respond that it is doubtful whether Pyongyang, if it had access to such goods, would use them to increase sanitation and food production. Pumps would likely end up being used to extract water out of illicit coal mines. Food-processing machinery would be dismantled to produce items that the regime believes are more crucial than food for survival, such as nuclear weapons.

This is all true. But on the ground, these rational considerations are of little comfort to humanitarian workers, who fear that the human collateral damage of sanctions is often ignored. The relationships between sanctions "targeters"—U.S. Treasury civil servants who impose penalties—and humanitarian workers are often frosty (at best). Most of the time, the two sides' standpoints look irreconcilable.

───── ⚬⚬⚬ ─────

Conscious of these flaws, in the early 2000s OFAC started to brainstorm about how to replace trade embargoes with something better.

The agency had three objectives in mind. Improved sanctions should be more targeted than blanket trade embargoes, sparing civilians while hurting well-connected elites. Enhanced penalties should prove more difficult to circumvent. And perhaps most important of all, revamped sanctions should hurt rogue regimes more than trade embargoes. With these aims in mind, OFAC started to do some thinking.

In 2003, while OFAC was undertaking these efforts, the agency's targeters detected that an obscure bank in Macau, Banco Delta Asia, was processing vast numbers of transactions for North Korea.[23] The agency felt that it was on to something. With the help of the rest of the intelligence community, OFAC started to dig a little deeper. After a thorough investigation, the pieces of the puzzle that the agency put together were astonishing. For more than 20 years,[24] the North Korean regime had been using networks of banks connected to Banco Delta Asia to conduct illegal business abroad and then repatriate illicit profits to Pyongyang.[25]

OFAC's targeters quickly realized that the sums at stake were huge. North Korea is a major (and probably the most skilled) global player in the forgery of US$100 banknotes. The country also excels at the smuggling of methamphetamine and heroin. In the early 2000s North Korea received around US$500 million per year from its banknote-counterfeiting activities and an additional US$100 million to US$200 million from drug trafficking.[26] The funds served to finance Pyongyang's military ambitions.

OFAC's investigation proved damning. The agency showed that Banco Delta Asia was involved in many of these transactions. The bank represented nothing less than the sole financial conduit between North Korea and the rest of the world. The arrangement between Pyongyang and Banco Delta Asia did not stop here. It also made it possible for North Korea to deposit bags of (counterfeit) cash on Banco Delta Asia's accounts.[27] North Korean smugglers and diplomats were then able to withdraw the money from ATMs anywhere in the world, undetected. In the mind of OFAC analysts, targeting Banco Delta Asia looked like an ideal way to apply pressure on Pyongyang. However, there was a catch: back then, the U.S. sanctions arsenal was limited to trade embargoes.

The agency had not yet invented any coercive measures to use against Banco Delta Asia.

At the time, shortly after 9/11, North Korea was not a top priority for OFAC. The agency was devoting a large share of its resources to tracking the financial transactions of terrorists. It cost Al-Qaeda around US$450,000 to finance 9/11;[28] in the early 2000s the terror group's annual budget stood at around US$30 million. Without access to international financial channels and banks willing to process illegal transactions, financing of terror attacks is difficult and more expensive. OFAC staff soon realized that the same reasoning could apply not only to terror groups but also to countries, such as North Korea.

Why not, OFAC officials thought, target the international bank on which Pyongyang was so dependent to finance its illicit activities? The reasoning went that by severing the ties between Banco Delta Asia and the international banking system, North Korea would not be able to launder and repatriate the proceeds from its illicit business activities abroad. Without cash, the regime would find it harder to finance nuclear weapons and, potentially, to survive. The concept of financial sanctions, which target banking ties, was born. They remain in effect to this day.

———— ∞∞∞ ————

The idea behind financial sanctions is beautifully simple. It is difficult to raise funds, conduct international business, or launder the proceeds from illicit activities without banks. Cash is king, but banknotes are bulky and impractical to carry around. For large amounts of money, wires, and therefore banks to process them, are needed. Instead of imposing trade embargoes that are difficult to enforce and easy to circumvent, the United States decided to go after the banks that process transactions for rogue regimes, starting with Banco Delta Asia.

The United States had no intention of freezing the accounts that North Korea held in Banco Delta Asia. At any rate, the United States had no jurisdiction to do so; for all its might, OFAC remains an American agency, which can freeze only U.S.-held bank accounts. Instead, OFAC chose to ask Banco Delta Asia to make a seemingly simple choice: the

financial institution could either stop conducting business with Pyongyang or be kicked out of the U.S. financial system. Across the world,
bank executives shuddered when they heard that a bank's ties to the U.S.
financial system could be severed: without such access, financial institutions cannot use the U.S. dollar. For banks, this amounts to a death
sentence, given the greenback's global clout.[29]

Undeterred, Banco Delta Asia chose the second option and continued its lucrative activities with Pyongyang (which it denied existed in
the first place). In turn, OFAC targeters imposed financial sanctions
on the bank, barring it from using the U.S. dollar. Rumors of potential
sanctions had previously triggered a run on the financial institution.
By the time Banco Delta Asia was effectively hit by U.S. penalties, its
clients had already withdrawn one-third of their deposits from the
bank's coffers.[30]

This was quite a blow, but OFAC did not stop here. The agency also
got in touch with international banks that used to work with Banco
Delta Asia. U.S. officials warned these banks of the risks of working with
dubious institutions. International banks got the message and started
to think twice before doing business with murky counterparts. Banco
Delta Asia soon became a pariah on the international financial scene
that no reputable financial establishment was willing to work with. A
string of international banks that had previously worked with Banco
Delta Asia on behalf of North Korea closed. (In late 2020 the United
States rescinded the sanctions on Banco Delta Asia.)[31]

Financial sanctions turned out to be much more effective than trade
embargoes in hurting North Korea. Targeting a single bank was all it
took to deal a severe blow to Pyongyang, destroying the sole conduit for
North Korea's international banking transactions. Since then, Pyongyang has refined its sanctions-busting tricks and found other ways to
finance its illegal activities across the globe. But as a North Korean senior
official admitted to a U.S. negotiator shortly after Banco Delta Asia was
hit, "You finally found a way to hurt us."[32] Financial sanctions were born.
They would soon be put to good use against Iran.

2

HITTING WHERE IT HURTS

The Era of Financial Sanctions

The success of the Office of Foreign Assets Control (OFAC) against North Korea proved resounding. By cutting the access of a single bank to the U.S. financial system, the agency dealt a serious blow to Pyongyang. OFAC officials were still celebrating this victory when they received instructions to start going after Iran. Like North Korea, the Islamic regime is high up in the global ranking of rogue countries. Tehran has long been sponsoring global terrorism via Hizbullah, its Lebanese political and military subsidiary. From Washington's perspective, Iran's support for paramilitary groups in Yemen, Syria, and Iraq also represents a threat to the stability of the Middle East.

Yet America's main worry, as in the case of North Korea, centers on Iran's nuclear ambitions. Tehran maintains that its nuclear program has purely civilian purposes, but most experts and Western governments think otherwise: they believe the Islamic regime wants to build a nuclear bomb. If Tehran manages to have nuclear weapons, the Israeli government is convinced that Israel will be wiped off the map. In such a scenario, there is also a distinct risk that other Middle Eastern countries, such as Saudi Arabia, Turkey, or Egypt, will want to become nuclear powers, too. This would undermine Washington's long-standing efforts to curb nuclear proliferation.[1]

Concerns about Iran's nuclear ambitions became especially acute in the early 2000s after a group of Iranian exiles revealed Tehran's clandestine efforts to build nuclear centrifuges.[2] By then, the country had already been the target of U.S. sanctions for more than two decades. In 1979 the Tehran hostage crisis prompted President Jimmy Carter to ban U.S. imports of Iranian oil and to freeze US$12 billion in Iranian assets held in U.S. banks.[3] In the 1980s Washington also imposed an arms embargo on Tehran in response to the Iran-Iraq war.

Tougher sanctions came in the 1990s, when President Bill Clinton imposed a full-fledged trade blockade on Iran to protest against the country's support for Islamist terror groups, such as Hamas in Palestine. The embargo was also a response to early indications that Iran was keen to launch a nuclear program. However, all of these sanctions proved only mildly effective. In the early 2000s Iran's global efforts to sponsor terrorism were only expanding, and so were the country's nuclear ambitions.

To OFAC's frustration, the approach that the agency used against Banco Delta Asia could not work against Iran. Pyongyang has long been a pariah on the global stage. By contrast, Tehran holds the world's largest oil and gas reserves, making Iran a significant player in global energy markets. In the early 2000s the Islamic regime had few ties to the United States as a result of Washington's long-standing trade embargo. However, Tehran had deep commercial relationships with European countries, such as Germany, as well as Middle Eastern neighbors, notably Dubai and Turkey.

As opposed to North Korea, Iran did not rely on a single financial channel to trade with the rest of the world; Tehran maintained links with multiple international banks, including many reputable European and Asian financial institutions. Targeting Banco Delta Asia, an obscure bank in Macau that worked with North Korea, was a reasonable endeavor. By contrast, imposing penalties on dozens of major financial institutions from allied countries was not realistic; such measures would almost certainly trigger a global financial crisis and badly hurt the U.S. economy along the way.

Thwarted, OFAC had another idea: how about going after Iranian banks instead? On paper, such a strategy appeared promising: in doing so, the United States would sever the ties between Iran and the global financial system, thereby choking the Iranian economy and slowing Tehran's nuclear ambitions. The United States had a powerful weapon at its disposal to implement this strategy: the U.S. dollar, which Iran used to conduct international trade and export oil. Like Banco Delta Asia, sanctioned Iranian banks would lose access to the greenback.

Such sanctions came with an added benefit, which made them easier to sell to U.S. policy makers: most of the Iranian banks that OFAC was keen to place under sanctions were also involved in the financing of Hizbullah's global terror operations,[4] such as the attack against American and French military barracks in Lebanon in 1983,[5] the hijacking of TWA Flight 847 in 1985,[6] or the 1992 bombing of the Israeli embassy in Buenos Aires.[7]

The proposed approach sounded good to the U.S. administration, and OFAC was soon busy imposing financial sanctions against Iran's largest banks. In 2006 the agency started with Bank Saderat, which represented the main financial link between Tehran and Hizbullah.[8] In the following months, OFAC added other Iranian banks to the list, including Melli (Iran's largest bank), Mellat, and Sepah.[9] These sanctions cut the access of these banks to global banking channels, making international transactions difficult. The process that eventually culminated in Iran's total financial isolation had started.

The United States had an ulterior motive to impose sanctions against Iranian banks. Washington wanted to send a strong signal to multinationals: the administration was determined to curb Tehran's ability to do business with the rest of the world, and the United States was watching all the transactions—legal or illegal—conducted in Iran. To monitor these transactions, the U.S. Treasury had an ace up its sleeve. OFAC had previously initiated a secret partnership with Swift, the Belgium-based cooperative that provides the infrastructure to process financial wires around the world.[10]

The covert scheme had a simple goal: gathering data on the activities of international companies in Iran. Given the long-standing U.S. embargo on Tehran, these firms could only be non-American ones. The United States maintains it was interested only in operations that could benefit Iranian-sponsored terror groups, such as Hizbullah or Hamas.[11] However, all financial transactions—many of them perfectly legitimate—were recorded. This was not an oversight. U.S. officials had a clear idea of how they could use these troves of data.

U.S. Treasury officials started to pay visits to bankers across the world, showing them that the U.S. Treasury had lists of all the transactions that the bankers' financial institutions had conducted with Iranian businesses. The message was clear: doing business with Iran was dangerous, and the United States was watching. If international banks were caught processing illegal transactions for Tehran, the United States would not hesitate to go after them and cut their access to the U.S. dollar. The subtext was also obvious: ditching all ties with Iran was the safest option. Many Western banks started to think twice before clearing wires involving Iranian companies.

Sanctions against Iranian banks were painful for Tehran. However, their impact was not severe enough to convince the Islamic regime to change tack. In 2012, six years after the United States started to slap sanctions on Iranian financial institutions, Western intelligence agencies were still filing reports about Iran's nuclear ambitions.[12] These developments alarmed Washington, but also European capitals and Israel. The Obama administration decided to act decisively. It threatened to put Swift under sanctions if the institution did not stop doing business with Iran.[13] Swift felt that it had no choice but to oblige, and it cut ties to Tehran. Processing international wires to or from Iran became almost impossible.

———— ◦◦◦ ————

By targeting Iranian banks and cutting Tehran's access to Swift, the United States effectively imposed a financial embargo against Iran. The lack of international banking ties put the Iranian economy under tremendous pressure. Some business transactions with Tehran remained legal despite the sanctions, but in the absence of financial infrastructure to process them, they could not take place. Iran became unable to conduct trade with Western countries. Worse still for Iranian leaders, without access to global banks Iran's ability to export oil—a crucial lifeline for the regime—became severely compromised.[14]

Growth collapsed. Iran's currency, the rial, sank. Inflation shot up to record-high levels. Living standards fell, and basic staples became hard to find in supermarkets.[15] The Iranian leadership had no choice but to acknowledge that sanctions were crippling the economy. Speaking on the topic of sanctions, in 2012 Iran's president Mahmoud Ahmadinejad declared that "The enemy has mobilized all its forces to enforce its decision, and so a hidden war is underway, on a very far-reaching global scale. . . . We should realize that this is a kind of war through which the enemy assumes it can defeat the Iranian nation."[16] Ahmadinejad's tone was pugnacious, but Iran was up against the sanctions wall.

Economic devastation was precisely the point of sanctions. The United States hoped that faced with such difficulties, the Iranian population would start to question whether the government's nuclear ambitions were really worth it. At some point, Washington expected, the Iranian leadership would have no choice but to change tack and abandon its nuclear program in exchange for sanctions relief. The U.S. bet was bold, but it proved to be a winning one.

❦

In 2013 Iranian voters elected Hassan Rouhani, a moderate pragmatist (by Iranian standards), as president. After eight years under the combative Ahmadinejad, this was quite a change. Rouhani's campaign manifesto included two pledges. His first promise was to negotiate a nuclear deal with the United States in return for the lifting of sanctions. His second commitment was that sanctions relief would prompt a swift economic recovery. For the rest of the world, Rouhani's election represented a promising development: it showed that Iranians felt that saving the economy was more important than realizing the leadership's nuclear ambitions.

On the day he took office, Rouhani vowed to put an end to the West's "oppressive sanctions."[17] Yet power in Iran is not fully in the hands of the president. The long-standing supreme leader, Ali Khamenei, is a much more powerful figure than short-lived presidents. At the time, Khamenei had been in power for nearly a quarter of a century. He was present at Rouhani's inauguration. The supreme leader bluntly reminded Rouhani that Iran had to "stand up to arrogance and bullies."[18] Khamenei was clearly talking about the United States. The path to negotiate a nuclear deal did not look straightforward.

Khamenei was a hard-liner, who appeared reluctant to make concessions around Iran's nuclear program. To him, negotiating a deal with Western countries was not only humiliating, but also a waste of time. Given the number of coups that American and British intelligence services are thought to have fomented on Iranian soil since the 1950s, the supreme leader probably believed that he could not trust America and Europe. In Khamenei's view, conflict with the United States also forms part of the regime's identity;[19] as he put it, Tehran "needs enmity with America, the [Islamic] revolution needs enmity with America."[20]

Khamenei's motives for opposing a nuclear deal went beyond politics. Hard-liners like him were close to Iran's Islamic Revolutionary Guard Corps (IRGC), which is officially a branch of Iran's armed forces. However, the IRGC's outreach goes well beyond the military sector. The paramilitary group also controls a large share of the Iranian economy, especially in the energy and construction sectors. Sanctions meant that the numerous companies the IRGC owned faced no competition from international businesses. The IRGC was not keen to see penalties being lifted: the long-sanctioned group was directly benefiting from them.

Khamenei was caught between reformists, who wanted a nuclear deal to save the economy, and hard-liners, who opposed the idea of negotiating with seemingly untrustworthy Western powers. The nuclear program used to be one of the most important items on Iran's policy agenda, even though it was pursued at the expense of economic development. Yet Khamenei soon had little choice but to shift tack. The Iranian economy was in a desperate state, and Iranian voters had expressed their desire to see sanctions lifted. Shortly after Rouhani's election, Khamenei gave Iranian diplomats the green light to negotiate a nuclear deal with Washington.[21]

Secret negotiations with the United States had started in Oman a few months before Rouhani's election. They had not proved constructive, to say the least. Disagreements between Iranian and American negotiators were numerous. The American side thought that Iranian demands were unrealistic, precisely to torpedo the possibility of holding productive talks. Khamenei's change of heart meant that from one day to another, this all changed. Armed with new instructions from Tehran, Iranian negotiators started to accept some limitations on their nuclear program that had previously represented nonstarters. Discussions remained diffi-cult, but at least they became productive.

Two years later, in 2015, Iran and the five permanent members of the UN Security Council signed the nuclear deal with great fanfare. In return for sanctions relief, Iran committed to curbs and checks on its nuclear program. Sanctions enthusiasts rejoiced: in their view, the con-clusion of the nuclear deal demonstrated the effectiveness of sanctions in bringing a rogue country to the negotiating table. To some, sanctions started to look like an almost magical tool to advance U.S. interests. At around the same time, Russia began to threaten Ukraine's territorial integrity. Unsurprisingly, America looked no further than sanctions to send a warning to Russian president Vladimir Putin.

In early 2014, while American and Iranian diplomats were busy nego-tiating a nuclear deal, Russia illegally annexed Crimea and started to back separatist rebels in eastern Ukraine. Moscow's brazen actions caused consternation in Western countries: why was the Kremlin risk-ing war with the West over a small peninsula that Soviet leader Nikita Khrushchev had given Ukraine 60 years earlier? Europe and America felt that they had to act fast to prevent Putin from seizing more of east-ern Europe.[22] Sanctions were in order.

Designing of sanctions entails carefully studying the strengths and weaknesses of their intended target. OFAC had long known that the energy sector represents Russia's greatest asset but also the country's Achilles' heel. Oil and gas extraction represents about one-third of Russia's economy, half of the country's fiscal revenue, and nearly two-thirds of its exports.[23] In turn, the targeting of Russia's energy sector looked like a sure way to deal a fatal blow to the Kremlin.

However, precisely because Russia's oil and gas sector is so big, American and European officials faced a tricky problem: if the United States cut the access of Russian energy firms to the U.S. dollar (possibly via sanctions on these companies or on Russian banks), Moscow would become unable to export hydrocarbons. Without access to Russian oil and gas, power plants and factories in many countries would simply come to a halt.

The imposition of embargoes against Cuba and North Korea, two minor players on the world economic scene, is one thing: the global economy will not suffer one iota. The global footprint of the Iranian economy is not negligible given Tehran's vast energy resources, but it remains limited, too. Going after Russia, which in 2014 was the sixth largest economy in the world and the biggest oil and gas producer, was an entirely different matter. If Western countries did not get their Russia sanctions right, they risked shooting themselves in the foot.

The situation was especially worrying for European governments. The Cold War legacy means that Russia has long been a minor trade partner for the United States; Washington could probably cut all ties with Moscow without doing much harm to the American economy. Europe, by contrast, finds itself in an entirely different situation. Russia is Europe's neighbor, and in 2014 Moscow supplied around one-third of the European Union's energy imports.[24] Sanctions against Russia's oil and gas sector would have been mostly painless for the United States but a catastrophe for the European Union.

This divergence of interests led to heated discussions between Washington and Brussels. The U.S. administration wanted to go hard against Russia, which meant targeting Moscow's oil and gas exports. Such a prospect was alarming for European countries, which pushed for milder penalties during countless (and often seemingly endless) late-night meetings. EU member states also worried that sanctions against Russia's energy exports would cause a spike in global oil prices, which would be damaging for the global economy. In the aftermath of the sovereign debt crisis in the euro zone, this was not a risk that the European Union was willing to take.

Something else in the timing of the crisis made European countries even more nervous. Tense transatlantic discussions to design sanctions against Russia started in the chilly month of February, during the colder winter period, when Europe's energy needs were greatest. The prospect of telling European citizens that they would have to endure several months without heating for the sake of Crimea, a land that few Europeans knew existed before Russia seized it, did not appeal to EU leaders.

Another headache for both the United States and the European Union was that many Western energy companies had a major presence in Russia, providing Moscow with top-notch technology to tap into ever more remote oil and gas fields. Britain's BP, the United States' Exxon, Italy's ENI, and France's Total, among others, had multibillion-dollar projects in Russia. They had no intention of losing their investments and made sure that their governments knew how strongly they opposed sanctions. How many jobs were at stake back home featured heavily in the case against sanctions that executives from these companies made to European governments.

A final hurdle remained. Russia was not Cuba, North Korea, or Iran, which had long been pariah states. In early 2014 Russia was a member of the then-G8 and the G20 as well as an ally for both Europe and, albeit to a lesser extent, the United States in the war on terror. Both sides of the Atlantic wanted to give Putin a face-saving way out to defuse or stop the conflict. After all, preventing the Ukrainian stand-off from escalating further was the very point of sanctions. At any rate, Russia was too big a target: going for stringent sanctions would be devastating for Moscow but also for Washington's European allies. A more nuanced form of sanctions was needed.

——∞∞∞——

The compromise that the United States found to maximize pressure on Russia while preserving Europe's economic interests represented a further refinement of financial sanctions. Instead of imposing blanket penalties on Russian banks, which would have prevented Moscow from exporting oil or gas by cutting their access to the U.S. dollar, Washington adopted a more targeted approach. America went after the three main pillars of the Russian economy: the energy, financial, and military sectors. To do so, OFAC created a new concept: sectoral sanctions. Such penalties target economic sectors, rather than individuals, banks or companies.

The U.S. approach restricted Russia's access to two crucial Western commodities: deep, well-functioning capital markets and technology for the extraction of oil and gas. Some of Russia's largest companies in energy (such as global oil major Rosneft), defense (such as Rosoboronexport, which serves as an intermediary for Russian arms exports), and finance (such as state-owned banks VTB and Sberbank) were barred from raising medium- and long-term debt in the United States—curbing their ability to finance themselves on capital markets. Crucially, however, their access to the greenback was untouched.

The most significant provisions of U.S. sanctions against Russia relate to the energy sector, however. As part of its Russia sanctions package, Washington restricted the ability of American energy companies to explore and produce hydrocarbons in the Arctic region, where most of Russia's untapped oil and gas reserves are located. The sanctions also banned the export of U.S.-made oil-drilling equipment to Russia. The measure was retroactive: even existing contracts had to be canceled.

For Moscow, development of energy fields in the Arctic is crucial: in the long term, these reserves are meant to replace maturing fields in the Urals and Siberia. Exploration of untapped resources in the Arctic is far from easy; energy fields are located deep under the Arctic Ocean, which is frozen for most of the year. To succeed, Russia knows that it needs ample financing as well as Western—and ideally American—technology. By barring Russian energy companies from raising debt in America and making U.S.-made technology off-limits for Moscow, sanctions have dealt a severe blow to Russia's energy sector.

If push comes to shove, Russia should be able to source the financing required from China; in 2016 Chinese banks lent US$12 billion to a Russian-led consortium of energy firms to salvage the US$27 billion Yamal gas megaproject after sanctions complicated its funding.[25] However, over time, securing financing from China might prove increasingly challenging. The financial terms extended by Chinese banks might also prove unattractive, but Russian energy companies will have no other alternatives.

The other challenge for Russia will be to source the required technology. Again, Chinese firms will be only too happy to help, but Chinese supplies might not meet Moscow's needs; Russian energy companies are used to working with Western-made, top-notch equipment, and adapting to other standards might be difficult. The bottom line is clear: by limiting financing options and access to American technology, the sanctions that the United States imposed on Moscow in 2014 will constrain Russia's ability to remain a major player on the global energy scene in the coming decades. For the Russian leadership, this represents an existential threat.

Since 2014 the United States has imposed several rounds of new sanctions against Russia, first in response to Moscow's meddling in the 2016 U.S. presidential election,[26] and then following Russia's invasion of Ukraine in 2022. The US imposed four seemingly stringent penalties after the military assault on Ukraine. It froze Moscow's U.S. dollar-denominated foreign-exchange reserves (a fairly small portion of the country's total reserves) and cut the access of several Russian banks to Swift. Washington also imposed restrictions on Russia's ability to raise sovereign debt (a measure that U.S. Treasury officials had previously opposed).[27] Finally, the Biden administration announced a ban on Russian oil imports. These measures made the headlines, but their impact will probably be limited.

Restrictions on Russia's access to its foreign-exchange reserves will curb the ability of the Russian central bank to prop up the value of the ruble. However, this will not bankrupt the Kremlin; the central bank holds roughly US$300 billion of reserves in renminbi, gold, and other non-Western currencies. Cutting the access of some Russian banks to Swift was a death penalty for these financial institutions, but the vast majority of Russian banks were spared and continued to process international transactions. Preventing Russia from raising sovereign debt will have only a symbolic impact; Moscow's public debt is among the lowest in the world. These penalties probably hurt American investment funds, which held around US$15 billion of Russian sovereign debt before the war, more than they hurt the Kremlin.[28] Finally, the U.S. ban on Russian oil imports was largely immaterial; America imports very little Russian oil.

The lack of bite of the 2022 vintage of U.S. sanctions showed that Washington had already implemented the most robust penalties in 2014, with measures targeting the energy sector being the most powerful U.S. weapon. The U.S.'s strategy has long been one aimed at a slow asphyxiation of the Russian economy. Washington knows that these measures will take decades to yield results, but the consensus among U.S. policy makers is that they will pay off in time. Shortly after dealing with Russia in 2014, OFAC turned to Venezuela. With Caracas the calculation proved entirely different. After some initial hesitation, the United States went for a policy of applying immediate, maximum pressure on Venezuela's financial lifeline.

America's first sanctions against Venezuela date back to the mid-2000s. At the time, Washington's grievances against Caracas were mild. Venezuela was not cooperating with U.S. anti-terror efforts (some Venezuelan individuals had been tied to Hizbullah), and the country served as a base for Colombian drug-traffickers (especially to launder money). A few years later, the Obama administration imposed further sanctions against Caracas, targeting Venezuelan officials in retaliation for human-rights abuses, drug smuggling, and support for international criminal networks. At the time, the White House also banned the export of

U.S.-made military equipment to Venezuela for fear that the authoritarian government of Hugo Chávez would use the gear to crush popular dissent. In truth, these penalties mainly had a symbolic purpose. In the grand scheme of things, Venezuela was simply not a foreign-policy priority for U.S. diplomats.

This all changed in March 2017, when Venezuela started to make international headlines. Supporters of the repressive regime of Chávez's successor, Nicolás Maduro, stripped the opposition-controlled parliament of its powers. International observers and opposition politicians saw this as a coup, and a severe political crisis that resembled a civil war between pro- and anti-government factions followed. On the ground, the human toll was high. Dozens of civilians died in demonstrations calling for free and fair elections.[29]

Five months later protests were still raging, sparking fears in Washington that the situation in Venezuela would spill over across Latin America. President Donald Trump had previously declared that he was not ruling out the military option to confront the Maduro regime.[30] However, sending in U.S. troops appeared risky, and at odds with the president's "America First" isolationist policy. Sanctions, which had by then become a tried and tested diplomatic tool, looked much more appealing. OFAC was put to work to see what form such penalties could take.

The agency's assessment was an easy one to make: Venezuela was nothing short of an economic mess, which left only a few pressure points against which to impose painful sanctions. The oil industry was the only sector that was still in decent shape. This made it look like a perfect target, especially as hydrocarbons were the financial lifeline of the Maduro regime: in 2017 Petróleos de Venezuela (PdVSA; the Venezuelan state-owned oil company) provided Caracas with 60 percent of fiscal income[31] and nearly all of the country's export revenues.[32] PdVSA also represented the regime's only source of hard currency, as the sale of oil was the only activity generating profits in U.S. dollars.

Importantly, OFAC noted that there was little risk that allies would oppose sanctions against PdVSA. Venezuela holds the world's largest reserves of oil, but decades of underinvestment mean that the country is not a major player on global energy markets. Asian and European economies import little hydrocarbons, if any, from Venezuela. This meant potential U.S. sanctions against PdVSA would not represent a problem for U.S. partners. However, there was a catch: at the time, American oil refineries bought one-third of Venezuela's oil exports, making the United States PdVSA's largest market.[33]

It did not take U.S. oil refiners long to grow alarmed about the prospect of sanctions on PdVSA. They had good grounds for objecting and getting a hearing in Washington. In their view, penalties against Venezuela's oil sector would lead to mass layoffs in U.S. refineries and raise domestic fuel costs.[34] Citgo, the eighth largest oil refiner in the United States, was particularly vocal in its opposition to potential sanctions on PdVSA.[35] This was not surprising. The firm is based in Texas, but it is fully owned by PdVSA, that is to say the Venezuelan government. Venezuelan oil is heavy, and thus hard to refine. Citgo had made massive investments to acquire the technology to process Venezuelan crude in giant refineries in Texas, Illinois, and Louisiana.[36] If the United States imposed sanctions on PdVSA, Citgo's survival appeared at stake. Alarmed, the company hired a team of lobbyists to make its case in Washington's corridors of power.

Another potential side effect of potential U.S. sanctions against Venezuela's oil exports soon emerged. It was even more alarming. PdVSA had just taken out a loan from Rosneft, the Russian state-owned oil giant. As collateral, PdVSA had offered 49.9 percent of Citgo's shares.[37] If PdVSA could not export oil anymore, it might default on this loan. In turn, Rosneft could soon own almost nearly half of Citgo's assets, including a wide U.S. network of gasoline stations, three oil refineries, several pipelines, and a few fuel terminals.

Such a scenario posed a myriad of problems. For one, these facilities provided thousands of jobs to U.S. workers. If Rosneft absorbed Citgo, there was a risk that these jobs would vanish overnight. Even more worryingly, Rosneft's largest shareholder is none other than the Kremlin. For the U.S. administration, letting Russia take control of a chunk of U.S. energy infrastructure was a nightmare scenario. It would also have been a public-relations disaster only a few months after Moscow's meddling in the 2016 presidential election. The risk that sanctions against PdVSA would backfire was simply too high. OFAC had to find something else.

—— ⊗⊗⊗ ——

Instead of going for the full-blown option—targeting Venezuela's oil sector—OFAC cut the country's access to international debt markets. As a result, Caracas was effectively barred from issuing sovereign debt in U.S. dollars. In theory, this strategy was a powerful one: it prevented the rollover of existing public debt, raising the chances of a sovereign default. As a government-owned entity, PdVSA was targeted by these restrictions, too. Citgo was also affected; the company was prevented from sending its U.S. profits back to Venezuela. On paper, these measures looked set to asphyxiate the Venezuelan regime financially. Yet sanctions specialists knew that these penalties mainly had a symbolic value.

Venezuela had long been facing problems to raise sovereign debt, and these had nothing to do with sanctions. Financial investors had no appetite for the debt of a rogue regime crippled by decades of chronic economic mismanagement. The interest rate on Venezuela's sovereign debt stood at nearly 30 percent, about ten times the average interest rate recorded in other emerging markets.[38] Despite having massive financing needs, Caracas had been able to tap international debt markets only twice in the year before U.S. penalties were imposed. Sanctions against Venezuela's sovereign debt looked great in theory, but they could not work in practice: the country's access to international debt markets was already nonexistent.

Experts also knew that blocking the repatriation of Citgo's dividends to Venezuela would not make much of a difference for the Maduro regime. Granted, Citgo represented Venezuela's largest and most profitable foreign asset. Before it was hit by sanctions, the U.S. energy firm used to send around US$1 billion in dividends back to Venezuela every year.[39] Every penny was much needed, but Venezuela's fiscal deficit was of an entirely different order of magnitude. It stood at nearly US$30 billion in 2017. Citgo's dividends were petty cash for Caracas.

Venezuela defaulted on its sovereign debt three months after U.S. sanctions were imposed. PdVSA started to miss debt repayments shortly afterward. The U.S. administration officially welcomed these developments, but OFAC officials knew that sanctions did not have much to do with this. Restrictions on PdVSA's oil exports were the only measure that could seriously weaken Caracas. However, U.S. oil refiners were vocally opposed to such penalties. OFAC shelved its files on PdVSA. The agency had to wait for a second chance to go after Venezuela's cash cow. Unbeknownst to American sanctions experts, this would not take long.

In January 2019 Juan Guaido, an opposition politician, declared himself as Venezuela's interim president until free and fair elections could be held. Guaido quickly received the support of the international community. However, Maduro resolutely held on to power. In Washington, the administration started to look for ways to send a powerful signal of its support to Guaido. The United States believed that regime change in Venezuela was possible, if not imminent. To speed up Guaido's installation, the United States looked no further than sanctions.

This time, proponents of sanctions against PdVSA had a solid narrative to offer to whoever would listen. They argued that sanctions against the Venezuelan energy firm would deprive the regime of crucial oil revenue. In their view, this could only accelerate the fall of Maduro's regime and encourage the installation of a Guaido-led administration. The reasoning was hard to resist. It also fitted neatly with the administration's foreign policy priorities, which included regime change in Venezuela. Support for sanctions against PdVSA started to gain traction within Washington.

There was another reason why the administration was more open to targeting PdVSA than had been the case two years before. Since 2018 the United States has been ramping up its domestic oil production and energy exports to historic highs. The rise in U.S. crude production meant that domestic oil refiners could replace Venezuelan oil with crude from the U.S. Gulf coast, something that they could not do back in 2017. From the perspective of the Trump administration, supporting the development of American oil producers could not be a bad idea. After two years of intense lobbying, Citgo's lobbyists lost the battle. The United States put PdVSA under stringent sanctions.

The United States' approach against PdVSA was intended to put Caracas under maximum pressure. Sanctions barred the Venezuelan oil company from exporting oil, including to U.S. refineries. For PdVSA's coffers, this was a catastrophe. American refiners used to pay cash for Venezuelan crude, providing PdVSA with around 70 percent of its cash income. Shipments to other buyers, such as Russia's Rosneft and China's CNPC, were less profitable; they were earmarked as repayment-in-kind for previous loans.[40] Cash from oil shipments to the United States vanished overnight, leaving a hole of US$11 billion in PdVSA's accounts.[41]

U.S. sanctions also cut out PdVSA's access to the U.S. financial system, barring the energy company from using the greenback and further complicating illicit oil exports to buyers willing to ignore U.S. sanctions (in return for a steep rebate). On top of this, U.S. companies that used to provide Venezuela with light crude were forbidden to do so.[42] This was a crucial part of the sanctions package: if it is not diluted with lighter crude, which often came from the United States, Venezuelan oil is so heavy that it cannot flow via pipelines. Without access to American light crude, PdVSA had no choice but to market Venezuelan oil at a discount until the firm could find alternative suppliers.

Even before Washington sanctioned PdVSA, Venezuela's oil production had been cut by half in the space of only two years, owing to chronic mismanagement and underinvestment. U.S. sanctions dealt a further blow to Caracas. U.S. companies stopped buying Venezuelan crude overnight. Most international buyers of Venezuelan oil also ditched their contracts with PdVSA after American diplomats paid them visits to (more or less gently) remind them to comply with U.S. sanctions. For PdVSA, repaying existing debt became difficult. Some analysts predicted that the company would prove unable to meet its financial commitments.

PdVSA's collapse looked possible. Such a scenario appeared to be a welcome development, but it kept some at OFAC awake at night. The agency wanted to make sure that Russia's energy giant Rosneft would not be able to seize Citgo's assets if PdVSA defaulted on its debt. U.S. officials had solid reasons to be worried. The Venezuelan firm had pledged half of Citgo's shares as collateral for a bond due to mature in 2020. PdVSA had used the other half of Citgo's shares to secure a loan from Rosneft. In late 2019 a US$928 million repayment on PdVSA's 2020 bond became overdue.

Creditors were growing impatient. They threatened to go after Citgo—the bond's collateral—to get their money back. If Citgo was dismembered during negotiations with creditors, there was a chance that the Russian oil company could seize the other half of the U.S. oil firm. The risk looked small, but Washington did not want to take any chances. Previous fears that Russia's state-owned oil giant could take control of U.S. energy infrastructure resurfaced. Some senators argued that such a scenario represented a threat to national security.[43]

Under tremendous pressure, the U.S. Treasury imposed a freeze on all transactions related to PdVSA's 2020 bond, effectively preventing investors from seizing half of Citgo to make up for the missed bond repayments.[44] The United States had the power to impose such a ban: the bond was denominated in U.S. dollars. This was another example of how the United States can leverage the greenback to impose its will in business negotiations between private creditors. With the ban in place, Citgo's assets remained off-limits for Rosneft.[45]

In Venezuela, targeting a single company is all that Washington had to do in order to weaken the regime. Cash receipts from PdVSA's oil exports vanished, and Caracas was left scrambling to find other customers for its crude. The regime initially managed to circumvent the penalties, but the United States gradually tightened the sanction screws to target illicit oil exports.[46] By early 2020, PdVSA's crude shipments represented only a fraction of what they used to be.[47]

All is not lost for Caracas. Unsurprisingly, Russia and China have stepped in to help Maduro. The Venezuelan government has also ramped up drug-trafficking and illegal mining activities to replace part of its lost oil revenues.[48] As a result, Maduro remains in power and is able to claim that U.S. sanctions are painless. In late 2020 he even regained control of parliament, the last institution that remained in the hands of the opposition. The reality is different, however. Sanctions will put the regime under tremendous pressure until Maduro gives in and comes to an agreement with the United States. Perhaps he will, or maybe not. In the meantime, Venezuela's prospects appear bleak.

3

HIT AND MISS

Why Sanctions Sometimes Work, but More Often Fail

I n 1969 America's relations with Libya's former ruler Muammar Gaddafi got off on the wrong foot. Shortly after overthrowing King Idris I, Gaddafi nationalized Libya's energy industry and booted U.S. oil companies out of the country. Ten years later, Libya epitomized what a rogue state could look like. Gaddafi's penchant for terrorism and desire to acquire chemical weapons worried Washington.[1] The autocratic ruler also had a tendency to murder his opponents on the streets of European capitals. On top of these assassinations, Gaddafi sponsored terror attacks in Western airports and worked with illegal proliferation networks to try to develop a nuclear arsenal for his country.

Washington saw Tripoli as an immediate threat to American security. In 1979 President Jimmy Carter added Libya to a list of states deemed to sponsor terror, prohibiting the export of U.S. military goods and financial assistance to the country. However, Gaddafi's behavior did not change. Two years later, Libyan fighter jets opened fire on U.S. airplanes involved in a naval exercise over international waters that Gaddafi claimed were Libya's. In retaliation, President Ronald Reagan stepped up pressure: he imposed a ban on Libya's oil exports to America. Washington also prohibited sales of U.S.-made oil and gas equipment to Tripoli. Reagan's strategy was clear: he sought to put maximum pressure on Gaddafi by targeting the powerhouse of the Libyan economy—the energy sector.

Gaddafi did not budge. In April 1986 it became painfully clear to Washington that sanctions had failed to deter the Libyan ruler from using terror attacks as a foreign-policy tool. Libyan intelligence officers planted a bomb in a Berlin disco that was popular among U.S. soldiers, killing three people (including two American servicemen) and injuring another 230. Ten days later, Reagan ordered retaliatory air strikes against Tripoli and Benghazi. Reagan's recourse to military force represented an admission by the White House that the effects of U.S. sanctions had not been severe enough to convince Gaddafi to change tack.

The limited impact of the penalties did not come as a surprise to the administration: Washington was sanctioning Tripoli on its own. European states lamented Gaddafi's behavior, but they did not see Libya as a security threat. In fact, U.S. allies were benefiting from America's row with Gaddafi. Sanctions meant that Tripoli could not export oil to the United States. This was not a problem for Gaddafi, who simply shifted export routes toward European buyers. Sanctions also prevented Libya from importing oil and gas technology from America. Gaddafi did not see this as an issue, either; he started to source such equipment from European companies, which were happy to oblige. The United States knew that sanctions against Libya had no chance of working without the support of European allies. Something had to change to convince Washington's partners to impose penalties on Tripoli, too.

The United States did not have to wait for long. In the late 1980s Libya added bombing of passenger jets to the long list of its murderous foreign-policy tools. Libyan intelligence officers took part in the 1988 bombing of Pan Am Flight 103 over Lockerbie, a small town in Scotland, killing 270 people (including the CIA's deputy station chief in Beirut). One year afterward, Tripoli downed a French airliner, UTA Flight 722, over Niger, murdering a further 170 people (including the wife of the U.S. ambassador to Chad). An international outcry followed, and the United States started to lobby for UN sanctions against Libya.

With American allies finally aboard, it was easy. A few weeks after the downing of the UTA Flight 722, the United Nations imposed stringent penalties against Tripoli. Western countries froze the assets that the Libyan government held abroad, depriving the regime of much-needed sources of cash. UN sanctions also prohibited all exports of oil and gas equipment, as well as arms sales, to Tripoli. Air travel to and from Libya was banned. The country became a pariah on the international stage. In these conditions, foreign energy companies started to exit Tripoli.

The impact of UN-mandated, multilateral sanctions on the Libyan economy proved to be severe. Libya's energy infrastructure soon started to crumble as investment and access to Western technology dwindled. Growth became a distant memory, raising the risk of social unrest as salaries stagnated amid skyrocketing inflation. Overall, Libyan government officials reckon that international sanctions cost the country around US$30 billion.[2] For Tripoli, this was too high a price to pay. Libya hung on for ten years before giving in to sanctions pressure.

In 1999 the country eventually handed over the two Libyan suspects in the bombing of Pan Am Flight 103 (one of them was sentenced to life imprisonment and the other was found not guilty). Gaddafi also announced that he would stop waging terror attacks and stayed true to his word. Libya's nuclear arsenal and stock of chemical weapons were dismantled under international supervision. In return, the United States and the United Nations lifted all sanctions against Tripoli.

For Washington, Libya represented a rare, unequivocal sanctions win: the country was one of a select group of rogue countries that managed to extricate themselves from U.S. penalties. For sanctions enthusiasts, Gaddafi's surrender was a clear demonstration that sanctions can be effective to force rogue countries to alter their behavior. However, the truth is that Libya was an exception. In most cases, sanctions do not work. In some instances, they may even backfire and hurt U.S. interests.

———— ∞ ————

In 1919 President Woodrow Wilson remarked that "A nation that is boycotted is a nation that is in sight of surrender. Apply this economic, peaceful, silent, deadly remedy and there will be no need for force. It does not cost a life outside the nation boycotted, but it brings a pressure upon the nation which, in my judgment, no modern nation could resist."[3] On this one, Wilson's judgment was wrong. Apart from a few high-profile wins such as Libya, there is little evidence that sanctions are as effective as policy makers would like. In fact, history shows that most of the time, nations resist and sanctions fail.

In a 2019 report, the Government Accountability Office (GAO) noted that the U.S. government does not know whether existing sanctions programs work, and what effects they have.[4] This is not surprising. The U.S. Treasury does not publish studies on the effectiveness of sanctions before they are imposed or after they have been in place for some time. Nor do the State and Commerce Departments. In fact, such assessments do not exist: before imposing sanctions, an administration checks only whether they could cause immediate humanitarian damage.[5]

Government officials are not to blame. They usually have to draft sanctions programs in a rush to respond to fast-unfolding diplomatic crises. Assessing whether sanctions are effective is also hard. Before sanctions are imposed, accurately predicting whether they will work is akin to looking into a crystal ball. Once sanctions are in place, determining whether they have been useful would require some form of access to alternative realities; such an assessment would have to be based on an impossible comparison between what could have happened (if sanctions had not been imposed) and what really happened (with sanctions in place).

It is feasible, however, to check whether what occurred after sanctions were imposed coincides with their initial goal. The results are not encouraging. A review of all U.S. sanctions programs since 1970 shows that targeted countries altered their behavior in the way that the United States hoped that they would only 13 percent of the time.[6] In an additional 22 percent of the cases, the policies of sanctioned states became somewhat—but not fully—more palatable to Washington.[7] Considering these figures, sanctions hardly represent a panacea; on average, they fail two-thirds of the time.

Examples of sanction failures are not hard to find. In Cuba, the regime of Fidel Castro is still in place after more than 60 years of a U.S. embargo. In North Korea, the Kim dynasty remains in power while the population is starving. In Iraq, international sanctions did not prompt Saddam Hussein to consider leaving Kuwait. Iran is still supporting Hizbullah and destabilizing the Middle East. Russia has never returned Crimea to Ukrainian control after seizing the peninsula in 2014. Instead, the Russian army invaded Ukraine eight years later. The reality is that sanctions are sometimes effective, but most often not, and it is hard to accurately predict if they will work.

Gauging whether sanctions will work is akin to fortune-telling. This does not mean that it is completely impossible to guess whether proposed penalties have at least a small chance of being effective. Experience shows that four factors may help to determine whether sanctions might work (or not): how long they have been in place; whether they have a narrow or a broad goal; the preexistence of trade ties between the United States and the targeted country; and, perhaps most important of all, whether allies are aboard.

First, sanctions work fast or never.[8] If penalties have not yielded results within two years, the target country usually has no intention of giving in. In 2018 Washington imposed sanctions on Turkey to protest against the detention of Andrew Brunson, an American pastor. Only two months later, Ankara bowed to U.S. pressure and released Brunson, prompting Washington to lift the related penalties. If sanctions are going to work, as turned out to be the case with Turkey, they do so fast.

Conversely, if sanctions have not proved effective after a couple of years, they are unlikely ever to yield results. After several years, sanctions become the new normal for targeted countries. They set up mechanisms to circumvent sanctions. Targeted states increase domestic production in order to reduce their reliance on imports. Since it fell under sanctions, Russia has been ramping up agricultural production to become self-sufficient in food supplies. Sanctioned countries also forge new ties with other trade partners. Over the past two decades, Iran has been reorienting exports away from the West, toward China, India, and Turkey.[9]

The vast majority of U.S. sanctions programs have been in place for more than two years, raising thorny issues. If these penalties have little chance of ever yielding results, should Washington lift them even if they have not achieved their stated goals? This would make theoretical sense, but also diminish U.S. leverage; in the future, sanctioned countries would assume that they just need to stick it out for a few years until Washington gave up and eventually lifted the penalties.

The objectives of sanctions are often vague, which makes lifting them—normally in return for a specific action, such as ditching a nuclear program—even trickier. Iran is a case in point. When the U.S. administration exited the nuclear deal and reimposed penalties against Iran in 2018, Washington initially outlined 12 steps that Tehran had to take for sanctions to be lifted, including withdrawing from Syria, releasing U.S. prisoners, and halting its ballistic missile program.[10] However, President Donald Trump contradicted his own administration shortly after these demands were made, tweeting that his only goal was to see Iran ditch nuclear weapons (the existence of which was never proved).

One year later Trump changed tack again. He implied that he was ready to lift Iran-related sanctions if Hassan Rouhani agreed to meet with him (the Iranian president declined the offer). Meanwhile, other U.S. officials kept hinting that the only acceptable outcome was regime change in Tehran.[11] In the light of these confusing statements, there was no way for Iran to gauge how it could alter its behavior in a way that would persuade the United States to lift the sanctions. Even in Washington, officials were hard pressed to give a definitive outline of the steps that Tehran had to take before sanctions could be lifted.

Another problem is that in addition to having poorly defined goals, many U.S. sanctions programs have no sunset clauses: once implemented, they can be in place forever without review. The Office of Foreign Assets Control (OFAC) has not updated Cuba-related sanctions much since their imposition in the 1960s, for instance. The penalties still reflect legacy concerns over Havana's association with the former Soviet Union. Terminating these sanctions would be difficult; American citizens and companies that had their assets seized by Castro's regime still have unsettled claims worth around US$8 billion against Cuba.[12] Yet an update of U.S. sanctions against Cuba, so they address current disputes rather than Cold War–era problems, appears long overdue.

The issues with legacy sanctions programs do not end there. The designations in decades-old programs often turn out to be out of date. This is not surprising; OFAC has been struggling with staff shortages for years.[13] After they have spent a few years gaining knowledge about sanctions, many OFAC officials choose to join the private sector, as salary packages in due-diligence companies are more attractive than OFAC's. Staff shortages mean that some Africa-related sanctions programs do not even have a single full-time staff member to administer them.[14] The situation is even worse at the State Department: around half of the department's positions for sanctions specialists were vacant in 2020.[15]

Coming back to the features of successful sanctions, the second characteristic of typically effective penalties is that they have a narrow purpose. Sanctions that have a limited objective, such as the release of a political prisoner or the settlement of a trade dispute, tend to work.[16] In 2018 penalties against Turkey worked in no small part because their goal was limited: the U.S. administration only wanted Ankara to release Pastor Brunson. By contrast, sanctions that have broader objectives, such as regime change in Cuba, North Korea, or Venezuela, tend to fail.

This explains why sanctions against dictatorships, which often try to foster a change in leadership, seldom work.[17] Since the 1950s nearly 90 percent of the U.S. penalties that have proved to be effective were imposed against states that have a multiparty electoral system.[18] This makes sense. By definition, authoritarian regimes have no intention of giving up power; in many cases, their leaders would be signing their death warrant. In addition, popular resentment is an important factor for sanctions to work. On paper, sanctions are not meant to affect the population of targeted countries, but the truth is that ordinary people often get poorer because of sanctions. Access to consumer goods shrinks. Travel becomes more difficult. Citizens soon start to ponder whether the policies of their government are worth the trouble. Hardship for voters becomes pressure on governments.[19]

This is precisely what happened in Iran in 2012–2015, for instance. Iranians resented the impact of sanctions, especially as the country used to enjoy decent living conditions. Crucially, Iranian citizens had a way to signal their displeasure with sanctions. Iran is a theocracy with a dismal human-rights record, but the country holds presidential elections (independent observers believe that these are not free and fair, but these polls still offer the population some say in governance[20]). In 2013 Iranians elected a reformist, Rouhani, as president, tasking him to get sanctions lifted. He delivered on his pledge by signing the nuclear deal in 2015.

Conversely, in countries where decision-making is not democratic, civilian pressure cannot bring results; there is no pathway for citizens to make their voices heard. Where dissent is suppressed, authoritarian regimes have no incentive to alter their behavior in a way that could prompt the lifting of sanctions. In fact, history shows that when dictatorships fall under sanctions, their human rights record tends to deteriorate. Disappearances, torture, and political imprisonment increase, as rogue governments double down on punishing those they think are colluding with the sanctioning enemy.[21]

The third characteristic of typically successful sanctions is that they target economic partners.[22] Again, U.S. sanctions against Turkey in 2018 fit this pattern. Washington and Ankara have long had significant economic links and are NATO allies. Sanctions were an anomaly that needed fixing. Conversely, if the United States targets a country with which it has few ties, the sanctioned country will have little incentive to alter its behavior. The severance of minor links will only represent the continuation of existing conditions. Partners have much to lose. Adversaries do not.

Finally, multilateral support is crucial for sanctions to be effective. Despite its unmatched economic power, the United States cannot sanction alone: from 1970 to 1990 only 13 percent of unilateral U.S. sanctions appear to have achieved their stated goals.[23] Penalties against North Korea illustrate this issue. More than 90 percent of North Korea's trade goes through China. The rest tends to go to Russia. If Beijing and Moscow are not aboard, sanctions on Pyongyang are useless; they will never be implemented on the ground.[24]

Multilateral support for sanctions at the United Nations is ideal. It means that all countries will (theoretically) impose the same restrictions. In turn, international firms around the world will need to comply with a unique set of common regulations for their dealings with the targeted country. For businesses, this is a crucial point: if sanctions are not multilateral, firms from non-sanctioning countries may benefit from the situation by seizing the market shares of companies headquartered in sanctioning states. This is what happened in Libya before allies joined the United States in imposing sanctions against Gaddafi. However, getting sanctions approved at the United Nations is often difficult.

Drafting of UN sanctions is a convoluted affair, not least because of the traditional reluctance of Russia and China—two permanent members of the UN Security Council—to go down the sanctions route. Moscow and Beijing are skilled at watering down UN-mandated sanctions against their allies, such as North Korea. In 2019 Russia and China blocked a resolution of the UN Security Council that condemned Pyongyang's imports of 3.5 million barrels of refined petroleum products—seven times the limit mandated by UN sanctions—in the previous year.[25]

Even if Russia and China are aboard, preparation of sanctions at the UN level involves agonizing debates over the choice of words to please everyone, including countries that may have close ties with the sanctioned state—such as Russia vis-à-vis Syria or China toward African dictatorships. This long process often presents an opportunity for targeted countries; in the meantime, they may take preemptive steps to lessen the impact of upcoming penalties, building up stocks, rerouting trade, and setting up sanctions-busting networks.[26]

In sum, typically effective sanctions are in place for the short term, have a narrow goal, target a democracy that has significant ties with the United States, and are backed by American allies. This is the exact opposite of most U.S. sanctions programs. The vast majority of Washington's penalties have been in place for years (if not decades), targeting dictatorships with which the United States has few ties. In many cases, U.S. sanctions have broad objectives, such as regime change. In many instances, these goals are not clear. In recent years the United States has also increasingly sanctioned on its own, as Washington's unilateral exit from the Iran nuclear deal in 2018 illustrates. On the basis of these metrics, many U.S. sanctions programs appear to be doomed to fail.

In 1990 the United States imposed sanctions on Pakistan in protest against the country's covert nuclear program. The penalties cut Washington's economic and military aid to Islamabad (America's support previously amounted to around US$600 million per year[27]). The United States halted the delivery of U.S. military equipment, including much-awaited F-16 jets, and canceled joint U.S.-Pakistan military exercises.[28] The consequences of sanctions against Islamabad turned out to be much more wide-ranging than the United States had expected. Sanctions against Pakistan diminished America's influence on the ground, with catastrophic consequences for national security. The Pakistan example highlights how sanctions can backfire and hurt U.S. interests.

Washington and Islamabad had collaborated closely during the 1980s to push the former Soviet Union out of Afghanistan.[29] Ties between the Pakistani and American military were extensive. Pakistan's officers used to receive training in the United States. In Islamabad, American and Pakistani officials maintained close relationships, exchanging information on sensitive topics over a drink or on the golf course. After the United States imposed sanctions on Islamabad, such military instruction programs and informal social encounters came to an end. Pakistani officials did not want to be seen as being on friendly terms with the United States anymore.

At around the same time, ISI, the Pakistani intelligence service, secretly started to support the rising Taliban movement in Afghanistan.[30] Despite Pakistan's denials, Washington suspected that the country was providing assistance to the Islamist movement. However, U.S. officials on the ground were struggling to collect much-needed information on this topic; sanctions had decimated their previously fruitful informal channels of discussion with Pakistani officials. Because of sanctions, American diplomats and intelligence officers found themselves in the dark, with no reliable Pakistani sources to tap into.

U.S. sanctions were not the reason why Pakistan started to support the Taliban; Islamabad's view that Afghanistan constituted an important buffer against a potential Indian military attack was a key motivating factor for Pakistani generals.[31] However, America's sanctions represented a turning point in the relationship between Washington and Islamabad.

The penalties led to a sharp deterioration in U.S.-Pakistan ties, destroying decades-old connections with a significant—although often murky and unreliable—regional power.[32] With U.S. influence in Islamabad greatly reduced, Washington found itself in a blind spot to track the rise of Al-Qaeda in Afghanistan. This came with disastrous consequences.

The Pakistan example is far from an isolated one. In many cases, America's sanctions foster anti-American sentiment instead of winning the hearts and minds of the citizens that they intend to save from rogue regimes. In Iran, U.S. penalties imposed after Washington exited the nuclear deal have managed to do what the regime had always dreamed of achieving: uniting Iranians against sanctions. In Venezuela, almost 60 percent of citizens oppose U.S. sanctions.[33] In fact, the rise in popularity in the early 2020s of Venezuelan president Nicolás Maduro may have been due to the vocal support of his opponent, Juan Guaido, for sanctions. In Russia, President Vladimir Putin's approval ratings went to record highs after the country was first placed under U.S. penalties in 2014.[34] Eight years later, Putin's popularity jumped again following the invasion of Ukraine.

In the long term, there is a risk that U.S. enthusiasm for sanctions will undermine the attractiveness of the American dream for those living in targeted countries. This is a dangerous development: because of sanctions, the United States is losing influence even among educated, urban young people in the countries that it targets. In a not-so-distant future, a significant share of the population of the countries that the United States has placed under sanctions might harbor anti-U.S. sentiment. Some of them may become easy prey for the recruiters of murderous terror groups such as Al-Qaeda or Islamic State.

In 1763 Founding Father Benjamin Franklin learned from a friend that the United Kingdom had found a new way to raise money. London was planning to raise taxes on the goods that its colonies, including the United States, imported from the United Kingdom. Surprisingly, Franklin was not alarmed. He wrote to his British friend, "you cannot hurt us without hurting yourselves.[35]" Nearly three centuries later, Franklin's reasoning still holds: a country cannot impose coercive economic measures on another one without hurting its own interests. This illustrates another reason why sanctions can backfire. In many cases, U.S. businesses bear the brunt of American coercive economic measures.[36]

The best-known example of how U.S. penalties can hurt American firms and workers dates back to 1980. Back then, Carter imposed a partial embargo on grain exports to the USSR to protest against the Soviet invasion of Afghanistan. Washington was making a bold bet: the White House hoped that the USSR would soon face difficulties sourcing wheat, soybeans, and corn, and thus feeding the Soviet population. Carter's assumption was that Moscow would feel it had no choice but to withdraw from Afghanistan in the hope of having the U.S. grain embargo lifted.

Carter's plan backfired. The United States used to supply around one-third of the USSR's grain imports. After the embargo was imposed, this share fell to about 20 percent.[37] Other countries were keen to win the market shares that the United States had lost. Argentina and Brazil ramped up their grain supplies to the Soviets. Even close U.S. allies, such as Canada and Australia, sensed a lucrative opportunity and increased their exports to the USSR. Meanwhile, U.S. farmers were left with a massive surplus of grains and no obvious countries to export them to. Commodities prices tumbled, and U.S. agricultural land values plummeted, driving many American farmers out of business.

Faced with such a dramatic situation, Reagan lifted the Soviet grain embargo after only one year. However, the damage was done, and U.S. farmers never regained Moscow's trust. The entire world also realized that Washington would not rule out using food supplies as a weapon. Countries that used to rely on imports of U.S. grains became more careful and sought to diversify their supplies. In the following years, the U.S. share of global exports for corn, soybean, and wheat all dropped.[38] The Soviet grain embargo was not the only reason behind this fall of U.S. market shares; the strength of the U.S. dollar, which made imports from the United States more expensive, also explained it. However, Carter's embargo was an aggravating factor.

Companies often mention the Soviet grain embargo, which many U.S. farmers continue to believe was "a catastrophic mistake,[39]" to explain why they believe that the United States is often shooting itself in the foot with sanctions. American firms argue that "they have been through this before [during the grain embargo], and it ends badly for both [companies] and taxpayers.[40]" The data show that from a purely economic standpoint, they are right.

In the mid-1990s an extensive study put the negative impact of sanctions on U.S. firms at almost US$20 billion per year.[41] This figure includes only lost exports, although it is hard to estimate whether U.S. companies were able to reroute part of their exports to non-sanctioned countries. The same research estimates that every year, more than 200,000 American jobs are also lost because of sanctions. Given how hard it is to reliably estimate the costs associated with sanctions, these data should be treated cautiously. However, these eye-popping numbers give an idea of the hidden costs of sanctions for American businesses.

These figures date back to almost 30 years ago. The real value of U.S. exports lost because of sanctions is probably much larger nowadays. A conservative estimate would stand at around US$50 billion per year (assuming that lost opportunities rose proportionately with exports since 1995[42]). The real figure may be much higher, however. Sanctions have become more widespread than they were in the 1990s, targeting larger economies—such as Russia's—than they used to. In addition, these estimates only refer to the trade of goods; they exclude exports of services, which today represent almost half of U.S. exports.

Other lost opportunities for American businesses are even harder to measure. International companies may believe that U.S. suppliers are unreliable because of sanctions, for instance. As a result, some foreign businesses report that they prefer to use non-American suppliers to avoid the risk of sanctions-induced supply-chain disruptions. Far away from rogue regimes, firms across America often pay the price of U.S. coercive economic measures. However, the costs that U.S. penalties impose on American businesses do not appear in government statistics, making sanctions look less costly than they really are.

In some worst-case scenarios, sanctions may even benefit U.S. foes or, ironically, other sanctioned countries. Penalties against Venezuela are a case in point. In January 2019 U.S. sanctions on Venezuela's oil exports created a global shortage of sour, heavy crude. Oil traders were quick to adapt. They saw Russia's Urals oil as an ideal replacement, as the Russian crude has similar characteristics to Venezuela's. For the first time in history, Russia's Urals oil started to trade at a premium over Brent crude, to the benefit of Russian—often sanctioned—energy companies.

The story does not end here. Three months afterward, the U.S. waivers that had allowed Iran to continue to export oil to a few countries (despite the U.S. withdrawal from the nuclear deal) expired, exacerbating the global shortage of heavy crude. The sanctions-fueled dearth of Venezuelan and Iranian oil was excellent news for Russia's energy firms; Urals oil was in even greater demand. As a result, Russian energy exporters received around US$1 billion in extra revenue.[43] Rosneft, Russia's largest oil firm, is state-owned. This means part of the extra money landed in Russia's state coffers, financing Moscow's military adventure in Syria or, ironically, supporting the cash-strapped Venezuelan government.

The benefits that Russia derives from U.S. sanctions against Venezuela go far beyond extra oil sales. After the United States imposed sanctions on Venezuela's oil exports, Moscow vowed to help Caracas to continue to export crude. For a while, the transactions went through two obscure, Switzerland-based subsidiaries of Rosneft.[44] At some point, these two companies handled around 70 percent of Venezuela's oil exports, conducting ship-to-ship transfers à la North Korea to hide the true destinations of illegal oil cargoes.[45]

Russia's help is not free, and Moscow has reaped rewards in return for its support. Rosneft has received stakes in at least six Venezuelan oil joint ventures and the in-kind repayment (in the form of oil) of billions of U.S. dollars of loans that the Russian energy giant had previously extended to Petróleos de Venezuela (PdVSA), the Venezuelan state-owned oil company.[46] The United States eventually imposed sanctions on the two firms that used to handle Venezuela's illegal oil exports. This has not deterred Moscow[47]: other Russian state-owned shell entities have taken over the lucrative process, playing a game of cat and mouse with OFAC.[48] When these companies fall under sanctions, new ones replace them—until Washington catches up with the new scheme.

In May 2019 Trump spent one hour on the phone with Putin. After the call, the U.S. president was adamant that Russia was "not looking at all to get involved in Venezuela, other than he'd like something positive to happen for Venezuela.[49]" Trump might have misunderstood what Putin believed would be "something positive" for Maduro. The Kremlin has every reason not to ditch Caracas; Moscow is getting profitable stakes in Venezuelan oil fields in return for its sanctions-busting support. In Venezuela, U.S. sanctions benefit Russia, which is also under stringent American penalties. Well-designed sanctions can backfire. In a worst-case scenario, they may even benefit U.S. foes.

II

SANCTIONS CROSSFIRE

4

COLLATERAL DAMAGE

When Sanctions Kill

I n August 1990 a U.S.-led international coalition launched Operation Desert Shield in response to Iraq's invasion of Kuwait. Unsurprisingly, sanctions formed part of the diplomatic and military arsenal that Washington and its allies deployed to put pressure on Iraqi leader Saddam Hussein. Four days after Operation Desert Shield started, the international community placed Iraq under stringent sanctions that cut off the country's access to humanitarian goods, such as food and medical supplies.

Within weeks, food staples became scarce and health care unavailable.[1] Malnutrition followed, and infant deaths reached record highs, inflaming popular opinion in Iraq against Western countries.[2] Malaria, typhoid, and tuberculosis, diseases that had previously almost disappeared, reemerged. Relief was slow to come. An "oil for goods" scheme that allowed Iraq to export limited quantities of oil in exchange for food and medicines was only signed five years later, in 1995.

Iraq's population paid a high price for these sanctions. The United Nations estimates that around half a million Iraqi children died because of the measures.[3] These figures are highly controversial, but it is an undisputed fact that several thousands of Iraqi kids died as a result of the sanctions.[4] In 1995 the then–U.S. ambassador to the United Nations, Madeleine Albright, stated that this death toll had been "worth it,[5]" given the need to apply pressure on Saddam Hussein. Albright subsequently retracted this statement, stating repeatedly that saying these words had been a "terrible mistake."[6]

Iraq is an extreme example of the negative humanitarian impact of sanctions. Since the 1990s the United States has taken steps to try to limit the damaging side effects of sanctions programs on the populations of targeted countries. Blunt embargoes—such as the one against Iraq—are seldom used anymore. The few trade blockades that remain in place—for instance on Cuba and North Korea—include (limited) provisions for the supply of humanitarian goods. Over the past decade, targeted sanctions against specific economic sectors, financial channels, and well-connected individuals have become the norm—as is the case in Iran, Russia, and Venezuela. Modern-day sanctions do not produce widespread starvation, but this does not mean that they are harmless. Civilians in targeted countries still suffer from the negative humanitarian side effects of sanctions.

⸎

Ask any Iranian, Russian, or Venezuelan, and they will say that inflation is the most obvious side effect of sanctions. In Iran, consumer prices rose by more than 30 percent per year in 2012–2013, when sanctions put Tehran under complete financial isolation.[7] Inflation jumped to around 15 percent in Russia in 2015—shortly after the country was placed under U.S. and EU penalties for annexing Crimea and backing separatist rebels in eastern Ukraine.[8] The record goes to Venezuela: inflation skyrocketed to more than 1,000,000 percent after the United States imposed stringent sanctions on Caracas in 2018.[9] The price of a single roll of toilet paper jumped to nearly 3 million bolivars, requiring a three-kilogram stack of 1,000 bank notes to pay for it.[10]

Economists say that such eye-popping price rises are not surprising. Sanctions restrict trade and prompt the depreciation of currencies, making imported products become both scarcer and more expensive. Sanctions also disrupt supply chains, fueling a rise in the number of intermediaries involved in the trade of goods, even for basic staples such as grains. As a result, imports become more expensive, as each middle-man wants to take a cut. In such conditions of scarcity, black markets often thrive, offering overpriced products of dubious quality (and further fueling the inflation spiral).

Penalties that restrict exports have an impact on inflation, too. Sanctions prompt a rise in consumer prices when they limit the ability of targeted countries to export commodities, such as oil in Iran's case. As a result of such embargoes, the central banks of sanctioned states see their foreign-exchange reserves fall, leaving them with few options to defend their currencies and to pay for imports.

The effects of higher inflation can be devastating for the population of targeted countries. The Democratic Republic of Congo (DRC) provides a good example of how the ripple effects of well-meaning sanctions may be detrimental to the local population.[11] In this poverty-stricken African country, where GDP per capita stands at around US$1,000 per year,[12] the probability of infant deaths in resources-rich regions that hold vast reserves of minerals, such as tin, gold, or tungsten, is twice as high as the national average.[13] This may sound counterintuitive: Why are babies dying at a faster rate in the areas that should be the richest in the country?

The explanation is that warlords involved in widespread human-rights abuses control these regions. In an attempt to tackle this issue, American penalties imposed under a clause of the 2010 Dodd-Frank Act force international companies to audit their supply chains in order to discourage them from sourcing warlords-controlled "conflict minerals." The aims of the legislation—reducing the revenues of militias and promoting peace in the DRC—are laudable. The Dodd-Frank Act has had some positive effects, not least in encouraging media attention around the plight of the DRC. However, the negative side effects of the legislation far outweigh the positive ones.

As soon as it was adopted, the legislation imposed a de facto ban on artisanal mining in the DRC, putting thousands of poor miners out of work.[14] Transport links to villages that produce fewer minerals were reduced, making food and infant health-care products become more expensive. As a result, parents cannot access basic staples for their children, who die of malnutrition or lack of medical care. The effects of higher inflation go well beyond increased child mortality.[15] Price rises also fueled an increase in poverty, leading to further violence,[16] such as banditry and kidnappings for ransom.[17]

As they were drafting their well-meaning legislation, Senator Chris Dodd and Congressman Barney Frank probably had no idea that they would drive up infant mortality in the DRC, thousands of miles away from Capitol Hill. Yet the unforeseen effects of the penalties appear to be punishing innocent Congolese families, rather than powerful war-lords whose power and fortunes do not seem to shrink.[18] More than one decade after the Dodd-Frank measures were imposed, war-torn DRC is no closer to peace, and U.S. penalties have not helped in reaching a settlement.

U.S. government officials usually have two ready-made answers when asked about the humanitarian impact of sanctions.[19] The first denies that sanctions have any adverse humanitarian effects, citing exemptions for food and medicines. This position is largely untenable, and often raises eyebrows. Most officials therefore prefer to flip the question, arguing that the behavior of the targeted country is what led the United States to impose sanctions in the first place. Whether the administration always realizes the full extent of the fallout from sanctions on the population of targeted countries remains an open question.

Policy makers are not to blame. In many instances, sanctions have a structural impact on targeted economies, which makes it difficult to disentangle their humanitarian effects from other causes of economic collapse. Iran illustrates this problem very well. In early 2020 what was then termed a novel coronavirus started to spread across the world, eventually leading the World Health Organization (WHO) to declare a pandemic in March. Iran quickly found itself among the worst-affected countries. Official Iranian statistics remain murky, but since early 2020 more than seven million Iranians have fallen ill with coronavirus,[20] resulting in hundreds of thousands of deaths.[21]

Even before the Covid-19 pandemic started, the humanitarian side effects of U.S. sanctions on the Iranian population were well documented.[22] American penalties were hindering Iran's access to medicines, for instance.[23] Chemotherapy drugs and treatments for epilepsy, cancer, and multiple sclerosis were notoriously hard to access; Western pharmaceutical companies restricted supplies, as they worried about falling foul of sanctions if they did business with Tehran.[24] Sanctions had also fueled inflation to such highs that the few medicines and spare parts for medical equipment that remained available had become prohibitively expensive.[25]

The pandemic only made a bad situation worse. Masks, symptoms-relief medicines, and personal protective equipment soon became in short supply—as also happened in many places across the world. The Islamic republic produces significant quantities of health-care products domestically, but factories struggled to meet expanding demand, necessitating imports from less-affected countries to meet demand. However, desperate attempts by Iranian hospitals to import critical medical supplies failed—something that, by contrast, did not happen in many countries.[26]

The poor response of the Islamic regime is the main reason why the coronavirus spread so quickly on Iranian soil. At the onset of the pandemic, the Iranian government tried to hide the true scale of the outbreak. Officials also delayed the imposition of social-distancing measures to curb the spread of the disease. In fact, Supreme Leader Ali Khamenei concocted his own conspiracy theory: the United States had created the coronavirus. He went as far as saying that America had used genetic data from Iranians to make the virus deadlier in Iran.[27]

Sanctions represented an ideal scapegoat for Tehran to explicate the terrible situation in the country. To explain why things had gone so wrong, a spokesperson from the Iranian health ministry declared, "Remember [Iran] is a country under sanctions."[28] The Iranian government had a solid narrative to offer. If sanctions prevented the import of medical equipment and medicines, the idea that they were responsible for the high coronavirus death toll appeared to be a reasonable assumption.

Across the world, media reports started to question whether the United States was right to continue with its policy of maximum pressure on Iran during the pandemic.[29] In late March the *New York Times* asked for an easing of sanctions against Tehran while coronavirus raged.[30] More than 30 members of Congress called on the administration to lift penalties against Iran on humanitarian grounds.[31] The United Nations also stepped in, stating that a relaxation of sanctions on Iran was "urgent."[32]

Tehran's behavior did nothing to win hearts and minds at the White House and in the administration, however. In a face-saving bravado, the Islamic regime turned down Washington's offer to help via the WHO. Adding another layer to his inventive conspiracy theories, Khamenei stated that American doctors wanted to come to Iran only to assess the effectiveness of their U.S.-made "poison."[33]

———— ∞ ————

The U.S. administration soon faced an intense media storm around the events in Iran, but U.S. officials staunchly maintained that Iran's difficulties in fighting the outbreak had nothing to do with sanctions. A State Department spokeswoman declared that "We have repeatedly said that U.S. sanctions do not impede the Iranian regime's response to the Covid-19 crisis."[34] On paper, she had a point. In 2000 U.S. farmers and pharmaceutical companies had successfully lobbied the Clinton administration to allow some limited sales of food and medicines to Iran.[35] In the 2010s the U.S. had further expanded the scope of medical goods that could be exported to Iran.

As a result, the 2020s vintage of U.S. sanctions on Tehran did not prohibit the export of masks, medicines, and some personal protective equipment. Such exports fall under general exemptions, that is to say automatic sanctions waivers that allow humanitarian trade to prevent a repeat of what happened in Iraq in the 1990s. American officials kept restating these talking points. The administration's stance was clear: sanctions would not be relaxed.

In early April the U.S. State Department released a memo titled "Iran's Sanctions Relief Scam."[36] The fact sheet argued that "Iran's slick foreign influence campaign to obtain sanctions relief is not intended for the relief or health of the Iranian people but to raise funds for its terror operations."[37] The United States' policy of maximum pressure on Iran looked set to continue. In the midst of the pandemic, Washington imposed additional sanctions on firms facilitating Iran's oil exports, further undermining the regime's ability to finance the import of medicines.[38]

Despite its apparently firm position, the administration knew that it would not get away from intense media scrutiny without announcing measures to show its goodwill. As the controversy mounted, the U.S. Treasury revealed that Tehran could use the normally frozen accounts that Iran's central bank holds abroad to process transactions related to the import of medical supplies. The Office of Foreign Assets Control (OFAC) also published clear guidance on what was permitted, or not, under Iran sanctions. This was a welcome step, as sanctions programs are typically detailed in obscure legal documents that cover hundreds of pages and may deter even the most determined exporters. The guidance repeated that exporting medical supplies to Iran was generally fine.

The administration had a final ace up its sleeve: the U.S. Treasury explained that humanitarian trade with Iran could freely flow through a "Swiss channel." This mechanism makes it possible for Swiss companies to export basic supplies, such as food and medicines, to Iran without having to worry about U.S. sanctions. Under this scheme, the Swiss government takes care of the due diligence, making sure that the exported goods do not fall into the hands of sanctioned Iranian entities.

On paper, the Swiss channel sounds promising. Despite the small size of the Swiss economy, the country is home to several pharmaceutical manufacturers, such as Roche and Novartis, and food companies, such as Nestlé. In addition, the Swiss mechanism was launched in early 2020, right when the pandemic started. Yet three months afterward, the Swiss channel had not registered a single transaction beyond a pilot one. For sanctions watchers, this did not come as a surprise. Companies willing to use the Swiss channel have to send extraordinary amounts of sensitive information to the U.S. authorities.[39]

Among other requirements, Swiss exporters have to provide OFAC with reports detailing the financial situation of the Iranian banks they intend to do business with. Such reports have to include details on the accounts that Iranian banks hold in foreign institutions. Many companies wonder what the United States intends to do with these troves of data; European officials have called the process a "fishing expedition"[40] to document the ties between Iranian and European banks. Even if exporters had been able to provide the data, gathering them would have taken months, rendering the channel impractical to tackle the pandemic.[41]

For all the faults of the Swiss mechanism, the administration hoped that announcing these steps would defuse the media controversy over the humanitarian impact of U.S. sanctions on Iran. It was wrong. Yet the truth is that the White House, Treasury and Congress could not have done much more than they did: U.S. sanctions formed part of the explanation for the shortage of medical equipment in Iran, but sanctions relief would not have helped during the pandemic. Sanctions have had such a deep, structural impact on trade between Iran and the rest of the world that fixing things would have been much more complex than simply lifting sanctions.

⸎

The problem that Iran faced was (at least) threefold. The first issue was that most businesses do not wish to trade under the general exemptions that allow the export of humanitarian goods to sanctioned countries. This is because such exemptions come with stringent conditions. Medical equipment must be recognized as a "device" in section 201 of the Federal Food, Drug, and Cosmetic Act and designated as "EAR99" in U.S. export administration regulations.[42]

As a result, general exemptions—which are capped at a mere US$500,000 per year—do not cover some equipment that was crucial to fight against the coronavirus, such as oxygen generators, laboratory machines, and medical-imaging equipment. OFAC considers these products as sensitive, which means that companies willing to export them to Iran need to apply for special export licenses.

Getting such licenses is far from easy. In 2016 lawyers estimated that a company asking OFAC for an export license had a roughly 50 percent chance of getting it.[43] Sanctions specialists thought that a solid application had a good chance of being approved. In 2019 the number of successful applications for OFAC's licenses had fallen to around 10 percent.[44] The figure was probably even lower at the onset of the pandemic, reflecting President Donald Trump's much-touted policy of maximum pressure on Tehran.

Firms willing to trade under general exemptions have other reasons to be cautious. Even when general exemptions apply, companies must check that they do not conduct business with sanctioned entities. This is time-consuming, but doable. However, there is a catch. Doing business with a company that has ties to a sanctioned entity is also prohibited. For firms willing to trade with Iran, investigating a prospective local Iranian partner is not enough. Businesses must also check who their potential Iranian partner does business with.

Given the opaque nature of business links in Iran, it is effectively impossible to know with certainty that a company does not have any ties to sanctioned entities. The sanctioned Islamic Revolutionary Guard Corps (IRGC) holds such a sway over the Iranian economy, for instance, that many Iranian firms have dealt with the paramilitary group at one point or another. At any rate, conducting thorough due diligence is both expensive and time-consuming. Most international businesses do not think that the potential benefits are worth the costs at the best of times, never mind during an urgent pandemic when lengthy investigations represent a nonstarter.

The second set of issues for Iran pertains to the financial sphere. Even under general exemptions, foreign banks cannot do business with Iranian financial institutions sanctioned on terrorism and nuclear proliferation grounds. With most Iranian banks being subject to such penalties, only four unsanctioned banks used to handle the transactions related to Iran's humanitarian imports. However, in October 2018, the United States imposed sanctions against the most important of them, Parsian Bank.[45]

Sanctions on Parsian Bank were a big blow for Tehran. The institution used to process most of the financial transactions related to Iran's imports of food and medicines. Even usually circumspect U.S. sanctions attorneys protested, arguing that the evidence to sanction Parsian Bank was thin;[46] the institution, which was known to have solid anti–money laundering procedures, was never found to be engaging in illicit activities.[47] According to OFAC, the issue was that an Iranian investment company called Andisheh Mevaran had bought and sold less than 0.3 percent of the shares of Parsian Bank. The investment company was not under sanctions, so the operation was not, in itself, an issue.

The problem was that Andisheh Mevaran had subsequently channeled the profits that it had derived from selling Parsian Bank's shares to the Basij network, a sanctioned paramilitary group. Parsian Bank maintained that it was not aware that Andisheh Mevaran intended to finance the Basij network, and that the bank could not reasonably be held responsible for the dealings of its 70,000 shareholders.[48] In addition, Andisheh Mevaran's transaction was for such a small amount that it fell below all regulatory thresholds. The United States was undeterred and called Parsian Bank a sponsor of terror.[49]

A second financial issue had to do with the reluctance of foreign banks to do business with Iran. Before the Covid-19 pandemic struck, the few banking transactions that were taking place between Iran and the rest of the Western world were processed by only a handful of European banks, most often on an ad hoc basis for a few trusted clients with whom the financial institutions had been doing business for years. Once the pandemic started, such limited financial channels were not enough for Iran to manage to ramp up medical imports.

The lack of financial ties between Iran and Europe, which had not reimposed sanctions against Tehran when the United States left the nuclear deal in 2018, reflected the fact that many international banks are reluctant to process transactions related to Iran, even when they are legal. Instead of taking the time to scrutinize potential transactions and check that they comply with sanctions, many financial institutions prefer to turn down any requests involving Iran (a process known as "de-risking" or "overcompliance").

Like companies, banks feel that they have too much to lose if they are found to be breaking U.S. sanctions, and not much to gain from doing business with Iran. The fear of falling foul of sanctions is only one aspect of the problem. After the global financial crisis of 2008–2009, most Western financial institutions cut banking ties with those Middle Eastern and African countries that were deemed to be both too risky from a compliance perspective and not lucrative enough in those cost-cutting times. Iran fit this category well.

In theory, the U.S. Treasury's "comfort letters," which offer foreign banks guarantees that they can process transactions without breaching sanctions, could help to solve the overcompliance issue. However, getting a comfort letter from OFAC has become so tricky since the late 2010s that many international banks have stopped trying. Just like the Swiss channel, comfort letters also come with onerous reporting requirements that many banks believe are at best not worth it and at worst a U.S. intelligence-gathering operation.

Even if foreign banks manage to get comfort letters from OFAC, their legal departments do not usually think that the documents offer strong enough guarantees. U.S. financial regulations are applied at both the federal and the state levels. This means the attorney general of a single state or the prosecutor of any given city may have another interpretation of sanctions rules than that of OFAC, which operates at the federal level.

Many European banks have painful memories of their dealings with federal and city prosecutors.[50] In 2014 French bank BNP Paribas was fined a whopping US$8.9 billion by a federal district judge in Manhattan for "large-scale, systematic violations"[51] of U.S. economic sanctions against Cuba, Sudan, and Iran. To be on the safe side, lawyers maintain that financial institutions would have to receive comfort letters from the financial authorities of every single U.S. state where they have some sort of presence before processing transactions with Iran.

The issues pertaining to the financial sphere do not stop here. Alongside North Korea, Iran remains on the black list of the Financial Action Task Force (FATF), the international body that oversees efforts against money laundering and the financing of terror or nuclear proliferation; the Islamic republic has not ratified international conventions against the financing of terror and organized crime. As a result, the FATF urges international banks to remain cautious about any transactions involving an Iranian counterpart. In plain English, this means ditching all ties with Iran.

A final financial deterrent is that international businesses often worry that they might not be paid for the products that they export to Iran, with good reason; Iranian companies struggle to get hold of hard currency to pay their foreign counterparts. The explanation lies with sanctions. U.S. penalties severely restrict Iran's oil exports, which normally represent the main source of foreign exchange for Tehran. In turn, international businesses can never be sure that their Iranian partners will be able to pay them quickly (and in full).

The third and last set of problems has to do with logistics. Even if a medical supplier were able to determine that its Iranian partner did not have links to targeted entities and managed to find a bank willing to process the related transaction, it would still have struggled to have the merchandise delivered to Tehran. Like banks, most shipping companies tend to "overcomply" with sanctions and prefer to turn down business with Iran. The few Western shipping firms that wanted to continue trading with Iran after the United States reimposed sanctions against Tehran in 2018 could not do so; their insurance companies disagreed, fearing that they could themselves be liable to sanctions.

Short of sending planes full of medical equipment, which was in short supply in the United States, there is little that Washington could have done to help Tehran combat the coronavirus pandemic. Sanctions relief could have benefited only those companies that already had well-established ties with Iran, as they would have been able to ramp up exports quickly. However, most medical firms had long exited the Iranian market for fear of falling foul of U.S. sanctions or of running into reputational issues.

Doing business with Tehran during the pandemic simply did not make sense, anyway. Demand for masks and personal protective equipment had skyrocketed, and medical-supplies companies were struggling to meet global demand. Many countries were willing to buy medical equipment at any cost: why would private firms have bothered exporting medical equipment to Iran given the risks?

The Iranian example shows how disentangling the negative human-itarian impact of sanctions from other factors is a complex endeavor. Addressing all of the ripple effects that sanctions had had over several decades could not have been done fast. Most of the time, sanctioned states have also been suffering from decades of chronic mismanage-ment, and Iran is no exception to the rule. Sanctions often make difficult situations worse for the populations of targeted countries.

Fixing these issues is far from a straightforward process. The side effects of penalties are often so deep and complex that sanctions relief—a mere legal act—is not enough to restore robust business, financial, and logistical ties. Reinstating business and financial ties also requires time and trust—ingredients that were in short supply during the pandemic. Perhaps counterintuitively, the fact that sanctions have such deep struc-tural effects may well make them less effective.

Sanctions work only if sanctions relief represents a credible option. If targeted countries know that the lifting of penalties will not deliver fast and tangible economic benefits, they have no reason to alter their behav-ior in a way that would meet U.S. demands. Overcompliance is also in the minds of the leaders of sanctioned countries: they know that there is virtually nothing that governments can do to persuade companies to reenter previously sanctioned markets. From the perspective of U.S. foes, the prospect of seeing sanctions being lifted is often less appealing than Washington would like.

The Iranian example confirms this reality. The country's experience with sanctions relief has been bitter, even during the short period when the United States was part of the nuclear deal. Tehran has little incentive to curb its nuclear ambitions or its ballistic missiles program to please the United States; the Islamic republic has long concluded that even when sanctions are lifted, companies remain too afraid to reenter the

Iranian market and bankers too panicked to process any transactions. In Iran's case, the very effectiveness of U.S. penalties could have negative consequences for the stability of the Middle East and America's security.

Iran is not an isolated example. Other rogues, chief among them North Korea, know that sanctions relief often fails to live up to expectations. Should Washington manage to open negotiations with Pyongyang to curb the country's access to nuclear weapons, it would be hard to convince the North Korean leadership that the potential lifting of sanctions would translate into immediate, tangible economic benefits. This could leave the United States more empty-handed than it seems to negotiate an agreement with North Korea.

If they are a weapon of U.S. diplomacy, which looks increasingly likely given their central role in economic warfare, sanctions could contradict international law. Under the Geneva Convention, weapons must discriminate between civilians and combatants. Even in war zones, soldiers cannot do as they please; they must abide by rules that seek to avoid the killing or harming of innocent civilians. The problem with sanctions may be that there are no global rules governing their use. If sanctions lead to the closure of factories and the death of citizens of rogue countries who are unable to access medical supplies, are they much different from other deadly forms of intervention? The lack of access to lifesaving medicines may kill as many people as a sustained military assault.

Is it even possible to design sanctions that do not have an adverse impact on civilians? Sanctions aim to put pressure on the populations of targeted countries to prompt policy changes by their governments. It follows that penalties that do not inflict pain would probably be worthless. This means that by design, sanctions are weapons that have damaging humanitarian consequences. They produce fewer deaths than conventional wars, but they kill nonetheless. Whether policy makers believe that this is an acceptable trade-off for advancing U.S. interests remains an open debate.

5

SANCTIONS OVERREACH

When Foreign Firms Get Caught in the Crossfire

Over the past two decades, U.S. sanctions have become a major concern for international businesses: companies fear that they could inadvertently fall foul of sanctions and become liable to astronomical fines or lawsuits in the United States. Keeping track of regulations is hard, which adds another layer of worries for business executives. Every year around 1,000 regulatory bodies issue about 60,000 regulatory alerts. This represents 240 new rules to take into account every working day.[1] According to Colin Bell, HSBC's chief compliance officer, "You have to build an industrial-scale operation just to digest all the regulatory changes."[2]

This avalanche of new regulations has fueled the development of internal compliance departments, especially within financial institutions. The number of people tasked with keeping track of legal requirements in international banks has tripled since the mid-2000s. Nowadays, about 15 percent of the staff of a major bank works in the compliance department, making sure that all transactions respect international rules. For a major bank such as Citi, this represents 30,000 people—roughly the size of a big university like Columbia.[3] HSBC's risk and compliance budget stands at US$1 billion per year—enough money to buy around 5,000 average houses in the United States.[4]

In the past, becoming a compliance officer was not an attractive prospect; the job was seen as a back-office role for naysayers. This is no longer the case: nowadays, chief compliance officers manage large teams, report directly to the CEO, and have a seat at management committees. When HSBC's board assesses the performance of the bank's CEO, compliance is the main factor that it takes into account. Profits and revenue growth come second and third.[5]

Specialized compliance firms are also growing fast, proof that compliance has become a full-fledged industry. Demand for such services, which range from providing legal advice to investigating potential business partners in far-flung countries, is rising by double digits every year. Tech start-ups are also investing in the field: they are developing artificial intelligence algorithms that can vet complex transactions in seconds, when a human being would take hours. Arachnys, a New York–based company, claims that it can automate all compliance checks, thereby eliminating human input from the process.[6]

Other tech companies go even further: some have created algorithms that scan large swaths of transactions to spot suspicious patterns. Such methods are especially useful to track North Korean sanctions evaders.[7] Pyongyang ranks among the most innovative and sophisticated sanctions busters; the regime uses thousands of front companies that are closed as soon as they are sanctioned. Scanning fast-outdated lists of sanctioned entities is of little use when trying to ensure conformity with North Korea–related sanctions. Tracking North Korean–like behaviors represents a much more effective approach.

⌖

U.S. sanctions are the biggest compliance headache for businesses. Perhaps surprisingly, this is especially the case for non-American companies. Mentioning U.S. sanctions with European or Asian business executives often produces angry, worried, or dreadful reactions. Many international firms feel that Washington is specifically targeting non-U.S. businesses when it comes to sanctions enforcement. Data seem to confirm these suspicions: since 2009 the Office of Foreign Assets

Control (OFAC) has imposed more than US\$4 billion in fines on foreign companies breaching sanctions; over the same period, U.S. firms had to pay less than US\$300 million in fines for evading sanctions.[8]

On paper, this stark difference could mean that the compliance departments of American firms are much better at their job than their foreign counterparts or that U.S. companies are simply more virtuous. However, a closer look at the data shows that this is not the case; U.S. firms breach sanctions just as much as foreign ones, but when they are caught, OFAC appears to be much more understanding. In recent years a foreign company caught evading sanctions could expect to receive a fine of US\$139 million. For American firms, the average fine was 70 times lower, at just US\$2 million.[9]

The United States has a long history of imposing sanctions that target the activities of non-American businesses. Such sanctions fall into two categories: extraterritorial penalties and secondary sanctions. Confusion usually reigns around whether a sanctions program is extraterritorial or includes a secondary component. Even though these two types of penalties share a similar objective—preventing all companies around the world from doing business with countries that are under U.S. sanctions—they are technically quite different.

U.S. extraterritorial laws are regulations that are applicable anywhere in the world. They are nothing new. In 1789 the United States adopted the Alien Tort Statute (ATS), which gave U.S. courts the right to hear lawsuits from foreigners for violations of U.S. or international law that did not take place on American soil.[10] In the eighteenth and nineteenth centuries the legislation mainly targeted piracy acts in international seas. In the twentieth century the United States issued other extraterritorial legislation on antitrust, banking, and labor regulations.[11] However, U.S. extraterritorial laws were mostly a minor phenomenon that interested only a few specialized attorneys.

In the early 1980s the situation changed.[12] The Paraguayan father of a young man who had been tortured and killed while in detention in Paraguay got word that one of his son's torturers, a Paraguayan policeman, was in the United States. The police officer had been living in New York City for nine months on a tourist visa, contravening U.S. immigration rules. The father got the policeman arrested for overstaying his U.S. visa. While the police officer was awaiting deportation back to Paraguay at the Brooklyn Navy Yard, the father brought a case against him under the ATS.

The procedure was a leap of faith; the ATS had never been invoked in such a situation. A U.S. federal court upheld the claim, stating that the ATS was relevant and that federal courts had jurisdiction over the suit even though the crime took place 5,000 miles away from America and no U.S. citizens were involved. The Paraguayan family was awarded US$10.4 million (however, it was never able to collect the money because the policeman did not have any assets in the United States). Since then, foreigners who have suffered human-rights abuses anywhere in the world have used the ATS to sue alleged perpetrators and obtain reparations in the United States.

<hr />

Until the mid-1990s Washington's sanctions programs were not extraterritorial. At the time, most U.S. sanctions were directed against entire countries, such as Cuba, or specific individuals and companies. Sanctioned persons and businesses were added to the Specially Designated Nationals (SDN) list that OFAC administers, barring them from using the U.S. dollar and from doing business in the United States or with American citizens. To comply with sanctions, U.S. firms simply had to check that they did not do business with an embargoed country and that their foreign business partners were not on the SDN list. Meanwhile, non-American entities did not have to worry about Washington's blockades and the SDN list; in theory, they are not supposed to respect U.S. law, including sanctions rules.

U.S. companies lamented this discrepancy, arguing that it put them at a disadvantage; when U.S. entities could not deal with a sanctioned country or firm, non-U.S. businesses were often happy to jump in. In 1996 this disparity started to come to an end. In February of that year the Cuban Air Force shot down two airplanes flown by Brothers to the Rescue, a Florida-based group of opponents of the Cuban regime.

In retaliation, the United States adopted the Helms-Burton Act, which extended the U.S. trade embargo that prevented American companies from doing business with Cuba to all international firms.

The Helms-Burton Act represented the first U.S. step toward making sanctions extraterritorial. With this measure, Washington sought to level the playing field between U.S. and non-U.S. companies: all business with Cuba was to be outlawed, not only for U.S. firms, but also for international ones. Unsurprisingly, European governments decried the Helms-Burton Act, saying that it infringed their sovereignty. The European Union lodged a complaint at the World Trade Organization (WTO). To Washington's alarm, the bloc also considered freezing some EU-held American assets and imposing visa requirements for U.S. business travelers.[13] Intense negotiations followed. In the end, President Bill Clinton backed down and waived the provisions of the Helms-Burton Act that applied to non-U.S. companies. However, the idea of U.S. extraterritorial sanctions was born.

The Helms-Burton Act sent shockwaves through global business communities. The legislation was the first hint that foreign businesses might one day have to comply with U.S. sanctions. Washington knew that it could leverage its global economic clout to force international companies to respect American penalties. No reputable firm could take the risk of becoming blacklisted in the world's biggest economy. Businesses were warned, but after Clinton backed down on the Helms-Burton Act, they gradually forgot about the threat.

It took the United States 14 years to revive the concept of extraterritorial sanctions, and when the country did so, it was with a twist. In 2010 Congress adopted a new round of sanctions against Iran. The United States had been waging a campaign of maximum pressure against the Islamic republic for several years. However, these new sanctions had a novel feature: they introduced the concept of secondary sanctions, which threaten to add foreign businesses that do not respect U.S. sanctions to the SDN list. As is the case for all entities on the SDN list, firms that are placed under secondary sanctions lose access to the U.S. dollar and must leave the American market. In addition, their executives may be subject to individual penalties.

The United States argues that secondary sanctions do not target non-American businesses, but that foreign companies must choose between the U.S. market and that of sanctioned countries. This is not really a fair choice; few global firms can afford to lose access to the greenback and to stop doing business with the world's largest economy.[14] As a result, almost all international companies comply with U.S. sanctions, for fear of becoming the target of sanctions themselves. Secondary sanctions magnify the reach of U.S. penalties beyond American borders: in practice, everyone has to follow U.S. rules.

Congress is the most enthusiastic backer of secondary sanctions. The majority of Congress-led recent sanctions programs against Iran, Russia, and North Korea include the possibility of imposing secondary sanctions. This is not surprising. In the foreign-policy sphere, lawmakers are often under intense pressure from their constituents and from NGOs to act decisively. For members of Congress, secondary sanctions look even more attractive than "regular" sanctions, as their effects go well beyond U.S. borders. Lobbying from U.S. companies also explains the interest of lawmakers in such far-reaching penalties; the threat of secondary sanctions means that non-U.S. businesses have to think twice before replacing American firms in sanctioned countries.

By contrast, U.S. presidents—including Barack Obama, Donald Trump, and Joe Biden—have traditionally displayed a much more cautious approach toward secondary sanctions. The White House is acutely aware of the tensions that secondary sanctions create with U.S. allies, which resent the damage these potential penalties do to their national companies. The divide over secondary sanctions between the White House and Congress has deepened in recent years. After having left the president in the driver's seat for foreign policy for decades, the legislative is trying to reassert its role in this area. The interest of lawmakers in secondary sanctions forms part of this trend.

⸎

Only a few non-American companies have, so far, been added to OFAC's blacklist as a result of secondary sanctions.[15] In 2018 the United States blacklisted a Chinese entity and its director for buying fighter jets and missile systems from Russia (U.S. sanctions prohibit the purchase of military equipment from Russia). Beyond a handful of such high-profile cases, sanctions programs on Russia, North Korea, and China have yielded few secondary sanctions designations over the past years. Doing business with Iran remains, by far, the likeliest path toward the SDN list. Chinese firms are the worst offenders. Since 2020 the United States has added a few dozen China-based companies to OFAC's sanctions list for buying Iranian oil despite U.S. penalties.[16]

Whether the United States imposes secondary sanctions is not what matters most, however. The simple threat of secondary sanctions is often more than enough to deter international companies from entering transactions that could trigger such penalties. Potential reputational problems are also too high to take any chances. U.S. policy makers are well aware that the power of secondary sanctions lies in their deterrent effect. In turn, they like to cultivate ambiguity around the criteria that the United States uses in order to decide when and why to impose secondary sanctions, further heightening uncertainty and boosting the dissuasive effect of secondary sanctions.[17]

In 2017 Congress adopted new sanctions against Russia, Iran, and North Korea that planned for automatic secondary sanctions against companies that conduct "significant transactions" with sanctioned entities in these countries. However, the United States did not provide a definition of what a "significant transaction" entails; OFAC only published a nonexhaustive list of examples of such transactions, mentioning—to the consternation of most lawyers—that true cases would be assessed on an individual basis, against unknown criteria.[18]

The U.S. president also has significant leeway in the imposition of secondary sanctions, further heightening uncertainty around what may trigger such penalties. In 2019 Turkey received air defense missiles from Russia, in violation of U.S. sanctions against Moscow. It is hard to imagine that the US$2 billion deal did not meet OFAC's threshold for what constitutes a "significant transaction." However, it took the White House two years to impose secondary sanctions on the Turkish entities and citizens involved in the deal. Ironically, international companies did not see this slow pace as a positive development; Washington's apparent restraint with Ankara only made it harder to decipher the criteria that are used to determine whether to impose secondary sanctions.

Proponents of secondary sanctions argue that this lack of predictability gives the United States leverage in diplomatic negotiations, for instance when Washington tried (but failed) to convince Turkey not to deploy the Russian missiles. This is a valid point. Secondary sanctions are usually meant to heighten the impact of primary penalties if these have not proved to be powerful enough. However, for foreign companies, the feeling of being held hostage to diplomatic negotiations they have nothing to do with may be hard to stomach.

Many non-American businesses also believe that they are at a disadvantage, compared to U.S. firms, when it comes to dealing with the uncertainty around secondary sanctions. OFAC's answers to the queries of foreign companies around the legality of potential transactions are painfully slow, if they materialize at all; there is no formal mechanism for foreign businesses to secure legal clarity as to whether a transaction is sanctions-proof or not. And when non-U.S. businesses receive clarifications, these are unlikely to be helpful. OFAC's answers are often worded in such a vague way that even seasoned lawyers are left scratching their heads; the agency's typical reply is that "it is up to the business community to conduct the necessary due diligence and make its own decisions about sanctions risk."[19]

To make matters worse, it is impossible for foreign firms to apply for sanctions waivers; only American businesses can.[20] OFAC argues that granting such waivers to non-U.S. firms would fuel the perception that U.S. sanctions are extraterritorial, something that the agency vehemently denies.[21] The U.S. government also does not want to appear to be authorizing transactions that might benefit sanctioned countries. However, seen from outside the United States, it is hard for foreign firms not to feel that the United States applies double standards between American and non-American firms.

—————⌾⌾⌾—————

Over the past decade, U.S. secondary sanctions have had a massive impact on the dealings—and strategy—of foreign firms. The fate of the European companies that had reentered the Iranian market after the nuclear deal was signed in 2015 is a case in point. Three years later, the United States unilaterally exited the nuclear deal and reimposed sanctions that included a secondary component on Tehran. The European Union remained in the nuclear deal. However, EU firms had no choice but to give in to U.S. demands and leave Iran. As Trump put it in a tweet shortly after the United States reimposed sanctions on Tehran, "The Iran sanctions have officially been cast. Anyone doing business with Iran will NOT be doing business with the United States."[22]

For most European businesses, the U.S. decision to reimpose sanctions on Iran was not a problem. Many firms had never had any dealings with Tehran. Those that had been present in Iran until 2010 had been extremely cautious about reentering the Iranian market after the nuclear deal was signed; they feared (for good reason) that the lifting of U.S. sanctions would only be temporary. However, some European companies intended to reenter the Iranian market. What happened to French oil major Total is a textbook example of how secondary sanctions may derail the business plans of non-American companies.

Total has a long history of facing issues with U.S. sanctions in Iran. In 1996 the U.S. Congress adopted the D'Amato-Kennedy Act, which imposed extraterritorial sanctions against Libya and Iran in an effort to curb their nuclear ambitions and support for terror. The act prohibited almost all international investments in the Iranian or Libyan energy sectors in an attempt to prevent non-U.S. energy companies from operating there. Previous U.S. sanctions against these countries did not apply to foreign firms, and non-U.S. businesses had proved eager to fill the void left by the departure of American companies. The D'Amato-Kennedy Act was meant to ensure that foreign firms would have to comply with U.S. law just as much as American ones.

In the mid-1990s, Total was already an active player in the Iranian energy sector. The French company was developing the second and third phases of the South Pars, a giant offshore gas field that Iran and Qatar share in the Persian Gulf.[23] For Total, the newly found extraterritoriality of U.S. sanctions represented a serious problem; the D'Amato-Kennedy Act threatened the involvement of the French company in the South Pars project. The European Union engaged in intensive lobbying with the United States to protect the interests of European firms, such as Total, in Iran and Libya.

European governments were all the more outraged because the United States had also just adopted the Helms-Burton Act, which intended to prevent European companies from doing business with Cuba. EU capitals regarded the D'Amato-Kennedy Act as a further escalation of the Helms-Burton Act, and a dangerous threat to European economic interests. Europe's condemnations did not deter the U.S. administration, however. Clinton was running for reelection, and he was keen to show that he was a staunch defender of American interests. In application of the D'Amato-Kennedy Act, OFAC started to investigate Total's operations in Iran—the first step toward a sanctions fine.

The United States expected that the European Union would give in and stop fighting against extraterritorial sanctions after a few months of inflamed rhetoric. Washington was wrong. Led by France, European governments mounted a counterattack against U.S. extraterritorial penalties. Brussels launched an EU-wide legislation that theoretically forbids European companies from complying with non-European laws. The so-called blocking regulation means that EU governments may sue European companies that comply with U.S. extraterritorial sanctions.

This was an odd move: threatening to impose fines on European companies caught in the sanctions crossfire was hardly a way to support them. In what proved to be a more constructive step, the European Union warned that it would start a dispute against the United States at the WTO; according to Brussels, the provisions of the D'Amato-Kennedy Act breached WTO rules.[24] Clinton eventually understood that the European Union would not back down. His administration advised him that the WTO case had a good chance of being successful, and that this could jeopardize future U.S. sanctions programs.

Back-pedaling looked like the wisest option for the United States. In 1998, after two years of transatlantic tensions, Clinton pledged that the D'Amato-Kennedy Act would not target the investments of European companies in Iran and Libya. In return, European governments dropped their WTO case and committed to support American efforts to combat Tehran and Tripoli's support for terror. Total went back to work on Iran's South Pars gas field. Unbeknownst to the French oil major, respite would prove to be short.

———— ∽∞∾ ————

In 2010 Total had to leave Iran a second time, as U.S. sanctions against Tehran's nuclear program introduced the threat of secondary sanctions on foreign firms that did business with the Islamic republic. At the time, Europe was aboard with respect to U.S. sanctions efforts; the bloc also imposed stringent penalties against Tehran. European companies had no choice but to withdraw from the Islamic republic, as their business dealings had become illegal from both the U.S. and EU perspectives. Total was the last international oil company to leave Iran. In fact, the firm did not fully exit the country; the French company kept an office in Tehran, betting that sanctions would be lifted, eventually.

Total's bet proved to be a winning one. Five years afterward, the nuclear deal was signed. Most European penalties and U.S. secondary sanctions against Iran were lifted (U.S. primary sanctions, however, remained in place, barring American firms from operating in Iran). International businesses could go back to Iran. Total scaled up its Tehran office, again. By then, work was needed on the eleventh phase of the South Pars gas field, an investment worth nearly US$5 billion.[25] Total was in a prime position to work on the project; the company had previously explored this slice of the gas field,[26] and it could invest US$1 billion cash to develop it.[27] Total's ability to finance the project on its own was crucial: despite the lifting of most Western sanctions, international banks remained wary of conducting business with Iran.

For Tehran, attracting investments in the oil and gas sector was a top priority. Iran hoped that ramping up energy exports could shield the country from a new round of Western sanctions in case relations with the United States and the European Union turned sour again. For Iranian policy makers, making Iran a major energy exporter was the best way to prevent future sanctions on the country's oil and gas sector; if Iran became one of the largest energy producers in the world, imposing such penalties would run the risk of destabilizing global oil and gas markets.

Iran's oil sector was also in dire need of Western investment and technology. The Islamic republic had not signed a major contract with an international oil company for ten years. Tehran reckoned that the energy sector needed around US$200 billion in investment.[28] The country was clearly unable to finance these investments on its own, making funding from foreign companies crucial. The timing was not ideal, however: given the sharp drop in oil prices in 2015–2016, energy companies were slashing investment budgets. Western technology was also much needed, especially for the development of liquefied natural gas.

Total could offer Tehran all that Iranian leaders could dream of—the French firm was a global energy major, with ample cash resources and easy access to top-notch technology. After two years of negotiations, in July 2017 Total came back to Iran to work on the South Pars megaproject in partnership with China's CNPC and Iran's Petropars. The agreement planned that Total would work on the giant gas field for 20 years, investing nearly US$5 billion in the project.

Iranian officials were pleased. They brandished the South Pars deal with Total as proof that Iran was able to attract global energy majors. Tehran hoped that other international companies would soon follow Total's example and bring in Western technology and financing to develop Iran's vast energy reserves. The Islamic regime was also keen to hedge its bets with Russian and Asian companies, which looked likelier to stay if Western countries reimposed sanctions on Iran. However, this carefully planned strategy fell foul of developments far beyond Iran's control.

In the meantime, thousands of miles away from Tehran, Trump had been elected as U.S. president. Total's management quickly realized that Trump's election was bad news for the company's plans in Iran, given his campaign pledge to reimpose sanctions against Tehran. Something else worried Total's lawyers. Technically, the United States had never lifted secondary sanctions on the Iranian energy sector; to work on South Pars, Total relied on special authorizations that the U.S. president had to renew every few months.[29] In normal times, the process was meant to be straightforward. However, with Trump at the White House, nothing looked set to be a routine procedure anymore.

Throughout 2017, Trump's cryptic declarations made it impossible to ascertain whether he would make good on his promise to exit the nuclear deal. If Trump decided to go down this path, Total knew that it would have to move quickly to salvage its investment in South Pars. There was a glimmer of hope that if the United States reintroduced sanctions against Iran, these would not include a secondary component. In such a case, Total would probably be able to continue developing the gas field. If secondary sanctions were reimposed, however, then Total's prospects looked gloomier; the company's only chance to stay in Iran was to secure the renewal of the special authorizations that foreign energy firms had been relying on to work in Iran after the nuclear deal was signed.

Preparations for a preemptive lobbying plan to salvage the South Pars project started at Total's Parisian headquarters. The strategy of the French energy major focused on strengthening ties with the United States. Total had long had a solid presence in North America: the French company's U.S. assets stood at around US$10 billion.[30] In late 2017 Total was finalizing a US$1.7 billion investment in a petrochemicals plant in Texas, creating 1,500 jobs for American workers.[31] This gave leverage to the French company, which also opened a government relations office in Washington, D.C. Five people were tasked, full-time, with "coordinating relations" (a synonym for "lobbying," in public-relations speak) with the Treasury and the State Departments.[32]

In early 2018 Patrick Pouyanné, Total's CEO, stepped up the company's lobbying efforts one notch further.[33] At the Davos Forum, Pouyanné told Trump over dinner to stick to the Iran nuclear deal or risk strengthening Iranian hardliners.[34] Total's CEO also hammered home to the U.S. president how South Pars was different from other energy projects: South Pars's gas was to be consumed in Iran. As a result, Tehran would not earn a single U.S. dollar from the field, which was not meant to boost the country's gas exports. According to Total's carefully drafted lobbying plan, the South Pars project was essentially a minor one that did not bolster Iran's standing as a global energy player.

The French energy group's hopes of salvaging its investment in South Pars were soon dashed. Three months after Pouyanné had dinner with Trump at Davos, the United States left the nuclear deal. OFAC immediately revoked the special authorizations that allowed Total and other foreign firms to operate in Iran, giving them six months to leave the country.[35] Total's worst-case scenario was fast becoming reality. In fact, the fresh round of U.S. sanctions was worse than those that the United States had imposed before the nuclear deal was signed: the export of Iran's natural gas was now banned, something that was not the case in the pre–nuclear deal era.

The European Union did not leave the nuclear deal, creating an odd situation for European companies. According to EU regulations, European companies had every right to operate in Iran. In fact, European governments tried to encourage them not to leave the Iranian market, in an attempt to salvage relations with Tehran. However, because of the threat of secondary sanctions, European companies halted operations in Tehran. Germany's Siemens, Denmark's Maersk, and France's Peugeot, among many others in the energy, finance, insurance, and shipping sectors, announced that they had no choice but to withdraw from the Iranian market. The threat of secondary sanctions meant that U.S. regulations had to prevail over EU ones.

In a last-ditch attempt to salvage its investment, Total put all its energy into securing an ad hoc U.S. authorization to continue working on South Pars.[36] The French government started to lobby the United States to support Total's case. However, Total also made it clear that if things did not work out with Washington, it would ditch South Pars in a heartbeat. The decision of the French firm was a no brainer: like most energy majors, Total relies on American banks—and in turn the U.S. dollar—for 90 percent of its financing operations.[37] Losing access to the greenback represented nothing less than a death threat for the company.

In parallel, France, Germany, and the United Kingdom made demands for a blanket sanctions exemption for European companies operating in Iran. The United States flatly denied the request.[38] In a letter to European governments, Secretary of State Mike Pompeo and Treasury Secretary Steven Mnuchin wrote that the United States would "seek to provide unprecedented financial pressure on the Iranian regime."[39] As a result, Pompeo and Mnuchin continued, the United States is "not in a position to make exceptions to this policy except in very specific circumstances where it clearly benefits [U.S.] national security." Paris, Berlin, and London, which had all been cautiously hopeful that a compromise with Washington could be found, were flabbergasted.

Pompeo and Mnuchin's letter sent a clear signal that the United States had no intention of allowing Total—or any other European company— to remain in Iran. After two months, the French firm notified the Iranian government that it had no choice but to exit from South Pars.[40] Ironically, Total's share in South Pars was initially transferred to China's CNPC.[41] The Trump administration had just started the trade war with Beijing, and U.S. secondary sanctions against Iran were benefiting a state-owned Chinese company, at the expense of a European one. However, after only a few weeks CNPC also stopped working on the project owing to the threat of U.S. secondary sanctions.[42]

In the end, the South Pars project went back under the control of Iran's Islamic Revolutionary Guard Corps (IRGC), which U.S. sanctions were meant to weaken. The long-sanctioned paramilitary group further strengthened its grip over the Iranian energy sector; gas forms the backbone of Iran's economy and is a crucial commodity for Iran's cement, steel, or petrochemical industries. The prediction that Pouyanné had made at Davos turned out to be accurate. Because of U.S. sanctions, the influence of hardliners over Iran's economy increased and that of reformers decreased.[43]

Throughout the Total saga, European governments did not hide their frustration with U.S. secondary sanctions. As a European diplomat put it, "We have a situation where there is a will to impose sanctions on Europeans and a resentment towards European companies who are now being accused of supporting a terrorist state."[44] European governments recalled that in 1986 the United States had quickly lifted an oil embargo against Libya for fear that the ban might hurt the interests of U.S. energy companies.[45] This time, however, no such relief was in sight for European firms caught in the sanctions crossfire in Iran.

The reasons that Trump gave to explain why the United States had left the nuclear deal were hard to stomach for European firms and governments. In the eyes of the U.S. president, the agreement was not benefiting American companies enough to represent a sound investment for Washington; as opposed to secondary sanctions, which were lifted, U.S. primary sanctions against Iran remained in place even after sanctions relief started in 2016, preventing American firms from reentering the Iranian market. Instead of trying to hold negotiations with Iran so the nuclear deal could benefit American companies, Trump rejected the agreement altogether so that no firm, U.S. or foreign, could benefit from the deal.

European capitals maintained that the United States had every right to leave the nuclear deal (although they insisted that Iran had complied with the terms of the agreement). However, they objected that threatening EU firms with secondary sanctions was taking things too far. The United States is the only country that imposes secondary penalties. This means American companies do not have to worry about European sanctions, but European firms need to comply with both EU and U.S. penalties. Washington's refusal to consider European requests for sanctions exemptions for European companies was also hard to swallow. Even when the economic interests of its allies were at stake, the United States was not prepared to make a single exception to its policy of exerting maximum pressure on Iran.

EU governments privately remarked that U.S. companies seem to fare better than international ones when they do business with sanctioned countries. While Total was leaving Iran, on the other side of the globe, Chevron, Halliburton, and several other U.S. oil services companies continued to operate in Venezuela even after the United States imposed stringent sanctions on Caracas's energy sector.[46] The U.S. Treasury had granted the American energy companies a string of supposedly temporary, three-month sanctions waivers. These waivers lasted for two years. By contrast, European companies had to unwind their operations in Iran within six months of the United States exiting the nuclear deal.

The Venezuelan example reinforces the widespread feeling among European policy makers that U.S. companies do not seem to have much to fear from sanctions. In their view, Exxon's Russian saga is a telling example of Washington's double standards between American and foreign firms with respect to sanctions. In 2011 Exxon signed a partnership with Rosneft, Russia's state-owned oil company. In return for the promise of several joint ventures in Russia, the U.S. energy major agreed to give Rosneft shares in six oilfields in Texas and the Gulf of Mexico.[47] For Rosneft, the deal represented a unique opportunity to get access to American oil-drilling technology and know-how.

Two years later, in 2013, Rosneft made good on its promise to give Exxon access to joint ventures in Russia. The projects were massive ones. The U.S. oil major planned to invest up to US$500 billion to develop Russian energy fields located deep under the Black Sea, in the Arctic, and in Siberia. Rex Tillerson, who was then Exxon's CEO, enthusiastically signed the deals. In recognition of Exxon and Rosneft's fruitful partnership, Russia's president Vladimir Putin went as far as awarding Tillerson the prestigious Russian Order of Friendship.[48]

A few months afterward, the United States started to impose sanctions against Moscow following Russia's annexation of Crimea and support for separatist rebels in Ukraine. Undeterred, Exxon pressed ahead with its megaprojects in Russia. At the company's annual meeting, Tillerson declared that "We do not support sanctions, generally, because we don't find them to be effective unless they are very well implemented comprehensively and that's a very hard thing to do."[49] This was an interesting comment to make for someone who, three years later, would become U.S. secretary of state (and a staunch supporter of sanctions).[50]

In spring 2014, while fighting was raging in eastern Ukraine, the American oil major doubled down on Russia and signed up for further joint ventures with Rosneft. The CEO of the Russian oil company, Igor Sechin, personally inked the deals even though he had just been placed under U.S. penalties. The transaction was legal, but it raised eyebrows.[51] Exxon was undeterred. The company continued to explore oil fields in the Russian Arctic. In September 2014 Exxon and Rosneft discovered a giant field, which they called Pobeda ("victory" in Russian). Exxon contributed US$600 million to Pobeda's drilling costs.[52]

It took Exxon seven months to put its partnership with Rosneft on hold after the United States started to impose sanctions on Russia.[53] Throughout this period, the American oil major begged the U.S. administration to water down sanctions on Russia's energy sector. However, Exxon's lobbying efforts backfired. OFAC started to investigate Exxon's deals with Rosneft to check whether they complied with sanctions. After three years of investigation, Exxon was fined US$2 million—exactly the average fine for U.S. companies that are caught busting sanctions—for what the U.S. Treasury called a "reckless disregard"[54] for sanctions.

The fine was the equivalent of an accounting rounding error for Exxon (in 2014 the oil giant's revenue amounted to US$412 billion[55]). Exxon nonetheless appealed the decision, arguing that the fine was "capricious"[56] and "fundamentally unfair."[57] Exxon's lawyers maintained that OFAC's guidance on Russia sanctions had been unclear, even though all other companies seemed to have got the message loud and clear that doing business with Russia had become a no-no. Exxon sued the U.S. government. The company won and never had to pay the US$2 million fine. Exxon finally pulled out of its partnership with Rosneft in 2018.

When it comes to secondary sanctions, European companies are asked to cancel their investments immediately or face the risk of being targeted by secondary sanctions. Intense lobbying from European governments is usually of no use, as foreign firms cannot even apply for sanctions waivers. By contrast, it took Exxon four years to exit its high-profile projects in Russia. In fact, Exxon finished ditching all of its Russian assets only in March 2022, after Russia invaded Ukraine. Until then, the company had continued to operate an oil and gas field in a joint venture alongside Rosneft on Sakhalin, an island in Russia's far east.[58]

The Exxon example is galling for America's European allies. The company's success in maintaining extensive operations in Russia for several years despite sanctions has convinced many in Europe that Washington applies double standards between U.S. and non-U.S. companies. Yet the impact of U.S. secondary sanctions goes well beyond forcing foreign companies to ditch investment projects. The penalties may also have far-reaching ripple effects on global energy and commodities markets.

6

SANCTIONS OVERKILL

When Sanctions Crash Global Commodities Markets

n 2007 Austria threatened to sue the Bank für Arbeit und Wirtschaft (BAWAG), the country's fifth largest bank. This was an odd move: Why would a government file a lawsuit against one of its own flagship financial institutions? The answer lay with U.S. sanctions. Cerberus, an American private equity fund, had just bought BAWAG. Worried about falling foul of the U.S. embargo against Cuba now that the bank was owned by an American investor, BAWAG had closed the bank accounts of around 100 Cubans. Under EU regulations, this represented unlawful discrimination on citizenship grounds.[1]

The Austrian government was furious that BAWAG seemed to consider that American rules mattered more than European ones. Vienna decided to invoke the EU's so-called blocking regulation, which (theoretically) forbids European companies from complying with America's extraterritorial penalties. In the words of Austria's foreign minister, "US law is not applicable in Austria. We are not the 51st of the United States."[2] BAWAG understood that it was in trouble and soon applied for waivers that rendered the U.S. sanctions moot. In the end, the Austrian government decided to drop the case after the bank reinstated all the accounts.[3]

Such cases tend to make the headlines in Europe, but they form only the tip of the iceberg when it comes to the ripple effects of U.S.

sanctions on firms around the world. In fact, the impact of sanctions is felt well beyond those firms that are caught in the sanctions crossfire. U.S. penalties on Russia-based Rusal, the world's largest producer of aluminum (outside China), ended up having unexpected side effects on commodities markets, and consequently hundreds of manufacturing companies in dozens of countries. The global ripple effects of sanctions on Rusal proved so massive that Washington had to backtrack in a rush after prompting an aluminum supply crash that derailed manufacturing value chains and threatened to put thousands of people out of work across the globe.

The Rusal saga started in 2017. In that year, the U.S. Congress adopted a broad sanctions package against three of the usual sanctions suspects—Iran, North Korea, and Russia. In Russia's case, the penalties were a retaliation for Moscow's behavior in Ukraine's Donbas region, arms sales to Syria, cyberattacks against American interests, and meddling in the 2016 presidential election. As part of these measures, Congress mandated the U.S. Treasury to publish a list of well-connected Russians who could be placed under individual sanctions. In early 2018 the Office of Foreign Assets Control (OFAC) duly published the list. This was the starting point of a one-year sanctions saga.

The U.S. Treasury list was initially met with widespread disbelief, for good reason. The file was a copy and paste of two documents: a list of 96 of the Russian businessmen who featured in the *Forbes* 2017 billionaires report and, perhaps even more bizarrely, the Kremlin public phone directory.[4] This was not a mistake. OFAC confirmed that its methodology was based on including all of the Russian individuals from the *Forbes* listing who had assets over US$1 billion.[5]

OFAC's methodology looked flawed, to say the least. The former editor of the Russian *Forbes* list called the agency's document a "disgrace," highlighting that the magazine's estimations of wealth were rudimentary.[6] The other source that OFAC had used—the Kremlin's phone directory—left sanctions watchers speechless. Many wondered whether

OFAC had done a rush job simply to fulfill Congress's demands; the agency released the listing in the middle of the night, only 11 minutes before the Congress-mandated deadline.

The Kremlin ridiculed what soon became known as the *Forbes* list. Russian president Vladimir Putin jokingly said that he felt "slighted"[7] that he had not been included. However, OFAC's list did not amuse Moscow's business community.[8] Russian executives worried about reputational risks, wondering whether international banks would continue to do business with them if they featured on a list of potential targets for U.S. sanctions. However, their greatest fear was that the U.S. Treasury had intentionally made the list appear random to a send a message to Moscow: everyone was at risk and could fall under sanctions, for no other reason than being both rich and Russian.

Across Russia, executives started to take preemptive steps to protect their assets. The Russian business community was right to worry. A few weeks later, OFAC announced sanctions on seven members of the *Forbes* list and on 12 companies that they owned or controlled. There was little doubt that some of these businessmen had murky business dealings and opaque connections to the Kremlin. However, why they were chosen out of a list of 96 potential targets remained a mystery despite the claims of Treasury Secretary Steven Mnuchin that the designation process had been "extremely thorough."[9]

The 89 other businessmen from the *Forbes* list had no idea whether they would be next in line or would be spared. Panic engulfed Moscow's business circles. Upon closer examination of the legal basis for the sanctions, businessmen grew even more concerned: Congress had not specified which criteria the Russian individuals placed under sanctions had to meet for the penalties to be lifted. This was unusual. It seemed that everyone in Russia could be targeted and that once someone made it to the list, sanctions could remain in place forever.

The *Forbes* list–driven sanctions package was the most significant increase in U.S. pressure on Russia since Washington had first imposed sanctions against Moscow four years earlier.[10] Many of the companies that OFAC had added to its blacklist were mostly operating in Russia; for them, losing access to the U.S. dollar was painful, but they could adjust by switching to the euro or the ruble. However, as part of the package, OFAC imposed penalties on Oleg Deripaska, a Kremlin insider whose net worth stood at around US$6.7 billion.[11] Deripaska owned and controlled several international companies via his holding, EN+, which was also placed under sanctions.

Rusal was one of these firms. The company, which produced 10 percent of the global supply of aluminum, made it onto the list of targeted entities.[12] To the consternation of lawyers, the legal basis to blacklist the Russian firm appeared shaky. OFAC made it clear that there was nothing wrong with Rusal, which was a well-respected, publicly traded, global business. The Russian state did not even own a single share of Rusal. In fact, Washington was not targeting Rusal. The administration had set its sights on Deripaska, who owned one-third of Rusal and was a close ally of Putin.[13]

The Russian company was a global player in the commodities sector, present across the whole production chain of aluminum,[14] from mining bauxite; then refining bauxite into alumina; and finally pouring alumina into smelters to turn it into aluminum. Rusal mined more than half of its bauxite output outside of Russian borders, including in Guyana, Jamaica, and Guinea. Two-thirds of Rusal's alumina production was refined outside Russia, in countries as diverse as Ukraine, Ireland, and Australia. Rusal's smelters in Russia, Sweden, and Nigeria finalized the production process, producing aluminum that manufacturing companies rely on to make cars, airplanes, and all types of metal objects, such as cans and power lines.

Washington's decision to target Rusal was a significant step; many manufacturing companies across the globe relied on aluminum supplies from Rusal to operate. The penalties also represented a departure from OFAC's traditional approach on sanctions; in the past, the U.S. had targeted the dealings of globally significant companies, such as Russia's energy firms, only via limited restrictions on their access to U.S. financial markets. By comparison, the ban on Rusal was total. After it was placed on OFAC's blacklist, the company could not use the U.S. dollar or do business in America.

The Congress-led sanctions against Rusal included a secondary component. All companies around the world had to ditch their dealings with the Russian aluminum giant or face the risk of being placed under sanctions, too. The threat of secondary sanctions instantly made Rusal a pariah. The firm's value collapsed by half on the Hong Kong stock exchange. American banks stopped processing payments for the company. As a last resort, Rusal asked customers to send payments in euros so these could be cleared by European financial institutions.

The ripple effects of the penalties on Rusal shook global metals markets. Upon news of the sanctions, aluminum prices jumped by 30 percent; traders and manufacturing companies switched to panic-buying mode, fearing that the penalties would cause a global shortage of aluminum. The London Metal Exchange, the global marketplace for nearly all metals, announced that it would not accept trading in Russian-made aluminum unless owners could prove that it had not been produced by Rusal. Down the road, aluminum-intensive companies saw their profit margins vanish as the price of aluminum soared. They warned that consumers would soon feel the pinch.

The timing of the U.S. sanctions could not have been worse. Other American policies had already put the aluminum sector under tremendous pressure. In an attempt to shore up domestic production, the United States had just imposed tariffs on aluminum imports, to which global metals companies were still adjusting.[15] On top of the American tariffs, Norway's Norsk Hydro, another global aluminum producer, had just shut a major Brazilian alumina refinery following the contamination of nearby waters.[16] The global supply of aluminum was running thin even before Rusal was hit by U.S. penalties. Sanctions made a bad situation much worse.

———— ⌘ ————

U.S. sanctions had an immediate impact on Rusal's global operations, putting thousands of jobs at risk across the world. Rusal owned Europe's largest alumina refinery, providing around 30 percent of the continent's alumina supply.[17] The Ireland-based facility stopped receiving bauxite, as the shipping industry canceled delivery contracts for fear of secondary sanctions. Rusal's Irish refinery had enough bauxite to operate for two months, but it warned that it would have to stop working afterward.[18]

The refinery's output had to be stockpiled, anyway. Fearing that they would breach American penalties, cargo ships refused to load alumina from Rusal's Irish plant to serve aluminum smelters in continental Europe. It was unclear whether the refinery would be able to continue to operate. Around 450 jobs were at stake, accounting for an annual wage bill of nearly US$60 million that supported local Irish businesses.[19] Overall, the plant contributed US$145 million annually to Ireland's economy.[20]

Elsewhere in Europe, Rusal's smelter in Sweden continued to produce aluminum, but it also had to stockpile its output, as shipping companies were not willing to touch it. This was the least of Rusal's worries in Sweden, however. Rusal's Swedish smelter was experiencing a massive power cut; Nord Pool, Europe's largest electricity market, refused to serve the plant for fear of breaching U.S. secondary sanctions. Instead, Rusal had to buy electricity directly from a local supplier, at a steep price. The Swedish smelter employed about 500 people. Many feared that the plant would have to close.

Rusal was not the only company struggling because of the U.S. penalties. Secondary sanctions disrupted the operations of other metals groups, too. Rio Tinto, an Anglo-Australian group of metals companies, had no choice but to invoke force majeure on its contracts with Rusal, leading to considerable financial losses.[21] In France and Iceland, Rio Tinto's aluminum smelters were reliant on Rusal-produced alumina. The smelters were left scrambling to find other suppliers amid record-high global demand. However, Rio Tinto had even bigger problems to deal with.

In Australia, Rio Tinto ran one of the world's largest alumina refineries in a joint venture with Rusal.[22] Upon news of the sanctions, Rio Tinto hastily declared that it had to review its ties with the Russian firm, which owned 20 percent of the Australian plant.[23] Many analysts feared that the

Australian refinery might have to close, at least temporarily. The plant employed hundreds of staff, for an annual wage bill of US$136 million. The refinery relied on a network of more than 350 local suppliers, whose operations were also at risk.

Beyond the metals sector, the ripple effects of sanctions against Rusal also had an impact on the shipping industry. Maersk and MSC, two of the world's largest shipping companies, immediately stopped working with the Russian firm.[24] Cargoes of Rusal-made aluminum that had departed from Europe to serve Asian customers before the sanctions were imposed stopped en route.[25] For Maersk and MSC, the loss in revenues was significant, but manageable. However, for other shipping firms that depended on doing business with Rusal, the impact of U.S. sanctions was much more serious.

Germany's Oldendorff was such a case. The shipping company operated tailor-made barges and tugs on Guyana's Berbice River to bring bauxite from Rusal's upstream mines down to coastal Atlantic cargo ships. Oldendorff also handled the maritime journeys of Rusal's Guyana bauxite to refineries in Ukraine and Ireland. With the threat of secondary sanctions looming, the German company had no choice but to suspend all operations with Rusal, putting its Guyanese staff out of work.[26] This was a serious blow for the 4,000-strong German business, which relied heavily on doing business with Rusal.[27]

Down the supply chain, aluminum producers across Europe warned that if Rusal's operations did not restart, they might have to shut down their aluminum smelters. This was far from trivial: shutting down a smelter is a costly, last-resort step. In such a scenario, aluminum production in Europe looked set to come to a halt. European carmakers, such as Audi, BMW, and Volkswagen, feared that they might be left without aluminum.[28] German business groups warned that car production might have to stop, putting 800,000 jobs at risk in Germany alone.[29]

U.S. penalties against Rusal created a serious mess. Aluminum prices spiked to record highs, and international manufacturing companies were struggling to source aluminum. Ironically, sanctions looked set to benefit Chinese metals producers; they had ample spare capacity and made it clear that they were keen to fill the void left by Rusal. By sanctioning Rusal, the United States was penalizing global aluminum consumers while inadvertently supporting Chinese metals makers.

Across the European Union, diplomats and treasury officials were furious. The United States had not consulted European allies before imposing sanctions against Rusal. The Russian company derived around half of its revenues from Europe, where it employed tens of thousands of people who feared they would soon lose their jobs. Down the supply chain, European manufacturing firms did not get any warnings from their governments that aluminum supply was at risk. U.S. allies learned about the Rusal sanctions from the media and had to enter into damage-control mode knowing virtually nothing about the strategy that the United States was pursuing.

Under tremendous business and diplomatic pressure, the United States had no choice but to make a U-turn. OFAC issued a general license that extended the deadline for foreign companies to wind down relations with Rusal. The sanctions remained in place, but the license temporarily waived them. As a result, Rusal was able to resume aluminum shipments, averting fears of a supply crisis. However, sanctions lawyers soon warned that dealings with the Russian firm were far from easy; every single transaction conducted with Rusal had to be reported to U.S. authorities.[30] The paperwork involved was massive: OFAC asked for reports that included the names and addresses of all the parties, the type and scope of the activities, and the dates of the transactions. This was enough to discourage even the most seasoned compliance officers.

Companies remained uneasy about doing business with Rusal, anyway. The U.S. general license that waived the sanctions was meant to be only temporary. OFAC could revoke it at any time or even decide to apply retroactive penalties on firms doing business with the Russian company. Fostering uncertainty was intentional. The U.S. Treasury had started negotiations with Deripaska for him to relinquish control of his holding EN+ and, in turn, Rusal. Severe disruptions of global metals markets represented useful leverage for Washington in the negotiations.

Deripaska had his back against the wall. He could either enter a deal with the United States to try to salvage his business empire or choose to stay put and see his companies lose contracts one after the other. Deripaska announced that he agreed to reduce his stake in EN+ below 50 percent (from 70 percent previously), thereby decreasing his share in Rusal to around 25 percent. In return, the United States agreed to lift sanctions against EN+ and Rusal (individual penalties against Deripaska, however, looked set to remain in place). Both sides concluded a deal a few months afterward. Deripaska's wealth shrunk by around US$3 billion, but EN+ and Rusal could continue to operate.[31] Aluminum consumers breathed a sigh of relief. However, a final hurdle remained to be cleared.

The implementation of the U.S. Treasury's deal with Deripaska required the approval of Congress, which had imposed the Rusal sanctions in the first place. Lawmakers had 30 days to scrutinize the Treasury's proposed agreement with the Russian businessman. In another nail-biting twist for the companies that relied on Rusal's aluminum supplies, members of Congress nearly rejected the agreement. The timing was poor, to start with: the 30-day period fell right during Christmas and New Year festivities, when lawmakers were on break.

More important, the terms of the deal appeared unpalatable to many in Congress. Deripaska was to retain a 44.95 percent share in EN+. This was short of a majority stake, but for many members of Congress this was still too much. The U.S. Treasury knew that this arrangement was not ideal, but it reflected a pragmatic truth: there was not enough appetite in the market to absorb Deripaska's entire stake in EN+. Other lawmakers feared that Deripaska would transfer his wealth and influence in EN+ to his children and friends—something that the proposed agreement did not entirely prevent, although the deal planned that Deripaska would transfer part of his share in EN+ to his charitable foundation.[32] This was a valid point. How was OFAC going to check what was happening behind closed doors in Russia?

Lawmakers needed 60 votes to reject OFAC's proposal to lift sanctions against EN+ and Rusal. They got 57.[33] The United States finally lifted sanctions on Rusal in January 2019. Four months later, Rusal announced plans to build a smelter in Kentucky to produce aluminum for American car plants—the first greenfield aluminum mill built in the United States in 37 years.[34] Deripaska remained under individual sanctions and was still Rusal's largest shareholder. However, this did not seem to matter anymore, now that U.S. jobs were at stake.

———⟨⟩———

On paper, the United States won the Rusal battle: the threat of secondary sanctions made dealings with Rusal toxic for virtually every company around the world, forcing Deripaska to give up control of his assets to save his business empire. This was a first: sanctions had never prompted a management and ownership overhaul in such a giant global firm as Rusal. However, Washington's victory came at a high price: sanctions prompted a spike in aluminum prices, nearly wiped out thousands of jobs across the globe, and left allied governments and business executives alike wondering whether the United States really knew what it was doing with sanctions.

That Washington imposed sanctions against Rusal without thinking they would have powerful side effects is doubtful. In fact, OFAC staff had warned that sanctions against the Russian company would shake global metals markets.[35] Nonetheless, the administration chose to proceed with sanctions, perhaps because Rusal did not own plants in the United States at the time. This left international companies thinking that the United States did not care about the potential side effects of sanctions. Other executives wondered out loud whether such a messy approach was the intended strategy, in an attempt to support American aluminum producers. After all, the administration had just imposed sweeping tariffs on U.S. aluminum imports.

The Rusal episode did some serious reputational damage to Washington. The ripple effects of sanctions against Rusal were so massive that the United States had to backtrack in a hurry by issuing a general license that effectively waived the penalties. International businesses welcomed such a U-turn, but it made America appear weak, with a sanctions strategy akin to "shoot first, aim later."[36] If penalizing a company owned by a wealthy Kremlin insider was the point, then the United States had achieved its goal and there was no need to lift the sanctions. That the administration changed tack in a hurry only created confusion about what the goal of the sanctions really was or if there even was a strategy at all.

The Rusal episode also highlighted the lack of preliminary consultations between the U.S. government and the private sector around sanctions.[37] In almost all policy areas, the administration holds consultations with companies to hear their views around planned regulations. The Commerce and State Departments, for instance, submit proposed tariffs or export controls for comment from the private sectors.[38] Even the U.S. Treasury's sensitive plans to tighten anti–money laundering procedures are discussed publicly. However, sanctions represent an exception: OFAC discusses sanctions plans behind closed doors with only a handful of well-connected American firms.

OFAC argues that submitting sanctions to a comment period would undermine their effectiveness. This is only partly true. It would certainly be counterproductive to announce individual penalties in advance; targeted people would rush to move their assets away from the United States during the consultation period. However, submitting proposed sanctions on companies or entire economic sectors to public comment would probably not undermine their effectiveness. Plans to impose such penalties are usually leaked in the media well before they are put into practice, not to mention that it is notoriously difficult to move a plant overnight.

Upon closer examination, the deal that the United States struck with Deripaska also raises thorny questions.[39] VTB, a sanctioned Russian state-owned bank, acquired part of Deripaska's former share in EN+. Instead of benefiting Deripaska, a share of EN+ profits now falls directly into the coffers of the Kremlin. From Putin's perspective, this was a good result. These extra revenues may serve to finance the very actions of the Russian state that prompted the United States to impose sanctions against Rusal in the first place, such as Moscow's cyberattacks against Washington and military intervention in Syria.

There are also legitimate concerns as to whether Deripaska has really relinquished his control of EN+, and in turn Rusal.[40] The deal that he signed with OFAC capped his voting rights in EN+ at 35 percent. However, Deripaska may still form informal alliances with other shareholders to influence strategic decisions. To prevent this from happening, the deal mandates that EN+ shareholders have to report any attempt by Deripaska to influence their votes. If Deripaska makes such moves, the United States is supposed to reimpose sanctions against Rusal. How OFAC intends to implement this policy remains a mystery: Why would Rusal's shareholders willingly report issues that may lead to the imposition of sanctions on the company that they have stakes in?

The U.S. Treasury appears in no rush to reimpose sanctions against Rusal, anyway. In late 2020 European governments informed the United States that they had intelligence showing that Deripaska was still involved in Rusal's day-to-day activities, using company staff and resources for his own business—such as launching a media campaign against China's presence in Africa.[41] Deripaska sent his lawyers to deny the allegations, which OFAC has so far not acted upon despite a request from a U.S. senator for a briefing on the European intelligence.[42] Even after Russia's invasion of Ukraine, Rusal has remained off the U.S. sanctions list. However, would the United States go down the sanctions road against Rusal a second time, now that the global ripple effects of penalties against the aluminum giant are well documented?

Meanwhile, Deripaska remains fairly busy. Shortly after OFAC lifted sanctions against Rusal, he launched a lawsuit against the U.S. Treasury to obtain some financial compensation for the US$7.5 billion worth of damages that he claims he suffered because of the penalties (he lost).[43] Deripaska's lawyers argued that "unlawful"[44] sanctions, based on "nothing more than false rumor and innuendo,"[45] led to the "wholesale devastation of [his] wealth, reputation, and economic livelihood."[46] Deripaska now likes to present himself as a tormented defender of the rule of law.[47] The latest *Forbes* ranking of billionaires has him pointing at the 1050th rank worldwide, with a net worth of around US$3 billion.[48] If U.S. sanctions were really meant to weaken Deripaska, something must have gone wrong somewhere in the process.

———— ◦◦◦ ————

The Rusal episode is not an isolated case. There are other examples of how U.S. sanctions nearly derailed supply chains across the globe. Only ten months after the United States lifted sanctions on the Russian firm, the administration imposed penalties against COSCO Shipping, a Chinese tanker company, for transporting oil from Iran despite U.S. sanctions.[49] COSCO's tricks were straight from the North Korean sanctions-busting playbook: oil cargoes with fake international identification numbers switched off their transponders to make dark voyages between Iran and China.[50] The penalties on COSCO included a secondary component. Almost 50 of the company's oil tankers were suddenly put out of work, as international firms were not willing to defy U.S. penalties.

The sanctions were a remake of those against Rusal: within hours, the penalties disrupted global shipping ties, fueling a roughly 30 percent hike in freight prices. Freight costs for oil transported from the United States to China reached their highest levels on record.[51] Oil firms that used to rely on COSCO tankers had to pay extortionate prices to book cargoes with other companies. COSCO has one of the world's biggest fleet of very large crude carriers, the equivalent of gigantic oil tankers. Most other shipping companies did not have such large vessels available, especially at the last minute. As a result, oil firms had to book several smaller oil carriers to make up for the lost capacity.[52]

The United States initially dismissed reports that the COSCO sanctions were having negative ripple effects on the shipping industry. An official from the U.S. State Department declared that he had not heard of any disruptions, adding that Trump's maximum pressure campaign against Iran was applied "without any harm."[53] OFAC officials were flabbergasted: they had never been in favor of imposing sanctions on COSCO in the first place, as they had learned a painful lesson from the Rusal story.

Political appointees from the U.S. State Department had been lobbying for the COSCO sanctions as part of Washington's maximum pressure campaign against Iran; as it turned out, the appointees had virtually no clue how sanctions worked and no idea about the potential side effects of the penalties.[54] As had happened with Rusal a few months before, OFAC was left on its own to clear up the mess and minimize the impact of the COSCO sanctions on the global shipping industry.

The remainder of the COSCO story looks very much like the Rusal saga. After three weeks, OFAC issued a general license giving international businesses time to unwind ties with COSCO. The United States lifted most of the sanctions against the Chinese firm a few months afterward.[55] The Rusal episode fueled doubts about Washington's ability to impose sanctions in a structured, coherent manner. To many foreign firms and U.S. allies, the COSCO debacle confirmed suspicions that the U.S. approach to Rusal was not an outlier, but proof that Washington does not care about the fallout from sanctions.

7

SANCTIONS DISPUTES

When Russian Gas Pipelines Divide Allies

I n 1981 President Ronald Reagan made an unusual request during the Ottawa G7 Summit. The U.S. president asked Zenko Suzuki, Japan's prime minister, to prevent Komatsu, a Japanese firm, from selling equipment to the USSR for the construction of a pipeline from Siberia to Europe. According to Reagan, the gas pipeline represented a national security threat for the United States: the White House claimed that the Kremlin would invest the export proceeds to boost the capabilities of the Soviet Army.[1] Komatsu had long been doing business with Moscow and was understandably reluctant to let go of the US$85 million contract. However, Suzuki agreed to Reagan's demands and asked the firm to put the deal on hold.[2]

Ten days later, the U.S. Commerce Department made an unexpected move: the agency granted an American company, Caterpillar, an export license for the very contract that Komatsu had been asked to cancel.[3] The Japanese government was flabbergasted. Across the globe, business executives wondered whether Washington's alleged security concerns about the pipeline were simply a ruse to promote America's commercial priorities. To the entire world, it looked like the United States was keen to use the national security narrative to advance its own economic interests, at the expense of its allies.

Nearly four decades later, U.S. partners had similar doubts about the motives behind American sanctions against Nord Stream 2, a gas pipeline connecting Russia to Germany. The United States opposed Nord Stream 2 on security grounds, arguing that the project represented a threat to Europe's security; Washington argued that in the event of a deterioration in EU-Russia relations, the Kremlin could block gas shipments to Europe.[4] Germany and several other EU countries saw things differently: they suspected that Washington's opposition to the pipeline formed part of a grand plan to boost American gas exports to Europe and argued that the U.S. unilateral measures infringed Europe's sovereignty. For several years, the Nord Stream 2 saga put the transatlantic relationship under serious strain.

The U.S.-EU dispute around Nord Stream 2 looked like a new departure when it erupted in the 2010s, but it was not the first time that America and Europe had argued over a Russian pipeline. In the early 1980s the construction of the Siberian Natural Gas Pipeline—the very project that Japan's Komatsu wanted to work on—had fueled transatlantic tensions. For Washington, concerns that the Kremlin would use the revenues to support the Red Army were only part of the problem. The U.S. Defense Department also worried about a deal that France's Thomson CSF had just signed: the French company had agreed to sell Moscow some high-tech computers to control gas flows within the pipeline. The United States saw this as a red flag: the Pentagon thought that the Soviets could covertly use the equipment for military purposes.[5]

On the other side of the Atlantic, European countries defended the pipeline: they argued that economic cooperation was the best way to engage with Moscow. Collaborating on the construction of the pipeline was a crucial component of the détente policy that they had adopted toward the Kremlin.[6] From Europe's perspective, the Siberian Natural Gas Pipeline was a way to diversify the mix of energy suppliers; the

European Union was keen to lessen its dependence on Middle East oil after the 1973 and 1979 oil shocks.

European governments had economic motives to back the project, too: French, Italian, West German, and British companies had inked contracts for around US$4 billion with the USSR to build various components of the pipeline, such as compressors and turbines.[7] The global economy was in a recession, making these deals crucial for the 20-odd European metallurgy and machinery firms involved.[8] EU governments hoped that the construction of the pipeline would help to curb high unemployment; in Germany alone, the project looked set to support around 1,000 jobs.[9]

American hawks were determined to do everything they could to prevent the construction of the pipeline. However, the Reagan administration was in a bind. Washington knew that it could not impose sanctions on the project without good reason. The only realistic option was to wait for a development that could serve as an excuse to impose sanctions on Moscow. The White House did not have to wait for long.

In December 1981 Communist Poland imposed martial law to crush pro-democracy protests. Demonstrations demanding social change and an improvement in working conditions were met with military force, and dozens of Polish activists were killed. The administration believed that the Kremlin had ordered the brutal crackdown. Reagan quickly seized the opportunity to impose sanctions on Moscow in an attempt to derail the construction of the Siberian pipeline.[10]

European companies were manufacturing the pipeline's turbines and compressors using U.S. technology. This had not escaped Washington's attention. The White House decided to act decisively: in late December the administration suspended the export licenses that allowed European companies to export components built using American technology to the Soviet Union. A modern equivalent of such a measure would be banning EU-based companies from using Apple computers or Microsoft software to manufacture products that they intend to export to Russia.

European governments were furious, not least because the United States had given them only five hours' notice before announcing the sanctions.[11] The measures looked set to delay the construction of the pipeline and, in turn, gas deliveries. The situation was serious, but it was not catastrophic: the export controls did not apply to preexisting contracts. Most European companies could continue to export parts of the pipeline to the USSR, provided they had already signed the related deals. However, Washington hinted that the sanctions could well become retroactive. In such a case, European firms would have no choice but to terminate existing deals. The potential financial losses looked considerable.

Washington knew that the threat to make sanctions retroactive gave it powerful leverage. The United States started to lobby European capitals to convince them to impose sanctions on the USSR in retaliation for the Polish developments. America's threat was thinly veiled. If Europe adopted stringent measures against Moscow, such as a trade embargo, then U.S. restrictions on technology exports to the USSR would not apply to existing contracts. European firms would be able to continue building the various parts of the Siberian pipeline. However, if European states refused to comply with U.S. demands, the administration would make the measures retroactive.

The European Union was caught between a rock and a hard place. The bloc wanted to support European manufacturing companies working on the pipeline, but member states had no appetite for cutting back trade ties with Moscow. European governments were also unsure that the former Soviet Union was behind the crackdown against Polish activists. It appeared to some that Reagan had used the situation in Poland as an excuse to derail the construction of the pipeline. In March 1982 the European Union announced a timid move. The bloc imposed an annual US$150 million cut in imports from the Soviet Union. This was a goodwill gesture toward Reagan, but it fell far short of American demands.

Washington was not impressed, and negotiations continued throughout June, culminating at the Versailles G7 Summit. Discussions were intense, but the two sides failed to reach an agreement.[12] Shortly after the G7 Summit concluded, the United States announced that the export controls that targeted the construction of the pipeline would apply to existing contracts. This was a first: until then, retroactive sanctions had been unheard of. European subsidiaries of U.S. companies would also have to comply with the measures. This was another first and an illegal move: the United States has no jurisdiction over the foreign subsidiaries of American firms.[13]

European governments were outraged. As the French foreign minister, Claude Cheysson, put it, "The United States has just declared what amounts to economic warfare on her allies in Western Europe."[14] The timing was poor. Reagan had recently announced that the United States was dropping its embargo on grain exports to the Soviet Union because the policy was hurting American farmers. The optics were disastrous: Washington appeared keen to sanction the USSR only as long as it did not hurt U.S. firms.

For all the heated diplomatic rhetoric, European businesses felt that they had no choice but to comply with the U.S. measures. The risk of falling foul of U.S. export controls did not appear to be worth taking. European companies started to inform Moscow that they had to withdraw from the pipeline project. America's plan seemed to be working. Protests from EU governments gradually became less frequent. However, this was only the calm before the storm. Britain, France, Italy, and West Germany were mounting a counterattack.

In July 1982 British prime minister Margaret Thatcher restarted the hostilities. In a speech to Parliament, she declared: "The question is whether one very powerful nation can prevent existing contracts from being fulfilled. It is wrong that it should prevent those contracts from being fulfilled."[15] The tone was set. European countries had no intention of caving in to U.S. pressure. European governments started to order their domestic firms to fulfill their contractual obligations with Moscow. The measure applied to the branches of American businesses, too; Dresser-France, the French subsidiary of U.S.-based Dresser Industries, received strict instructions from Paris to deliver the pipeline parts to the USSR.[16]

If companies refused to deliver the components to the Soviet Union, the French and British governments had a plan B. Paris threatened to requisition the businesses that complied with American sanctions.

London proceeded similarly with four British firms.[17] European companies got the message loud and clear. They swiftly restarted delivering the various parts of the Soviet pipeline. Washington retaliated by imposing sanctions on 12 European firms, barring them from doing business in the United States.[18]

The transatlantic row had turned into a standoff. European countries were united in their opposition to U.S. sanctions. By contrast, support for the penalties was crumbling in Washington. The administration was deeply divided as to whether imposing sanctions on allies was an appropriate move.[19] Secretary of State Alexander Haig resigned, arguing that the sanctions on the Soviet pipeline were causing an unnecessary split in the transatlantic alliance.[20] A young Columbia and Harvard graduate named Antony Blinken, who would later become the U.S. secretary of state under the presidency of Joe Biden, shared the same view. He wrote a book explaining why blocking the construction of the pipeline should be less important for the United States than maintaining strong ties with European allies.[21]

In Washington, those who opposed the sanctions argued that they were at best ineffective and at worst counterproductive: despite the penalties, the European Union's determination to stand up to American demands meant that the Soviet pipeline looked set to be built.[22] Part of the administration also feared that the measures were hurting U.S. companies, which had to stop selling technology to European businesses; estimates put the short-term losses for American firms, such as Caterpillar and General Electric, at more than US$2 billion (equivalent to US$6 billion in today's money when adjusted for inflation).[23]

The potential long-term reputational damage to U.S. businesses looked set to be even worse: foreign companies started to wonder whether they should use American technology at all in case this might expose them to Washington's sanctions. These worries made sense. Soviet authorities hinted that European firms using U.S.-made know-how would not be eligible for future contracts.[24] Facing intense lobbying from industrial companies, Congress started to draft legislation to reverse the sanctions on the Soviet pipeline and to force the White House to seek the approval of allies for similar measures.

In November 1982, after nearly a year of transatlantic tensions, Reagan decided that the controversy had lasted for too long. Martial law was still in place in Poland, but he canceled the sanctions. The Soviet pipeline was completed two years later, on schedule, and remains in operation. The damage to American companies proved long-lasting: European firms remained wary of using U.S. technology for fear of new rounds of retroactive sanctions. As Thatcher put it, the measures were "harmful ultimately to American interests because so many people will say there is no point in making a contract to secure materials, machinery and equipment from the U.S. if at any time they can just cancel that contract."[25]

Fast-forward nearly 40 years later, to the late 2010s: the quarrel over Nord Stream 2 looked like a repeat of the 1982 dispute.[26] A pipeline connecting Russia to Europe was being built. The United States was seeking to apply pressure on Moscow and imposed sanctions to derail the project. European companies were caught in the crossfire and EU governments were incensed, arguing that the measures were an infringement of their sovereignty. Transatlantic tensions ensued. The squabble was pointless: the pipeline would be built and then eventually scrapped.[27]

On paper, Nord Stream 2 had nothing to do with the United States. The project aimed at doubling the capacity of Nord Stream 1, another gas pipeline between Russia and Germany. Gazprom, the Russian state-owned gas giant, financed half of Nord Stream 2's hefty price tag of US$11 billion.[28] The five European companies that signed up to receive gas via the new pipeline funded the other half of the construction costs. For the European Union, the project was a huge one: around 150 European firms were involved in one way or another.[29] However, for the United States, Nord Stream 2 was much more than a purely business-driven enterprise.

From Washington's perspective, the pipeline represented a potential Russian weapon against Europe. The administration worried that Nord Stream 2 would deepen the European Union's dependence on Russian energy; at the time, Europe sourced around 40 percent of its gas imports from Russia.[30] The United States believed that this was already too much and that a further increase in Moscow's market share in the European gas market would boost the Kremlin's leverage over Europe. Other critics noted that the new pipeline would be operated by the same company—Nord Stream AG—as the existing Nord Stream 1 pipeline, which ran close to the proposed route of Nord Stream 2. Europe could lose nearly half of its gas supplies if a cyberattack targeted Nord Stream AG or if an explosion were to occur on either Nord Stream 1 or 2.[31]

Opponents of the pipeline argued that the project was dangerous not only for Europe, but also for Ukraine. Kyiv had stopped importing Russian gas several years earlier, but Nord Stream 2 looked set to put a strain on the Ukrainian budget: the pipeline meant that Russian gas exports could go directly to Europe instead of transiting through a network of existing pipelines that often crossed Ukraine. Nord Stream 2 skeptics argued that this would do great economic damage to cash-strapped Kyiv, which would lose the roughly US$3 billion in transit fees that Moscow used to pay every year.

Gazprom and its five European partners announced the construction of Nord Stream 2 in 2015. Preparatory works, such as the issuance of tenders to select suppliers of steel pipes, started shortly afterward. Congress first tried to derail the project two years later, in 2017, when a fresh legislative package threatened to impose secondary sanctions on international companies that provided funding or support for Russian energy projects.[32] The measures targeted the European energy firms that financed half of Nord Stream 2. However, for several weeks, it was not clear whether the threat of secondary sanctions would apply retroactively.

As is often the case, the wording of Congress's legislation was unclear and remained open to interpretation. European companies involved in Nord Stream 2 anxiously waited for the United States to issue some explanatory guidance. Under intense diplomatic pressure, Washington backed down: the State Department announced that the sanctions would not apply to energy projects that had already started. European businesses breathed a sigh of relief. Nord Stream 2 was spared, and preparatory work for the construction of the pipeline could continue.[33]

Pipe-laying operations began in September 2018. Only a few weeks later, U.S. energy secretary Rick Perry resurrected the sanctions threat.[34] While visiting Moscow, he declared that penalties against Nord Stream 2 were still an option for Washington. A few weeks later, U.S. ambassador to Germany Richard Grenell doubled down; he wrote letters to the European companies that were financing part of Nord Stream 2, urging them to ditch the project.[35] EU policy makers and energy companies held their breath again, thinking that sanctions were in the cards. Yet nothing happened. Work on the pipeline continued throughout 2019. Progress was fast. By the end of the year, segments of the pipeline in Sweden, Finland, and Russia were completed. The pipeline looked set to start operations some time in 2020.

Congress eventually imposed sanctions on Nord Stream 2 in the final days of 2019, when lawmakers adopted legislation threatening to impose secondary sanctions on companies laying undersea pipes for Russian energy projects. After two years of vain attempts, Congress had finally managed to threaten the completion of Nord Stream 2.[36] The ultimatum worked: a few hours after Congress's vote, AllSeas, the Swiss-Dutch company that had been providing highly specialized megaships to lay the 200,000 pipes that would make up the pipeline, exited the project in a rush.[37]

The threat of secondary sanctions dealt a blow to Nord Stream 2. Sanctions watchers wondered whether the American measures would derail the project. They did not have to wait for long to get the answer. The penalties were painful, but not enough to convince Gazprom and European energy firms to abandon the pipeline. Despite AllSeas' exit, Gazprom had a plan B for laying the pipes. Three years earlier, while preparatory work on the pipeline was taking place, the Russian gas company had conveniently bought a pipe-laying vessel, the *Akademik Cherskiy*.

In early 2020 the *Akademik Cherskiy* was sailing north of Japan in the Sea of Okhotsk, waiting to start work on Russia's nearby Sakhalin gas fields. Gazprom immediately sent the ship on a four-month journey around the world, going all the way from Japan to the Baltic Sea via the Cape of Good Hope (the crane of the *Akademik Cherskiy* was too high for the vessel to transit below the Suez Canal bridge).[38] For the Kremlin, securing the ship's voyage was a top priority; Moscow enlisted the Russian Navy to escort the vessel, which safely arrived in the Russian enclave of Kaliningrad in May.

Gazprom knew that the *Akademik Cherskiy* was slower than AllSeas' ships, but swift progress in 2019 meant that only around 100 miles (or about 5 percent) of undersea pipes remained to be laid. This seemed feasible. Russia's prime minister Dmitry Medvedev argued that there was "nothing catastrophic" about the U.S. sanctions.[39] According to Moscow, the construction of the pipeline was delayed, but not derailed. However, developments in the Baltic Sea meant that it was hard to be sure that work on Nord Stream 2 would continue.

Throughout May and June 2020, the *Akademik Cherskiy* did not a lay a single pipe. Rumor had it that the ship was being upgraded with some advanced pipe-laying equipment, but some analysts believed that the tightening of U.S. sanctions had killed Nord Stream 2. No information was coming from Russia, except that Gazprom had hired an additional pipe-laying ship, the *Fortuna*. However, sanctions watchers were unsure that the *Fortuna* would ever be allowed to lay pipes in the Baltic Sea.

The *Akademik Cherskiy* was a formidable ship: it was able to lay down pipes nearly 700 feet under the sea with a high degree of accuracy even in stormy waters. The vessel had advanced capabilities that assessed its position in real time on the basis of current, wave motion, and wind patterns. However, it was painfully slow. By contrast, the *Fortuna* was faster, but it did not have the same positioning technology as the *Akademik Cherskiy*. As a result, the *Fortuna* required multiple anchorages to lay undersea pipes accurately.[40]

This was a serious problem: the only work that remained for Nord Stream 2 to be completed was to be done in German and Danish waters. However, Copenhagen usually forbids anchored vessels from doing work in Danish waters for fear that ships will moor on unexploded World War II mines. To the consternation of the United States (and after long delays that some observers believed were due to U.S. pressure), in early

July 2020 Copenhagen gave the green light for the *Fortuna* to lay pipes.[41] For Gazprom, this was brilliant news. The *Fortuna* and the *Akademik Cherskiy* were soon en route to the small German port of Mukran to load up steel pipes before restarting the construction work.

The U.S. administration decided to step up pressure on Nord Stream 2 one notch further. In mid-July the State Department issued revised guidelines stating that previous sanctions that had targeted companies working on Russian energy projects back in 2017 would apply retroactively.[42] For European firms working on Nord Stream 2, the updated guidance was alarming. It meant that ports such as Mukran that welcomed pipe-laying vessels, the companies that insured the ships, and the banks that processed transactions related to Nord Stream 2 could become the targets of U.S. secondary sanctions.[43]

The State Department's change of heart was a bitter blow for Europe: the 2017 vintage of sanctions explicitly mentioned that U.S. measures against energy projects had to be coordinated with allies.[44] The United States reneged on this commitment.[45] It was hard to see how the updated guidance could be enforced: lawyers thought that it was likely to be challenged in international courts.[46] However, spooked by the risk of sanctions, the Russian owner of the *Fortuna* withdrew from the project. The *Akademik Cherskiy* left the pipeline's construction site and returned to Kaliningrad. Speculation about Nord Stream 2's prospects reached record highs. All bets were off as to whether the pipeline would ever be completed.

The following weeks proved intense as the United States appeared to gain the upper hand in the Nord Stream 2 saga. In early August some U.S. senators declared that they would not shy away from imposing "crushing"[47] sanctions on Mukran, the German port that had been providing pipes and other supplies to the pipe-laying ships. The move was extraordinary: the senators went as far as threatening to impose sanctions on the employees of the Baltic port. The threat to sanction German port stevedores prompted consternation across Europe. Even those who opposed Nord Stream 2 began to wonder whether the U.S. senators were really serious.

In the 1950s the small port of Mukran was a thriving fishing community and a popular destination for Swedish holidaymakers. Seven decades later, the port was only a shadow of its former self, with many living below the poverty line owing to a dearth of positions that paid more than the minimum wage. The town was desperate to create new jobs, but most of those available involved working on Nord Stream 2.[48] If the project was canceled, the annual US$2 million in local taxes that the local authorities had penciled in would also vanish.[49] For Mukran, economic ruin loomed.[50]

Threatening to impose sanctions on German port employees badly damaged Washington's credibility. For Mukran's inhabitants, who learned Russian at school and used to live in Communist East Germany, the ultimatum confirmed negative stereotypes about American imperialism. Germany's left-wing party sent a letter to Congress asking how Washington would react if Berlin threatened to impose sanctions on American ports.[51] The Russia-friendly German Far Right went even further. The party asked for the sanctions that the European Union had imposed against Moscow following the annexation of Crimea to be lifted altogether.

The abrasive declarations of the U.S. senators backfired. The threat to sanction German workers made building the pipeline a matter of pride against what many in Europe were increasingly seeing as a U.S. abuse of power. The construction of the pipeline was still on pause, but some European policy makers were starting to believe that completing the project was the best way to send Washington a message about the European Union's determination to stand up to U.S. demands. However, another development that had nothing to do with gas, pipe-laying vessels, or sanctions intervened to complicate matters further.

─── ⟨⟨⟩⟩ ───

In August 2020 Alekseï Navalny, Russia's most prominent opposition leader, fell critically ill after he was exposed to a nerve agent.[52] Given the

Kremlin's track record of silencing opponents, suspicions quickly arose that the Russian government was responsible for Navalny's poisoning. On both sides of the Atlantic, those who opposed the construction of Nord Stream 2 sensed an opportunity: while Navalny was being treated in Berlin, they called on Germany to ditch the pipeline in retaliation for the attack.

The German government faced a difficult situation. On the one hand, Berlin did not want to appear to downplay the seriousness of Navalny's condition or to minimize concerns about what looked like an attempt from the Kremlin to murder an opponent (it was later confirmed that members of the Russian security services were involved in the attack). On the other hand, Germany was adamant that Nord Stream 2 was a private business project that had to be completed to meet Europe's energy needs. Berlin also felt that it was pointless to argue with Russia about something that could not be reversed—Navalny had been poisoned and nothing could change this fact.[53] For Chancellor Angela Merkel, the only way was forward.

There was probably another reason why Germany was reluctant to cancel Nord Stream 2. Even if she was never a fan of the pipeline project, Merkel wanted to avoid giving the impression that Berlin had finally caved in to U.S. pressure on Nord Stream 2—something that Congress and the White House would have loudly hailed as a major victory for sanctions. At the time, only a few people in Washington understood what this really meant: if even the attack on Navalny did not derail the project, then U.S. sanctions had almost no chance of succeeding.

Germany chose to bide its time and to wait for the Navalny story to gradually disappear from the media. Work on the pipeline remained on hold, however. Again, experts were scratching their heads to figure out what was happening. Had the threat of secondary sanctions on European companies working on Nord Stream 2 really halted the completion of the pipeline? This appeared unlikely, but it was hard to know for sure. Perhaps Washington had also issued covert warnings to the Kremlin; the CIA had just claimed that it had the capability to switch off the lights in Moscow.[54]

Ship movements around Kaliningrad held the answer: far from withdrawing from the project, Gazprom was busy gathering an armada of Russian boats that looked set to become supply and rescue vessels for pipe-laying ships.[55] This was a smart move: with support from these boats, the pipe-laying vessels would be able to complete the pipeline with virtually no help from the shore. The German port of Mukran would not have to be involved, neutralizing Congress's sanctions threat.[56] Gazprom put the ships under a tough testing regimen to make sure that they would be able to withstand the freezing temperatures and fierce winter storms of the Baltic Sea. The *Fortuna* had just changed hands and rejoined the party, too.

Work on Nord Stream 2 looked set to continue. Congress tried to tighten sanctions against "Putin's pipeline"[57] again; in October 2020 the administration issued guidance that further widened the scope of previous sanctions rounds.[58] However, it was clear that these penalties would not bite much; by then, Gazprom had made the construction of Nord Stream 2 a purely Russian enterprise. The United States could sanction the entire armada of pipe-laying ships and supply and rescue boats as much as it liked; their Russian captains would gladly accept the measures as a badge of honor. Washington was starting to sound like a broken record.

In late 2020 the *Fortuna* restarted work on the last two incomplete German and Danish segments of the pipeline in a race to the finish line.[59] The Office of Foreign Assets Control (OFAC) imposed sanctions on the vessel, to no avail. After years of uncertainties, the United States had no more options to tighten sanctions further. Nord Stream 2 looked set to be built, and Russia's press agency announced that the pipeline would be completed in 2021.[60] However, this was not the end of the story: experts were still making bets as to whether gas would ever run in the pipes.

Gazprom could complete the construction of the pipeline by making the process a Russian affair. However, no gas could flow in Nord Stream

2 until the pipeline was both certified and insured. In early 2021 the United States adopted a new round of sanctions that targeted insurance and certification companies that worked on the project; only Western firms had the required certification expertise, and defying U.S. penalties was not a risk that they were willing to take. It looked like the pipeline was going to be built, but that American sanctions would prevent it from operating. Things were in a standstill. However, in Washington, the political landscape had just changed dramatically.

Biden had recently become U.S. president. Blinken, the Columbia and Harvard alumni who had written a book on the Soviet pipeline, had been named secretary of state. After four years of tensions under the presidency of Donald Trump, the White House knew that finding a compromise over Nord Stream 2 presented a rare opportunity to reset badly strained transatlantic ties. Washington was also acutely aware that any attempts from the Biden administration to address Russia's behavior would prove futile if European allies were not aboard. However, as long as the United States and Germany were arguing over the pipeline, cooperating over dealing with Moscow would prove difficult.

Shortly after Biden's inauguration, rumors started to circulate about a potential agreement between Washington and Berlin about Nord Stream 2. It seemed that the United States and Germany might come to a compromise about the commercial modalities of the pipeline's operations—by, say, putting a cap on the share of Russian gas in the European energy mix in return for the lifting of sanctions.[61] Another much-touted option was that Germany could sign up for a mechanism that would interrupt gas deliveries via Nord Stream 2 if Russia ratcheted up tensions with Ukraine or other European countries.

That Washington and Berlin might come to an agreement on Nord Stream 2 looked like a breakthrough, but it was far from new. The United States had always left the door open for such negotiations; even the most stringent sanctions packages against Nord Stream 2 planned for transatlantic "consultations" to find an arrangement over the issue. Beyond politics, the White House also knew that starting negotiations was the most logical step. Before the war in Ukraine made Russia a pariah in 2022, it was unrealistic to expect that European energy firms, let alone

Gazprom, would abandon Nord Stream 2 given the billions that they had invested in the project.

At the time, leaving the pipeline to rot in the Baltic Sea was not seen as an option, anyway; such a scenario entails significant safety and environmental risks. To its chagrin, Washington also realized that Biden's arrival at the White House meant that Berlin had the upper hand; given the need to mend transatlantic ties after the animosity of the previous administration, there was little chance that the United States would dare to go down the sanctions route if Berlin ordered German firms to certify and insure the pipeline.

Such a situation would have been a repeat of the 1982 row between America and Europe over the Soviet pipeline. From this perspective, negotiations on Nord Stream 2 represented a face-saving exercise for America, even though the administration tried to look tough. Berlin knew it and Merkel had every intention of showing the United States that she would stand firm on this topic. The end of the story was clear: Washington had lost the battle, and U.S. sanctions had failed to derail the pipeline project.

Four months after taking office, the Biden administration lifted penalties on Nord Stream 2 after a report from the State Department assessed that it was in the U.S. national interest to waive the measures. The construction of the pipeline was completed in September 2021. However, the likeliest scenario is that Russian gas will never flow through the pipes. In early 2022, after Russia invaded Ukraine, the German government pulled the plug on Nord Stream 2, confirming once again that the fate of the pipeline was only ever going to be determined by Berlin.

⸺ ∞ ⸺

The Nord Stream 2 episode highlighted deep divisions among EU member states regarding relations with Moscow. Some East European countries, including staunch Russia critics such as Poland and the Baltics, argued that building the pipeline was a dangerous endeavor that would make Europe overly dependent on Russian gas. The European Parliament also opposed the project. The legislative body adopted several nonbinding resolutions calling for a halt in the construction of the pipeline and an urgent rethink of ties with Moscow.[62]

Meanwhile, European governments that tend to have a softer stance toward Russia, such as Germany and Austria, argued that building Nord Stream 2 would help to secure Europe's long-term energy supplies at a low environmental cost compared to alternatives, such as coal. (Germany started to decommission nuclear plants following the Fukushima nuclear disaster in 2011. As a result, the country relied on polluting coal-fired power plants to produce electricity.) However, almost all Europeans agreed on one thing: Washington took things a step too far by imposing sanctions on the pipeline.

Germany believed that it did not need U.S. permission to boost gas imports from Russia. As the German foreign minister put it, "The U.S. administration is disrespecting Europe's right and sovereignty to decide itself where and how we source our energy."[63] This is a two-way street: Berlin has never given Washington advice as to which energy supplier to choose. Some German policy makers wondered how the United States would react if the European Union imposed sanctions on pipelines that run on American soil.

The German government also found it infuriating that Washington started to impose stringent sanctions on Nord Stream 2 four years after the project was launched, at a time when billions had already been invested in the construction of the pipeline. The United States argued that it was targeting Nord Stream 2 because America saw itself as the ultimate guarantor of Europe's security. If this was really the case, some European officials wondered why America had to wait for several years before coming to Europe's rescue against what Washington believed was a major threat to European security.

Before the war in Ukraine started, some European officials also noted that receiving more gas directly from Russia represented a positive development for Europe's energy security: in their view, thanks to Nord Stream 2, the European Union would have been able to extricate itself from Russia-Ukraine gas wars. The Kremlin knew that the threat to cut gas exports to Ukraine was powerful precisely because such a measure had a direct impact on European countries. If EU member states received less Russian gas via Ukraine, they had fewer chances of being held hostage of disputes between Moscow and Kyiv. This was probably one of the key reasons why Berlin was so reluctant to cancel the project.

American concerns about the financial impact of Nord Stream 2 on Ukraine appeared harder to dismiss. Kyiv was in dire need of Gazprom's money to, among other things, fight against Russian-backed separatist rebels. However, before Russia's invasion of Ukraine prompted a rethink of ties to Moscow, some European policy makers thought that the construction of Nord Stream 2 could well turn out to be beneficial to Ukraine in the long term: as the country ceased to be a transit state for Russian gas exports, Moscow's leverage over Kyiv looked set to greatly decrease.

Throughout the Nord Stream 2 saga, Berlin also liked to think that it was already doing enough to support Ukraine. In the five years to 2019, the European Union was the largest donor to Kyiv; the bloc had sent Ukraine an annual average of US$710 million in aid since Russia's illegal annexation of Crimea in 2014—twice as much as the United States.[64] European countries also supported Ukraine on a bilateral basis. Germany's assistance to Kyiv totaled more than US$1 billion in 2014–2019.

⸎

From a European perspective, the reasons the United States gave for sanctioning Nord Stream 2 were not convincing, fueling suspicions that Washington had other motives for derailing the project. Some EU member states surmised that these were commercial: they believed that the United States was trying to boost American exports of liquefied natural gas (LNG) to Europe. In support of this view, European officials noted that Nord Stream 2 was one of the few topics of disagreement between Russian president Vladimir Putin and Trump; the U.S. president's top priority was always to boost U.S. exports even if this meant imposing coercive economic measures, such as tariffs, on allies.

The declarations of several American officials only appeared to confirm Europe's theory. As energy secretary Rick Perry put it, "the United States is again delivering a form of freedom to the European continent [. . .], and rather than in the form of young American soldiers, it's in the form of liquefied natural gas."[65] U.S. senator Ted Cruz, who had led the charge against the German port of Mukran, agreed. In his view, "It's far better for Europe to be relying on energy from the United States than to be fueling Putin and Russia and dependent on Russia and subject to economic blackmail."[66]

The recent rapid development of the U.S. LNG sector further fueled Europe's suspicions that Washington was targeting Nord Stream 2 to boost American gas exports. In 2019 the United States was the world's fourth largest exporter of LNG,[67] on track to claim the top spot by 2025. However, America provided only a fraction of Europe's gas imports in 2019, while Russia supplied about 40 percent of them.[68] U.S. LNG terminals located on the East Coast, within easy reach of Europe, had plenty of spare capacity. Seen from this perspective, the European Union represented a natural battleground for American and Russian gas exports, with U.S. gas companies seeking to take over Russia's market share. However, if Russian gas started to flow through Nord Stream 2, Europe would not need America's LNG.

If the pipeline had become operational, supply from Nord Stream 2 would have amply covered European gas needs in the coming decades, not to mention that Russian gas is much cheaper than American LNG. Seen from this perspective, the U.S. strategy to do everything it could to try to prevent the construction of Nord Stream 2 appeared sound. This reasoning would help to explain why the United States started to grow concerned about Nord Stream 2 only in 2017, when Trump came to power and vowed to do everything he could to make the United States the world's largest exporter of LNG.

The possibility that Washington used sanctions to boost LNG exports to Europe also helped energy experts to make sense of an intriguing feature of U.S. measures against Russia. Sanctions packages that Congress adopted in 2019 threatened to impose penalties on Russian energy projects worth more than US$250 million. However, for the construction of Russian gas or LNG infrastructure, the threshold was far lower: Congress set it at only US$1 million.[69] To many sanctions watchers, it looked like Washington did not care much about sanctioning Russian energy projects, unless they competed with U.S. gas exports.

For Europe, the Nord Stream 2 saga appeared to confirm long-standing fears that in some cases, the United States does not shy away from using sanctions to advance America's economic interests. Washington vehemently denied this, arguing that American sanctions first and foremost hurt U.S. companies by preventing them from doing business in dozens of countries. From this perspective, U.S. secondary sanctions on foreign firms are a minor matter, which pales in comparison with the restrictions with which U.S. firms have to comply. Whether or not the United States targeted Nord Stream 2 to boost American LNG exports may not be the most important point, however.

That European allies suspected that this could be the case highlighted the lack of trust between the two parties and put a further strain on the transatlantic relationship. This was a dangerous development. Such tensions undermined ties between Washington and European capitals, preventing both sides from working together on other issues, such as—precisely—Russia's behavior in the run-up to its invasion of Ukraine. Cracks in the partnership only benefit U.S. foes—Russia in Nord Stream 2's case.

<hr />

As was the case for the Soviet pipeline in the early 1980s, U.S. sanctions failed to prevent the construction of Nord Stream 2. This was hard to predict. However, the United States could probably have guessed that the measures would divert attention away from Washington's understandable concerns around the pipeline, turning the debate into a discussion about the legitimacy and motives—real or supposed—of U.S. sanctions on the activities of its allies.[70] For America, the fight against Nord Stream 2 cost time, energy, and credibility. All the efforts of U.S. diplomacy failed to convince European partners to ditch the pipeline.

For Europe, the Nord Stream 2 saga was a wakeup call. It underlined the need for the bloc to stand ready to defend its economic interests. Coupled with other contemporaneous developments, such as the impact of U.S. secondary sanctions on European companies in Iran, the Nord Stream 2 episode further reinforced Europe's determination to resist

U.S. extraterritorial measures. That U.S. sanctions failed to derail the project also exposed their limits; sanctioned states will not have failed to notice that Gazprom continued building the pipeline despite facing U.S. penalties.

The U.S. decision to impose unilateral sanctions on Nord Stream 2 also set a dangerous precedent: How would Washington react if China chose to follow the U.S. example and imposed unilateral penalties on American companies? The United States tends to believe that it is always on the right side of moral arguments. There is no reason to think that China does not share the same belief. However, in many instances Washington and Beijing happen to disagree, making the risk of Chinese unilateral sanctions credible. America's track record of sanctioning Nord Stream 2 on its own makes it difficult to argue that China has no right to do something similar if it so wishes.

III

SANCTIONS BLUES

8

SANCTIONS-BUSTING

Avoidance Schemes from U.S. Friends and Foes

I n the summer of 2020 the U.S. Congress published a report detailing how wealthy Russians had been dodging U.S. sanctions for years.[1] The investigation showed that businessmen close to the Kremlin had used the opaque, unregulated American art market to access the U.S. financial system and flout sanctions.[2] The report made the headlines, as its implications were huge: If sanctioned Russians could buy and sell art in America undetected, what else could they do under the radar? Were Washington's measures against Moscow effective or were they easy to circumvent?

Capitol Hill has long been concerned that sanctions against Russia might not be watertight. When they commissioned the report, lawmakers wanted to understand how U.S. penalties could be improved. Congressional investigators first thought that they would take a broad look at sanctions loopholes, such as the use of obscure Belarusian front companies to hide dealings with Russia. After reviewing a few transactions, the researchers narrowed down their search much closer to American soil, to the U.S. art market. Within this niche area, the activities of two Russian brothers, Arkady and Boris Rotenberg, caught Congress's attention.

The Rotenbergs are no small fry; their combined wealth stands at more than US$3 billion.[3] They form part of the inner circle of Russian president Vladimir Putin: Arkady, Boris, and Vladimir went to the same gym in St. Petersburg to practice judo when they were teenagers.[4] Since then, they have remained close friends. Arkady regularly lends his Black Sea mansion to Putin. Today, the Rotenbergs count among the most powerful businessmen in Russia. The various companies that they own in the energy sector work closely with Gazprom, the Kremlin-backed gas giant.[5]

The Rotenbergs' reach extends far beyond the oil and gas sector. When the Olympic Games took place in Russia in 2014, the Russian government awarded the brothers' construction companies around US$7 billion in contracts.[6] A few years later, Arkady's firm built a bridge connecting Crimea to the Russian mainland after Moscow illegally annexed the Ukrainian peninsula.[7] A few months after that, Boris sued Finnish financial institutions that had refused to open a bank account for him because he was under American—but at the time not European—sanctions (he lost).[8] When they are not working hand in hand with the Kremlin, the brothers share a hobby: buying art masterpieces.

The Rotenbergs were among the first Russian businessmen that the United States placed under sanctions in March 2014.[9] In theory, the brothers cannot conduct any transaction in the United States, or with American counterparts, or using the U.S. dollar. Congress believed that the Rotenbergs repeatedly ticked all three boxes over the course of several years: starting in 2014, the businessmen spent US$91 million buying high-value paintings from American auction houses. The brothers did not deal directly with the likes of Sotheby's and Christie's; they used intermediaries (who acted on their behalf) and shell entities (which hid their identities).

The auction houses did not do anything wrong. The U.S. art market is huge, with roughly US$30 billion in sales every year. It is also murky. U.S. law does not require auction houses to check who will own the paintings that they sell; auctioneers simply need to make sure that the intermediaries they deal with are not under sanctions. If auction houses ask further questions, go-betweens usually refuse to reply. It is also up to auctioneers to decide whether to run anti–money laundering checks on art buyers and sellers. Even when these verifications take place, they are of little value: auction houses may perform checks on the intermediaries, but not on the people who stand behind them. The identity of buyers and sellers remains secret.

The Rotenberg episode caused consternation in Washington, but what the investigation uncovered should not really have come as a surprise. As long as the United States imposes sanctions on wealthy, well-connected individuals, these people will find inventive ways to circumvent penalties with the help of creative lawyers and accountants. Such sanctions-skirting schemes tend to attract a lot of attention, but they do not seriously undermine the effectiveness of U.S. sanctions; rather, they form part of the natural order of things.

Illicit schemes such as those set up by the Rotenberg brothers do not keep American policy makers awake at night. Their fears lie elsewhere: over the past few years, Washington's enthusiasm for sanctions has fueled the development of state-backed mechanisms aimed at circumventing America's coercive measures. U.S. allies and foes alike are openly taking steps to evade American sanctions, which they often believe are an abuse of power. These sanctions-busting mechanisms vary, but they have one thing in common: they all seek to build alternative financial channels that bypass the U.S. dollar.

In March 2020 finance ministers of the Shanghai Cooperation Organization (SCO) met in Moscow. The alliance seldom makes the headlines in Western countries, but it carries significant weight: the club of like-minded emerging countries covers half of the world's population and includes major powers such as China, India, Pakistan, and Russia. During their meeting, the ministers took what they believed was a long overdue, and seemingly innocuous, decision: they agreed to expedite the setting up of processes to conduct trade in national currencies, such as the Chinese renminbi, the Indian rupee, and the Russian ruble.[10]

Finance ministers of the SCO had a clear objective in mind when they agreed to set up mechanisms to foster trade in local currencies: encourage a move away from U.S. dollar–denominated payments in an attempt to evade U.S. sanctions. Any transaction conducted in U.S. dollars has to go through an American bank at some point, making it sensitive to U.S. penalties. The U.S. Treasury routinely orders banks to freeze wire transfers that look suspicious or in breach of sanctions. For the many members of the SCO that have frosty relations with the United States, this was a problem that needed to be addressed.

A few months later, readers of Russian statistics noticed an unusual trend: for the first time in history, more than half of Russia-China trade was settled in a currency other than the U.S. dollar.[11] Moscow and Beijing had stayed true to their word and started to establish an alternative payments system; firms in Russia and China had expanded their use of the ruble and the renminbi for international transactions. In Moscow and Beijing, this was cause for celebration: the majority of Russia-China trade had become immune to U.S. sanctions. As Putin put it, "We aren't aiming to ditch the dollar. The dollar is ditching us."[12] For American policy makers, however, there was no reason to rejoice. This development only highlighted how keen U.S. foes are to skirt the greenback.

The easiest option for countries wishing to protect themselves from the risk of falling foul of U.S. sanctions is to avoid the U.S. dollar altogether. Russia, where the greenback used to be traded as easily as vodka on the street, leads the way. In 2019 Rosneft, the Russian state-owned oil giant, announced that it would abandon the U.S. dollar for all of its export contracts and use the euro instead.[13] Rosneft's CEO Igor Sechin did not try to conceal that the move intended to evade U.S. sanctions. As he put it, "this is a forced measure aimed at protecting ourselves [. . .] from the effect of US sanctions."[14] However, few international companies are able to ditch the U.S. dollar as Rosneft did.

The global role of the U.S. dollar rests not only on America's economic preeminence but also on the lack of financial channels in other currencies. Most central banks have no direct ties with each other, making trade in local currencies impossible. There is no system in place to exchange, say, Indian rupees directly for South African rands. Using a third currency, which most of the time is the widely available greenback, is a must. Indian rupees are first converted into U.S. dollars, which are then exchanged for South African rands. As a result, it is usually more practical for companies to invoice each other directly in U.S. dollars, exposing their transactions to potential U.S. sanctions along the way. However, things are changing fast.

Central banks across the globe, especially in emerging countries, are keen to become less reliant on the U.S. dollar so as to diversify their financial ties and to boost the use of their own currency—something that they believe will bolster their international standing. As Washington develops its sanctions arsenal, many central bankers are also becoming acutely aware of the risks that come with using the U.S. dollar. The danger may not be immediate, but taking preemptive steps in case relations with the United States take a turn for the worse makes sense. As a result, dozens of countries across the world are fast-tracking the development of government-backed mechanisms to avoid the greenback.

Bilateral currency swaps feature prominently in the minds of central bankers intent to lessen their dependence on the U.S. dollar. Such deals make it possible for central banks to exchange their local currency directly with those of other countries, without having to use the U.S. dollar (or any other currency) as an intermediary. Currency swap agreements came to the spotlight during the 2008–2009 financial crisis. At the time, the U.S. Federal Reserve agreed to have an open line to send U.S. dollars to the European Central Bank. On both sides of the Atlantic, the two central banks shared the same goal: avoiding a potentially disastrous shortage of U.S. dollars in developed economies.

The global financial crisis is long gone, but the American, European, and Japanese central banks have continued to develop currency swap deals over the past decade. The Fed has active swap agreements worth US$450 billion with a long list of (mostly) advanced economies.[15] Emerging markets, including Brazil, China, India, and Turkey, are entering the field, too. This reflects their growing global economic clout and willingness to build financial channels that do not rely on those that Western countries developed when they used to rule the world.

China stands at the forefront of this trend: with 60 currency swap agreements worth nearly US$500 billion, the People's Bank of China has more swap lines than the Fed, for a much larger amount of money.[16] China has inked deals with a long list of U.S. allies and foes alike, including Argentina, Australia, Canada, New Zealand, Pakistan, Russia, South

Africa, South Korea, Turkey, the United Arab Emirates, and the United Kingdom. The United States does not feature in this listing. This is not surprising: China is using currency swap deals to circumvent American financial channels. In the short term, China wants to escape Washington's financial monitoring. In the long run, Beijing intends to evade the threat of U.S. sanctions and to reduce the centrality of the U.S. dollar in the global financial system.

China's enthusiasm for bypassing the U.S. dollar does not come unexpected given the frosty relations between Washington and Beijing. However, U.S. allies, especially in Asia, are also making currency swap arrangements at a fast pace. In 2018 New Delhi signed a US$75 billion megaswap deal with Japan's central bank.[17] Just like China, India and Japan acknowledge openly that these agreements will allow them to avoid U.S. financial channels when they need to do so.

New Delhi has already put its currency swap agreements to good use. In 2019 India finalized negotiations to buy air defense missiles from Russia.[18] For the United States, this was a blow; Washington was always hoping that India would choose U.S.-made Patriot or THAAD gear. The US$5 billion transaction between New Delhi and Moscow should normally have triggered U.S. sanctions; Washington prohibits countries from buying Russian-made military kit. However, New Delhi and Moscow were quick to find a fix.

India and Russia resurrected a bilateral currency swap agreement that dated back to Soviet times. India bought the Russian missiles using a mix of Russian rubles and Indian rupees, skirting the U.S. dollar and American banks. The deal was hard to swallow for Washington. India, a key U.S. ally in Asia, defied American sanctions to buy weapons from Russia, a U.S. foe.[19] New Delhi's avoidance of the U.S. dollar may not be enough to escape U.S. sanctions, which theoretically apply to all sales of Russian-made military equipment (regardless of the invoice's currency). However, with bilateral currency swaps, many foreign governments believe that they have found a way around America's coercive economic measures.

Ditching the U.S. dollar to skirt U.S. sanctions looks like a quick fix for countries at odds with the United States. Yet it would be of no use for them to get rid of the U.S. dollar if they continue to use Western financial channels, such as Swift. The undisputed leader for financial messaging services, Swift is a cooperative that links virtually all banks.[20] The messaging service acts like a global Rolodex of financial institutions, helping to route wires to the right bank anywhere across the globe. In the financial world, Swift is everywhere: the roughly 11,000 institutions that form part of the cooperative's network send each other around 440 messages every second to process an estimated US$6 trillion in payments every day.[21]

Swift's headquarters are in Belgium, but the institution needs to maintain close ties to the United States: around 40 percent of the payments that the cooperative processes are denominated in U.S. dollars.[22] If Swift wishes to keep access to the greenback, it has no choice but to collaborate with Washington and block payments that breach American sanctions. In extreme cases, Swift may have no alternative but to cut all ties with sanctioned countries. This happened in 2012, when Swift, under intense U.S. pressure, removed Iranian banks from its network. Sending or receiving money became nearly impossible in Iran. U.S. foes took note and did their homework to develop financial mechanisms that bypass Swift. Unsurprisingly, China leads the way.

Only three years after Swift cut Iran's access to its systems, China announced that it had built its own financial messaging service, called CIPS, to process international payments in renminbi. In the small world of global banking, the move attracted a lot of attention: heavyweights BNP Paribas, Citi, Deutsche Bank, and HSBC formed part of the founding members of the network. Swift even lent a helping hand to Beijing to design CIPS.[23] With this mechanism, China set itself two goals: fostering the internationalization of the renminbi and shielding Chinese firms from potential U.S. sanctions.[24] As a side benefit, CIPS may also serve to conceal some sensitive transactions from Swift (and the United States).

Despite the fanfare, China's initial hopes of competing with Swift were soon dashed.[25] In the *entire* year of 2016 CIPS processed transactions for a mere US$700 billion, around 10 percent of Swift's *daily* turnover.[26] CIPS was suffering from a number of issues. The system linked only 20 banks around the world. The service was impractical; it was open for only 11 hours a day and could not process securities purchases or investment flows. Worse still, to many bankers, CIPS sounded like a fad.[27] International banks had been relying on Swift as the sole financial messaging service for decades, and the system functioned perfectly well. Why would financial institutions get rid of something that works to try a new, untested arrangement?

CIPS's initial difficulties did not deter Chinese policy makers. They continued to try to convince financial institutions, one after the other, to join the mechanism. As China's economic clout grew, Asian banks soon signed up, convinced that CIPS would eventually become unavoidable for those doing business with Beijing. Emerging countries that receive high investment inflows from China, such as South Africa and Kenya, soon became interested in the scheme, too. Within five years, CIPS signed deals with more than forty African banks, outnumbering the number of CIPS-connected financial institutions in North America.

Beijing's efforts paid off, eventually.[28] In 2021 CIPS processed more than US$12 trillion in transactions.[29] This is only a fraction of Swift's turnover, but this still represents a seventeenfold jump in five years. Around 1,300 banks in more than 100 countries have now joined the framework. Banks that the United States has sanctioned also form part of the scheme: Russia's bank VTB, which has been under American sanctions since 2014,[30] joined CIPS in 2016.[31] Since then, two dozen more Russian banks—including some that got excluded from Swift following Russia's invasion of Ukraine—have signed up for CIPS.[32] This is exactly in line with Beijing's goals: offering an alternative to Swift for countries that want to, or need to, circumvent Western financial channels.[33]

There is little chance that CIPS will ever catch up with Swift given how deeply the Belgian cooperative is embedded in global financial channels. However, with CIPS, China is preparing for the day when it can dispense with Swift. As Cornell University's Eswar Prasad puts it, "what matters is it's there."[34] CIPS comes with added benefits, too: there is little doubt that Chinese security services monitor all of the transactions that go through the system, giving Beijing the capability to track financial flows across the world. In the long term, China is also building the capacity to cut off countries from renminbi-denominated payments—and the Chinese economy.[35] With China set to become the world's largest economic power in the early 2030s, this will give Beijing crucial leverage to advance its interests.[36]

CIPS focuses on cross-border payments, but alternatives to Swift are also emerging at the national level. In 2016 the Indian central bank launched Unified Payments Interface (UPI), a domestic payments framework. Only four years later, the system had been widely adopted across India. In 2021 UPI processed almost 35 billion transactions worth a total of nearly US$1 trillion.[37] In a country where around 40 percent of the people each live on about US$3 per day, such a turnover is no small feat.[38] Like CIPS, the system has no links to American financial channels, making it U.S. sanctions proof.

India's efforts to develop a domestic alternative to Swift are not an isolated phenomenon. Russia, another BRICS country, has similar plans. In 2015 Moscow launched a domestic payment card, Mir, that sought to rival Western-led Visa and Mastercard.[39] More than 30 percent of Russian-issued payment cards use the system, making the related transactions immune to U.S. scrutiny and penalties.[40] In the same year, Moscow also forced Visa and Mastercard to use a Russian scheme, the National Card Payment System, to process domestic transactions. This localization push was certainly a prescient move for the Kremlin; it ensured that card payments kept flowing even after Visa and Mastercard left Russia in 2022.

In the long term, BRICS countries are making plans to develop their own, BRICS-led financial channels. Demand for such systems is high, especially in Moscow and Beijing.[41] The supply of financial transactions that could go through the system appears guaranteed. Kirill Dmitriev, the head of Russia's sovereign fund, remarked in 2019 that BRICS countries "make up over 20 percent of the global inflow of foreign direct investment."[42] The launch of BRICS-owned payment systems will not happen overnight, if it happens at all. However, such mechanisms would be game-changing for global payments: they would bypass both the U.S. dollar and Swift, impeding the reach of American sanctions.

It is not surprising that BRICS countries are keen to develop their own financial channels. Even if U.S. sanctions did not even exist, emerging countries would probably still want to develop their own payments systems to strengthen their global standing. However, U.S. sanctions have certainly encouraged the turn to alternative payment systems. For two of the BRICS states, Russia or China, defying U.S. sanctions is a matter of economic survival. For the three others, Brazil, India, and South Africa, the experience of China and Russia serves as a cautionary tale, highlighting the need to avoid dependence on American financial channels.

Individual currency swap agreements and alternative payments systems will not have much of an impact on their own. However, taken together, these innovations will fragment the global financial landscape and slowly erode the U.S. dollar's dominance. Only a small drop in the share of transactions settled using the greenback may be enough to dent the effectiveness of U.S. sanctions. Perhaps even more alarmingly for American policy makers, efforts to bypass sanctions do not come solely from the emerging world. The European Union, Washington's closest ally, is also making strides in this direction.

European resentment of U.S. sanctions dates back several decades. There was the Siberian pipeline debacle in the 1980s. In 1996 the U.S. decision to impose extraterritorial penalties against Cuba, Iran, and Libya deepened mistrust between both sides. Starting in 2017, Congress-led attempts to target the (now defunct) Nord Stream 2 gas pipeline connecting Russia to Germany further fueled tensions. President Donald Trump's exit from the Iran nuclear deal in 2018 was the straw that broke the camel's back.

The decision by the Trump administration to reimpose penalties on Tehran unilaterally highlighted how deep the transatlantic rift over sanctions has become. Trump was not the source of the problem; he merely turned the spotlight on existing issues. For European leaders, the Trump presidency was a wakeup call; many EU countries realized that they could no longer assume that America would always be a reliable ally. How can European countries be sure that the United States will never elect another president who wants to make America great again at the expense of everyone else?

Even with the election of Joe Biden, very little changed. A few weeks after Biden's inauguration, some top European diplomats went as far as publicly calling for travel bans on American officials who impose extraterritorial sanctions that have an impact on EU firms, retaliatory freezes of the assets that Washington holds in Europe, and even the removal of U.S. banking institutions from the European Union.[43] Taking such steps would be absurd: they would be extremely hard (if not impossible) to put into practice and risk triggering a financial crisis. However, these far-fetched proposals highlight the fury of allies with U.S. sanctions. Despite significant cooperation after Russia invaded Ukraine in 2022, the long-term picture for transatlantic collaboration on sanctions does not look promising.

To be fair, the United States also takes issue with EU sanctions.[44] American policy makers regard Europe's approach to sanctions as being narrow and ineffective.[45] Washington usually points out the lack of a pan-European sanctions policy and the reluctance of some (although not all) EU countries to enforce penalties aggressively.[46] When Europeans protest that U.S. sanctions are too harsh, Americans usually respond that the real issue is that Europeans have never been serious about sanctions.

The European Union is a complex beast, made up of 27 member states that like to disagree with each other. All member states have to adopt sanctions unanimously. This is no small feat. By the time all European capitals approve sanctions packages, these have usually been watered down; every member state is keen to adopt sanctions unless they penalize its domestic companies (and constituencies). And once member states have adopted sanctions, it is up to them to ensure compliance with the measures; there is no European agency responsible for the implementation of sanctions.

The implementation of EU sanctions at the member-state level also means that there is no European mechanism to issue sanctions waivers. In practice, this implies that some EU member states may be more lenient than others in granting exemptions, making the enforcement of EU sanctions far from uniform across the bloc. Seven member states, including France and Germany,[47] have waived penalties on the EU-based subsidiaries of some of the Russian banks that fell under European sanctions after Russia's annexation of Crimea, for instance.[48] To Washington's dismay, European regulators argued that they preferred to create a massive sanctions loophole rather than risk harming Europe's financial stability.[49]

U.S. officials also lament that sanctions enforcement is generally less aggressive in Europe than in America. Sometimes the United States spots sanctions evasion in EU countries before European intelligence services do. In 2013 the Office of Foreign Assets Control (OFAC) exposed a Greek scheme to bust Iran-related sanctions that Greece had never uncovered. Greek citizens and companies had managed to buy eight megatankers undetected and to smuggle oil from Iran at a time when both European and American sanctions forbade Tehran from exporting oil.[50] Since then, Americans have been wondering out loud whether Europe is really serious about sanctions.

The apparent willingness of European judges to overturn sanctions designations does not reassure Washington, either: in 2016 the European Court of Justice (ECJ) ruled that EU sanctions against Arkady Rotenberg, one of the Russian brothers who like to buy high-value art in America, were unlawful. The ECJ argued that it could not find conclusive evidence that Rotenberg had anything to do with Russia's illegal annexation of Crimea. To American policy makers, this was a baffling conclusion: while European judges were deliberating, Rotenberg's company was building the bridge connecting the Ukrainian peninsula to the Russian mainland. (In 2017 the European Union reinstated sanctions on Arkady Rotenberg.)

American officials also often mention that they cannot find a single high-profile case where European courts punished sanctions busters.[51] Europeans argue that this is because the implementation of EU sanctions is not public—sanctions-related court cases are confidential. Yet U.S. concerns are valid. Overall, the European Union implements sanctions much less aggressively than does the United States. However, Europe's more lenient approach vis-à-vis sanctions is unlikely to harm American interests and companies. The European Union's worries about U.S. sanctions are of another order of magnitude. Europe views American sanctions as a threat to the bloc's global standing and to European firms.

Brussels believes that U.S. sanctions undermine Europe's sovereignty and international credibility.[52] The recent proliferation of U.S. secondary sanctions means that European companies often have to prioritize respect for American demands over EU legislation. For Europe, this is problematic. If European businesses have to comply with U.S. penalties at the expense of European regulations, where does that leave Europe's foreign policy? Will third countries ever have an interest in negotiating with Brussels if Washington really has the upper hand in the decisions taken by European firms?

In 2018 the U.S. decision to reimpose sanctions on Iran despite the vocal protestations of European allies proved to be a turning point. To protect EU companies from Washington's penalties against Tehran, Europe started to design mechanisms aimed at circumventing American sanctions.[53] Coming from U.S. allies, this was an extraordinary move: the United States and the European Union used to cooperate to design and implement sanctions. Nowadays, it sometimes looks like they are on opposing sides.

Shortly after Washington left the nuclear deal, the European Union announced that it had decided to design a mechanism to evade U.S. sanctions. From Europe's perspective, this made sense on at least two accounts. The bloc wanted to try to salvage the nuclear deal with Tehran. Perhaps more important, Brussels also intended to support European firms that could not remain in Iran because of the threat of U.S. secondary sanctions, even though their business dealings in the Islamic republic were legal from a European perspective.

After nearly a year of negotiations, EU member countries launched the Instrument in Support of Trade Exchanges (Instex).[54] Instex represents the first brick in what looks set to become, over time, a European edifice to escape American penalties. France, Germany, and the United Kingdom back the scheme: they figured that the United States would not dare to sanction sovereign states with which it has strong relations. For Washington, the support of Europe's biggest powers for a mechanism that openly aims at circumventing U.S. sanctions should have represented a red flag: it revealed how deeply U.S. allies resented American sanctions. However, Washington shrugged off Instex as a matter of little importance.

American policy makers have every reason not to be impressed by Instex, which essentially represents a modern version of barter. The scheme functions as a clearinghouse for trade between the European Union and Iran that does not use the U.S. dollar and completely bypasses Swift. European companies that wish to export goods to Iran get paid by European firms that need to import products from Iran. On the Iranian side, the scheme is similar. In the end, no money ever leaves Iran or Europe. Instex is not a bank. The mechanism merely acts as an intermediary between all parties: it puts importers and exporters across Europe and Iran in touch and keeps ledgers of the transactions.

Instex may sound clever on paper, but it has serious flaws. Most European companies are not willing to use the system for fear of retaliation from the United States. The only firms that use Instex are small EU businesses that either operate under the radar or have no presence in the United States. For these companies, the Iranian market may be an important one—a source of crucial revenue to maintain jobs or keep production lines open. However, even combined, the trading volumes of mom-and-pop European firms will always remain a drop in the ocean.

Another issue is that Instex relies on barter, so trade between the European Union and Iran would need to be balanced for the scheme to work smoothly. This is not the case: Iran imports more from Europe than

Europe imports from Iran.[55] If Instex covered energy trade, this problem would be solved; Europe would be able to import Iranian oil under the scheme (something that U.S. measures forbid unless the nuclear deal is revived). However, Instex facilitates transactions only for so-called humanitarian goods such as food or medicines, which U.S. sanctions do not target. The European Union does not defy U.S. sanctions with Instex. The system exclusively processes transactions that comply with American penalties.

Whether Instex works (or not) may not be the most important thing to consider, however. Instex is the most tangible symbol of Europe's frustration with U.S. sanctions. The scheme may be flawed, but it represents a first attempt, by an American ally, to create an official, state-backed mechanism to bypass U.S. sanctions. Instex has been around for only a few years. Effective schemes may take several decades to emerge. Just like China's CIPS payments system, what really matters is that Instex is there. The barter scheme was only a first step for the European Union and a sign of things to come.

⸺ ∞ ⸺

In 2021 Brussels struck again. European leaders drafted a policy paper stating that Europe needs to "shield [itself from] the effects of unlawful extraterritorial application [of sanctions]."[56] European policy makers did not mince their words: they called extraterritorial measures "abusive," denouncing the "short-term pursuit of unilateral interests by specific actors."[57] In line with the conclusions of the report, the bloc made protecting itself from American sanctions a priority.[58] To achieve this goal, the European Union shares the same assumption as U.S. foes: the bloc needs to reduce its reliance on the U.S. dollar. However, this is easier said than done.

The energy field offers a glimpse of the many challenges that lie ahead. Around 80 percent of Europe's energy imports are invoiced in U.S. dollars, although only 2 percent of these imports come from the United States.[59] The European Union's dependence on the U.S. dollar in the energy sector is not surprising. Almost all of the global oil trade and a large chunk of gas sales are settled using the greenback. The entire financial framework for energy derivatives also relies on the U.S. dollar. However, Europe believes that it needs to invest precisely in the energy sector to lessen its dependence on America's currency.

Climate change is fostering the development of new sources of energy, such as hydrogen. In this field, the European Union wants to establish global benchmarks that rely on the euro, much as the global oil trade relies on the U.S. dollar. Focusing efforts on the energy sector to bolster the use of the European currency is a smart bet. The European Union is the largest energy importer in the world.[60] In Europe's gas sector, the share of euro-denominated contracts doubled between 2018 and 2020, reaching two-thirds. This is partly because Russian gas giant Gazprom, which used to supply roughly 40 percent of Europe's gas imports, started to draft its global export contracts in euros instead of U.S. dollars.[61] (Unsurprisingly, the move was intended to protect Gazprom from U.S. sanctions.)

Strengthening the role of the euro is only one element of the European Union's strategy to shield itself from U.S. sanctions. The bloc also plans to beef up mechanisms that protect European companies from extraterritorial penalties. Europe intends to resurrect the long-dormant blocking statute, which theoretically forbids European firms from respecting extraterritorial sanctions. In a nod to Washington, the European Union also wants to tackle claims that Europe does not enforce sanctions seriously. The bloc agreed to launch a pan-EU database to foster information-sharing about sanctions. A European agency will coordinate the enforcement of penalties across the bloc. National authorities will also automatically report sanctions breaches to the European Court of Justice.

Europe's plans to boost the use of the euro in the energy field are unlikely to yield results for many years or even decades. It is not clear how the European Union will convince companies to prioritize European rules over American sanctions, given Instex's failure and the well-documented fiasco of the existing blocking regulation (to escape the blocking rule, European companies pretend that they are not interested in doing business with, say, Iran, and insist that this has absolutely nothing to do with sanctions). However, the European Union's recent moves indicate the broad direction in which the bloc intends to move in the long term.

Europe released its paper on strategic autonomy on the eve of Biden's presidential inauguration. This was not random. The document went largely unnoticed in Washington, but it made the headlines across the European Union. Europe's message to the United States was clear: four years of Trump had convinced European governments that they should stop relying on America's financial system. For America, this is a sure sign of trouble ahead: if Europe and the U.S. cannot collaborate on sanctions, U.S. sanctions will lose their bite.

Step by step, U.S. foes and allies alike are setting up the infrastructure to circumvent American sanctions. If the European Union, the world's largest economic power, takes the lead in designing such mechanisms, things may well change more quickly than the United States would like. Europe's approach is garnering support: Russia, China, India, Turkey, South Korea, and Japan have expressed interest in Instex.[62] China and Russia have also joined Europe's ranks to lessen the reliance of the energy sector on the U.S. dollar. In 2018 Beijing ordered Chinese banks to start invoicing oil imports in renminbi.[63] In 2019 Russia announced that it was seeking to get rid of the U.S. dollar for all oil and gas exports—a shift that the war in Ukraine will accelerate.[64] Taken together, such moves will, over time, inevitably have an impact on energy markets. There is every chance that these developments will spill over to other economic sectors, too.

In the long term, the development of government-backed initiatives to lessen the global dependence on the U.S. dollar, coupled with the rise in bilateral currency swaps and alternatives to Swift, will probably decrease the effectiveness of American coercive measures. None of these developments will be a game changer on its own, which makes the threat hard to grasp and even harder to combat for U.S. policy makers. Instead, it is the combined effect of mechanisms that do not rely on the U.S. dollar that may prove more powerful than America would like. For Washington, this means the golden age of sanctions may be coming to an end.

9

DOING DOWN THE DOLLAR

The Rise of Digital Coins and Other Reserve Currencies

I n 2019 diplomats, academics, and government officials gathered at Harvard University for a war-gaming exercise.[1] The scenario was the following: in the not-so-distant future, a Chinese cryptocurrency has undermined the global dominance of the U.S. dollar, pulling the rug from under American sanctions. Hackers have stolen US$3 billion from Swift, the cooperative that provides the infrastructure to process wires around the world. With this spectacular operation, the hackers have undermined confidence in the global financial system, encouraging a turn to China's digital currency.[2]

Meanwhile, North Korea has used Chinese crypto coins to escape sanctions and build nuclear weapons that the CIA believes will target American soil within three to six months.[3] The U.S. National Security Council holds an emergency meeting: What should Washington do? This script may sound far-fetched, but it really is not. In fact, many of the things it describes are already under way. For one, Swift is not hack-proof; in 2016 North Korean hackers used the cooperative's infrastructure to steal US$81 million from an account that the central bank of Bangladesh held in the United States.[4]

The rest of the script focused on the risks that the emergence of a Chinese-backed cryptocurrency would pose. Here, too, the assumptions were realistic. In 2020 the Chinese leadership launched a sovereign cryptocurrency, the digital renminbi.[5] As in Harvard's war-gaming exercise, China is banking on its virtual currency to erode the global dominance of the U.S. dollar. In parallel, the rise of "traditional" currencies, chief among them the (physical) renminbi and the euro, could also threaten the hegemony of the U.S. dollar. A fragmented—instead of U.S. dollar dominated—global currency landscape could emerge and undermine the effectiveness of American sanctions. Given how important sanctions have become in Washington's foreign-policy toolkit, this would be bad news for U.S. policy makers.

<hr />

Cryptocurrencies may sound complex, but their underlying principles are simple. Instead of carrying cash or debit and credit cards, people make payments using coins that they have bought online. Everything is virtual; people buy and sell cryptocurrencies on the Internet, and there is no such thing as a physical crypto coin. Another key feature of cryptocurrencies is that they have nothing to do with central banks. This means virtual coins are not linked to a country as the U.S. dollar is to America or the yen is to Japan. The final characteristic of cryptocurrencies is that their users hide behind pseudonyms, boosting privacy (in theory).

Cryptocurrencies are often dismissed as a fad, but this assessment appears to be increasingly at odds with the latest developments. The combined value of the ten largest crypto coins stands at around US$1 trillion, or roughly the size of Saudi Arabia's economy.[6] Bitcoin, with about US$500 billion in virtual money, is by far the world's largest cryptocurrency. It is becoming increasingly popular in countries where the local currency is volatile (such as Argentina) or where the greenback is in scarce supply (such as Nigeria).[7] Other major players include Ethereum, Tether, and BNB. Most people will not have heard these names, but in the long term they could become as familiar as the U.S. dollar. America's bank Citi believes that Bitcoin could soon become the preferred currency for global trade.[8]

For U.S. enemies, crypto coins appear to provide a means of evading sanctions or engaging in illicit activities.[9] Iranian firms have been using cryptocurrencies for years to escape sanctions.[10] In 2014 North Korean hackers stole US$1.3 billion in cash and cryptocurrency from banks around the world.[11] Pyongyang likely used the proceeds to finance the development of nuclear and ballistic weapons. In 2016 Moscow used Bitcoins to pay for the computers that were used to hack into the servers of the Democrat Party and access the emails of U.S. presidential candidate Hillary Clinton.[12] In 2017–2018 North Korea struck again and stole around US$500 million in five Asian cryptocurrency exchanges.[13] After invading Ukraine in 2022, Russia announced that it would accept Bitcoins as payment for oil and gas exports. However, the idea that cryptocurrencies represent a magic tool to evade sanctions and facilitate illegal activities may be overblown.[14]

In practice, crypto coins are not the panacea that Tehran, Pyongyang, and Moscow are hoping for. Europe's criminals launder around US$4 billion per year using cryptocurrencies.[15] This may sound like a lot, but this represents only 3 percent of the total amount that European thieves launder every year. This points to the first (and probably main) weakness of cryptocurrencies. For all the hype, trade in crypto coins remains negligible in the grand scheme of things; cryptocurrencies cannot match the liquidity and volumes of transactions—around US$10 trillion every working day—that conventional banks process.[16]

A second problem for wannabe sanctions busters is that the pseudonyms that cryptocurrencies offer do not guarantee anonymity. Far from it. All crypto transactions are publicly viewable, unless virtual coins include advanced cryptography methods. Monero, a minor cryptocurrency that North Korea likes to use to launder Bitcoins into untraceable cryptocurrencies, has such capabilities.[17] However, it is an exception rather than the rule.

A final issue for sanctioned states is that after a slow start, the United States has stepped up scrutiny of cryptocurrencies. In 2018 the Office of Foreign Assets Control (OFAC) added Iranian individuals, complete with their cryptocurrency addresses, to its sanctions list. The Iranians had been involved in more than 7,000 illicit Bitcoin transactions worth millions of U.S. dollars.[18] In 2019 North Korean money launderers who used cryptocurrencies to escape America's financial surveillance also joined OFAC's blacklist. In 2020 the agency added to its sanctions list the cryptocurrency addresses of the Russian hackers who had accessed Hillary Clinton's emails.

The ability of the U.S. Treasury to track illegal activities involving cryptocurrencies will undoubtedly rise in the coming years. Cryptocurrency addresses may well become a common feature in OFAC's designations. For America's enemies, this is bad news: crypto coins will be of only limited value to do illicit business undetected. However, a new form of cryptocurrency is emerging in China-backed research centers. Its creators are going to great lengths to ensure that it will remain beyond the purview of the United States.

The Chinese leadership has set its sights on cryptocurrencies to challenge the supremacy of the U.S. dollar, with a twist: Beijing is placing its hopes in a state-backed cryptocurrency—the digital renminbi.[19] China's interest in crypto coins is not new: the country's five-year development plan for 2016–2020 identified cryptocurrencies as a top priority, paving the way for the Chinese central bank to launch a research lab on this topic in 2017.[20] Since then, the research center has filed more than 130 patents, placing China at the top of the global league table for cryptocurrency-related patents.[21] Close to Shanghai, Hangzhou has emerged as the Chinese capital for all things related to cryptocurrencies. In this city alone, investment in crypto companies tops almost US$2 billion, with 30 percent of the sum coming from the Chinese government.[22]

China's efforts to develop crypto coins are paying off. In a move that has gone largely unnoticed, China started issuing its own sovereign cryptocurrency in 2019. A state-backed cryptocurrency is different from a regular one: everything is done online, but the Chinese central bank keeps ledgers of all the transactions, making it easy for the Communist leadership to trace them back to specific individuals or companies. The digital renminbi simply represents a virtual, but fully trackable version of China's physical coins and notes. For Beijing, such surveillance capabilities are of paramount importance.

If cash and payment cards become obsolete in China, everyone in the country will have to use a mobile phone to make payments, including visiting foreigners (and U.S. intelligence officers). All transactions will be recorded and traceable. The troves of personal data that the crypto renminbi generates will greatly enhance the capabilities of China's security services. Instead of offering greater privacy, as some cryptocurrencies may do, China's crypto coin promises to help Beijing record every move of everyone in China.[23]

Beijing is pushing hard to develop the scheme. Nearly 300 million Chinese citizens—or almost one-quarter of China's population[24]—already use the crypto renminbi in ten cities,[25] including Beijing, Shanghai, and Shenzhen.[26] Users of the scheme may withdraw cash, pay bills, and transfer money using their mobile phone number. At the moment, Chinese people must open a digital account from a commercial bank to access digital renminbis on their phone wallets. Over time, China's central bank may well decide to centralize the process by getting rid of intermediaries. The idea of depositing cash within a physical bank would become obsolete.

Chinese consumers tend to be early adopters of new forms of digital payments. Mobile transactions are already the norm across China: they account for around half of in-store sales and three-quarters of online payments.[27] Alibaba and WePay, two giant Chinese tech firms, run payments systems that nearly all Chinese online consumers use.[28] With its digital renminbi, the Chinese leadership hopes to emulate the success of these platforms before eclipsing them and regaining full control over the country's financial scene.[29]

Such a goal is less far-fetched than it may seem. The Chinese leadership designated the 2022 Winter Olympics in Beijing to serve as a test of the digital renminbi on a large scale, including with foreigners.[30] If a subsequent assessment shows that the results were promising, China plans to gradually replace all physical coins and bills with virtual money.[31] Beijing believes that digital currencies will become the new normal as people spend most of their time online.[32] American bank Goldman Sachs agrees; its analysts think that the digital renminbi will attract 1 billion users within a decade.[33]

Other states may choose to adopt similar schemes in the coming years. Numerous countries, including Ecuador, El Salvador, Estonia, Iran, Russia, Singapore, Sweden, and Venezuela, have more or less developed plans to launch a sovereign cryptocurrency. However, the Chinese Communist leadership will have a massive advantage over every other government: China will have been the first mover in the field, giving Beijing a head start to become the global leader in cryptocurrency technology and software.

This will help China to achieve its second goal: ensuring that the crypto renminbi has a global reach.[34] For shops around the world, catering to hordes of Chinese tourists will provide an incentive to adopt the digital renminbi as a means of payment. However, Beijing's plans to internationalize the digital renminbi go well beyond having Chinese tourists use a cryptocurrency to buy souvenirs or luxury products in Paris, London, or New York.

China's Belt and Road Initiative (BRI) infrastructure project includes a cryptocurrency component that will enable trade with Ethereum, the world's second biggest cryptocurrency.[35] China could demand that BRI countries receive payments in digital renminbi. The Communist leadership may not even need to ask. For companies operating in BRI countries, the ability to quickly settle transactions with Chinese suppliers from a mobile phone may be appealing. Chinese laborers working on BRI projects may also find that the digital renminbi is the easiest way to send money back home.

In the coming decade, there is every chance that Beijing's digital currency will attract companies doing business with China from all around the world. The Chinese central bank is testing the waters; in 2021 it launched partnerships with its counterparts in the United Arab Emirates and Thailand to see how the digital renminbi could be used to settle trade.[36] For many exporters, use of China's cryptocurrency for their dealings with Chinese firms will make sense: it will be faster and cheaper than paying a visit to the local branch of a traditional bank. Demand will not be hard to find: China already is the largest trade partner of most countries around the world.[37]

The rise of the digital renminbi will have far-ranging global implications. The Chinese cryptocurrency will operate outside of traditional banks and Western financial channels, such as Swift. The world's financial infrastructure currently centers on New York, given the dominant role of the U.S. dollar and American banks in the global economy. However, cryptocurrencies have nothing to do with the United States, which is not in the driving seat for such innovations; the Federal Reserve believes that there is "no need to rush" to develop a U.S. dollar–based cryptocurrency.[38] Over time, the rise in state-backed cryptocurrencies, be it from China or elsewhere, could erode America's ability to write the financial rules of the world.

Innovations such as cryptocurrencies mean that the U.S. dollar could gradually lose its hegemonic status. China's central bank does not hide that this is the goal of the crypto renminbi; the People's Bank of China sees its digital currency as a crucial tool to break the global monopoly of the U.S. dollar.[39] This shift will not happen overnight, if it takes place at all; China's digital renminbi is growing fast, but it remains a minor phenomenon so far. However, this may make the threat even more dangerous to American policy makers: slow changes are often hard to detect, and politicians are seldom keen to address threats that could become acute long after they have left office.

China's digital currency is only one aspect of Beijing's long-term strategy to challenge the dominance of the greenback. Beijing is also trying to boost the use of the (traditional) renminbi, and it has a strong basis for doing so. China is the world's biggest manufacturer and the largest economic partner of more than 120 countries[40] (compared to only 57 countries for the United States[41]). The country's growth is resilient; in 2020, at the height of the coronavirus pandemic, China was one of only two G20 countries not to experience a recession (the other one was Turkey). Despite uncertainties around the country's demographic outlook, China's GDP looks set surpass that of the United States in the early 2030s.[42]

Recent trends in the financial sector highlight the growing clout of the renminbi. At around US$40 trillion,[43] the global stock of redbacks is already almost twice as big as that of greenbacks.[44] Chinese banks were virtually invisible globally only a decade ago. Their assets, worth US$40 trillion, are now larger than those of American or European banks.[45] China also has a massive financial trump card: it is gradually opening its US$19 trillion bond market—the second largest in the world—to foreign investors.[46] Investment funds are interested: China is one of the few low-risk countries where interest rates stand well above zero.

Subtle changes show that the global reach of the renminbi is already expanding. In 2019 China settled 15 percent of its trade in renminbi, compared to next to nothing only ten years earlier.[47] This share is rising steadily, with most of the growth in renminbi-denominated payments coming from emerging markets, especially in Asia, Africa, and the Middle East. However, some developed countries are keen to use the redback, too: France, a longtime U.S. dollar basher, settles 20 percent of its trade with China in renminbi.[48]

China's Belt and Road Initiative will further fuel the growth in renminbi-denominated payments, especially across emerging markets. In 2019 Chinese companies invested US$15 billion in BRI projects, a quarter of which was disbursed in renminbi.[49] Over the long term, all of these trends will likely add up, boosting the global role of the Chinese currency. Such changes will take time, though, and in the short term, the renminbi will not threaten the greenback's monopoly. However, China is not the only source of competition for the U.S. dollar. The European Union is also keen to bolster the global role of its currency, the euro.

———— ✦✦✦ ————

Few in Washington realize that the euro is used just as much as the U.S. dollar for global trade; both have roughly a 40 percent market share.[50] For a currency that is only two decades old, this is not a bad performance. The rapid rise of the euro since its full launch in 2002 should not be surprising. Europe is the biggest export market for 80 countries and the second largest player in terms of global trade (behind China, but above the United States).[51] The single-currency area is the world's leader for both inbound and outbound foreign investment flows. The bloc is home to four of the seven major global oil companies. It also has a vast, well-run banking system. As an added benefit for international firms, EU sanctions are not extraterritorial; even if they use the euro, companies that are not based in the European Union do not have to comply with European sanctions.

These factors may explain why the U.S. dollar and the euro are on a par when it comes to trade, a short-term activity. However, for debt and foreign-exchange reserves, which tend to be held for much longer periods, the greenback remains king; around 60 percent of global debt and currency reserves are denominated in U.S. dollars, compared to about 20 percent in euros.[52] This reflects a trust issue: over the past two decades, financial investors have often believed that the euro would soon disappear. Placing long-term bets on a fairly new currency that sometimes looked like it might go bust was a risk too far for many investors.

The European Union's recent history is one of successive crises, including the Greek debt saga, fears around the sustainability of Italy's sovereign debt, and, more recently, Brexit. The European Union also lacks a fiscal union, which means that there is no solidarity between member states on financial matters. Given the high debt piles in many southern EU member states, this may sound alarming to cautious investors. To make matters worse, until recently there were no pan-European sovereign bonds; fund managers who wanted to add European debt to their portfolios had to buy separate bonds from France, Italy, Germany, Spain, or Portugal. However, the coronavirus pandemic means that all of this is changing.

The outbreak has brought European economies to their knees, highlighting the need for more solidarity between richer (northern) and poorer (southern) member states. In 2020 the European Union launched a US$900 billion rescue fund to help its weakest members cope with the year's economic downturn. To finance this fund, the bloc will issue debt maturing in more than three decades, in 2058. Beyond the economic impact that the scheme will have, this is a powerful symbol: EU member states signaled that they intend to stick together for the long term. Faced with such a strong political commitment, investors increasingly struggle to argue that the euro might disappear.

The EU rescue fund is also likely to enhance the euro's global leverage in other ways: sovereign debt from various member states will start to be pooled. The first pan-European bond, worth €100 billion, was launched in October 2020. It turned out to be a massive success, attracting the largest number of orders ever recorded across Europe's financial markets.[53] This means a deep European bond market will gradually develop, for an amount that could eventually be neck and neck with that of U.S. public debt.[54] The dominance of U.S. Treasury bonds as the global safe asset of choice will probably start to diminish.

Pandemic-induced social-distancing measures have also prompted the European Central Bank to speed up existing plans to launch a digital version of the euro, following in the footsteps of the Chinese.[55] Christine Lagarde, the European Central Bank's governor, hopes that a digital euro could be launched by 2025.[56] This is an ambitious timeline, which will probably be missed. However, Europe's direction is clear. The bloc wants to reap the benefits of being the first Western power to invest seriously in the development of digital currencies. Over time, Europe's digital currency will help the bloc to challenge the global hegemony of the greenback.[57]

⸎⸎⸎

The current supremacy of the U.S. dollar rests on several factors. The United States is the world's largest economy. American firms play a leading role in global supply chains. U.S. investment funds have a massive international footprint. New York is the world's leading financial hub. The depth and liquidity of U.S. financial markets are unmatched. The Fed, the Securities and Exchange Commission (SEC), and the U.S. Treasury write the financial rules of the world. For all of these reasons, the U.S. dollar has no credible challenger, for now.

America's policy makers have long assumed that the United States would always be the world's economic superpower. On the basis of this premise, there is virtually no chance that the U.S. dollar could lose its position as the world's leading currency. In the short term, this is a safe assumption: the ascendancy of the U.S. dollar will not be seriously threatened in the coming decade or so, unless the United States makes a currently inconceivable move, such as entering into a direct conflict with China. The longer-term prospects for the U.S. dollar, however, appear much less certain.

As Mark Carney, the former governor of the Bank of England, put it, "Even a passing acquaintance with monetary history suggests that this [U.S. dollar] centre won't hold."[58] Carney knows that the British pound offers a cautionary tale of how a currency may slowly lose its global standing. Sterling's slow decline started in the 1920s, when the global preeminence of the British Empire began to fade; 30 years later, the U.S. dollar had replaced the pound as the world's leading currency.[59] There is no reason to believe that such a scenario cannot happen again, this time at the expense of the greenback. In fact, many factors point in this direction.

America's global economic clout is decreasing. The American economy is not shrinking, but China and other (mostly Asian) emerging countries are growing much faster. The U.S. share of the global economy stood at around 30 percent in the 1950s, when the U.S. dollar replaced the British pound as the world's leading currency.[60] America's footprint in the global economic landscape is half smaller now, at around 15 percent. By 2050 China and India will count among the world's three largest economies. The United States will likely be in second position in the global GDP league table.[61] Three decades from now, almost half of the world's output will be produced in Asia. China's share in the global economy will stand at nearly 20 percent, one-third higher than that of the United States.[62]

Also, the International Monetary Fund (IMF) has long been issuing warnings about the long-term prospects of the U.S. economy. The main problem is that the trajectory of U.S. public debt appears unsustainable[63]; America's liabilities to the rest of the world stand at more than two-thirds of the country's output—a level that often denotes a coming financial crisis.[64] The U.S. corporate sector is dangerously overleveraged, too. It is not clear how American companies will manage to repay the mountains of debt that they have contracted. The IMF also worries about America's large income inequalities, which look set to increase even further in the coming years.

Financial investors have other, more immediate, worries. Many investment funds have doubts about the extent of the Fed's independence from political interference; these were fueled by the Trump administration's calls for the Fed to boost the economy. Investment funds also think that America's byzantine regulatory environment is a turn-off; already complex federal and state laws may not match, making it difficult to navigate through a complex web of financial regulations. None of these issues would be enough on their own to undermine trust in the greenback. Taken together, however, they reduce appetite for investing in the United States.

The coronavirus outbreak dented America's reputation, too. In late spring 2020 European countries were discussing the contours of a solidarity fund, and China was lifting lockdown measures. Meanwhile, the United States was becoming the global hot spot of the pandemic. Despite a fast rollout of coronavirus vaccines from late 2020, the United States has suffered the world's highest death toll from the pandemic, by far.[65] The country's poor management of the outbreak has shaken confidence in U.S. institutions and weakened the world's trust in America's ability to respond to crises. The largest economic power in the world appeared to be less capable of dealing with a pandemic than many other, including some much poorer, countries.

Perceptions of how a country responds in a crisis matter and are almost always reflected in global financial markets. After an initial rally around the U.S. dollar at the start of the pandemic, the greenback started to sink against the euro around May, after it became clear that America was in a bad way.[66] The year 2020 turned out to be an awful one for the greenback. For the first time in recent history, the U.S. dollar lost its safe-haven status; investors ditched the U.S. dollar and turned to gold instead. Previous warnings about investors one day losing faith in the greenback appeared to be becoming a reality.

The debate about the long-term role of the U.S. dollar as the global reserve currency is often framed in black-and-white terms. It is assumed that there is space for only one reserve currency for the world. On the basis of this assumption, the U.S. dollar's position remains assured, at least for now. However, matters have become more complex in recent years. The global geopolitical landscape is fragmenting. China, and also Russia, are increasingly challenging the traditional, Western-led, global order that emerged after World War II.

The coronavirus pandemic has accelerated the trend toward fragmentation, not only in the geopolitical arena but also in the economic sphere. Throughout 2020–2021 the virus caused disruptions to global supply chains, as entire regions of China and Europe were in lockdown. As a result, a growing number of multinationals are considering relocating their production lines closer to consumers in an attempt to enhance security of supply and resilience to future shocks; regional supply chains serving the Americas, Europe, and Asia are likely to replace seemingly unreliable global ones.[67] This means economic fragmentation will intensify.

Currencies will probably mirror these geopolitical and economic trends, paving the way for the emergence of a fragmented currency landscape that may allow for several global reserve currencies. Under this scenario, the U.S. dollar, the euro, and the renminbi would function in parallel to each other, each with a regional footprint: the greenback would rule in the Americas, the euro would dominate over Europe and part of Africa, and the redback would be unchallenged in the Asia-Pacific and most of Africa. In some way, this would be a return to the situation that existed in the eighteenth and nineteenth centuries, when the British pound, the Dutch guilder, and the French franc coexisted as the main global currencies.[68]

Shifts in the composition of foreign-exchange reserves across the globe tend to give early hints of future changes. Things do not look good for the greenback. In the early 2000s central bankers kept more than 70 percent of their reserve assets in U.S. dollars. This share has now decreased to less than 60 percent—a 25-year low.[69] Central banks appear increasingly keen to diversify their reserve portfolios and to replace their greenback holdings with assets in euros and renminbis. This shift is taking place at a slow pace, but it is nonetheless real.[70] Some analysts even predict that the renminbi will become the world's third-largest reserve currency (after the U.S. dollar and the euro) as soon as 2030.[71]

This is not far-fetched. In 2016 the IMF added the renminbi to its basket of leading reserve currencies, alongside the U.S. dollar, the euro, the yen, and the British pound.[72] Across the world, more than 70 central banks already hold renminbi as part of their foreign-exchange reserves. There are good reasons to believe that this number will continue to rise over the coming decades. China's reliance on exports as a major driver of economic activity is waning, partly as a result of sluggish growth across developed markets. In parallel, the Chinese population is aging, which means it is saving less, boosting consumption and imports. As a result, China will soon become a net importer of capital. This should boost demand for renminbi-denominated bonds from global investors and central banks.

This is a plausible scenario, but it remains far from certain. Using a currency for trade, a short-term transaction, is one thing. Storing strategic currency reserves is another matter: long-term trust in the value of the chosen reserve currency is the most important factor. So far many investors are not fully reassured that the value of the renminbi will always remain steady. Investment funds may also be wary of investing in Chinese bonds, owing to U.S.-China tensions. Beijing's push to liberalize Chinese financial markets may also take longer than expected. However, the trend is clear: traditionally cautious central bankers increasingly feel the need to diversify their assets away from the U.S. dollar.

———— ✦ ————

The global reach of U.S. sanctions depends on the hegemonic role of the greenback. If, say, Tajikistan imposed sanctions on countries and companies using the Tajik currency, these measures would not have much of an impact across the globe. By contrast, the impact of sanctions that apply to every company that wishes to use the world's leading currency—the U.S. dollar—is massive. However, the current reliance of American sanctions on the use of the greenback means that only a subtle uptick in the market share of other currencies would be enough to weaken the effectiveness of U.S. penalties.

A dual financial world—with some companies using the U.S. dollar while others do not—could emerge. This is already happening. Some Chinese banks do business in U.S. dollars and therefore respect American regulations, while others do not touch the greenback to shield themselves from Washington's demands. Europe is taking a similar path. Most European banks have no choice but to keep access to the American market. However, a few financial institutions are choosing not to use the U.S. dollar. At a time when the vast majority of European banks steer clear of Iran for fear of falling foul of Washington's sanctions, these small banks process most of Europe's trade with Iran, under the radar.

For America, the emergence of such a fragmented global financial system—with some channels controlled by the United States, while others escape Washington's scrutiny—represents a dire threat. Such a shift will not happen, if it takes place at all, for several decades. This slow, incremental pace of change is not good news: it makes the threat harder to grasp and more difficult for the United States to counter. The consequences could be huge. Foreign companies would have no trouble side-stepping the U.S. dollar to do business, including with America's foes. Perhaps even more worryingly, if North Korea and other rogue states have access to well-developed financial systems over which the United States has no oversight, it will become even harder to keep track of nuclear proliferation.

Trouble would not end there for Washington. If American companies have to use currencies other than the U.S. dollar to conduct trade abroad, they will become exposed to the threat of extraterritorial or secondary sanctions from other major economic powers, such as the European Union or China. Given Europe and China's economic clout, such penalties would have a big, negative impact on American firms, excluding them from two of the world's largest markets. Faced with a choice between conducting business with the United States on the one hand, and the European Union and China on the other hand, many foreign firms could choose to abandon the American market.

European sanctions that applied to U.S. firms using the euro or doing business in Europe would carry heavy symbolic weight. From the European Union's perspective, such penalties might sound appealing: they would give the European Union leverage over Washington. How would the United States react if American firms that do not follow Europe's demands are barred from accessing the European market? The reality is that such a scenario is extremely unlikely to happen: the European Union is staunchly opposed to extraterritorial regulations, which it insists are illegal under international law. However, history shows that policy U-turns happen, even if they do not seem at all likely in the short term.

Sanctions from Beijing look likelier. This is a recent development; until two decades ago, the Communist leadership opposed the use of sanctions, in line with the country's noninterventionist stance. Pragmatic considerations explained this posture. When China was a minor economic power, restricting access to the Chinese market ran counter to Beijing's economic and development goals. However, getting access to China's vast middle class has now become crucial for many international companies. This gives a new form of powerful leverage to Beijing to advance economic, political, or foreign-policy goals.[73]

The Communist leadership is making quick strides in this direction. In 2011 Chinese officials had a seemingly innocuous meeting with OFAC. Many at the U.S. agency still remember it: for several hours, the Chinese asked the Americans detailed questions related to the technicalities of U.S. sanctions. It turned out that China was in the process of developing its own sanctions legislation.[74] Since then, Chinese scholars and officials have published a flurry of papers discussing how Chinese sanctions could work and why they represent attractive tools. China will likely put its newly designed sanctions laws to work, eventually. American firms will probably be prime targets.

South Korea offers a cautionary tale of what may happen when China decides to punish a country or its businesses. In 2016–2017 Beijing's retaliation against the deployment of U.S. missile systems in South Korea cost Lotte, a South Korean conglomerate, nearly US$2 billion.[75] For the South Korean economy as a whole, losses amounted to nearly US$16 billion.[76] For China, such measures were probably only modest, tentative steps. In the future, Beijing will likely use its growing global economic clout to ensure that Chinese sanctions have an impact not only on firms operating in China but also on foreign firms elsewhere in the world. In a few decades, the reach of Chinese sanctions could be on a par with that of American ones.

In the coming years, the United States will probably have to find new tools to replace less-effective financial sanctions. America's coercive toolkit could gradually switch to measures that do not depend on the use of the greenback. Secondary sanctions are an obvious contender: they target multinationals that cannot survive if they do not have access to the American market. However, increasing the use of secondary penalties will further strain ties with allies and fuel foreign efforts to develop mechanisms to circumvent sanctions. It could also fuel China's willingness to design its own secondary sanctions regime and to impose such penalties on American (and possibly foreign) firms.

In a digital world where U.S.-based companies such as Meta (the parent company of Facebook, Instagram, and WhatsApp), Google, and Twitter hold vast swaths of sensitive data, another option is that future sanctions could target digital flows. This would make the impact of sanctions both less severe (shortages of goods would be unlikely) and more dangerous for U.S. foes (telling hundreds of millions of people that they do not have access to Facebook anymore would be a political challenge). However, given the current domination of American tech firms over the digital landscape, pursuing such an option would probably be akin to shooting itself in the foot for Washington.

Investment restrictions and export controls, especially on crucial technology staples, are a final option to replace financial sanctions. These economic weapons look appealing, on paper. They are highly effective, given America's technological lead. In addition, these measures do not rely on the widespread use of the U.S. dollar, but on America's economic clout, which is unlikely to decline all that much even in the long term (as long as the United States can maintain its lead at the technological frontier). The United States has been hard at work targeting China with precisely such measures over the past few years. This strategy carries significant risks for the Chinese economy, but even more so for U.S. interests.

10

HIGH-TECH FUTURE

Are Export Controls the Sanctions of Tomorrow?

I n the summer of 2020 massive wildfires erupted in California and Oregon. Forest fires are a yearly occurrence in the region. Yet amid devastation and chaos, the thousands of firefighters that were battling the flames quickly noticed that something was different from other years. Controlled burning, a crucial tool to prevent wildfires, had not taken place during the spring. Something else was amiss: there were no drones available to monitor how quickly the flames were spreading. If firefighters had known why there had been no controlled burns, and why drones were missing, they would probably have been surprised. It had nothing to do with forests, environmental policies, or perennial budget cuts. It was all about China.

A few months earlier, the Trump administration had ordered U.S. government agencies to stop using a fleet of more than 800 drones that previously helped to monitor fires and to conduct controlled burns across America.[1] The drones worked perfectly well, but they were made by DJI, a Chinese company.[2] Using unmanned aircraft from DJI is nothing special: the firm supplies more than 70 percent of the world's civilian drones.[3] However, the administration worried that the drones might covertly send sensitive information to China, allowing Beijing to see exactly what the drones could see.[4]

DJI had vigorously denied these claims and taken steps to relocate production to the United States. Staff from the Interior Department had warned that halting controlled burning would likely result in catastrophic wildfires. Yet the administration had chosen to ignore these warnings and to go even further with its China-proofing strategy: Washington also halted the acquisition of 17 high-tech systems, called Ignis, which help to start controlled fires.[5] The technology was American. Three years earlier, the U.S. government had added Ignis to a top list of "Made in America" innovations.[6] However, there was a catch: the Ignis systems include Chinese-made components. For the administration, this was too much of a risk to take.

The decision to shelve the fire-monitoring equipment derailed the activities of the Office of Wildland Fire; the administration was not able to identify alternative suppliers of controlled-burning systems that had no tie to China.[7] With drones grounded and Ignis systems missing, the Office of Wildland Fire was able to carry out only a quarter of the controlled-burning operations that it had arranged to undertake in 2020. The backup plan would have been to use aircraft manned by firefighters, but this option was quickly abandoned: it imperiled human lives when there was a risk-free alternative.

The lack of drones was a tangible illustration of the ripple effects of the U.S.-China conflict.[8] It came with catastrophic consequences. It is unlikely that using drones would have prevented the fires, which were due to an unusual combination of strong winds and extreme heat. However, perhaps it could have helped to lower the death toll (nearly 40 people died) and to reduce the scope of the damage (which stood at nearly US$2 billion).[9] Was mitigation of unsubstantiated risks that China may use the drones to spy on U.S. soil worth such a high price? For Washington, the answer was apparently a clear yes.

American concerns around China's technological rise—and the industrial espionage and cyber theft that go with it—date back to the early

2000s. They came to the fore in 2018, when the U.S. trade representative issued a lengthy report summarizing China's perceived offenses against the United States.[10] The document highlighted Washington's realization that the Chinese economy is not market-driven, but fully state-led.[11] According to the U.S. government, China's economic strategy focuses on attracting foreign firms, stealing their technology, and indigenizing it before forcing the companies out of the Chinese market. In the view of U.S. policy makers, this process involves only a few, well-documented steps.

First, the Chinese government forces global companies that want to gain access to China's market to form joint ventures with Chinese firms. These local companies have one single objective: siphoning the technological secrets of their foreign counterparts. This is a well-known issue; as the U.S. Office of the National Counterintelligence Executive put it, "Chinese actors are the world's most active and persistent perpetrators of economic espionage"[12] (to be fair, the United States is probably not far behind). Alternatively, China may also force Western firms to sell their know-how to their Chinese partners at ridiculously low prices.

Once Beijing has gathered the technology it is looking for, Chinese companies replicate it. This is the famous moment when foreign businesses realize that a factory closely resembling their own has just opened down the road. Strangely, the Chinese plant happens to manufacture exact replicas of the Western products. Washington believes that Beijing eventually plans to kick foreign companies out of China. This makes sense, in theory: once Chinese companies have gotten hold of foreign technology, Beijing may see little reason to let competing foreign firms remain in its domestic market.

These unfair practices are widely acknowledged, but they form only one aspect of American concerns toward China. In recent years, the U.S. government has also become increasingly worried that letting Chinese technological companies operate on U.S. soil or having U.S. government agencies use Chinese-made technology puts national security at risk. This was the reasoning behind the grounding of the controlled-burning drones on the West Coast. The issue is far from limited to drones, however. The argument goes that all of China's high-tech companies have ties to the Chinese state and may be compelled to secretly gather data on their Western consumers.

On paper, these concerns appear valid. Although there are no (public) records of such an occurrence, China's national security law may force Chinese companies that operate in the United States to collect information on American citizens or businesses and to send these data back to Beijing. Chinese firms have no choice but to cooperate with Beijing; according to China's regulations, the companies have no right to appeal such requests.[13] Many American firms already take these issues seriously. Technological supplies to Google and Facebook, for instance, have to be China-proof.[14]

From this perspective, Chinese-made cell-phone towers installed near government buildings, such as federal offices or military bases, pose an especially acute threat. This is the crux of the debate around Beijing's participation to the global rollout of 5G telecommunications networks. Defense hawks believe that China could use the infrastructure to spy on sensitive installations. China's backers are quick to point out that these concerns are both theoretical and unsubstantiated. However, there are precedents: on two separate occasions,[15] China was accused of spying on the Ethiopian headquarters of the African Union. Beijing and the Chinese companies that are suspected of having been involved have denied the accusations, which the African Union has also—albeit inexplicably—downplayed.[16]

The American security establishment's worst-case scenario looks even more worrying. Some experts fear that installing Chinese-made telecommunications equipment on U.S. soil may enable Beijing to pull the plug on America's phone or Internet networks.[17] Most analysts believe that this is not really feasible. At any rate, this sounds unlikely: China's growth would tank if the U.S. economy crashed. If China took such an extreme step, Beijing's long-term ability to convince countries to install Chinese telecommunications equipment would also suffer. However, if the United States and China became embroiled in a direct military conflict, for instance over Taiwan, Beijing would have nothing to lose.

The Trump administration brought China-related concerns to the fore, but these will not end under the presidency of Joe Biden (and beyond). Trump did not prompt any change in thinking around Beijing; despite his bombastic claims, he merely highlighted the shift in consensus around China within the American establishment.[18] After years of debates and hopes that the Chinese leadership would live up to its World Trade Organization (WTO) commitments, Democrats and Republicans now agree that China and the United States are competitors. The consensus in Washington is that there is little chance that relations between both countries may improve in the coming decades.[19] To the United States, China is no longer the useful, cheap factory of the world.

The bipartisan view in America's corridors of power is that China is rolling out a revamped version of economic imperialism, just like Great Britain in the nineteenth century or Japan after World War II. To retain its role as the world's sole superpower, Washington believes that it has to stop Beijing in its tracks.[20] Some Americans go as far as seeing the U.S.-China clash as a generational one, on a par with conflicts against the former Soviet Union or Islamist terror. The reality may be less dramatic. The conflict between America and China is one for economic dominance between an incumbent economic superpower and its rising challenger.

In this economic war, the United States is unsurprisingly keen to put all forms of economic coercion to good use. The Trump administration imposed tariffs on US$360 billion of American imports from China; Biden has made it clear he is not lifting these.[21] The United States has also sanctioned Chinese individuals linked to human-rights abuses against both the Uyghur minority in Xinjiang and pro-democracy protesters in Hong Kong. In the financial sphere, U.S. lawmakers are pondering whether to de-list more than US$1 trillion worth of shares of Chinese companies on U.S. stock exchanges.[22] Congress is also considering barring the Thrift Savings Plan, which manages the pensions of millions of federal government employees, from investing in Chinese companies.[23]

Taking such stringent measures on China is highly significant. The United States has become used to imposing economic sanctions, but this time these are not meant to punish a rogue state such as North Korea, Syria, or Venezuela. Instead, American penalties target a demographic giant that is a permanent member of the UN Security Council and the second biggest economy in the world (China will become the world's largest economy in the early 2030s[24]). U.S. sanctions against China also have a direct impact on the livelihoods of nearly 2 billion American and Chinese citizens; when tariffs are imposed, consumers almost always pay the bill.[25] However, the reality is that these measures remain mild in the grand scheme of things.

Tariffs hurt consumers, but they may be canceled at the stroke of a pen. Financial sanctions against Chinese individuals do not bite much, as the targeted people almost invariably have no ties to the United States. Threats to de-list Chinese companies from the New York Stock Exchange carry little more than symbolic weight, too: China's firms would simply raise capital elsewhere, for instance in London, Tokyo, or Hong Kong, further diluting U.S. leadership over global financial places. Finally, Beijing will not care about Congress's plans to prevent U.S. federal employees from investing their pension pots in Chinese companies: American investors own only a fraction of Chinese stocks.

America's restraint highlights the fact that in China's case, financial sanctions remain unlikely. Imposing sanctions on major Chinese banks and companies or even banning China from using the U.S. dollar would deal Beijing a serious blow. However, such measures would also destabilize the global economy. This explains why U.S. policy makers have never really seriously considered going down that road: they know that potentially triggering another financial crisis would hurt Washington at least as much as it would harm Beijing.[26]

China is not Iran, Venezuela, or even Russia. The Chinese economy has grown far too big for America to sanction Beijing with its usual toolkit. America needs something else to advance its interests against China. The U.S.-China confrontation is playing out in the three areas that make or break economic influence nowadays: trade, finance, and technology. The United States has probably explored all the potential trade tools— mainly tariffs—that it can use against China, and financial sanctions appear highly unlikely. The only remaining option for Washington is to focus efforts on the technological sector.

—⁂—

In 2016 the Chinese leadership announced that it planned to spend US$150 billion over ten years to develop a Chinese semiconductor industry.[27] The U.S.-China conflict had not started in earnest by then, but Beijing's announcement raised alarm bells across the American defense establishment. U.S. experts warned that China's plan to beef up its presence in the semiconductor sector put America's national security at risk: in a few decades, Chinese firms could become able to manufacture microchips that are more advanced than those that the United States can make. As a result, China's missiles, lasers, or air defense systems could become the most sophisticated in the world.

Semiconductors, which are also called computer chips, microchips, or integrated circuits, are the brains that power all modern high-tech gadgets.[28] These components are 2,000 times thinner than the breadth of a human hair, but they are just as important as oil, gas, or coal in today's tech-dependent economy. Without microchips, virtually all modern products, including mobile phones, computers, planes, trains, servers, tablets, pacemakers, cars, wind turbines, or even rice cookers, cannot work. Without semiconductors, the Internet, telecommunications networks, and power plants would not exist.

Semiconductors are also crucial in the military sector. The defense industry buys only a tiny fraction of global semiconductor supplies, but fighter jets, submarines, and missile-launching pads are full of microchips.[29] As former U.S. under secretary of defense for research and engineering Michael Griffin put it, "Superiority in [microchip] technologies . . . is the key to deterring or winning future conflicts."[30] If Chinese semiconductor capabilities become more advanced that those of the United States, America may lose its military superiority.[31]

The widespread use of products that rely on semiconductors means that the global microchip sector has become a gigantic one, recording annual sales of around US$600 billion (more than Sweden's, Ireland's, or

Israel's GDP).[32] The sector looks set to record double-digit growth in the coming decade; tomorrow's economy will rely on the Internet of Things (IoT), cell phones, and high-speed telecommunications, all of which are huge consumers of computer chips. The country that will control the technology and know-how to produce the most-advanced semiconductors will hold tremendous economic and political leverage.

Semiconductors are the Achilles' heel of the Chinese economy. Beijing buys more than US$300 billion of foreign-made semiconductors every year, making computer chips China's largest import, far above oil.[33] This reflects the fact that Chinese factories import 85 percent of the microchips that they need to build electronic goods.[34] Most of these semiconductors are manufactured using American technology. For Washington, this makes export controls a seemingly ideal tool to deprive Beijing of U.S. innovation and know-how in the manufacture of semiconductors. Such restrictions function in a similar fashion to financial sanctions: they seek to curb the access of America's adversaries to U.S.-made staples—the greenback for financial sanctions or computer chip technology for export controls—that have become so crucial that few countries can do away with them.

Washington knows that it has a massive trump card to play in the semiconductor sector: virtually every microchip around the world has some link to the United States, be it because it was designed with American software, produced using U.S.-made equipment, or inspected with American tools.[35] This is not surprising: the United States is the birthplace of the semiconductor industry. The sector was born in the 1950s to meet the growing tech needs of the American military as it started to confront the former Soviet Union. Around 70 years later, U.S. microchip firms are worth more than US$1 trillion.[36] Simply put, America dominates the field.[37]

American firms manufacture only around 10 percent of the computer chips sold across the world. The world's leading microchip foundries (as semiconductor assembly lines are called) are located in Asia, mainly in

Taiwan and South Korea.[38] However, a handful of U.S. companies control all of the higher, upstream echelons of the supply chain. Before a chip is manufactured, three steps have to take place: software to design microchips has to be created; semiconductors have to be designed using these computer programs; and equipment to manufacture and test the computer chips has to be produced.[39]

Three U.S.-based businesses—Cadence Design Systems, Synopsys, and Mentor Graphics—control 85 percent of the market for microchip design software, the first step in the creation of a semiconductor.[40] In the view of industry insiders, these firms are irreplaceable; virtually every semiconductor across the world was designed using software from one of these American businesses.[41] Cadence Design Systems and Synopsis are the only two companies that are able to provide integrated, end-to-end solutions for complex designs. Meanwhile, Mentor Graphics fans boast that the firm has the best back-end tools on the market.

The companies involved in the second, chip-design step are bound by American rules, too. In this step, engineers use software from Cadence Design Systems, Synopsys, and Mentor Graphics to draw a map of all the components of a given microchip, complete with manufacturing instructions for foundries. Arm, a British firm that America's Nvidia tried (but failed) to buy in 2020, provides such a blueprint for around 90 percent of chips around the world.[42] Arm was sensitive to U.S. export controls long before Nvidia announced its intention to swallow it for US$40 billion; the UK-based firm has always had a strong presence in the United States, which means that it has to comply with America's rules. Beyond Arm, the other leaders in this sector are American and include Qualcomm and Broadcom.

Once a microchip is designed, the final step before it may be manufactured and tested is to gather the sophisticated industrial tools that equip foundries. Again, the market leaders are American: Applied Materials, Lam Research, and KLA-Tencor control nearly half of the market for semiconductor manufacturing equipment.[43] Two other firms, the Netherlands' ASML and Japan's Tokyo Electron, make up another third of the sector.[44] On paper, foreign firms such as ASML or Tokyo Electron do not have to respect U.S. export controls, as these only apply to

American companies.[45] However, in practice, these global firms know that U.S. pressure to force them to comply with Washington's restrictions may be intense.

The U.S. domination over the semiconductor sector also extends to other highly specialized parts of the manufacturing chain; American suppliers control around 80 percent of the market of such obscure, yet unavoidable, technical processes as etching, wafer inspection, chemical vapor deposition, rapid thermal processing, chemical-mechanical planarization, or metrology.[46] For the materials and chemicals that foundries use on their manufacturing lines, the picture is the same: U.S. businesses, such as 3M, Corning, Cree, Honeywell, and Rogers, dominate the sector.

The fabrication of a microchip usually involves a process spanning several specialized companies, which in turn creates complex supply chains[47]: on average, American semiconductor firms work with around 16,000 suppliers.[48] However, some major tech businesses like to design, manufacture, and test semiconductors using their own software, technology, and production lines. Five of these so-called integrated device manufacturers (IDMs)—Samsung, Intel, TSMC, Qualcomm, and Apple—dominate the market, with annual revenues higher than those of their 249 competitors combined. Again, the United States runs the show in the IDM sector. Three of these giants—Intel, Qualcomm, and Apple—are American.[49] The other two—South Korea's Samsung and Taiwan's TSMC—are based in countries that are close U.S. allies, making them sensitive to U.S. export regulations.

⸺ ❦ ⸺

Given America's dominance over the microchip sector, Washington knows that measures curbing China's access to U.S. semiconductor technology have every chance to deal a blow to Beijing's technological ambitions. In 2018 Congress started to put this strategy into practice, quietly adopting a flurry of regulations meant to cut China's access to American know-how.[50] The hostilities began when lawmakers ordered the Commerce Department to start controlling the export of "emerging and foundational" technology.[51] This represented the first step toward the resurrection of Cold War–era export controls. However, instead of targeting defense exports—as was mostly the case with the former Soviet Union—these restrictions applied to the U.S. civilian, high-tech sector. China was not mentioned in Congress's legislation, but it was the only country that lawmakers had in mind.

The measure had more bark than bite. For one, Congress failed to define what an "emerging or foundational technology" is, leaving it to the White House to do some thinking around this issue.[52] Semiconductors were obvious contenders, but the legislation remained open to interpretation. There was another problem, too. Measures to monitor U.S. exports could only be applied, in the words of lawmakers, to technologies that are "essential to the national security of the United States." Again, defining what this meant was easier said than done and certainly open to a myriad of debates. However, the Congress-mandated controls on "emerging or foundational" technologies were only a start.

A few weeks later, Congress struck again, tightening the legislative framework to scrutinize foreign investments in the United States.[53] Lawmakers chose to broaden the definition of what constitutes national security.[54] They also included minority investments in the scope of the foreign takeovers that the White House can control or even block.[55] Again, there was no mention of China in the deliberations of Congress. However, Chinese investments in U.S. tech companies in Silicon Valley were the obvious—if not sole—target of these updated regulations.

Capitol Hill assumed that depriving China of the possibility of buying American technology start-ups would slow down Beijing's ability to innovate. To be fair, Chinese investments in the United States were already in free fall because of trade tensions—they stood at a mere US$5 billion in 2018, down from almost six times more in 2017.[56] As a result, the legislation probably had only a limited impact.[57] However, American lawmakers knew that they were sending Beijing a clear message: "we are watching what you're doing and intend to take steps to stop you in your tracks."

Congress's steps to scrutinize U.S.-China ties in the tech sector went mostly unnoticed. In May 2019 it was the Trump administration's turn to strike a blow to Chinese technological firms. This one was much more high profile. The administration put its sights on Huawei, China's telecommunications giant. The Commerce Department added the Chinese firm and dozens of its subsidiaries to its so-called entity list; the agency argued that Huawei had violated U.S. sanctions against Iran (something that the Chinese company denies).[58] In practice, the step amounted to imposing export controls on Huawei; American firms were barred from selling high-tech products to the Chinese firm without a license that—as is the case with most export licenses—was tricky to get.[59]

The decision to cut Huawei from U.S. innovation sent shockwaves through the global technology sector. The U.S. move was striking: the Commerce Department had initially designed the entity list to target murky proliferators of weapons of mass destruction. Huawei was clearly in another league. With around 200,000 employees and annual revenues of US$100 billion, the Chinese firm is the world's biggest maker of telecommunications equipment.[60] Like virtually every Chinese technology firm, Huawei is almost fully dependent on foreign shipments to meet its microchip needs. With access to U.S.-made semiconductors suddenly curtailed, the United States reckoned, Huawei would soon prove unable to manufacture high-tech products.[61] However, there was a catch.

It was reasonably easy for semiconductor businesses to go around U.S. export controls against Huawei.[62] Huawei's presence on the entity list meant that selling semiconductors directly to the Chinese firm was a no-no for American businesses. However, it remained possible to sell U.S.-made microchips to a third party, which in turn sold them to another firm that finally delivered them to Huawei.[63] The Chinese company could also still buy off-the-shelf U.S. computer chips that had not been specifically designed for its needs. America's first attempt to impose export controls on Huawei had failed.

Something else was needed for the penalties to work. The administration realized that measures against Huawei had to become extraterritorial and apply not only to American firms but also to foreign ones, just like financial sanctions. Imagining what form such regulations could take was not hard: the measures had to target not only the sale of micro-chips but also that of all the U.S.-made software and equipment required to produce them. This was a logical move: Washington knew that many of the tools that global chipmakers and foundries use to design and manufacture microchips rely on American technology. The Commerce Department got to work to see what could be done.

In May 2020 the Trump administration announced that it was barring all microchip manufacturers from forging chips for Huawei, anywhere across the world, if they used U.S. technology.[64] Three months later, the Commerce Department further tightened the rules to ban all micro-chip sales to Huawei.[65] In the remainder of the year, the administration broadened the restrictions to target dozens of other Chinese firms; these included SMIC, the largest Chinese foundry of microchips.[66] The measure closely resembled financial sanctions. The difference was that instead of targeting global companies using the greenback, Washington was applying coercive measures to firms, American and foreign, using U.S. technology.

Like financial sanctions, these export regulations sought to force countries and companies to choose sides between the United States and the sanctioned country—in this case China. The United States bet that the world's largest microchip producers, such as South Korea's Samsung or Taiwan's MediaTek and TSMC, would side with America and stop working with Chinese companies. Alternatively, these foreign firms could maintain ties to China, but this came at a high price: using American technology to design or manufacture microchips for Chinese firms had become impossible. Continuing to serve the Chinese market entailed rebuilding entire, U.S.-proof manufacturing lines for Chinese customers, at a cost of several billion dollars.

Both in the United States and abroad, the ripple effects of U.S. export controls against Chinese technological firms proved colossal, probably even more than the Commerce Department had expected. Huawei had to stop a number of its production facilities, as many of them relied on U.S.-made equipment.[67] Faced with high levels of uncertainty, SMIC slashed spending and investment plans.[68] Outside China, the manag-ers of microchip foundries frantically started to check whether their equipment used American technology. If this was the case, working with dozens of firms from China, the world's largest importer of semiconductors, had become illegal.

In some rare instances, the production lines of global tech firms did not rely on American technology. In theory, this shielded these companies from U.S. measures. However, Washington intended to see to it that all Western companies ditched their contracts with Beijing. Foreign tech firms all remembered that only a few months earlier, the Netherlands' ASML had learned the lesson the hard way. The company builds machines capable of carving out microchips using extreme ultraviolet light. The U.S. administration pressed the Dutch government hard to ensure that Amsterdam would forbid ASML from working with Chinese companies. The Netherlands eventually gave in to U.S. pressure and revoked ASML's export license to China.[69]

For Beijing, issues with ASML were a sure sign of problems to come: the Dutch firm is the only company in the world that masters the extreme ultraviolet technology that SMIC needs to manufacture highly advanced chips. For the Dutch business, this development was bad news, too.[70] The equipment cost more than US$20 billion to develop, and the fast-growing Chinese market was one of the most promising.[71] In a phone call with investors that took place a few weeks afterward, ASML's CEO hinted that the company was looking at making its supply chains fully U.S.-proof.[72]

Export controls against Huawei were not meant to have an impact in America, but they also had ripple effects on U.S. soil. American rural cell-phone and Internet providers had long understood that they were in trouble.[73] The cheap Huawei gear they had bought to connect remote and sparsely populated places to the Internet abruptly stopped to receive crucial software updates or replacement parts from U.S. firms. This was a death sentence: without these updates or spare parts, the Huawei cell-phone towers and Internet networks will, over time, simply stop working.

On the other side of the Pacific, Beijing knows that Washington's new export measures will pose a host of new problems to address. For the Chinese leadership, semiconductors are especially important in two areas: the manufacturing of cell phones and the roll-out of 5G networks on Chinese soil. The United States does not seem intent to curb China's ability to manufacture cheap, basic cell phones, as these do not pose a security threat to the United States[74]; the White House has extended export licenses to a number of American and foreign companies so they can continue to deal with Huawei for such unsophisticated products.[75] However, Washington appears keen to apply export controls to their fullest extent when it comes to highly advanced, ultrasmall chips.

For China, this will be a major headache in the coming years. High-tech microchips are a crucial component of much-touted 5G telecommunications networks. America's willingness to restrict Beijing's access to advanced semiconductors will likely hamper China's development of 5G infrastructure. The Chinese leadership will probably be able to prioritize the roll-out of 5G in a few high-profile cities and regions, such as Beijing, the Yangtze delta around Shanghai, or the Pearl River delta near Shenzhen.[76] However, the rest of the country will probably have to wait for longer than expected to get access to the innovations that fifth-generation networks enable, such as self-driven vehicles or smart electric grids.

Such ripple effects, both in China and the United States, are likely to be only the tip of the iceberg. The consequences of export controls restricting China's access to U.S. technology will be witnessed only over several decades. Innovation tends to come with long-term industrial investments that involve meticulously arranged supply chains and manufacturing processes. U.S. export controls will alter these plans.

The world's leading microchip manufacturers, including Taiwan's TSMC (which controls around half of the global production capacity) and South Korea's Samsung (which specializes in the most advanced microchips), are already redesigning their global supply chains with U.S. export controls in mind.[77] TSMC plans to open a giant, US$12 billion foundry in Arizona by 2024; the U.S.-subsidized plant will probably only serve the American market, while other TSMC factories will continue to do business with Chinese firms.[78] Samsung's latest projects also reflect this new reality: the South Korean firm plans to build two foundries in the coming years, one in Texas for US$17 billion and another one in Xian, in central China, for US$15 billion.[79]

Even if U.S.-China tensions were to recede, which appears highly unlikely, the long-term nature of such massive investment programs means that the effects of export controls will prove both long-lasting and hard to unwind. Adding to an already complicated picture, in the U.S.-China conflict, America is not the only country that is looking at export controls to fight against the other side.[80]

In 2019, at the height of the trade war, Chinese leader Xi Jinping paid a visit to a rare-earths mine in Jiangxi, a province in southeast China. Most China watchers got the message loud and clear: Beijing intended to signal that China held tremendous leverage over America in the form of rare-earth minerals, such as scandium, yttrium, and gadolinium. In case things were not explicit enough, following the visit, a Chinese government–controlled mouthpiece made the threat unambiguous: "Don't say you weren't warned."[81] China had already used the sentence twice before: to warn India against war over a disputed Himalayan border in 1962 and before starting a conflict with Vietnam in 1979.

China knows that it has an ace up its sleeve with rare earths.[82] The country controls 80 percent of the global production of the 17 metals that technological companies rely on to build semiconductors and other electronic products, including smartphones, televisions, electric vehicles, computer screens, or wind turbines.[83] The list of applications also extends to the military sector: building an F-35 fighter jet, for instance, requires 417 kilograms of rare earths.[84] A Virginia-class submarine needs ten times this amount of rare earths.[85] America may dominate the semiconductor sector, but China controls access to the commodities needed to build all modern electronic gear.

As Chinese leader Deng Xiaoping remarked in 1992, "the Middle East has oil, China has rare earths."[86] Beijing holds 40 percent of the global stock of the crucial minerals. By contrast, America owns only 1 percent of the world's known reserves of rare earths.[87] Mining rare earths is only part of the equation; China also controls 85 percent of the world's refining capacity for the metals.[88] In fact, the only U.S. rare-earths mine sends its production to China for processing (the California-based mine also happens to be partly owned by a Chinese investor).[89]

The idea that China could restrict America's access to rare earths to fight back against U.S. coercive measures is not far-fetched.[90] In 2010 Beijing banned the exports of rare earths to Tokyo amid a conflict over disputed islands in the East China Sea.[91] Since then, Beijing's threats have become more open. In 2019 the country launched a precise survey of China's production of rare earths, in what looked like a first step toward the imposition of export controls.[92] In 2020 the Chinese leadership adopted new legislation restricting sensitive exports, chief among them rare earths.[93]

The United States knows about this threat. In early 2022 a group of American senators introduced legislation that would force U.S. defense companies to stop buying Chinese rare earths beginning in 2026.[94] The Pentagon has long been pushing to develop rare-earths mines in Australia, Burundi, or Myanmar to reduce dependency on China.[95] However, matching the Chinese production capacity would take a decade, at least; it takes around ten years for a rare-earths mine to achieve good yields (if it ever does). Most experts also agree that America cannot even consider challenging China's supremacy without massive federal financing. However, public funding is slow to come.

The pandemic federal aid package included US$800 million of fresh money for the diversification of America's sources of critical minerals, including rare earths.[96] This was a start, but it is likely to be too little; a rare-earths project requires at least US$1 billion in investment.[97] Money is not the only problem. The sector is so notoriously environmentally unfriendly that developing U.S.-based production and refining lines would likely meet strong pushback (rare earths often come mixed with dangerous radioactive materials). Another issue is that the know-how to mine and process rare earths is mostly Chinese, so far.

The only thing left for American policy makers is to hope that China would not take the risk of wiping out its rare-earths industry by restricting exports. Beijing also knows that so-called rare earths are not that scarce. Over time, the United States would likely be able to rebuild rare-earths supply chains; since the 2010 dispute, Japan has cut its reliance on

Chinese rare earths by a third.[98] These factors will play a role in Beijing's calculations. However, China may also believe that temporarily curbing the United States' access to rare earths is a reasonable price to pay to deal a blow to America's tech sector.

———— ∽∞∾ ————

The Sino-American conflict over technology will take place across several decades, probably well beyond 2050. Export controls look set to form the bulk of Washington's arsenal to defend U.S. interests, especially in the technological sector. The measures illustrate the growing shift toward an environment where technological leadership is the main driver of political influence and economic power, as well as a crucial determinant of military might.[99]

Over time, export controls against Chinese firms are likely to prompt global technological companies to have two different sets of supply chains: one for the United States and other Western countries, and another one for China and emerging countries. Such a process, which has been dubbed "decoupling," would effectively cut ties between the American and Chinese economies. In a decoupled world, the utility of export controls would become limited; Chinese-controlled supply chains would effectively be U.S.-proof. Worse still, a U.S.-China decoupling may turn out to be beneficial to Beijing's interests.

11

WHEN SANCTIONS WORK TOO WELL

Why Decoupling from China Would Backfire

n 2014 the U.S. Commerce Department published a report assessing the benefits of the International Traffic in Arms Regulation (ITAR), a set of export controls meant to protect the know-how of American aerospace companies, such as Boeing, Northrop Grumman, or Lockheed Martin.[1] The conclusions of the study turned out to be surprising. Most U.S. firms believed that ITAR had hurt them; 35 percent of companies even reported that they had lost contracts because of the regulations. In countless interviews, executives explained that the measures had only served to encourage the development of cutting-edge space technology outside the United States, out of reach of America's export controls. A respondent noted that without ITAR, "it is unlikely that the European space industry would have grown so significantly, so quickly."[2]

To the embarrassment of the Commerce Department, hard data appeared to support the complaints of American businesses. The U.S. share of the global space market stood at 75 percent in 1998, when Washington started to enforce the ITAR rules. Within ten years, America's global market share for space equipment, such as satellites, had dropped to less than 50 percent. As part of the survey, one firm bluntly reported that the regulations had been "very successful in creating a global network of companies making competing products while ensuring U.S. companies cannot compete."[3] Three years after publication of the report, the administration scrapped ITAR in an attempt to restore the competitiveness of the U.S. space industry.[4]

More than two decades later, U.S. tech firms worry that history looks set to repeat itself. This time, Washington's export controls target semiconductors; the United States has made these restrictions its tool of choice to fight Beijing's technological rise by depriving China of access to American microchip technology. As the Department of Commerce keeps imposing more and more export controls, "decoupling" has become a buzzword in Washington. Definitions vary, but President Donald Trump's words are a good summary of the theory. As he put it, "We lose billions of dollars and, if we didn't do business with [China], we wouldn't lose billions of dollars. It's called decoupling."[5]

In practice, decoupling would entail cutting links between the U.S. and Chinese economies, especially in the technological sector. This concept rests on a simple idea: fewer ties with China are better for America's economy and security. Under a decoupling scheme, American companies would re-shore production to U.S. soil instead of outsourcing manufacturing lines to cheaper Chinese factories. Apple, for instance, would relocate factories to the United States instead of producing iPhones in China. If decoupling becomes reality, America's shipments to China would be curbed, too, in line with Washington's export restrictions on semiconductors.

On paper, America would kill two birds with one stone through decoupling: Washington would cut the access of Chinese high-tech firms to the U.S. market (thereby addressing national security concerns linked to the use of Chinese-made equipment for U.S. telecommunications infrastructure) and halt the rise of China's technology companies (by depriving them of access to crucial U.S. know-how). In theory, America would also narrow its large trade deficit: the many U.S. firms that have outsourced manufacturing lines to China would relocate production to U.S. soil, providing jobs to tens of thousands of Americans.

Decoupling enthusiasts point out that dealing a blow to Chinese firms is only one of many good reasons to decouple from China. The consensus view among Fortune 500 companies is no longer that cheaper is better to attract consumers.[6] American citizens and businesses are getting increasingly concerned about poor employment practices and lax environmental regulations in China and other emerging countries. Growing calls to cut carbon footprints also entail producing closer to consumers. Rising levels of automation form a final aspect of the equation: if robots can manufacture products in the United States, a cheap labor force in emerging countries becomes less of an attraction.

Many U.S. policy makers see the semiconductor sector as a top-priority area for decoupling. In their view, cutting China's access to microchips would be a sure way to deal a blow to the country's technology sector. If Chinese firms run out of semiconductors, they will be unable to produce electronic goods. Export controls on microchips mean that the United States also has a seemingly cheap and effective tool to decouple from China in this field. This reasoning looks appealing. However, it does not hold up to scrutiny. In fact, decoupling is both a bad idea and poor policy.[7]

Cutting the extensive ties that exist between American and Chinese semiconductor companies would be difficult and expensive. It would also hurt U.S. technology firms, cutting them out of global innovation and depriving them of opportunities to shape technology standards. Losing access to the Chinese market would also entail a steep drop in revenues for U.S. semiconductor firms, which would have no choice but to cut R&D. As a result, the United States could lose its technological, and in turn military, superiority. Instead of addressing national security risks and weakening the Chinese high-tech sector, decoupling would create new challenges and unintentionally bolster Beijing's rise.

To state the obvious and take a broad view beyond the sole microchip industry, decoupling from China would be tremendously difficult. The United States designed export controls to deal with Moscow in the Cold War era, when the American and Soviet economies had virtually no ties. At the time, the United States and the Soviet Union were already decoupled; in fact, they had never really been coupled. During the Cold War, Soviet products were absent from America's supermarkets. U.S.-Soviet technology exchanges were few and far between. Moscow did not buy American tech firms in a Silicon Valley that did not even exist. However, China is a vastly greater opponent than the former Soviet Union ever was.

The U.S. and Chinese economies are fully intertwined.[8] China is the world's largest manufacturer of goods, with an output equivalent to that of all American, German, and Japanese factories combined.[9] China is also the United States' largest trading partner, with a turnover of more than half a trillion U.S. dollars every year; Beijing represents the third biggest export market for American firms (after Canada and Mexico) and the main source of U.S. imports.[10] Links between companies on both sides of the Pacific are extensive. Cargo ships endlessly make return journeys between the Californian ports of Los Angeles or Long Beach and those of Shanghai, Shenzhen, or Guangzhou.

Economic ties between the United States and China go far beyond trade. American and Chinese supply chains have been integrated for more than two decades; the production lines of most U.S. technology firms span across both sides of the Pacific, making use of America's edge over innovation and of China's competitive advantage when it comes to (cheap) production. Apple's iPod may look like an American product, for instance, but it is really made by hundreds of different firms in dozens of countries, including China.[11]

In addition to being difficult, decoupling would be long. Judging by the time it took Japanese, South Korean, and Taiwanese high-tech companies to move their supply chains to China in the 1990s, relocating the production lines of American technology firms to U.S. soil could take more than 20 years.[12] Decoupling enthusiasts point out that this might not be an issue: many of the events that shaped the global economy took decades to unfold, as was the case for the development of personal cars, the rise of the Internet, or the democratization of cell phones. However, American businesses object that decoupling has nothing to do with innovation-led, profit-generating progress.

Decoupling would not present American companies with an opportunity to grow and become more profitable. Cutting ties with China would come with a hefty price tag for U.S. businesses. A conservative estimate puts the price of moving away from China at US$1 trillion over five years.[13] Tax breaks and other financial incentives could help micro-chip companies to swallow the decoupling pill, but many firms would still have to raise (and then repay) huge amounts of debt to finance such an operation, weighing on their profits for many years—unless American consumers foot the bill.

—— ⚮ ——

The challenges that decoupling would pose would be even greater in the microchip sector. Cutting ties to China would be costly for U.S. semi-conductor firms: they design microchips in America but have them produced in Asian foundries, which manufacture three-quarters of the world's computer chips.[14] Building a foundry is far from cheap: it costs around US$10 billion.[15] Decoupling would entail relocating dozens of such manufacturing facilities from China to the United States. Some-thing else would compress the profits of U.S. semiconductor companies if they get out of China. At the moment, the manufacture of microchips cannot be fully automated. This means losing access to the compara-tively cheap Chinese workforce would increase production costs.

Relocating semiconductor production lines to the United States would be expensive, but American microchip firms, such as Intel, Texas Instruments, or Qualcomm, worry even more about something else: if Washington cuts ties to Beijing, U.S. microchip companies would gradu-ally lose access to the Chinese market. This would represent a death war-rant for American semiconductor firms; China accounts for one-third of global demand for computer chips.[16] Without access to the buoyant Chinese market, many U.S. semiconductor businesses could go bust.

The extensive presence of American microchip companies in China reflects this commercial reality: American semiconductor firms have US$700 billion in assets, such as factories and research centers, booked on Chinese soil. American technology giant Intel illustrates how crucial China has become to U.S. microchip companies. The business has US$5 billion worth in factories across China, which is Intel's largest market; the country accounts for more than a quarter of Intel's global revenues.[17]

Intel is only one example: virtually all American companies have a similarly large footprint in China. As one insider puts it, "The idea that we can decouple from China and our industry will still be successful is not tethered to reality."[18]

For U.S. semiconductor firms, losing access to the Chinese market could cause their market shares to drop in other countries, too. Washington's growing export controls arsenal means that foreign companies are increasingly wary of doing business with U.S. companies. Over time, some international businesses could feel that avoiding American microchip technology altogether is a safer option. This is already happening; some global chip producers already market some of their semiconductors as "EAR free," meaning that they do not include American technology and are therefore not sensitive to U.S. Export Administration Regulations.[19]

Losing access to China, the largest market for semiconductors, while inadvertently fostering the rise of foreign semiconductor firms represents a dire threat for U.S. technological companies.[20] In the long term, decoupling from China could translate into a nearly 40 percent loss in the revenues of American microchip businesses.[21] To stay afloat, most U.S. makers of computer chips could have no choice but to cut down on some seemingly unnecessary investments, such as research and development. However, such a step would come with catastrophic consequences.

American microchip companies currently spend around 20 percent of their revenues in R&D. In the ten years to 2020, this represented more than US$300 billion.[22] Such huge investments form part of a virtuous circle. The more American microchip firms invest in R&D, the more they cement their global technological lead. The more cutting-edge the technology of American companies is, the more these firms sell computer chips, which, in turn, subsidizes more R&D. However, if revenues from China and possibly other countries disappear, this virtuous circle could become a vicious one.[23]

The production of computer chips is among the most R&D-intensive in the world, more than that of pharmaceutical products or airplanes for instance.[24] This means even a small drop in R&D expenses comes

with huge consequences. If they cut R&D budgets, American companies would prove unable to keep developing ever more innovative technology. Meanwhile, their foreign competitors would gain new contracts
in the markets that cannot (or do not want to) work with U.S. companies anymore. As a result, these rivals would be able to double down on
R&D. Over time, U.S. semiconductor firms could lose their position as
the global leaders for sophisticated microchip technology, to the benefit
of their competitors.

This may sound like a far-fetched scenario, but it would only be
a repeat of a well-known story.[25] In the late 1990s three American
firms—Lucent, Nortel, and Motorola—dominated the global telecommunications sector. These three giants looked too big to fail, until
the bursting of the tech bubble in the early 2000s prompted a sharp
drop in their revenues. As a result, the American telecommunications
behemoths felt that they had no choice but to cut R&D spending to
stay afloat. Meanwhile, Chinese companies started to flood the global
market with cheap cell phones that proved highly popular, especially
in developing countries.

Within only ten years, the American telecommunications sector
became only a shadow of its former self, lagging behind its European and
Asian peers regarding innovation. Lucent, Nortel, and Motorola were
bought a few years later by their European competitors, for a fraction
of their previous valuations. Nowadays, not a single world-class telecommunications company is American. As a result, the United States
depends on foreign companies, such as Sweden's Ericsson, Finland's
Nokia or South Korea's Samsung, to install the telecommunications
infrastructure that forms the backbone of today's economy and security.

This cautionary tale might well repeat itself in the microchip sector.
It highlights the fact that the decoupling-induced risk to America does
not really come from losing its technological advance to China outright.
At any rate, this is unlikely to happen; as things stand, Chinese semiconductor firms remain far less advanced than their U.S. competitors.
Instead, the danger that decoupling poses stems from the loss in revenues that not being able to serve the Chinese market and losing contracts in other countries would entail. With profits severely curtailed,

U.S. technology firms would probably struggle to remain ahead of the global game for semiconductor innovation.

Within a few decades, Washington could have no choice but to do business with foreign companies to meet its advanced semiconductor needs. Taiwanese and South Korean firms, which are the world's leading chip manufacturers, will be all too happy to sell semiconductors to American firms for civilian purposes. However, the situation may be different regarding military gear. Would foreign countries sell their most advanced microchips to the United States or would they prefer to keep their best technology for their own defense forces? Could Beijing apply pressure on Taipei and Seoul to prevent sensitive exports to the United States? Decoupling from China to protect U.S. national security could have the exact opposite effect and heighten military vulnerabilities.

The race to design technical standards for emerging technologies is another overlooked aspect of the U.S.-China confrontation. As Werner von Siemens, who later founded the Siemens empire, put it, "He who owns the standards, owns the market."[26] Nowadays, there are standards for nearly every appliance, including the gauge of railways, the frequencies of mobile phones, and the shape and voltage of electrical plugs. Without common global rules, a cell phone that works in the United States would not have any reception in, say, Brazil. Setting up technical standards used to be a boring affair. Amid U.S.-China tensions, geopolitics now plays an oversized role in what has become a highly sensitive exercise. In a decoupling scenario, America's ability to promote the adoption of U.S.-made standards could decrease.

The United States, Japan, and European countries have long been the sole rule-makers for global technical standards. China, by contrast, is a latecomer to the party. Until recently, the country had virtually no presence in international standard-setting bodies, such as the International Organization for Standardization (ISO; in charge of promoting the adoption of unified standards across the world), the International Telecommunications Union (ITU; focused on telecommunications norms), and the International Electrotechnical Commission (IEC; tasked with defining standards for all electronic items).

This changed in 2015, when the Chinese leadership set out to turn China from a minnow into the global leader for the design of technical standards. Beijing had two goals in mind: influencing innovation across the world and promoting the use of Chinese technology. To achieve these objectives, Beijing beefed up the role of its Ministry of Industry and Information Technology (MIIT), tasking it to centralize the work of various Chinese research institutes and companies on standards. As one industry insider explains, "We participate in standardisation to influence how the market will shape up."[27] China would be foolish to miss such a golden opportunity to advance its interests and those of its high-tech companies.

China's efforts to influence the design of global technological standards turned out to be fruitful. Despite Beijing's initial difficulties to find qualified personnel to hold leadership positions in international technical bodies, China's presence in the main rules-setting organizations has grown sharply in recent years.[28] In 2015 Zhang Xiaogang became the first Chinese president of ISO. In the same year, Zhao Houlin began an eight-year stint as the secretary-general of the ITU. Shu Yinbiao has been the IEC's president since 2020.

China has made good use of its newly found presence in rules-setting bodies. Chinese experts have become assiduous members of their various working groups: the country is the third most active participant in ISO technical committees (after France and the United Kingdom), and the second most dynamic member of IEC panels (after Germany). In all of these working groups, China's representatives strive to promote Chinese-made technical standards, which may run counter to American ones. For instance, China has long tried to support the development of WAPI, a competitor to WiFi. In doing so, Beijing intends to advance its own domestic surveillance goals.

Tech experts believe that under WAPI, governments enjoy a great amount of control of what users do while browsing the Internet. Many Chinese government agencies and key state contractors already use the intrusive standard. Starting in 2003, Beijing tried to go further and to have WAPI replace WiFi on a global scale.[29] So far these efforts have failed; ISO has judged that WAPI may not be rolled out internationally, as WiFi is already widely available. However, there will probably be other WiFi/WAPI dilemmas in the future. In addition, China knows that it has a trump card to promote Chinese technological standards.

Beijing is rolling out made-in-China technology in the 70-odd countries that form part of the Belt and Road Initiative (BRI) infrastructure project. Alongside investments in roads, ports, and railways, China has launched a "digital silk road" that promotes Chinese technology in dozens of so-called smart cities across several countries, including Serbia, Pakistan, or Egypt.[30] The concept of smart cities is all about surveillance: participating capitals get Chinese-made security cameras, 5G networks that transmit the data of cameras in real time, and facial recognition software.[31] The amounts at stake are massive; Beijing has already invested nearly US$80 billion in the scheme.[32] In some years, China's funding for digital infrastructure in Africa is higher than that provided by all multilateral agencies and Western governments combined.[33]

The coronavirus pandemic has given a new urgency to this push, as many governments have curbed or monitored the movements of their populations in an attempt to contain the outbreak. Beijing has sensed an opportunity and resurrected long-held plans to launch a "health silk road" alongside the digital one. In Ecuador, for instance, the scheme comes with Huawei-made Covid-19 diagnostic tools for hospitals (the technology sends lung scanners to China-based servers before an artificial intelligence algorithm assesses the severity of the patient's condition).[34]

All of the equipment that smart cities use as part of the digital silk road relies on Chinese technology. Governments might not even realize that they are signing up for a Chinese-made set of technological standards. Many cash-strapped BRI states are lured by the cheap prices that China is able to offer for high-tech gear, especially for the roll-out of 5G networks. Chinese technology may be genuinely better, too: in 165 countries, Beidou, the Chinese competitor to America's GPS, is up to three times more accurate (perhaps this should not come as a surprise: in Chinese, the word *beidou* means "big dipper").[35]

Once the Chinese networks are up and running, it is too late (and too expensive) for BRI governments to change their mind. Emerging countries find themselves locked in with Chinese technology, giving a long-term advantage to Beijing's firms over American ones. China also hopes that its willingness to set up and fund research centers in BRI states will ensure that scientists from developing countries take part in research and cooperation programs solely with their Chinese counterparts, effectively cutting out American firms from such exchanges. In the long term, Beijing is betting that increased influence in the emerging world will also help to secure the support of developing countries for Chinese-made standards in rules-setting bodies.

There is no consensus in Washington's corridors of power on the merits or risks of decoupling. Some policy makers believe that cutting ties with China is a necessity to protect America's national security and curb China's technological rise. Other officials are more circumspect. They usually cite the negative side-effects that such a policy would involve and mention the intense lobbying of U.S. semiconductor firms against decoupling plans. However, on the other side of the Pacific, the decoupling question is not an "if" but a "when." Beijing believes that decoupling is inevitable. The Communist leadership is getting ready for what it sees as the new normal.

America's export controls focus on the semiconductor sector, which has become one of the many battlefields of the U.S.-China conflict. In this area, Beijing believes that it has to take decisive steps to address a life-or-death issue. A potential dearth of semiconductors could decimate China's technology firms. As a result, the Chinese leadership intends to put an end to the country's reliance on U.S. microchip technology.[36] This will not be easy. So far China produces only 15 percent of the microchips it needs, making the country a minor global player for semiconductors.[37] However, America's decoupling plans have made China's self-sufficiency ambitions for computer chips pressing. Beijing calls this process the new

"Long March." Communist media go further, dubbing the process the "Great semiconductor leap forward."[38]

China's road toward autonomy for computer chips will be long. High-tech innovation tends to be a networking exercise, with private firms, universities, and research centers working together to develop cutting-edge technology.[39] So far, China lacks such a high-tech ecosystem when it comes to microchips. The country will have to build a semiconductor industry from scratch. Chinese microchip makers currently rely on U.S. technology to produce even moderately advanced semiconductors. Innovation in microchips is a race to the smallest: today's smartphones have 100,000 times more processing power than the NASA computer that sent *Apollo 11* to the moon in 1969.[40] However, ever smaller microchips are hard to make.

As things stand, Chinese firms cannot produce semiconductors of a smaller size than 40 nanometers (that is to say smaller than the average growth of a nail over one minute) without American know-how.[41] This may sound minuscule, but this remains too big by today's standards: the most sophisticated microchips are about eight times smaller, and China does not have a clue how to produce these in high volumes, let alone with low manufacturing error rates. The United States is cashing in on years of research and development in the microchip sector. However, Chinese firms have every intention to catch up.

American firms currently dominate the semiconductor market, but Beijing believes that they are not irreplaceable. The U.S. Semiconductor Industry Association, which is supposed to boast about America's leadership for computer chips, shares this sanguine assessment. The lobbying group believes that China may find non-American suppliers for around 70 percent of its microchip needs.[42] For Beijing, this estimate is excellent news. To build a semiconductor sector that will be U.S.-proof, China simply has to focus its efforts on acquiring technology and building up production lines for the remaining 30 percent.[43] For the second largest economy in the world, this sounds doable.

Chinese tech firms know that their survival is at stake. As a result, they are doubling down on R&D spending to boost their technological

capabilities. In 2020 Huawei became the world leader for patent applications at the UN-backed World Intellectual Property Organization;
the Chinese firm applied for 5,464 patents, nearly double the amount of
South Korea's Samsung, which was the second-biggest applicant. Only
one U.S. firm, Qualcomm, featured in the otherwise Asia-dominated
global top five.[44] By early 2021 Huawei held around 100,000 technology
patents, an increase of nearly 20 percent in only one year.

This investment push is already yielding results. Huawei has managed
to make its production lines for 40-nanometer microchips fully U.S.-
proof.[45] The Chinese company aims to design and build 20-nanometer
semiconductors—small enough for high-tech 5G equipment—without using any American technology by early 2023.[46] Most tech experts
believe that these are ambitious targets, which Beijing could well miss
by a few months or even years. However, in the grand scheme of things,
China's direction is clear: in the long run, the Communist leadership
will do everything it takes to ensure that it does not have to rely on U.S.
know-how to design and build semiconductors.

Beijing has established two milestones for its microchip self-sufficiency
plans, setting a first signpost for 2035.[47] By that year, China plans to have
reached parity with the United States in the microchip sector and to play
a leading role in setting global standards for semiconductors. The Communist leadership did not set this target randomly: it took South Korea
and Taiwan 15–20 years to become global leaders for computer chips.[48]
Even if Beijing needs more time than Seoul and Taipei to develop its
semiconductor industry, owing to a lesser degree of access to U.S. technology, China should still make it broadly on time for its self-imposed
2035 deadline. However, China's plans go way beyond 2035.

By 2049—the centenary of the birth of the People's Republic—Beijing
intends to have replaced the United States as the world leader in the
semiconductor industry. At a time when the United States struggles to
think with a longer time horizon than that of a four-year presidential
term, China is playing the long game. Beijing knows that reaching this

ambitious goal will not be easy; Chinese microchip firms will struggle in the short term, for lack of know-how.[49] To make up for the shortage of skills and the need to build a semiconductor ecosystem from scratch, the Chinese leadership has unveiled a massive investment push.

Beijing's so-called "dual circulation" industrial strategy forms the most visible layer of this plan.[50] It is all about autonomy, reducing China's current reliance on exports as an engine of growth and making domestic consumption the main pillar of the Chinese economy. As part of this program, the Chinese leadership has committed to spending US$120 billion to improve self-sufficiency in the energy, health care, and high-tech industries, with a focus on microchips.[51] The investment plan goes with ten-year tax breaks, cheap loans, and eye-popping levels of government subsidies for chipmakers.[52] Beijing plans to channel public funding to Chinese firms through 1,800 "government guidance funds" valued at more than US$600 billion.[53]

This may sound like a lot, but this amount pales in comparison with the US$1.4 trillion investment plan for semiconductors that Chinese president Xi Jinping unveiled on the day after the U.S. imposed export controls on Huawei.[54] Even if half of this amount forms part of a rebranding operation—pretending that previously planned funds are newly created—the sums at stake remain colossal. Other initiatives will complement this plan, with a national semiconductor fund valued at US$29 billion[55] and state-sponsored investment funds meant to support microchip start-ups.[56] Overall, these amounts are so high that they almost guarantee long-term progress.[57]

By comparison, U.S. public and private funding for semiconductor R&D looks negligible. In the microchip sector, China's investment plans outspend those of the U.S. government by almost 50 to 1.[58] Even under an optimistic scenario, U.S. federal funding for semiconductors will not go much above US$50 billion in the coming years.[59] Adding the R&D expenses of American microchip firms does not change the overall picture. All told, America's spending in the semiconductor sector represents only a fraction of China's investment push. However, many American tech experts remain unconvinced that Beijing's colossal investments will pay off.

Skeptics argue that a large share of the funds that Beijing is putting on the table will be wasted. They are probably right. Around 22,000 Chinese companies registered as microchip firms in 2020 to get hold of government subsidies.[60] Many of them have little to no experience in the semiconductor industry; Chinese government records show that some used to sell auto parts, while other specialized in seafood or online gaming.[61] This means many of China's wannabe microchip companies will likely fail. Generous government subsidies mean that other businesses will stay afloat even though they are not profitable, raising the risk of a "zombification" (as the survival of unhealthy companies is known) of the sector.

Critics also point to recent scandals to argue that China's push to invest in computer chip companies is at best a scam and at worst a fraud. Examples of flagship microchip projects that have gone wrong abound. Partially built factories that were supposed to form part of multibillion-dollar semiconductor hubs have popped up throughout China. In many cases, the owners of the production plants had managed to negotiate billions in grants from the Chinese government.[62] Months afterward, only a few half-finished buildings and a couple of cranes stood at what were supposed to become world-class innovation centers.[63] However, the Communist leadership could not care less.

There is an old saying in Chinese: "If you build the nest, the birds will come." Beijing knows that if only 1 percent of the tens of thousands of newly created semiconductor firms succeed, this will be enough to create an ecosystem of a few hundred successful Chinese microchip companies. As Lu Lei, the secretary-general of a Shanghai-based industry group, said in a television interview, "We must not view that as waste. We must look at it as the price you have to pay to develop an industry. It's a natural process that has to happen, you must have quantity to arrive at quality.[64]"

⸗

China's end goal is to rebuild an entire, U.S.-proof supply chain for semiconductors. So far Chinese firms remain way behind their American competitors, which control the upper echelons—the design of chip-creation software, the utilization of such software to sketch semiconductors, and the manufacturing of equipment to produce microchips—of the value chain. The small number of well-established, mostly U.S., players in this niche area will make it difficult for Chinese companies to enter the market. But over several decades, there is no reason to think that China will not be able to catch up. To achieve this goal, Beijing is betting that its massive investment push will foster the rise of national champions.

For chip software design, the first step for the creation of a microchip, China's state-owned Huada Empyrean and Beijing-based Cellixsoft aim to replace America's Synopsys, Cadence Design Systems, and Mentor Graphics. For chip design, HiSilicon, a Huawei subsidiary, is trying to compete with U.S.-based Qualcomm and Broadcom. And for semiconductor manufacturing equipment, Naura Technology Group and AMEC want to dethrone California-headquartered Applied Materials and Lam Research.[65] All of these Chinese companies are much smaller than their U.S. competitors so far, but they are growing fast; their combined revenues have grown fourfold over the past decade.[66]

China has left no stone unturned to rebuild an entire microchip supply chain. Beyond replacing U.S. giants, Beijing is also creating an entire ecosystem of smaller, highly specialized companies. These new firms work in such obscure fields as vapor deposition (Shenyang Piotech), lithography (Shanghai Micro Electronics Equipment), rapid thermal processing (Mattson Technology), chemical-mechanical planarization (Hwatsing and Sizone Technology), wafer cleaning (ACM Research), or metrology (Shanghai Precision Measurement Semiconductor Technology).[67]

China's ambitions go even further: within a few decades, the Communist leadership wants to compete with global, integrated device manufacturers (IDMs) such as Intel, IBM, or Samsung. These world giants host most of the semiconductor fabrication chain in-house, designing, manufacturing, and selling microchips directly to smartphone makers or data centers. Beijing has an answer to these firms, called Yangtze Memory Technologies. The business looks set to work exactly like other IDMs, centralizing all design and manufacturing processes in house.

Despite concerns around the financial situation of its parent company, Yangtze Memory Technologies appears to be making quick progress.[68] In 2020 the Wuhan-based firm announced that it had managed to build a highly sophisticated microchip that could reasonably compete with Samsung's top-notch technology.[69] Analysts remain skeptical; so far Yangtze Memory Technologies lags behind its foreign competitors when it comes to stability and reliability. However, experts agree that the company is catching up. The firm has expanded the capacity of its US$24 billion semiconductor plant in Wuhan to meets its goal of doubling microchip production.[70]

Over several decades, Beijing might become nearly self-sufficient for semiconductors.[71] China would likely be able to get rid of U.S. microchips and to claim one of the top three global spots in the sector, alongside Taiwan and South Korea. Chinese firms would probably continue to struggle to build super-small microchips. This would not be a problem. Taiwanese and South Korean firms would likely specialize in cutting-edge semiconductors for sophisticated products, such as smartphones; both countries already hold 100 percent of the world's production capacity for semiconductors smaller than 10 nanometers.[72] Meanwhile, China would flood the world with cheaper, good-enough chips for most electronic equipment.

Gradually cash-strapped, and in turn less innovative, U.S. microchip firms would be relegated to a distant fourth place in the global league for semiconductor players. In retrospect, dethroning America in the microchip sector has long been the goal of the Chinese leadership, with investment plans in the sector dating back to the 1980s. The previous aspirations of the Communist leadership floundered, but the U.S. push to decouple from China makes it more likely that Beijing's semiconductor ambitions could finally succeed. Washington's decoupling plans, meant to choke the Chinese tech industry, have every chance to backfire. It is American firms that would choke, for China's benefit.

In the words of Xi Jinping, the global economy is undergoing changes "unseen in a hundred years."[73] From his perspective, decoupling is unavoidable, and China's seemingly unstoppable rise may only trigger America's fall. Like many of his fellow Chinese citizens, Xi Jinping hopes that over time, China will manage to overcome its current technological reliance on the United States. The Communist leader knows that there is little chance that the reverse may ever be true: China's oversized role as the world's manufacturing powerhouse, producing two-thirds of consumer electronics worldwide, means that the United States would struggle to reduce its dependence on Chinese products.[74]

The impact of a potential decoupling would go way beyond the United States and China. If the U.S. and Chinese economies were to part ways, every country around the world would have to choose sides, eventually. In some ways, this would be a repeat of what happened during the Cold War, when all states had to pick a camp between Washington and Moscow. Many countries would want to refrain from doing so, but reality would soon catch up: nonaligned states would not be able to operate two 5G telecommunications networks—one with U.S. standards and another one with Chinese technology—for instance. For consumers, this would be bad news.

To take the 5G example, such a scenario would not entail lower costs for customers as a result of increased competition. The parallel development of technology standards that do not work from one country to another or even within the same country would actually drive up costs. If a business signed up to a given standard for, say, phone lines, its clients would have to use compatible technology to get in touch. Prices might drop, as competition increases, but costs would likely double as people would need to use two technology standards (and in turn two phones) instead of one.

It is hard to predict which countries would side with the United States and which would go with China, but it is possible to sketch out broad trends. The economies of many Asian countries have become too dependent on China, which concentrates more than half of the region's economic output, to cut ties with Beijing. In fact, 15 Asian states—including close American allies such as Japan, Australia, and South Korea—have recently signed up to a massive regional free-trade agreement with China.[75] Beijing's rising clout over Asia would come at a heavy price for the United States; if Asian countries feel that they have no choice but to side with China, the U.S. military presence in the region could wane (except in a few spots such as Japan and South Korea). This would leave China with a freer hand to advance its territorial ambitions in the region.

In the rest of the developing world, including in Africa and Latin America, the calculation might prove easier for many countries: years of U.S. withdrawal, coupled with growing economic ties with China, mean that aligning with Beijing might feel like the most natural path. Vaccine diplomacy, as China's widespread use of coronavirus shots to advance its geopolitical interests is known, offers a glimpse of such a scenario; since early 2021 Beijing has been sending hundreds of millions of Chinese-made jabs to dozens of emerging countries, making China the world's largest exporter of Covid-19 vaccines. Many developing countries are genuinely grateful to have received China's jabs. Beijing can only rejoice, as vaccine diplomacy will only further boost its global influence and leverage.

Europe, for its part, would find itself stuck between the United States and China and try to tread carefully between the two giants. Resentment against U.S. extraterritorial sanctions and increased dependency on China for trade (the Chinese economy is the European Union's largest trade partner) could at times tilt the balance in favor of Beijing. The strain that the Trump administration put on transatlantic ties would undoubtedly be on the mind of European leaders, too; many Europeans now assume that America's reliability varies depending on who lives at the White House. However, if the United States and China entered into a direct conflict, Europe would almost certainly side with Washington.

For the European Union, this would be a nightmare scenario.[76] If Washington and Beijing went to war, for instance following a miscalculation in the South China Sea, the United States would have no qualms imposing stringent financial sanctions on Chinese firms and state-owned banks. These would likely include a secondary component, leaving European firms squeezed in the middle; EU companies would have to choose between the American and Chinese markets, which, combined, make up nearly half of the global economy. In such a situation, many European businesses might not be able to survive.

Even short of a military conflict, decoupling would make cooperation between the United States and China even more difficult. This would have a negative effect on global stewardship over crucial topics where no progress may realistically be made without both the United States and China at the negotiating table. Such issues include climate change, nuclear proliferation, or the fight against tomorrow's pandemics. Cutting ties with Beijing would also leave the United States with only little leverage over China in these discussions; seeing American firms flock away from the Chinese market or losing access to U.S. technology would not be a risk anymore for Beijing.

In such a decoupled global landscape, U.S. sanctions that target economic, financial, and technological exchanges would become moot. Beijing could simply ignore Washington's threats to impose such measures. As a result, China would find that it has much greater room for maneuver to advance its interests. The potential cost of intervening militarily in the South China Sea or in Taiwan would become lower, for instance. This is especially dangerous for Taipei, which is the main global hub for the production of semiconductors.

So far, China needs to keep ties to Taiwan in order to retain access to the semiconductors that Chinese firms cannot yet produce.[77] From this perspective, microchips act as a deterrent against Beijing's military ambitions over the Taiwan Strait—China regularly sends fighter jets to Taiwan's air defense zone, prompting U.S. military commanders to warn that China could try to take control of the island by 2027.[78] Decoupling makes this threat even more credible.

America's decoupling plans have convinced China that it needs to build its own microchip industry. Once this is done, Beijing will have only few reasons not to intervene in Taiwan.[79] The United States may well be caught off guard: decoupling also means that Washington would have less and less visibility over China's actions and intentions as time unfolds. If a China-Taiwan conflict were to erupt, Washington would have to go to war with Beijing or face the risk of losing its credibility as a defense ally. A military conflict between the United States and China would be a global catastrophe. Instead of protecting U.S. national security, Washington's plans to decouple from China may well make the world a less safe place.

CONCLUSION

A s I write these lines the year 2022 has just started, marking the third anniversary of this book project. Authors often worry that their topic will go out of fashion. We anxiously follow the news to make sure that the media have not moved on to a different issue. While I put the finishing touches to my manuscript, Russia's invasion of Ukraine means that my fears were, sadly, unfounded. Besides Russia, there are also no shortages of sanctions-related news about China, Venezuela, and Iran. Despite the front-page headlines, the real sanctions story has yet to be told: the days of unilateral U.S. sanctions are numbered.

❧

When it comes to sanctions, economic size matters. This is not good news for Washington. In the early 2030s the Chinese economy will displace that of the United States as the world's largest. China's economic dominance will turn the threat of U.S. sanctions against Beijing into mere rhetoric: sanctioning the world's biggest economy would damage the United States at least as much as it would hurt China. In recent years, Beijing has also set up the infrastructure to survive potential U.S. sanctions. The country boasts a growing tech sector, a digital currency, and

U.S.-proof financial channels. In the U.S.-China conflict, America will need other weapons besides sanctions.

The consequences of China's economic supremacy on the effectiveness of U.S. sanctions will extend beyond Chinese borders. When America ruled the world, U.S. sanctions were a powerful tool; nobody ever wants to get on the wrong side of the global policeman. However, times have changed. Now that China has emerged as an economic superpower, sanctioned countries have an alternative partner to turn to. Beijing's willingness to help others—chief among them Russia—evade the consequences of U.S. sanctions creates a vicious circle, further diminishing America's clout and undermining the impact of U.S. penalties.

Looking ahead, the United States will find itself fighting a losing battle if it sanctions alone. As Moscow kept the world guessing about its intentions in Ukraine in early 2022, the threat of more sanctions being imposed against Russia was everywhere in the news. However, it soon became clear that the threat of U.S. sanctions had lost its potency and would not deter Russian president Vladimir Putin. Since America first imposed sanctions on Russia in 2014, the Kremlin has taken steps to insulate the country's economy from the United States. It has established financial channels that circumvent the U.S. dollar. The greenback no longer features prominently in the composition of Moscow's foreign-exchange reserves. Trade ties with the United States have dwindled to next to nothing.

The Kremlin's efforts to reduce Russia's exposure to America have effectively disarmed the threat of U.S. sanctions, leaving Washington with little leverage in negotiations with Moscow. Only the threat of guaranteed, joint U.S.-EU penalties could have had a chance of making Putin think twice before invading Ukraine. However, long-standing sanctions disputes and transatlantic tensions made him bet that Europeans would be wary of going down the sanctions road with Washington. Putin was wrong: following the start of the war in Ukraine, Western collaboration on sanctions has been robust. This is good news for the effectiveness of sanctions: Russia cannot afford to go up against both America and Europe.

The 2022 vintage of Russia sanctions highlights that after decades of going it alone, America needs its allies to implement sanctions too. This shift away from unilateralism will call for a reinvention of U.S. diplomacy. Multilateral sanctions, supported by the United States, the European Union, Japan, and other like-minded powers, will probably become the only option. Drafting these measures is more difficult, but they have greater legitimacy and they are harder to circumvent. Such sanctions would also avoid the danger of antagonizing partners because (almost) everybody would be aboard.

Having allies aboard will come with an added benefit for the United States in helping to ensure that sanctions policy becomes less unpredictable. When the United States imposes sanctions on a whim, trust sinks to such low levels that targeted countries have no incentive to comply with U.S. demands. They simply do not believe that America will keep its side of the bargain and lift sanctions if they change their behavior. This lack of trust undermines the effectiveness of sanctions, which are not meant to be used as sticks to punish rogue countries, but as carrots to reward those foes that change their ways.

The Iranian example comes to mind. Since 2021 the glacial pace of negotiations to revive the nuclear deal has shown that the rulers of the Islamic republic are in no hurry to resurrect the agreement. They know that the country has little to gain from U.S. sanctions relief. Experience has taught them that even if all Western sanctions were to be lifted, multinationals would not return to the Iranian market. International firms remember that the United States unexpectedly reimposed sanctions on Iran in 2018 despite the country's compliance with the nuclear agreement. When sanctions policy is so unpredictable, countries have little incentive to comply with Washington's demands, undermining U.S. diplomacy.

In a best-case scenario, the development of multilateral penalties will foster the establishment of a global framework to improve the effectiveness of sanctions while limiting their side effects. The United States could push for the creation of an international institution overseeing sanctions. Similar organizations deal with issues that require global collaboration, such as maritime law, the war on drugs, and the resettlement of refugees. Why not set up one for sanctions? However, there is a catch. The emergence of a Western-led sanctions alliance would further deepen the divide between U.S.-aligned countries and China-leaning states.

———— ✸ ————

The time of peak U.S. sanctions has passed. American diplomats will soon be deprived of their favorite weapon to cajole, threaten, or punish U.S. enemies. In coming years, Washington will have to learn to collaborate with partners and to negotiate with adversaries without having the sanctions ace up its sleeve. The demise of U.S. unilateral sanctions reflects both their potency (targeted countries were always going to try to find ways to circumvent such powerful measures) and the erosion of America's position as the world's sole superpower. Washington's lack of interest in the side effects of its unilateral policies also united both friends and enemies against U.S. sanctions. For American policy makers, the loss of the previously all-powerful sanctions weapon will be a seismic change.

ACKNOWLEDGMENTS

My first thanks go to Columbia University Press, where I greatly benefited from the early enthusiasm and encouragement of Jason Bordoff, Monique Briones, and my editor Caelyn Cobb. I was lucky to work with a brilliant production team, including Susan Pensak (production editor), Ben Kolstad (project manager), and Christopher Curioli (copyeditor), who took this project across the finish line. Thank you also to the design team for the beautiful cover and to Zachary Friedman and Peter Barrett for their work marketing the book. Finally, many thanks to my anonymous peer reviewers, whose insights helped to improve the final manuscript.

I owe a debt of gratitude to those in sanctioned countries who accepted to chat with me about sanctions over the past years, even when I was on the sanctioning side. I am also grateful to the sanctions experts and practitioners who generously shared their insights, including Esfandyar Batmanghelidj, Ellie Geranmayeh, Nigel Gould-Davies, Jonathan Hackenbroich, Kadri Liik, Chris Miller, Erica Moret, Richard Nephew, Maria Shagina, and Juan Zarate. Some sources have chosen to remain anonymous given the sensitivity of the topic; you know who you are.

My book adventure took more than three years from start to finish. This book would never have taken shape without the patience and support of my colleagues, friends, and family, who were always here to remind me that this project was—hopefully—worthy of my (and their) time. This was a collective effort. Some helped choosing the cover. Others guaranteed last-minute additions made sense. One person even ensured my book files were always safe (and backed up—every day). I am especially grateful to the few trusted friends and family members who read various versions of the entire manuscript (often on short notice), giving me brutal feedback, useful food for thought, and much-needed advice along the way. Merci.

NOTES

PREFACE

1. Gary Hufbauer and Barbara Oegg, "New Frontier in the Sanctions Debate," Peterson Institute for International Economics, May 2002, https://www.piie.com/publications /policy-briefs/capital-market-access-new-frontier-sanctions-debate.
2. "Civil Penalties and Enforcement Information," U.S. Treasury, accessed May 7, 2020, https://www.treasury.gov/resource-center/sanctions/CivPen/Pages/civpen-index2 .aspx.
3. Philip Stephens, "Sanctions Are Donald Trump's New Way of War," *Financial Times*, October 17, 2019, https://www.ft.com/content/86eb2db4-f016-11e9-ad1e-4367d8281195.
4. Taehee Whang, "Playing to the Home Crowd? Symbolic Use of Economic Sanctions in the United States," *International Studies Quarterly* 55, no. 3 (2011): 787–801, https://doi .org/10.1111/j.1468-2478.2011.00668.x.

1. FROM EMBARGOES TO SANCTIONS

1. "Western Use of Targeted Sanctions Is Intensifying," Oxford Analytica, March 30, 2021, https://dailybrief.oxan.com/Analysis/GA260544/Western-use-of-targeted-sanctions -is-intensifying.
2. Abigail Eineman, "Sanctions by the Numbers, the Geographic Distribution of U.S. Sanctions," Center for a New American Security, June 15, 2020, https://www.cnas.org /publications/reports/sanctions-by-the-numbers-1.
3. Abigail Eineman, "Sanctions by the Numbers, Spotlight on Iran," Center for a New American Security, September 15, 2020, https://www.cnas.org/publications/reports/sanctions -by-the-numbers-spotlight-on-iran.

4. "Donald Trump Uses Sanctions More Keenly than Any of His Predecessors," *Economist*, November 24, 2019, https://www.economist.com/united-states/2019/11/24/donald -trump-uses-sanctions-more-keenly-than-any-of-his-predecessors.

5. "Issuance of Executive Order 'Blocking Property with Respect to the Situation in Burma,' Burma-Related Designations and Designations Updates," U.S. Treasury, February 11, 2021, https://home.treasury.gov/policy-issues/financial-sanctions/recent-actions/20210211.

6. Gary Hufbauer, "Sanctions-Happy USA," *Washington Post*, July 12, 1998.

7. Jesse Helms, "What Sanctions Epidemic? U.S. Business' Curious Crusade," *Foreign Affairs*, January/February 1999, https://www.foreignaffairs.com/articles/1999-01-01 /what-sanctions-epidemic-us-business-curious-crusade.

8. Hufbauer, "Sanctions-Happy USA."

9. "Presidential Documents—January 1 to June 30," Public Papers of the Presidents of the United States, no. 01 (1998): 998, https://www.govinfo.gov/content/pkg/PPP-1998-book1 /pdf/PPP-1998-book1.pdf.

10. Nick Wadhams and Saleha Mohsin, "Trump Set Record Sanctions Use That Biden Is Likely to Keep," Bloomberg, December 10, 2020, https://www.bloombergquint.com /business/trump-set-record-sanctions-use-that-biden-is-likely-to-maintain.

11. "Donald Trump Uses Sanctions," *Economist*.

12. Chad Bown, "Russia's War on Ukraine: A Sanctions Timeline," Peterson Institute for International Economics, accessed April 15, 2022, https://www.piie.com/blogs/realtime -economic-issues-watch/russias-war-ukraine-sanctions-timeline.

13. The Editors of Encyclopaedia Britannica, "Napoleonic Wars," *Encyclopaedia Britannica*, https://www.britannica.com/event/Napoleonic-Wars.

14. "U.S. Trade Embargo Has Cost Cuba $130 Billion, U.N. Says," Reuters, May 9, 2018, https://www.reuters.com/article/us-cuba-economy-un-idUSKBN1IA00T.

15. "Cuba Country Forecast," Economist Intelligence Unit, 2020.

16. "Cuba Country Forecast," Economist Intelligence Unit.

17. "Report of the Panel of Experts Established Pursuant to Resolution 1874," UN, March 5, 2019, https://www.undocs.org/S/2019/171.

18. Marianna Parraga, Rinat Sagdiev, and Parisa Hafezi, "Special Report: Phantom Oil Buyers in Russia, Advice from Iran Help Venezuela Skirt Sanctions," Reuters, November 10, 2020, https://www.reuters.com/article/venezuela-oil-exports-special-report/special-report -phantom-buyers-in-russia-advice-from-iran-help-venezuela-skirt-sanctions -idUSKBN27Q2CB.

19. "Report of the Panel of Experts Established Pursuant to Resolution 1874," UN.

20. Eleanor Albert, "What to Know About Sanctions on North Korea," Council on Foreign Relations, last updated July 16, 2019, https://www.cfr.org/backgrounder/what-know -about-sanctions-north-korea.

21. "Review of Maritime Transport 2019," UN, October 30, 2019, https://unctad.org/en /PublicationsLibrary/rmt2019_en.pdf.

22. "Report of the Panel of Experts Established Pursuant to Resolution 1874," UN.

23. Juan Zarate, *Treasury's War* (New York: Public Affairs, 2013), 219.

24. "Finding That Banco Delta Asia SARL Is a Financial Institution of Primary Money Laundering Concern; Notice Financial Crimes Enforcement Network; Amendment

to the Bank Secrecy Act Regulations—Imposition of Special Measure Against Banco Delta Asia SARL; Proposed Rule," U.S. Treasury, September 20, 2005, https://www.fincen.gov/sites/default/files/shared/finding_banco.pdf.

25. Dianne Rennack, "North Korea: Economic Sanctions," Congressional Research Service, October 17, 2006, https://fas.org/sgp/crs/row/RL31696.pdf.

26. Raphael Perl, "Drug Trafficking and North Korea: Issues for U.S. Policy," Congressional Research Service, January 25, 2007, https://fas.org/sgp/crs/row/RL32167.pdf.

27. Zarate, Treasury's War, 226.

28. John Roth, Douglas Greenburg, and Serena Wille, "Monograph on Terrorist Financing," National Commission on Terrorist Attacks Upon the United States, 2004, accessed June 17, 2020, https://govinfo.library.unt.edu/911/staff_statements/911_TerrFin_Monograph.pdf.

29. Marc Aubouin, "Use of Currencies in International Trade: Any Changes in the Picture?" World Trade Organization, May 2012, https://www.wto.org/english/res_e/reser_e/ersd201210_e.pdf.

30. Mark Gaylord, "The Banco Delta Asia Affair: The USA PATRIOT Act and Allegations of Money Laundering in Macau," Crime Law and Social Change 50 (2008): 293–305, https://doi.org/10.1007/s10611-008-9127-3.

31. "Financial Crimes Enforcement Network; Repeal of Special Measure Involving Banco Delta Asia (BDA)," Federal Register, October 8, 2020, https://www.federalregister.gov/documents/2020/08/10/2020-17143/financial-crimes-enforcement-network-repeal-of-special-measure-involving-banco-delta-asia-bda.

32. Zarate, Treasury's War, prologue, x.

2. HITTING WHERE IT HURTS

1. Thomas Friedman, "Biden Made Sure 'Trump Is Not Going to Be President for Four More Years,'" New York Times, December 2, 2020, https://www.nytimes.com/2020/12/02/opinion/biden-interview-mcconnell-china-iran.html.

2. "Implementation of the NPT Safeguards Agreement in the Islamic Republic of Iran," IAEA Report to the Board of Governors, June 6, 2003, https://www.iaea.org/sites/default/files/gov2003-40.pdf.

3. Kenneth Katzman, "Iran Sanctions," Congressional Research Service, accessed April 25, 2020, https://fas.org/sgp/crs/mideast/RS20871.pdf.

4. "Fact Sheet: Designation of Iranian Entities and Individuals for Proliferation Activities and Support for Terrorism," U.S. Treasury, October 25, 2007, https://www.treasury.gov/press-center/press-releases/Pages/hp644.aspx.

5. "Bombings in Beirut," New York Times, October 25, 1983, https://www.nytimes.com/1983/10/25/nyregion/tuesday-october-25-1983-bombings-in-beirut.html.

6. Carla Humud, "Lebanese Hezbollah," Congressional Research Service, accessed March 18, 2021, https://crsreports.congress.gov/product/pdf/IF/IF10703.

7. Matthew Levitt, "Hezbollah: A Case Study of Global Reach, Remarks to a Conference on Post-Modern Terrorism: Trends, Scenarios, and Future Threats," American Civil

Liberties Union, September 8, 2003, https://www.aclu.org/sites/default/files/field
_document/ACLURM001616.pdf.

8. "Treasury Cuts Iran's Bank Saderat Off from U.S. Financial System," U.S. Treasury,
    September 8, 2006, https://www.treasury.gov/press-center/press-releases/Pages/hp87
    .aspx.

9. "Fact Sheet: Designation of Iranian Entities," IU.S. Treasury.

10. Juan Zarate, *Treasury's War* (New York: Public Affairs, 2013), 49–60.

11. Zarate, *Treasury's War*, 272.

12. James Risen and Mark Mazzetti, "U.S. Agencies See No Move by Iran to Build a Bomb,"
    New York Times, February 24, 2012, https://www.nytimes.com/2012/02/25/world/middleeast
    /us-agencies-see-no-move-by-iran-to-build-a-bomb.html.

13. Mark Dubowitz and Annie Fixler, "'SWIFT' Warfare: Power, Blowback, and Harden-
    ing American Defenses," Foundation for Defense of Democracies, July 2015, https://
    s3.us-east-2.amazonaws.com/defenddemocracy/uploads/publications/Cyber_Enabled
    _Swift.pdf.

14. Katzman, "Iran Sanctions."

15. Djavad Salehi-Isfahani, "Impact of Sanctions on Household Welfare and Employment,"
    Johns Hopkins University, accessed December 10, 2020, https://static1.squarespace
    .com/static/5f0f5b1018e89f351b8b3ef8/t/5fd0e13ca4b4ef2db6b17e06/1607524670688
    /IranUnderSanctions_Salehi-Isfahani.pdf.

16. Zarate, *Treasury's War*, prologue, ix.

17. Damien McElroy, "Hassan Rouhani Vows to Lift Sanctions on Iran," *Telegraph*, August 3,
    2013, https://www.telegraph.co.uk/news/worldnews/middleeast/iran/10220564/Hassan
    -Rouhani-vows-to-lift-sanctions-on-Iran.html.

18. Mohammad Davari, "Iran's Rowhani Takes Office with Vow to Rescue Economy,"
    Agence France Presse, August 3, 2013, https://sg.news.yahoo.com/rowhani-set-become
    -irans-7th-president-073501208.html.

19. Karim Sadjapour, "How to Win the Cold War with Iran," *Atlantic*, March 25, 2021,
    https://www.theatlantic.com/ideas/archive/2021/03/how-win-cold-war-iran/618388.

20. Karim Sadjapour, "Iranian Supreme Leader Ali Khamenei Is One Despot Trump Might
    Not Win Over," *Time*, October 3, 2019, https://time.com/5691642/iran-supreme-leader
    -ali-khamenei-trump.

21. Richard Nephew, *The Art of Sanctions, a View from the Field* (New York: Columbia
    University Press, 2018), 122.

22. Kadri Liik, "Into the Jungle," *Berlin Policy Journal* (January/February 2019), https://
    berlinpolicyjournal.com/into-the-jungle.

23. Author's calculations using Economist Intelligence Unit data, March 2021.

24. "From Where Do We Import Energy and How Dependent Are We?," Eurostat, accessed
    February 15, 2021, https://ec.europa.eu/eurostat/cache/infographs/energy/bloc-2c
    .html.

25. James Marson, "Russian Natural-Gas Project Gets Funding from China," *Wall Street
    Journal*, April 29, 2016, https://www.wsj.com/articles/russian-natural-gas-project-gets
    -funding-from-china-1461934776.

26. "Countering America's Adversaries Through Sanctions Act," U.S. Treasury, accessed April 26, 2020, https://www.treasury.gov/resource-center/sanctions/Programs/Pages /caatsa.aspx.

27. John Dizard, "Russia Sanctions—Easy to Announce, Hard to Implement," *Financial Times*, March 25, 2021, https://www.ft.com/content/0d16212a-2d52-49f1-af5d-80e43d1be5b7.

28. Dmitry Kulikov and Natalia Porokhova, "US Residents Hold 8 Percent of Russian Sovereign Debt," Analytical Credit Rating Agency, August 17, 2018, https://www.acra -ratings.com/research/868.

29. "Crackdown on Dissent: Brutality, Torture, and Political Persecution in Venezuela," Human Rights Watch, November 2017, https://www.hrw.org/sites/default/files/report _pdf/venezuela1117web_0.pdf.

30. Brian Ellsworth, "Trump Says U.S. Military Intervention in Venezuela 'an Option'; Russia Objects," Reuters, February 3, 2019, https://www.reuters.com/article/us-venezuela -politics-idUSKCN1PS0DK.

31. Igor Hernández and Francisco Monaldi, "Weathering Collapse: An Assessment of the Financial and Operational Situation of the Venezuelan Oil Industry," Center for International Development at Harvard University, November 2016, https://growthlab.cid .harvard.edu/files/growthlab/files/venezuela_oil_cidwp_327.pdf.

32. Collin Eaton and Luc Cohen, "Explainer: U.S. Sanctions and Venezuela's Trade and Oil Industry Partners," Reuters, August 14, 2019, https://www.reuters.com/article/us -venezuela-politics-crude-sanctions-ex/explainer-u-s-sanctions-and-venezuelas -trade-and-oil-industry-partners-idUSKCN1V420P.

33. "US Sanctions Rosneft Subsidiary Over Venezuela," Economist Intelligence Unit, February 24, 2020, https://country.eiu.com/article.aspx?articleid=79103591&Country =Venezuela&topic=Economy.

34. Clifford Krauss, "White House Raises Pressure on Venezuela with New Financial Sanctions," *New York Times*, August 25, 2017, https://www.nytimes.com/2017/08/25/world /americas/venezuela-sanctions-maduro-trump.html.

35. Richard Nephew, "Evaluating the Trump Administration's Approach to Sanctions, Case: Venezuela," Columbia/SIPA Center on Global Energy Policy, June 17, 2020, https:// energypolicy.columbia.edu/research/commentary/evaluating-trump-administration -s-approach-sanctions-venezuela.

36. Luc Cohen and Carina Pons, "New Venezuela Sanctions Protect Citgo, Encourage Debt Talks: Opposition," Reuters, August 6, 2019, https://www.reuters.com/article/us -venezuela-politics-usa-citgo/new-venezuela-sanctions-protect-citgo-encourage-debt -talks-opposition-idUSKCN1UW1YK.

37. Kenneth Vogel, "Lewandowski's Firm Quietly Inked Deal with Venezuela-Owned Company," Politico, March 5, 2017, https://www.politico.com/story/2017/05/03/corey -lewandowski-citgo-deal-237960.

38. Dany Bahar, Sebastian Bustos, Jose R. Morales, and Miguel A. Santos, "Impact of the 2017 Sanctions on Venezuela, Revisiting the Evidence," Brookings, May 2019, https:// www.brookings.edu/wp-content/uploads/2019/05/impact-of-the-2017-sanctions-on -venezuela_final.pdf.

39. Marianna Parraga, "Exclusive: As Citgo Profit Rises, Pressure to Restore Dividend Grows—Sources," Reuters, December 4, 2019, https://www.reuters.com/article/us-citgo -dividends-exclusive/exclusive-as-citgo-profit-rises-pressure-to-restore-dividend -grows-sources-idUSKBN1Y82SQ.

40. "A Closer Look at US Oil Sanctions," Economist Intelligence Unit, February 21, 2019, http://country.eiu.com/article.aspx?articleid=1017682885&Country=Venezuela&topic =Economy_1.

41. Marie Delcas, "Venezuela: quelles seront les conséquences des sanctions américaines contre Maduro," Le Monde, January 29, 2019, https://www.lemonde.fr/international /article/2019/01/29/venezuela-les-etats-unis-durcissent-les-sanctions-contre-maduro _5416029_3210.html.

42. Brian Scheid, "US Set to Sanction Rosneft Oil, Fuel Trade with PDVSA: Senior Trump Administration Official," S&P Global Platts, August 15, 2019, https://www.spglobal .com/platts/es/market-insights/latest-news/oil/081519-us-set-to-sanction-rosneft-oil -fuel-trade-with-pdvsa-senior-trump-administration-official.

43. Clifford Krauss, " 'It's the Only Way to Get Paid': A Struggle for Citgo, Venezuela's U.S. Oil Company," New York Times, October 17, 2019, https://www.nytimes.com/2019/10/17 /business/energy-environment/citgo-venezuela-creditors.html.

44. "US Treasury Extends Block on Takeover of Citgo," Argus Media, accessed December 1, 2020, https://www.argusmedia.com/en/news/2123539-us-treasury-extends-block-on -takeover-of-citgo.

45. "U.S. Judge Rules PDVSA's 2020 Bonds Are Valid, Citgo Still Protected," Reuters, October 16, 2020, https://uk.reuters.com/article/us-venezuela-debt/u-s-judge-rules-pdvsas -2020-bonds-are-valid-citgo-still-protected-idUKKBN2712DG.

46. "Treasury Targets Sanctions Evasion Network Supporting Corrupt Venezuelan Actors," U.S. Treasury, June 18, 2020, https://home.treasury.gov/news/press-releases /sm1038.

47. "Major Drop in OPEC+ Supplies," Economist Intelligence Unit, accessed December 1, 2020, http://industry.eiu.com/handlers/filehandler.ashx?mode=pdf&issue_id =1059705889.

48. "Venezuela Country Report," Economist Intelligence Unit, 2020.

3. HIT AND MISS

1. Richard Nephew, "Libya: Sanctions Removal Done Right? A Review of the Libyan Sanctions Experience," Columbia/SIPA Center on Global Energy Policy, March 2018, https://energypolicy.columbia.edu/sites/default/files/pictures/Libya%20Sanctions%20 Removal_CGEP_Report_031918.pdf.

2. Lisa Anderson, "Rogue Libya's Long Road," Middle East Report, no. 241 (2006): 42–47, https://doi.org/10.2307/25164764.

3. Joseph Feliciano, "The Economic Instrument of Power and Globalization," U.S. Army War College, March 24, 2011, https://apps.dtic.mil/dtic/tr/fulltext/u2/a560021.pdf.

4. "Economic Sanctions: Agencies Assess Impacts on Targets, and Studies Suggest Several Factors Contribute to Sanctions' Effectiveness," U.S. Government Accountability Office, October 2019, https://www.gao.gov/assets/710/701891.pdf.

5. Richard Nephew, "Collateral Damage: The Impact on Pakistan from U.S. Sanctions Against Iran," Columbia/SIPA Center on Global Energy Policy, August 2017, https://energypolicy.columbia.edu/sites/default/files/CGEPSanctionsandtheRisk%20of CollateralDamageTheImpactofUSIranSanctionsonPakistan0717.pdf.

6. Kimberly Ann Elliott, "Evidence on the Costs and Benefits of Economic Sanctions," Subcommittee on Trade, Committee on Ways and Means, U.S. House of Representatives, October 23, 1997, https://www.piie.com/commentary/testimonies/evidence-costs-and -benefits-economic-sanctions.

7. Elliott, "Evidence on the Costs and Benefits of Economic Sanctions."

8. Marteen Smets, "Can Economic Sanctions Be Effective?" WTO Staff Working Paper, No. 2018/03 (Geneva: World Trade Organization, 2018), https://dx.doi.org/10.30875 /0b967ac6-en.

9. Esfandyar Batmanghelidj, "Resistance Is Simple, Resilience Is Complex: Sanctions and the Composition of Iranian Trade," Johns Hopkins University, accessed December 10, 2020, https://static1.squarespace.com/static/5f0f5b1018e89f351b8b3ef8/t/5fd0e4a906d 21916ed79ba75/1607525546925/IranUnderSanctions_Batmanghelidj.pdf.

10. Richard Nephew, "Evaluating the Trump's Administration's Approach to Sanctions, Case: Iran," Columbia/SIPA Center on Global Energy Policy, November 8, 2019, https://www .energypolicy.columbia.edu/research/commentary/evaluating-trump-administration -s-approach-sanctions-iran.

11. Gérard Araud, *Passeport Diplomatique, Quarante Ans au Quai d'Orsay* (Paris: Grasset, 2019), 165.

12. Peter Harrell, "Cuba: U.S. Sanctions Policy After the Embargo," Columbia/SIPA Center on Global Energy Policy, November 2016, https://energypolicy.columbia.edu/sites /default/files/Cuba%3A%20US%20Sanctions%20Policy%20After%20the%20Embargo .pdf.

13. "Economic Sanctions: Treasury and State Have Received Increased Resources for Sanctions Implementation but Face Hiring Challenges," U.S. Government Accountability Office, accessed May 10, 2020, https://www.gao.gov/assets/710/701891.pdf.

14. Hilary Mossberg, "Beyond Carrots, Better Sticks," The Sentry, October 2019, https:// cdn.thesentry.org/wp-content/uploads/2019/10/SanctionsEffectiveness_TheSentry _Oct2019-web.pdf.

15. James Gibney, "Trump's Sanctions Are Losing Their Bite," Bloomberg, April 2, 2020, https://www.bloomberg.com/opinion/articles/2020-04-02/trump-s-overuse-of -sanctions-is-weakening-their-effectiveness.

16. Christian Gianella, Magali Cesana, Audrey Cezard-Assouad, et al., "Economic Sanctions: What Have We Learned from the Recent and Not so Recent Past?," *Trésor-Economics*, no. 150 (2015), https://www.tresor.economie.gouv.fr/Articles/2015/07/29/tresor-economics -no-150-economic-sanctions-what-have-we-learned-from-the-recent-and-not-so -recent-past.

17.   Gary Hufbauer, Jeffrey Schott, Kimberly Ann Elliott, and Barbara Oegg, *Economic Sanctions Reconsidered*, 3rd ed. (Washington, DC: Peterson Institute for International Economics, 2009).

18.   Kim Nossal, "Liberal-Democratic Regimes, International Sanctions, and Global Governance," in *Globalization and Global Governance*, ed. Raimo Väyrynen (Lanham, MD: Rowman & Littlefield, 1999), 127–49.

19.   Richard Nephew and Colin Rowat, "ExxonMobil Just Challenged Trump to Get Serious with Russia Policy," *Fortune*, April 30, 2017, https://fortune.com/2017/04/30/sanctions-waivers-donald-trump-russia-exxonmobil.

20.   "Iran: Threats to Free, Fair Elections," Human Rights Watch, May 24, 2013, https://www.hrw.org/news/2013/05/24/iran-threats-free-fair-elections.

21.   Dursun Peksen, "Better or Worse? The Effect of Economic Sanctions on Human Rights," *Journal of Peace Research* 46, no. 1 (January 2009): 59–77, https://doi.org/10.1177/0022343308098404.

22.   Nigel Gould-Davies, "Russia, the West and Sanctions," *Survival: Global Politics and Strategy* 62 (February–March 2020): 7–28, https://doi.org/10.1080/00396338.2020.1715060.

23.   Elliott, "Evidence on the Costs and Benefits of Economic Sanctions."

24.   Peter Harrell, "Is the U.S. Using Sanctions Too Aggressively? The Steps Washington Can Take to Guard Against Overuse," *Foreign Affairs*, September 11, 2018, https://www.foreignaffairs.com/articles/2018-09-11/us-using-sanctions-too-aggressively.

25.   Edith Lederer, "Russia, China Block UN from Saying North Korea Violated Sanctions," Associated Press, June 19, 2019, https://apnews.com/article/cb6be1337d2a48ecbde14dac590be083.

26.   Smets, "Can Economic Sanctions Be Effective?."

27.   "Sixty Years of US Aid to Pakistan," *Guardian*, July 11, 2011, https://www.theguardian.com/global-development/poverty-matters/2011/jul/11/us-aid-to-pakistan.

28.   Nazia Malik, "Economic Sanctions Imposed on Pakistan and Their Impact (1979–2001)," Lee Kuan Yew School of Public Policy, National University Singapore, accessed May 20, 2020, http://www.ipedr.com/vol39/028-ICITE2012-K00006.pdf.

29.   Steve Coll, *Ghost Wars: The Secret History of the CIA, Afghanistan and Bin Laden, from the Soviet Invasion to September 10, 2001* (London: Penguin, 2004), 164–69.

30.   Coll, *Ghost Wars*, 296–300.

31.   Coll, *Ghost Wars*, 406.

32.   Coll, *Ghost Wars*, 313.

33.   Francisco Rodríguez, "Why More Sanctions Won't Help Venezuela," *Foreign Policy*, January 12, 2018, https://foreignpolicy.com/2018/01/12/why-more-sanctions-wont-help-venezuela.

34.   Michael Birnbaum, "Putin's Approval Ratings Hit 89 Percent, the Highest They've Ever Been," *Washington Post*, June 24, 2015, https://www.washingtonpost.com/news/worldviews/wp/2015/06/24/putins-approval-ratings-hit-89-percent-the-highest-theyve-ever-been.

35.   Robert Middlekauff, *Benjamin Franklin and His Enemies* (Oakland: University of California Press, 1998), 57.

36.   Richard Haass, "Economic Sanctions: Too Much of a Bad Thing," Brookings, June 1, 1998, https://www.brookings.edu/research/economic-sanctions-too-much-of-a-bad-thing.

37. Kathryn Zeimetz, "USSR Agricultural Trade, August 1991," *Statistical Bulletin* 808 (August 1991): 15, https://ageconsearch.umn.edu/record/154704/files/sb808.pdf.

38. Carl Zulauf, Jonathan Coppess, Nick Paulson, and Gary Schnitkey, "U.S. Corn, Soybean, Wheat Exports and USSR Grain Embargo: Contemporary Implications," *farmdoc daily* 8, no. 129 (July 2018), https://farmdocdaily.illinois.edu/2018/07/us-corn-soybean-wheat-exports-and-ussr-grain-embargo-contemporary-implications.html.

39. Frank Morris, "Farmers Swept Up in Trade Wars Remember '80s Grain Embargo," National Public Radio, August 16, 2018, https://www.npr.org/2018/08/16/639149657/farmers-caught-up-in-u-s-trade-war-s-remember-80-s-grain-embargo.

40. Morris, "Farmers Swept Up Iin Trade Wars."

41. Gary Hufbauer, Kimberly Ann Elliott, Tess Cyrus, and Elizabeth Ann Winston, "US Economic Sanctions: Their Impact on Trade, Jobs, and Wages," Peterson Institute for International Economics Working Paper (Washington, DC: Peterson Institute for International Economics, April 1997), https://www.piie.com/publications/working-papers/us-economic-sanctions-their-impact-trade-jobs-and-wages.

42. Author's calculations using Economist Intelligence Unit data, March 2021.

43. Dina Khrennikova and Anna Andrianova, "Trump's Oil Sanctions Leave Russian Exporters $1 Billion Richer," Bloomberg, August 16, 2019, https://www.bloomberg.com/news/articles/2019-08-16/trump-s-oil-sanctions-leave-russian-exporters-1-billion-richer.

44. "Treasury Targets Additional Russian Oil Brokerage Firm for Continued Support of Maduro Regime," U.S. Treasury, March 12, 2020, https://home.treasury.gov/news/press-releases/sm937.

45. Clare Ribando Seelke, "Venezuela: Overview of U.S. Sanctions," Congressional Research Service, accessed April 23, 2020, https://fas.org/sgp/crs/row/IF10715.pdf.

46. "Factbox: Oil, Loans, Military—Russia's Exposure to Venezuela," Reuters, January 24, 2019, https://www.reuters.com/article/us-venezuela-politics-russia-factbox/factbox-oil-loans-military-russias-exposure-to-venezuela-idUSKCN1PI1T4.

47. Иван Ткачёв, "Танкеры с пропиской в России подключились к перевозке венесуэльской нефти," *РБК*, December 14, 2020, https://www.rbc.ru/economics/14/12/2020/5fce9d879a79471c1e8cb6b4.

48. Gabrielle Tétrault-Farber and Olesya Astakhova, "Rosneft Sells Venezuelan Assets to Russia After U.S. Sanctions Ramp Up," Reuters, March 28, 2020, https://www.reuters.com/article/us-russia-rosneft-venezuela/rosneft-sells-venezuelan-assets-to-russia-after-u-s-sanctions-ramp-up-idUSKBN21F0W2.

49. Aaron Blake, "Trump Echoes Putin on Venezuela—and Contradicts His Own Secretary of State," *Washington Post*, May 3, 2019, https://www.washingtonpost.com/politics/2019/05/03/trump-echoes-putin-venezuela-contradicts-his-own-secretary-state.

4. COLLATERAL DAMAGE

1. "Economic Affairs—Second Report," House of Lords, April 24, 2007, https://publications.parliament.uk/pa/ld200607/ldselect/ldeconaf/96/9606.htm#a8.

2. Wilfrid Kreisel, "Health Situation in Iraq," World Health Organization, February 26, 2001, https://apps.who.int/disasters/repo/6386.doc.

3. Sarah Zaidi and Mary Smith Fawzi, "Health of Baghdad's Children," *Lancet* 346, no. 8988 (1995): 1485, https://doi.org/10.1016/s0140-6736(95)92499-x.

4. Tim Dyson and Valeria Cetorelli, "Changing Views on Child Mortality and Economic Sanctions in Iraq: a History of Lies, Damned Lies and Statistics," *BMJ Global Health* (July 2017), https://dx.doi.org/10.1136/bmjgh-2017-000311.

5. David Rieff, "Were Sanctions Right?," *New York Times*, July 27, 2003, https://www.nytimes.com/2003/07/27/magazine/were-sanctions-right.html.

6. Joy Gordon, *Invisible War: The United States and the Iraq Sanctions* (Cambridge, MA: Harvard University Press, 2010), 200.

7. "Iran Country Report," Economist Intelligence Unit, 2021.

8. "Russia Country Report," Economist Intelligence Unit, 2021.

9. "Venezuela Country Report," Economist Intelligence Unit, 2020.

10. Richard Partington, "14m Bolivars for a Chicken: Venezuela Hyperinflation Explained," *Guardian*, August 20, 2018, https://www.theguardian.com/world/2018/aug/20/venezuela-bolivars-hyperinflation-banknotes.

11. "Why It's Hard for Congo's Coltan Miners to Abide by the Law," *Economist*, January 23, 2021, https://www.economist.com/middle-east-and-africa/2021/01/23/why-its-hard-for-congos-coltan-miners-to-abide-by-the-law.

12. "Democratic Republic of Congo Country Report," Economist Intelligence Unit, 2021.

13. Dominic Parker, Jeremy Foltz, and David Elsea, "Unintended Consequences of Sanctions for Human Rights. Conflict Minerals and Infant Mortality," *Journal of Law and Economics* 59, no. 4 (November 2016): 731–74, https://doi.org/10.1086/691793.

14. Lauren Wolfe, "How Dodd-Frank Is Failing Congo," *Foreign Policy*, February 2, 2015, https://foreignpolicy.com/2015/02/02/how-dodd-frank-is-failing-congo-mining-conflict-minerals.

15. Nik Stoop, Marijke Verpoorten, and Peter van der Windt, "More Legislation, More Violence? The Impact of Dodd-Frank in the DRC," *PloS ONE* 13, no. 8 (August 2018), https://doi.org/10.1371/journal.pone.0201783.

16. Jeffrey Bloem, "The Unintended Consequences of Regulating 'Conflict Minerals' in Africa's Great Lakes Region," World Bank Blogs, November 25, 2019, https://blogs.worldbank.org/impactevaluations/unintended-consequences-regulating-conflict-minerals-africas-great-lakes-region.

17. Mvemba Phezo Dizolele, "Dodd-Frank 1502 and the Congo Crisis," Center for Strategic and International Studies, August 22, 2017, https://www.csis.org/analysis/dodd-frank-1502-and-congo-crisis.

18. Nik Stoop, Marijke Verpoorten, and Peter van der Windt, "Trump Threatened to Suspend the 'Conflict Minerals' Provision of Dodd-Frank. That Might Actually Be Good for Congo," *Washington Post*, September 27, 2018, https://www.washingtonpost.com/news/monkey-cage/wp/2018/09/27/trump-canceled-the-conflict-minerals-provision-of-dodd-frank-thats-probably-good-for-the-congo.

19. Richard Nephew, "The Humanitarian Impact of Sanctions," Columbia/SIPA Center on Global Energy Policy, April 29, 2015, https://energypolicy.columbia.edu/sanctions-blog-columbia-s-center-global-energy-policy-post-six.

20. "COVID-19 Dashboard," Center for Systems Science and Engineering (CSSE) at Johns Hopkins University (JHU), accessed April 18, 2022, https://coronavirus.jhu.edu/map.html.

21. "The Pandemic's True Death Toll," Economist, accessed January 23, 2022, https://www.economist.com/graphic-detail/coronavirus-excess-deaths-estimates.

22. Erica Moret, "Humanitarian Impacts of Economic Sanctions on Iran and Syria," European Security 24, no. 1 (2015), https://doi.org/10.1080/09662839.2014.893427.

23. Siamak Namazi, "Sanctions and Medical Supply Shortages in Iran," Woodrow Wilson Center, February 2013, https://www.wilsoncenter.org/sites/default/files/media/documents/publication/sanctions_medical_supply_shortages_in_iran.pdf.

24. "Iran: Sanctions Threatening Health," Human Rights Watch, October 29, 2019, https://www.hrw.org/news/2019/10/29/iran-sanctions-threatening-health.

25. Declan Butler, "How US Sanctions Are Crippling Science in Iran," Nature 574 (October 2019): 13–14, https://media.nature.com/original/magazine-assets/d41586-019-02795-y/d41586-019-02795-y.pdf.

26. Esfandyar Batmanghelidj and Abbas Kebriaeezadeh, "As Coronavirus Spreads, Iranian Doctors Fear the Worst," Foreign Policy, March 3, 2020, https://foreignpolicy.com/2020/03/03/iran-coronavirus-spreads-sanctions-covid19-iranian-doctors-fear-worst.

27. Jon Gambrell, "Iran Leader Refuses US Help, Citing Virus Conspiracy Theory," Associated Press, March 22, 2020, https://apnews.com/2cffa4c49cbf085562a71cd36a4e4378.

28. Maggie Michael, "Doctors and Nurses Suffered as Iran Ignored Virus Concerns," Associated Press, May 12, 2020, https://apnews.com/6c7715f300797502329f6117e1141503.

29. Editorial Board of the New York Times, "This Coronavirus Crisis Is the Time to Ease Sanctions on Iran," New York Times, March 25, 2020, https://www.nytimes.com/2020/03/25/opinion/iran-sanctions-covid.html.

30. Editorial Board of the New York Times, "This Coronavirus Crisis Is the Time to Ease Sanctions on Iran."

31. "House & Senate Members Call on President Trump to End Sanctions Against Iran During Covid-19," Congressman Jared Huffman, accessed May 13, 2020, https://huffman.house.gov/media-center/press-releases/house-and-senate-members-call-on-president-trump-to-end-sanctions-against-iran-during-covid-19.

32. "Bachelet Calls for Easing of Sanctions to Enable Medical Systems to Fight COVID-19 and Limit Global Contagion," United Nations, accessed May 12, 2020, https://ohchr.org/EN/NewsEvents/Pages/DisplayNews.aspx?NewsID=25744&LangID=E.

33. Gambrell, "Iran Leader Refuses US Help."

34. "Coronavirus: Iran and the US Trade Blame Over Sanctions," BBC News, April 17, 2020, https://www.bbc.com/news/world-middle-east-52218656.

35. Peter Harrell, "Cuba: U.S. Sanctions Policy After the Embargo," Columbia/SIPA Center on Global Energy Policy, November 2016, https://energypolicy.columbia.edu/sites/default/files/Cuba%3A%20US%20Sanctions%20Policy%20After%20the%20Embargo.pdf.

36. Rachel Oswald, "Calls Grow for Trump to Relax Humanitarian Sanctions on Iran," CQ Roll Call, April 9, 2020, https://www.rollcall.com/2020/04/09/calls-grow-for-trump -to-relax-humanitarian-sanctions-on-iran.

37. "Iran's Sanctions Relief Scam," U.S. Department of State, accessed January 6, 2021, https://www.state.gov/irans-sanctions-relief-scam.

38. Richard Nephew, "Reconsidering US Sanctions Policy Amid the Coronavirus Crisis and the Oil Market Crash," Columbia/SIPA Center on Global Energy Policy, March 2020, https://energypolicy.columbia.edu/sites/default/files/file-uploads/Sanctions_CGEP _Commentary_033120-2.pdf.

39. Esfandyar Batmanghelidj and Sahil Shah, "As Iran Faces Virus, Trump Admin Fails to Use Swiss Channel to Ease Medical Exports," European Leadership Network, May 6, 2020, https://www.europeanleadershipnetwork.org/commentary/as-iran-faces-virus -trump-admin-fails-to-use-touted-swiss-channel-to-ease-medical-exports.

40. Erin Cunningham, "As Coronavirus Cases Explode in Iran, U.S. Sanctions Hinder Its Access to Drugs and Medical Equipment," Washington Post, March 29, 2020, https:// www.washingtonpost.com/world/middle_east/as-coronavirus-cases-explode-in-iran -us-sanctions-hinder-its-access-to-drugs-and-medical-equipment/2020/03/28/0656a196 -6aba-11ea-b199-3a9799c54512_story.html.

41. Oswald, "Calls Grow for Trump to Relax Humanitarian Sanctions on Iran."

42. Scott Flicker, Lauren Kelly Greenbacker, Talya Hutchison, and Holly Flynn, "Human- itarian Aid to Iran Under Existing Sanctions–An Important Reminder in a Time of Pandemic," Paul Hastings, April 21, 2020, https://www.paulhastings.com/publications -items/details/?id=84f02f6f-2334-6428-811c-ff00004cbded.

43. Cunningham, "As Coronavirus Cases Explode in Iran."

44. Cunningham, "As Coronavirus Cases Explode in Iran."

45. "Iran-Related Designations and Updates; Counter Terrorism Designations and Updates; Administrative Removals from Executive Order 13599 List," U.S. Treasury, accessed May 10, 2020, https://www.treasury.gov/resource-center/sanctions/OFAC -Enforcement/Pages/20181016.aspx.

46. Samuel Rubenfeld, "U.S. Sanctions Listing Could Hurt Humanitarian Trade with Iran," Wall Street Journal, October 19, 2018, https://www.wsj.com/articles/u-s-sanctions-listing -could-hurt-humanitarian-trade-with-iran-1539941400.

47. Erin Cunningham, "Fresh Sanctions on Iran Are Already Choking Off Medicine Imports, Economists Say," Washington Post, November 17, 2018, https://www.washingtonpost .com/world/middle_east/fresh-sanctions-on-iran-are-already-choking-off-medicine -imports-economists-say/2018/11/17/c94ce574-e763-11e8-8449-1ff263609a31_story.html.

48. Maziar Motamedi, "Parsian Bank CEO: US Treasury Made 'Mistake' in Iran Sanctions Designation," Bourse and Bazaar, October 21, 2018, https://www.bourseandbazaar .com/articles/2018/10/21/parsian-bank-ceo-us-treasury-made-mistake-in-iran-sanctions -designation.

49. Esfandyar Batmanghelidj and Ellie Geranmayeh, "America's Latest Wave of Iran Sanc- tions," European Council on Foreign Relations, November 6, 2018, https://www.ecfr .eu/article/commentary_americas_latest_wave_of_iran_sanctions.

50. Gérard Araud, *Passeport Diplomatique, Quarante Ans au Quai d'Orsay* (Paris: Grasset, 2019), 158.

51. "BNP Paribas Agrees to Plead Guilty and to Pay \$8.9 Billion for Illegally Processing Financial Transactions for Countries Subject to U.S. Economic Sanctions," U.S. Department of Justice, accessed April 20, 2020, https://www.justice.gov/opa/pr/bnp-paribas -agrees-plead-guilty-and-pay-89-billion-illegally-processing-financial.

5. SANCTIONS OVERREACH

1. "Regulatory Intelligence Desktop," Thomson Reuters, accessed June 13, 2020, https:// legal.thomsonreuters.com/content/dam/ewp-m/documents/legal/en/pdf/brochures /tr_regulatory_intelligence_desktop_digital_us.pdf.

2. "The Past Decade Has Brought a Compliance Boom in Banking," *Economist*, May 4, 2019, https://www.economist.com/finance-and-economics/2019/05/02/the-past-decade -has-brought-a-compliance-boom-in-banking.

3. "The Past Decade," *Economist*.

4. "Banks: A New Approach to Risk? Governance, Culture and Risk in a Revamped Banking Industry," Schroders, January 2015, https://www.schroders.com/en/sysglobalassets /digital/insights/pdfs/banks-a-new-approach-to-risk.pdf.

5. "The Past Decade," *Economist*.

6. "Providing Frictionless AML for a Global Bank's 3,000 Analysts," Arachnys, September 15, 2019, https://www.arachnys.com/providing-frictionless-aml-for-a-global-banks -3000-analysts.

7. Elizabeth Rosenberg and Neil Bhatiya, "Busting North Korea's Sanctions Evasion," Center for a New American Security, March 4, 2020, https://www.cnas.org/publications /commentary/busting-north-koreas-sanctions-evasion.

8. Bryan Early and Keith Preble, "Trends in U.S. Sanctions Enforcement During the Trump Administration," New York University School of Law Program on Corporate Compliance and Enforcement, accessed August 7, 2020, https://wp.nyu.edu/compliance _enforcement/2019/01/30/trends-in-u-s-sanctions-enforcement-during-the-trump -administration.

9. Early and Preble, "Trends in U.S. Sanctions Enforcement."

10. Duane Windsor, "Alien Tort Claims Act," *Encyclopaedia Britannica*, accessed April 9, 2022, https://www.britannica.com/topic/Alien-Tort-Claims-Act.

11. Sascha Lohmann, "Extraterritorial U.S. Sanctions, Only Domestic Courts Could Effectively Curb the Enforcement of U.S. Law Abroad," Stiftung Wissenschaft und Politik, February 2019, https://www.swp-berlin.org/fileadmin/contents/products/comments /2019C05_lom.pdf.

12. "Filártiga v. Peña-Irala," Center for Constitutional Rights, accessed March 27, 2021, https://ccrjustice.org/home/what-we-do/our-cases/fil-rtiga-v-pe-irala.

13. Richard Nephew, "Decertification of the JCPOA and the Risk of European Union 'Blocking Regulation,'" Columbia/SIPA Center on Global Energy Policy, October 31, 2017,

https://energypolicy.columbia.edu/research/commentary/decertification-jcpoa-and
-risk-european-union-blocking-regulations.

14. Ellie Geranmayeh and Manuel Lafont Rapnouil, "Meeting the Challenge of Secondary
    Sanctions," European Council on Foreign Relations, June 2019, https://www.ecfr.eu
    /page/-/4_Meeting_the_challenge_of_secondary_sanctions.pdf.

15. Samantha Sultoon and Justine Walker, "Secondary Sanctions' Implications and the
    Transatlantic Relationship," Atlantic Council, September 2019, https://www.atlantic
    council.org/wp-content/uploads/2019/09/SecondarySanctions_Final.pdf.

16. Jason Bartlett and Megan Ophel, "Sanctions by the Numbers: U.S. Secondary Sanc-
    tions," Center for a New American Security, August 26, 2021, https://www.cnas.org
    /publications/reports/sanctions-by-the-numbers-u-s-secondary-sanctions.

17. Geranmayeh and Rapnouil, "Meeting the Challenge."

18. "Section 231 of the Countering America's Adversaries Through Sanctions Act of 2017: Pub-
    lic Guidance/Frequently Asked Questions," U.S. Department of State, accessed March 27,
    2021, https://www.state.gov/countering-americas-adversaries-through-sanctions-act
    /public-guidance-frequently-asked-questions.

19. Richard Nephew, "Issue Brief: The Future of Economic Sanctions in a Global Economy,"
    Columbia/SIPA Center on Global Energy Policy, May 21, 2015, https://www.energypolicy
    .columbia.edu/research/report/future-economic-sanctions-global-economy.

20. "Top 10 Things to Know About Expanded US Sanctions on Iran," Latham & Watkins,
    November 6, 2018, https://www.lw.com/thoughtLeadership/lw-top-10-things-to-know
    -expanded-us-sanctions-iran.

21. Simond de Galbert, "Transatlantic Economic Statecraft," Center for a New American
    Security, June 21, 2016, https://www.cnas.org/publications/reports/transatlantic-economic
    -statecraft-the-challenge-to-building-a-balanced-transatlantic-sanctions-policy-between
    -the-united-states-and-the-european-union.

22. Donald Trump (@realDonaldTrump), Twitter, accessed June 19, 2020, https://twitter
    .com/realDonaldTrump/status/1026762818773757955.

23. David Jalilvand, "Progress, Challenges, Uncertainty: Ambivalent Times for Iran's Energy
    Sector," Oxford University Institute for Energy Studies, April 2018, https://www.oxfordenergy
    .org/publications/progress-challenges-uncertainty-ambivalent-times-irans-energy-sector.

24. Stefaan Smis and Kim Van Der Borght, "The EU-U.S. Compromise on the Helms-Burton
    and D'Amato Acts," *American Journal of International Law* 93, no. 1 (1999): 227–36,
    https://doi.org/10.2307/2997968.

25. Jalilvand, "Progress, Challenges, Uncertainty."

26. Stanley Reed, "Total Signs Deal with Iran, Exposing It to Big Risks and Rewards,"
    New York Times, July 3, 2017, https://www.nytimes.com/2017/07/03/business/energy
    -environment/iran-total-france-gas-energy.html.

27. "2017 Factbook," Total, accessed June 20, 2020, https://www.total.com/sites/g/files/nytnzq111
    /files/atoms/files/factbook-2017_web_0.pdf.

28. Babak Dehghanpisheh, "Foreign Funds for Iran's Oil Sector a Top Priority: Oil Min-
    ister," Reuters, August 20, 2017, https://www.reuters.com/article/us-iran-oil-zanganeh
    -idUSKCN1B00T0.

29.   Bate Felix, "Oil Major Total Says Final Iran Project Investment Decision Depends on Renewal of U.S. Waivers," Reuters, February 9, 2017, https://www.reuters.com/article/iran-total-sanctions-idUSL5N1FU1VT.

30.   "US Withdrawal from the JCPOA: Total's Position Related to the South Pars 11 Project in Iran," Total, May 16, 2018, https://www.total.com/media/news/press-releases/us-withdrawal-jcpoa-totals-position-related-south-pars-11-project-iran.

31.   "U.S.: Total, Borealis and NOVA Chemicals Sign Definitive Agreements to Form a Joint Venture in Petrochemicals," Total, February 19, 2018, https://www.total.com/media/news/press-releases/us-total-borealis-and-nova-chemicals-sign-definitive-agreements-form-joint-venture-petrochemicals.

32.   Ron Bousso and Bate Felix, "France's Total Opens Washington Office as Iran Risks Loom," Reuters, November 3, 2017, https://www.reuters.com/article/us-total-usa/frances-total-opens-washington-office-as-iran-risks-loom-idINKBN1D31H2.

33.   Sarah White, "Head of France's Total Urged Trump to Stick with Iran Nuclear Deal: FT," Reuters, February 12, 2018, https://www.reuters.com/article/us-total-iran-trump/head-of-frances-total-urged-trump-to-stick-with-iran-nuclear-deal-ft-idUSKBN1FW0NL.

34.   David Keohane and Andrew Ward, "Total Chief Told Trump to Stick with Iran Nuclear Deal," *Financial Times*, February 11, 2018, https://www.ft.com/content/f3c2d084-0e83-11e8-8cb6-b9ccc4c4dbbb.

35.   David Jalilvand, "The US Exit from the JCPOA: What Consequences for Iranian Energy?," Oxford University Institute for Energy Studies, June 2018, https://www.oxfordenergy.org/publications/us-exit-jcpoa-consequences-iranian-energy.

36.   David Keohane, "Total Vows Iran Pullout Over Trump Sanctions Threat," *Financial Times*, May 16, 2018, https://www.ft.com/content/cf9a7ef8-5912-11e8-bdb7-f6677d2e1ce8.

37.   "US Withdrawal from the JCPOA," Total.

38.   "Iran Nuclear Deal: US Rejects EU Plea for Sanctions Exemption," BBC News, July 16, 2018, https://www.bbc.co.uk/news/world-us-canada-44842723.

39.   Dan De Luce, Abigail Williams, and Andrea Mitchell, "U.S. Refuses European Requests for Exemptions from Its New Sanctions on Iran," NBC News, July 14, 2018, https://www.nbcnews.com/news/world/u-s-refuses-european-requests-exemptions-its-new-sanctions-iran-n891371.

40.   David Keohane and Najmeh Bozorgmehr, "Threat of US Sanctions Pushes France's Total Out of Iran," *Financial Times*, August 20, 2018, https://www.ft.com/content/6baba178-a459-11e8-926a-7342fe5e173f.

41.   "Iran Says China's CNPC Replacing France's Total in Gas Project," Reuters, November 25, 2018, https://www.reuters.com/article/us-oil-iran-cnpc/iran-says-chinas-cnpc-replacing-frances-total-in-gas-project-idUSKCN1NU0FP.

42.   Chen Aizhu, "CNPC Suspends Investment in Iran's South Pars After U.S. Pressure: Sources," Reuters, December 12, 2018, https://www.reuters.com/article/us-china-iran-gas-sanctions/cnpc-suspends-investment-in-irans-south-pars-after-u-s-pressure-sources-idUSKBN1OB0RU.

43.   Ellie Geranmayeh, "Reviving the Revolutionaries: Trump's Maximum Pressure Is Shifting Iran's Domestic Politics," European Council on Foreign Relations, June 2020,

https://www.ecfr.eu/page/-/reviving_the_revolutionaries_how_trumps_maximum
_pressure_is_shifting_irans.pdf.

44. Sudip Kar-Gupta and John Irish, "France's Total to Quit Iran Gas Project if No Sanc-
     tions Waiver," Reuters, May 16, 2018, https://www.reuters.com/article/us-iran-nuclear
     -france-total-idUSKCN1IH1XK.

45. Richard Nephew, "Libya: Sanctions Removal Done Right? A Review of the Libyan
     Sanctions Experience," Columbia/SIPA Center on Global Energy Policy, March 2018,
     https://energypolicy.columbia.edu/sites/default/files/pictures/Libya%20Sanctions%20
     Removal_CGEP_Report_031918.pdf.

46. Brian Scheid, "Chevron's Venezuela Sanctions Waiver Extended to April: US Trea-
     sury," S&P Global Platts, January 18, 2020, https://www.spglobal.com/platts/en/market
     -insights/latest-news/oil/011820-chevrons-venezuela-sanctions-waiver-extended-to
     -april-us-treasury.

47. Andrew Kramer, "Exxon Reaches Arctic Oil Deal with Russians," New York Times,
     August 31, 2011, https://www.nytimes.com/2011/08/31/business/global/exxon-and-rosneft
     -partner-in-russian-oil-deal.html.

48. Atle Staalesen, "These Are Rex Tillerson's Assets in Arctic Russia," Barents Observer,
     December 2016, https://thebarentsobserver.com/en/arctic-industry-and-energy/2016
     /12/these-are-rex-tillersons-assets-arctic-russia.

49. Bradley Klapper, "Trump's Choice for Top Diplomat Is no Fan of Sanctions," Associated
     Press, December 15, 2016, https://apnews.com/ba5a55b4956846b5af90962c290679ac
     /trumps-choice-top-diplomat-no-fan-sanctions.

50. David Brunnstrom, "Tillerson: Evidence Sanctions 'Really Starting to Hurt' North Korea,"
     Reuters, January 17, 2018, https://www.reuters.com/article/us-northkorea-missiles-tillerson
     /tillerson-evidence-sanctions-really-starting-to-hurt-north-korea-idUSKBN1F62UV.

51. Clifford Krauss, "Exxon Mobil Seeks U.S. Sanctions Waiver for Oil Project in Russia,"
     New York Times, April 19, 2017, https://www.nytimes.com/2017/04/19/business/energy
     -environment/exxon-mobil-russia-sanctions-waiver-oil.html.

52. Atle Staalesen, "They Found One of Russia's Biggest Arctic Oil Fields, but Now Abandon
     It," Barents Observer, March 2018, https://thebarentsobserver.com/en/industry-and
     -energy/2018/03/they-found-one-russias-biggest-offshore-arctic-oil-field-now-abandon
     -it.

53. Ed Crooks and Jack Farchy, "Exxon Considers Its Course After Sanctions Hit Rus-
     sian Ambitions," Financial Times, September 30, 2014, https://www.ft.com/content
     /586ae5c0-487c-11e4-ad19-00144feab7de.

54. Alan Rappeport, "Exxon Mobil Fined for Violating Sanctions on Russia," New York
     Times, July 20, 2017, https://www.nytimes.com/2017/07/20/us/politics/exxon-mobil-fined
     -russia-tillerson-sanctions.html.

55. "Financial Statements and Supplemental Information," ExxonMobil, accessed May 8,
     2020, https://corporate.exxonmobil.com/-/media/Global/Files/investor-relations/annual
     -meeting-materials/financial-statements/2014-financial-statements.pdf.

56. Yeganeh Torbati and Ernest Scheyder, "Exxon Sues U.S. Over Fine Levied for Russia
     Deal Under Tillerson," Reuters, July 20, 2017, https://www.reuters.com/article/us-exxon
     -mobil-usa-ukraine-idUSKBN1A51UH.

57.   Jaclyn Jaeger, "Exxon Wins Legal Battle with OFAC Over Sanctions Violation," Compliance Week, January 3, 2020, https://www.complianceweek.com/sanctions/exxon-wins-legal-battle-with-ofac-over-sanctions-violation/28258.article.

58.   Vladimir Soldatkin, "Exxon Pursues Cost Cuts at Russia's Sakhalin-1 Project," Reuters, May 8, 2020, https://uk.reuters.com/article/health-coronavirus-russia-exxon/update-1-exxon-pursues-cost-cuts-at-russias-sakhalin-1-project-idUKL8N2CQ1TR.

6. SANCTIONS OVERKILL

1.   "BAWAG Restores Cuban Accounts After Public Uproar," Reuters, May 4, 2007, https://www.reuters.com/article/austria-bawag-cuba-idUSL0450488520070504.

2.   "Austria Charges Bank After Cuban Accounts Cancelled," Reuters, April 27, 2007, https://www.reuters.com/article/austria-bawag/austria-charges-bank-after-cuban-accounts-cancelled-idUSL2711446820070427.

3.   "Foreign Ministry Ceases Investigations Against BAWAG Bank," Austrian Federal Ministry for European and International Affairs, June 21, 2007, https://www.bmeia.gv.at/en/the-ministry/press/announcements/2007/foreign-ministry-ceases-investigations-against-bawag-bank.

4.   Andrew Roth and Carol Morello, "Kremlin Reacts with Anger and Ridicule to Treasury List of Influential Russians," Washington Post, January 30, 2018, https://www.washingtonpost.com/world/kremlin-reacts-with-anger-and-ridicule-to-treasury-list-of-influential-russians/2018/01/30/f5405586-05c7-11e8-8777-2a059f168dd2_story.html.

5.   Igor Bosilkovski, "Treasury Department's Russia Oligarchs List Is Copied from Forbes," Forbes, January 30, 2018, https://www.forbes.com/sites/igorbosilkovski/2018/01/30/treasury-departments-russias-oligarchs-list-is-copied-from-forbes.

6.   Leonid Bershidsky, "The U.S. List of Russian Oligarchs Is a Disgrace," Bloomberg, January 30, 2018, https://www.bloomberg.com/opinion/articles/2018-01-30/the-u-s-list-of-russian-oligarchs-is-a-disgrace.

7.   Roth and Morello, "Kremlin Reacts with Anger and Ridicule."

8.   Christian Caryl, "Why Treasury's 'Oligarch List' Is Driving Russian Tycoons Crazy," Forbes, January 30, 2018, https://www.washingtonpost.com/news/democracy-post/wp/2018/01/30/why-the-treasurys-oligarch-list-is-driving-russian-tycoons-crazy.

9.   Courtney Weaver, Katrina Manson, and Max Seddon, "Trump and Putin: Inside the Muddled American Policy on Russia," Financial Times, July 10, 2018, https://www.ft.com/content/31bccode-8102-11e8-bc55-50daf11b720d.

10.   Ashish Kumar Sen, "Trump Administration Targets Russian Oligarchs," Atlantic Council, April 6, 2018, https://www.atlanticcouncil.org/blogs/new-atlanticist/trump-administration-targets-russian-oligarchs.

11.   Nigel Gould-Davies, "Russia, the West and Sanctions," Survival: Global Politics and Strategy 62 (February–March 2020): 7–28, https://doi.org/10.1080/00396338.2020.1715060.

12.   "Treasury Designates Russian Oligarchs, Officials, and Entities in Response to Worldwide Malign Activity," U.S. Treasury, April 6, 2018, https://home.treasury.gov/news/press-releases/sm0338.

13. Brian O'Toole and Samantha Sultoon, "Memo to Congress: Treasury's Plan to Lift Sanctions on Russian Oligarch's Companies Is a Good One," Atlantic Council, January 11, 2019, https://www.atlanticcouncil.org/blogs/new-atlanticist/memo-to-congress-treasury-s-plan-to-lift-sanctions-on-russian-oligarch-s-companies-is-a-good-one.

14. Ole Moehr, "US Sanctions' Global Impact—A Case Study of RUSAL's Supply Chain," Atlantic Council, May 18, 2018, https://www.atlanticcouncil.org/blogs/econographics/us-sanctions-global-impact.

15. "Section 232 Investigation on the Effect of Imports of Steel on U.S. National Security," U.S. Department of Commerce, accessed March 26, 2021, https://www.commerce.gov/section-232-investigation-effect-imports-steel-us-national-security.

16. Terje Solsvik, "Russia, Brazil Woes Could Lead to Aluminum Supply Shortage: Hydro CEO," Reuters, April 16, 2018, https://www.reuters.com/article/us-norsk-hydro-aluminium/russia-brazil-woes-could-lead-to-aluminum-supply-shortage-hydro-ceo-idUSKBN1HN18G.

17. Arthur Beesley, "US Sanctions Puts Future of Aughinish Plant in Doubt," *Irish Times*, April 23, 2018, https://www.irishtimes.com/business/energy-and-resources/us-sanctions-puts-future-of-aughinish-plant-in-doubt-1.3470888.

18. "Aughinish Alumina Supply Contract Hit by Russian Parent's US Sanctions," *Irish Times*, April 13, 2018, https://www.irishtimes.com/business/energy-and-resources/aughinish-alumina-supply-contract-hit-by-russian-parent-s-us-sanctions-1.3460988.

19. Beesley, "US Sanctions Puts Future of Aughinish Plant in Doubt."

20. Peter O'Dwyer, "State Vows to Fight for Alumina Plant," *Sunday Times* (London, UK), January 29, 2019, https://www.thetimes.co.uk/article/state-vows-to-fight-for-alumina-plant-qzv89rf6g.

21. Neil Hume, Henry Sanderson, and Arthur Beesley, "Rio Tinto Declares Force Majeure on Rusal Deals," *Financial Times*, April 13, 2018, https://www.ft.com/content/6a56584e-3f38-11e8-b9f9-de94fa33a81e.

22. Nicole Mordant, "Rio Tinto Reviewing Rusal Ties, Mum on Queensland Venture," Reuters, April 10, 2018, https://www.reuters.com/article/us-rio-tinto-rusal/rio-tinto-reviewing-rusal-ties-mum-on-queensland-venture-idUSKBN1HH2C7.

23. "Rio Tinto Reviews Arrangements with Rusal," Rio Tinto, April 13, 2018, https://www.riotinto.com/news/releases/Rusal-arrangements-reviewed.

24. "Sanctions on UC Rusal Hit Shipping," *Maritime Executive*, April 20, 2018, https://www.maritime-executive.com/article/sanctions-on-uc-rusal-hit-shipping.

25. Melanie Burton, "Rio Tinto Stands to Win from Rusal Sanctions; U.S. Consumers to Lose," Reuters, April 9, 2018, https://www.reuters.com/article/us-rusal-sanctions-aluminium/rio-tinto-stands-to-win-from-rusal-sanctions-u-s-consumers-to-lose-idUSKBN1HG1NL.

26. Denis Chabrol, "Oldendorff Closing Bauxite Transshipment Operations in Guyana Due to US Sanctions Against RUSAL," Demerara Waves, April 19, 2018, https://demerarawaves.com/2018/04/19/oldendorff-closing-bauxite-transshipment-operations-in-guyana-due-to-us-sanctions-against-rusal.

27. Jonathan Saul, "Ship Firm Oldendorff Halting Guyana Operation Due to Rusal Crisis," Reuters, April 20, 2018, https://www.reuters.com/article/us-usa-sanctions-oldendorff

/ship-firm-oldendorff-halting-guyana-operation-due-to-rusal-crisis-idUSKB-
N1HR2AD.

28.   Neil Hume and David Sheppard, "Supply Deals with Rusal's Irish Plant to Restart as
Sanctions Ease," *Financial Times*, April 24, 2018, https://www.ft.com/content/c4ace960
-479f-11e8-8ee8-cae73aab7ccb.

29.   Angharad Parry, "Rusal Sanctions: Market Turmoil and Legal Fall-out," Essex Street,
April 2018, https://twentyessex.com/wp-content/uploads/2019/06/Rusal-sanctions.pdf.

30.   Paul Marquardt and Sameer Jaywant, "OFAC Reporting Still Required for Transactions
with EN+, Rusal, and EuroSibEnergo," Cleary Gottlieb, January 31, 2019, https://www.cleary
tradewatch.com/2019/01/ofac-reporting-still-required-transactions-en-rusal-eurosibenergo.

31.   Barry O'Halloran, "Deal to Lift Sanctions Against Aughinish Alumina Refinery at
Shannon in the Balance," *Irish Times*, November 12, 2018, https://www.irishtimes.com
/business/manufacturing/deal-to-lift-sanctions-against-aughinish-alumina-refinery
-at-shannon-in-the-balance-1.3694140.

32.   Ole Moehr, "A Breakdown of the Sanctions Deal Between the United States and Oleg
Deripaska," Atlantic Council, February 6, 2019, https://www.atlanticcouncil.org/blogs
/econographics/us-sanctions-lifted-coles-2.

33.   Jeremy Herb and Ted Barrett, "Senate Democrats' Effort to Block Trump Move on Russia Sanctions Fails," CNN, January 16, 2019, https://edition.cnn.com/2019/01/16/politics
/senate-democrats-sanctions-russia/index.html.

34.   Polina Devitt, "Russia's Rusal Lands First U.S. Investment Since Sanctions Lifted," Reuters, April 15, 2019, https://www.reuters.com/article/us-russia-rusal-usa/russias-rusal
-lands-first-u-s-investment-since-sanctions-lifted-idUSKCN1RR09V.

35.   Erin Banco, "Treasury Department Chaos Leads to Exodus of Key Staffers," Daily Beast,
January 9, 2019, https://www.thedailybeast.com/treasury-department-chaos-leads-to
-exodus-of-key-staffers.

36.   Richard Nephew, "Evaluating the Trump's Administration Approach to Sanctions,
Case: Iran," Columbia/SIPA Center on Global Energy Policy, November 2019, https://
energypolicy.columbia.edu/sites/default/files/file-uploads/IranSanctions_CGEP
_Commentary_110819.pdf.

37.   Richard Nephew, "Transatlantic Sanctions Policy: From the 1982 Soviet Gas Pipeline
Episode to Today," Columbia/SIPA Center on Global Energy Policy, March 22, 2019,
https://energypolicy.columbia.edu/research/report/transatlantic-sanctions-policy-1982
-soviet-gas-pipeline-episode-today.

38.   Peter Harrell, "Is the U.S. Using Sanctions Too Aggressively? The Steps Washington
Can Take to Guard Against Overuse," *Foreign Affairs*, September 11, 2018, https://www
.foreignaffairs.com/articles/2018-09-11/us-using-sanctions-too-aggressively.

39.   Richard Nephew, "U.S. Sanctions Relief: Good for Russian Companies but Bad for Policy?,"
Columbia/SIPA Center on Global Energy Policy, January 11, 2019, https://energypolicy.columbia
.edu/research/commentary/us-sanctions-relief-good-russian-companies-bad-policy.

40.   Polina Devitt and Arshad Mohammed, "Questions Linger Over Deripaska's Rusal
Influence After U.S. Deal," Reuters, February 4, 2019, https://www.reuters.com/article
/us-usa-russia-sanctions-rusal-analysis-idUSKCN1PT0K9.

41. Alan Katz, Kitty Donaldson, and Stephanie Baker, "Oleg Deripaska's Rusal Role Spurred Europe Sanctions Warning to U.S.," BNN Bloomberg, December 17, 2020, https://www.bnnbloomberg.ca/oleg-deripaska-s-rusal-role-spurred-europe-sanctions-warning-to-u-s-1.1537929.

42. Stephanie Baker, "U.S. Senator Asks Treasury for Sanctions Briefing on Deripaska," Bloomberg, December 23, 2020, https://www.bloomberg.com/news/articles/2020-12-23/u-s-senator-asks-treasury-for-sanctions-briefing-on-deripaska.

43. Andrew Harris, David Voreacos, and Stephanie Baker, "Deripaska Sues Over U.S. Sanctions, Claims $7.5 Billion Loss," Bloomberg, March 15, 2019, https://www.bloomberg.com/news/articles/2019-03-15/deripaska-sues-u-s-treasury-to-block-sanctions-against-him.

44. Kevin Breuninger, "Putin Ally Oleg Deripaska Sues Treasury and Steven Mnuchin to Lift Sanctions, Claiming 'Utter Devastation' of His Wealth," CNBC, March 15, 2019, https://www.cnbc.com/2019/03/15/putin-ally-deripaska-sues-treasury-to-block-sanctions-says-hes-lost-billions.html.

45. Breuninger, "Putin Ally Oleg Deripaska Sues Treasury."

46. Sam Meredith and Natasha Turak, "Putin Ally Oleg Deripaska Denies Kremlin Encouraged His Lawsuit Against US Treasury Sanctions," CNBC, March 18, 2019, https://www.cnbc.com/2019/03/18/putin-ally-deripaska-explains-why-hes-suing-us-treasury-department.html.

47. Benjamin Quenelle, "Sanctions: le "roi de l'aluminium" russe accuse Washington," Les Echos, February 14, 2020, https://www.lesechos.fr/finance-marches/marches-financiers/sanctions-loligarque-de-laluminium-accuse-washington-1171891.

48. "Real Time Net Worth, No. 1050, Oleg Deripaska," Forbes, accessed April 17, 2022, https://www.forbes.com/profile/oleg-deripaska.

49. Humeyra Pamuk and Timothy Gardner, "U.S. Lifts Iran Sanctions on One Unit of Chinese Shipping Giant COSCO," Reuters, January 31, 2020, https://www.reuters.com/article/us-iran-nuclear-usa-cosco/u-s-lifts-iran-sanctions-on-one-unit-of-chinese-shipping-giant-cosco-idUSKBN1ZU04I.

50. Byron McKinney, "COSCO Shipping & OFAC Sanctions—The Nightmare in the Haystack," IHS Markit, October 8, 2019, https://ihsmarkit.com/research-analysis/cosco-shipping-ofac-sanctions.html.

51. Jonathan Saul and Chen Aizhu, "Unipec Replaces Ship Charters After U.S. Sanctions COSCO Tanker Units: Sources," Reuters, September 26, 2019, https://www.reuters.com/article/us-iran-nuclear-usa-china/unipec-replaces-ship-charters-after-u-s-sanctions-cosco-tanker-units-sources-idUSKBN1WB1XY.

52. Greg Miller, "Sanctions Are Cleaving the Global Shipping Fleet in Two," American Shipper, September 30, 2019, https://www.freightwaves.com/news/sanctions-are-cleaving-the-global-shipping-fleet-in-two.

53. Saul and Aizhu, "Unipec Replaces Ship Charters."

54. Pamuk and Gardner, "U.S. Lifts Iran Sanctions."

55. Brian Scheid, "End of Cosco Sanctions Shows US Reluctance for Penalizing Key Oil Market Players: Analysts," S&P Global Platts, February 3, 2020, https://www.spglobal.com/platts/en/market-insights/latest-news/oil/020320-end-of-cosco-sanctions-shows-us-reluctance-for-penalizing-key-oil-market-players-analysts.

7. SANCTIONS DISPUTES

1. "The Soviet Gas Pipeline in Perspective," U.S. Central Intelligence Agency, September 21, 1982, https://www.cia.gov/library/readingroom/docs/19820921.pdf.

2. "Caterpillar Gets Export License," *New York Times*, December 10, 1981, https://www.nytimes.com/1981/12/10/business/caterpillar-gets-export-license.html.

3. Lisa Martin, *Coercive Cooperation, Explaining Multilateral Sanctions* (Princeton, NJ: Princeton University Press, 1992), 208.

4. Alan Riley, "Nord Stream 2: Understanding the Potential Consequences," Atlantic Council, June 2018, https://www.atlanticcouncil.org/wp-content/uploads/2018/06/Nord_Stream _2_interactive.pdf.

5. Patrick DeSouza, "The Soviet Gas Pipeline Incident: Extension of Collective Security Responsibilities to Peacetime Commercial Trade," Yale University Law School, accessed July 28, 2020, http://digitalcommons.law.yale.edu/cgi/viewcontent.cgi?article =1317&context=yjil.

6. "Bonn Needs the Business Even More than the Gas," *New York Times*, August 16, 1981, https://www.nytimes.com/1981/08/16/weekinreview/bonn-needs-the-business-even -more-than-the-gas.html.

7. John Tagliabue, "Europeans in Pact on Soviet Gas," *New York Times*, September 30, 1981, https://www.nytimes.com/1981/09/30/business/europeans-in-pact-on-soviet-gas .html.

8. Paul Lewis, "A Soviet Project Tempts Europe," *New York Times*, May 30, 1982, https://timesmachine.nytimes.com/timesmachine/1982/05/30/173299.html?pageNumber =156.

9. DeSouza, "The Soviet Gas Pipeline Incident."

10. John Hardt, "Energy Equipment Sales to U.S.S.R.," Congressional Research Service, October 22, 1982, https://www.everycrsreport.com/files/19821022_IP0219S_d8bc44 c63e6d2816a3fc8cbe261e4338ac65de49.pdf.

11. Richard Nephew, "Transatlantic Sanctions Policy: From the 1982 Soviet Gas Pipeline Episode to Today," Columbia/SIPA Center on Global Energy Policy, March 22, 2019, https://energypolicy.columbia.edu/research/report/transatlantic-sanctions-policy -1982-soviet-gas-pipeline-episode-today.

12. "Declaration of the Seven Heads of State and Government and Representatives of the European Communities," G7 Summit, Versailles, June 6, 1982, http://www.g8.utoronto .ca/summit/1982versailles/communique.html.

13. Gary Perlow, "Taking Peacetime Trade Sanctions to the Limit: The Soviet Pipeline Embargo," *Case Western Reserve Journal of International Law* 15, no. 253 (1983), https://scholarlycommons.law.case.edu/jil/vol15/iss2/4.

14. Nephew, "Transatlantic Sanctions Policy."

15. "European Council," British Parliament Archives, accessed July 28, 2020, https://api .parliament.uk/historic-hansard/commons/1982/jul/01/european-council#S6CV0026P0 _19820701_HOC_153.

16. Perlow, "Taking Peacetime Trade Sanctions to the Limit."

17. Rita Dallas, "Britain Orders Firms to Defy Pipeline Ban," *Washington Post*, August 3, 1982.

18. Emmanuel Mourlon-Druol and Angela Romano, "The Iran Nuclear Deal Crisis: Lessons from the 1982 Transatlantic Dispute over the Siberian Gas Pipeline," Bruegel, May 2018, https://www.bruegel.org/2018/05/the-iran-nuclear-deal-crisis-lessons-from-the -1982-transatlantic-dispute-over-the-siberian-gas-pipeline.

19. Oliver Dziggel, "The Reagan Pipeline Sanctions: Implications for U.S. Domestic Policy and the Future of International Law," *Towson University Journal of International Affairs* L, no. 1 (2016), https://cpb-us-w2.wpmucdn.com/wp.towson.edu/dist/b/55/files /2017/11/REAGAN-PIPELINE-SANCTIONS-19q4sd1.pdf.

20. Bernard Gwertzman, "Lifting of U.S. Sanctions," *New York Times*, November 15, 1982, https://www.nytimes.com/1982/11/15/world/lifting-of-us-sanctions-news-analysis .html.

21. Antony Blinken, *Ally Versus Ally: America, Europe, and the Siberian Pipeline Crisis* (Westport, CT: Praeger Publishers, 1987).

22. Bernard Gwertzman, "Reagan Lifts Sanctions on Sales for Soviet Pipeline; Reports Accord with Allies," *New York Times*, November 14, 1982, https://www.nytimes.com/1982 /11/14/world/reagan-lifts-sanctions-on-sales-for-soviet-pipeline-reports-accord-with -allies.html.

23. Richard Weintraub, "President Lifts Sanctions on Soviet Pipeline," *Washington Post*, November 14, 1982, https://www.washingtonpost.com/archive/politics/1982/11/14 /president-lifts-sanctions-on-soviet-pipeline/f04df97a-bbb9-4ef6-acae-4484effd0282.

24. Lewis, "A Soviet Project Tempts Europe."

25. James Feron, "Mrs Thatcher Faults U.S. on Siberia Pipeline," *New York Times*, July 2, 1982, https://www.nytimes.com/1982/07/02/world/mrs-thatcher-faults-us-on-siberia -pipeline.html.

26. Maria Shagina, "A Tale of Two Pipelines," Riddle Russia, January 13, 2021, https://www .ridl.io/en/a-tale-of-two-pipelines.

27. "Putin Says Nord Stream 2 Link Ready to Calm Gas Prices," Reuters, December 29, 2021, https://www.reuters.com/markets/commodities/putin-declares-nord-stream-2-ready -gas-exports-2021-12-29.

28. Paul Belkin, Michael Ratner, and Cory Welt, "Russia's Nord Stream 2 Pipeline: A Push for the Finish Line," Congressional Research Service, accessed March 18, 2021, https:// fas.org/sgp/crs/row/IF11138.pdf.

29. Jean-Pierre Stroobants, Faustine Vincent, Benoît Vitkine, et al., "Nord Stream 2, le gazoduc russe qui sème la zizanie en Europe," *Le Monde*, February 26, 2021, https:// www.lemonde.fr/international/article/2021/02/26/nord-stream-2-le-gazoduc-russe -qui-seme-la-zizanie-en-europe_6071337_3210.html.

30. "From Where Do We Import Energy and How Dependent Are We?" Eurostat, accessed February 15, 2021, https://ec.europa.eu/eurostat/cache/infographs/energy/bloc-2c.html.

31. Agnia Grigas and Lukas Trakimavičius, "Nord Stream 2 Is a Bad Deal for Europe," Atlantic Council, July 10, 2018, https://www.atlanticcouncil.org/blogs/new-atlanticist /nord-stream-2-is-a-bad-deal-for-europe.

32. Henry Foy, "Nord Stream 2 Pipeline Targeted in US Sanctions Broadside," *Financial Times*, June 15, 2017, https://www.ft.com/content/03a9fd6a-51d8-11e7-bfb8-997009366969.

33. "Background Story: Pipeline Construction—Nord Stream 2," Nord Stream 2, accessed February 7, 2021, https://www.nord-stream2.com/media/documents/pdf/en/2018/10/background-story-pipeline-construction-en.pdf.

34. Alastair Macdonald, "U.S. Envoy Warns Sanctions Still an Option Against Nord Stream 2," Reuters, November 13, 2018, https://www.reuters.com/article/us-eu-gazprom-nordstream-usa-idUSKCN1NI1FY.

35. "US-Botschafter Grenell schreibt Drohbriefe an deutsche Firmen," *Der Spiegel*, accessed July 30, 2020, https://www.spiegel.de/politik/deutschland/richard-grenell-us-botschafter-schreibt-drohbriefe-an-deutsche-firmen-a-1247785.html.

36. Aime Williams, "US Congress Passes $738bn Defence Spending Bill," *Financial Times*, December 17, 2019, https://www.ft.com/content/d144c6ec-20e8-11ea-b8a1-584213ee7b2b.

37. "Allseas Suspends Nord Stream 2 Pipelay Activities," AllSeas, December 21, 2019, https://allseas.com/wp-content/uploads/2019/12/2019-1221-Media-statement-Allseas-discontinues-Nord-Stream-2-pipelay.pdf.

38. Maria Grabar, "Russian Pipe-Laying Vessel Moors at Nord Stream 2 Hub in Germany: Data," Reuters, May 18, 2020, https://www.reuters.com/article/us-germany-gas-nord-stream-2/russian-pipe-laying-vessel-moors-at-nord-stream-2-hub-in-germany-data-idUSKBN22U1TZ.

39. "Russia Says 'Nothing Catastrophic' About U.S. Sanctions on Nord Stream 2," Reuters, December 23, 2019, https://www.reuters.com/article/us-usa-russia-nord-stream-medvedev/russia-says-nothing-catastrophic-about-u-s-sanctions-on-nord-stream-2-idUSKBN1YR1Q8.

40. Benjamin Schmitt, "Hot Issue—They're Gonna Need a Bigger Boat: The Curious Voyage of the Akademik Cherskiy," Jamestown Foundation, March 31, 2020, https://jamestown.org/program/hot-issue-theyre-gonna-need-a-bigger-boat-the-curious-voyage-of-the-akademik-cherskiy.

41. Vladimir Soldatkin and Natalia Chumakova, "Russian Vessel Able to Complete Nord Stream 2 Pipeline Departs from German Port," Reuters, July 8, 2020, https://www.reuters.com/article/us-nordstream-vessel/russian-vessel-able-to-complete-nord-stream-2-pipeline-departs-from-german-port-idUSKBN2491WE.

42. "CAATSA/CRIEEA Section 232 Public Guidance," U.S. Department of State, accessed July 28, 2020, https://www.state.gov/caatsa-crieea-section-232-public-guidance.

43. Demetri Sevastopulo, Henry Foy, and David Sheppard, "US Steps Up Threats over Nord Stream 2 Pipeline," *Financial Times*, July 15, 2020, https://www.ft.com/content/ff3edd61-a404-48b0-adb8-65b91bc90486.

44. Daniel Fried and Brian O'Toole, "The New Russia Sanctions Law, What It Does and How to Make It Work," Atlantic Council, September 29, 2017, https://www.atlanticcouncil.org/wp-content/uploads/2017/09/The_New_Russia_Sanctions_Law_web_0929.pdf.

45. Brian O'Toole and Daniel Fried, "US Opens Door to Nord Stream II Sanctions and Transatlantic Tensions," Atlantic Council, July 15, 2020, https://www.atlanticcouncil.org/blogs/new-atlanticist/us-opens-door-to-nord-stream-ii-sanctions-and-transatlantic-tensions.

46. Diane Pallardy, "US Threatens Nord Stream 2 Gas Pipe Investors with Sanctions," Independent Commodity Intelligence Services, July 16, 2020, https://www.icis.com/explore/resources/news/2020/07/16/10530894/us-threatens-nord-stream-2-gas-pipe-investors-with-sanctions.

47. Frank Jordans, "US Senators Take Aim at German Port over Russia Pipeline," Associated Press, August 6, 2020, https://apnews.com/93f980822fdc4ed8f53d6dfef380746f.

48. Melissa Eddy and Steven Erlanger, "German Town Fears Ruin by U.S. Effort to Stop Russian Pipeline," *New York Times*, August 25, 2020, https://www.nytimes.com/2020/08/25/world/europe/nord-stream-2-germany-us-russia.html.

49. Thomas Wieder, "En Allemagne, la peur d'un abandon du gazoduc Nord Stream 2," *Le Monde*, January 28, 2021, https://www.lemonde.fr/international/article/2021/01/28/en-allemagne-la-peur-d-un-abandon-de-nord-stream-2_6067944_3210.html.

50. "US Senators Threaten Germany's Port Town of Sassnitz over Nord Stream 2 Gas Project," Deutsche Welle, August 14, 2020, https://www.dw.com/en/us-sanctions-nord-stream-2-gas/a-54565504.

51. Erika Solomon and Katrina Manson, "US Senators' Letter on Nord Stream 2 Sparks Outrage in Germany," *Financial Times*, August 19, 2020, https://www.ft.com/content/f43fa079-bf7f-4efa-8f72-ae9fd4a5368f.

52. Michael Schwirtz and Melissa Eddy, "Aleksei Navalny Was Poisoned with Novichok, Germany Says," *New York Times*, September 2, 2020, https://www.nytimes.com/2020/09/02/world/europe/navalny-poison-novichok.html.

53. Steven Erlanger and Melissa Eddy, "Navalny Poisoning Raises Pressure on Merkel to Cancel Russian Pipeline," *New York Times*, September 3, 2020, https://www.nytimes.com/2020/09/03/world/europe/navalny-poisoning-merkel-nord-stream.html.

54. Paul Kolbe, "With Hacking, the United States Needs to Stop Playing the Victim," *New York Times*, December 23, 2020, https://www.nytimes.com/2020/12/23/opinion/russia-united-states-hack.html.

55. "Труба пришла в движение," *Коммерсантъ*, October 14, 2020, https://www.kommersant.ru/doc/4530356.

56. Meghan Gordon, "US Steps Up Sanctions Pressure on Nord Stream 2 Gas Pipeline Contractors," S&P Global Platts, October 20, 2020, https://www.spglobal.com/platts/en/market-insights/latest-news/natural-gas/102020-us-steps-up-sanctions-pressure-on-nord-stream-2-gas-pipeline-contractors.

57. Diane Francis, "US Expands Sanctions Against Putin's Pipeline," Atlantic Council, October 22, 2020, https://www.atlanticcouncil.org/blogs/ukrainealert/us-expands-sanctions-against-putins-pipeline.

58. Gordon, "US Steps Up Sanctions Pressure."

59. Henry Foy and Erika Solomon, "Gazprom to Restart Nord Stream 2 Construction," *Financial Times*, January 10, 2021, https://www.ft.com/content/d3f86ba6-95ce-496a-b323-62109775364d.

60. "Russia's Gazprom Expects Nord Stream 2 Launch in 2021: RIA," Reuters, February 11, 2021, https://www.reuters.com/article/us-gazprom-nordstream2/russias-gazprom-expects-nord-stream-2-launch-in-2021-ria-idUSKBN2AB1JL.

61. Daniel Fried, Richard Morningstar, and Daniel Stein, "Reconciling Transatlantic Differences over Nord Stream 2," Atlantic Council, February 2, 2021, https://www.atlantic council.org/blogs/energysource/reconciling-transatlantic-differences-over-nord -stream-2.

62. Stuart Elliott, "European Parliament Reiterates Call for Nord Stream 2 Gas Link to Be Halted," S&P Global Platts, January 21, 2021, https://www.spglobal.com/platts/en /market-insights/latest-news/natural-gas/012121-european-parliament-reiterates-call -for-nord-stream-2-gas-link-to-be-halted.

63. Stanley Reed and Lara Jakes, "A Russian Gas Pipeline Increases Tension Between the U.S. and Europe," *New York Times*, July 24, 2020, https://www.nytimes.com/2020/07/24 /business/nord-stream-pipeline-russia.html.

64. Iain King, "Not Contributing Enough? A Summary of European Military and Development Assistance to Ukraine Since 2014," Center for Strategic & International Studies, September 26, 2019, https://www.csis.org/analysis/not-contributing-enough-summary -european-military-and-development-assistance-ukraine-2014.

65. "'Freedom Gas': US Opens LNG Floodgates to Europe," Euractiv, updated August 28, 2019, https://www.euractiv.com/section/energy/news/freedom-gas-us-opens-lng -floodgates-to-europe.

66. "Sen. Cruz: 'The Administration Needs to Immediately Begin Implementing These Sanctions' on Nord Stream 2 Pipe-Laying Vessels," Senator Ted Cruz, December 12, 2019, https://www.cruz.senate.gov/?p=press_release&id=4818.

67. "Statistical Review of World Energy 2019," BP, accessed May 8, 2020, https://www .bp.com/content/dam/bp/business-sites/en/global/corporate/pdfs/energy-economics /statistical-review/bp-stats-review-2019-full-report.pdf.

68. "EU Imports of Energy Products—Recent Developments," Eurostat, accessed May 8, 2020, https://ec.europa.eu/eurostat/statistics-explained/index.php/EU_imports_of _energy_products_-_recent_developments#Overview.

69. Richard Nephew, "Understanding and Assessing the New US Sanctions Legislation Against Russia," Columbia/SIPA Center on Global Energy Policy, February 15, 2019, https://energypolicy.columbia.edu/research/commentary/understanding-and-assessing -new-us-sanctions-legislation-against-russia.

70. Matthew Karnitschnig, "Germany Blames Trump in Pursuit of Nord Stream 2 Pipeline," Politico, August 10, 2020, https://www.politico.eu/article/germany-plays-trump-card -in-pursuit-of-russian-nord-stream-2-pipeline-dream.

8. SANCTIONS-BUSTING AVOIDANCE SCHEMES FROM U.S. FRIENDS AND FOES

1. "The Art Industry and U.S. Policies That Undermine Sanctions," U.S. Congress, July 29, 2020, https://www.hsgac.senate.gov/imo/media/doc/2020-07-29%20PSI%20Staff%20 Report%20-%20The%20Art%20Industry%20and%20U.S.%20Policies%20that%20 Undermine%20Sanctions.pdf.

2. Kelly Crow, "How Two Sanctioned Russian Billionaire Brothers Bought Art Anyway," *Wall Street Journal*, July 29, 2020, https://www.wsj.com/articles/how-two-sanctioned -russian-billionaire-brothers-bought-art-anyway-11596035186.

3. "Real Time Net Worth, No. 1548, Arkady Rotenberg," *Forbes*, accessed April 17, 2022, https://www.forbes.com/profile/arkady-rotenberg. "Real Time Net Worth, No. 2526, Boris Rotenberg," *Forbes*, accessed April 17, 2022, https://www.forbes.com/profile/boris -rotenberg.

4. Jim Mustian, "Report: Oligarchs Skirt US Sanctions Through Shady Art Sales," Associated Press, July 29, 2020, https://apnews.com/85e77f9b520cefc1f536bc417d9099cc.

5. Maria Grabar, "Russia's Rotenberg Denies Buying Gazprom Stake," Reuters, August 7, 2019, https://uk.reuters.com/article/us-russia-gazprom-rotenberg/russias-rotenberg -denies-buying-gazprom-stake-idUKKCN1UX1VP.

6. Graham Bowley, "Senate Report: Opaque Art Market Helped Oligarchs Evade Sanctions," *New York Times*, July 29, 2020, https://www.nytimes.com/2020/07/29/arts/design/senate -report-art-market-russia-oligarchs-sanctions.html.

7. Joshua Yaffa, "Putin's Shadow Cabinet and the Bridge to Crimea," *New Yorker*, May 29, 2017, https://www.newyorker.com/magazine/2017/05/29/putins-shadow-cabinet-and-the -bridge-to-crimea.

8. Anne Kauranen and Jussi Rosendahl, "Russian Oligarch Under U.S. Sanctions Files Suit Against Nordic Banks," Reuters, October 22, 2018, https://www.reuters.com/article /us-finland-russia-sanctions/russian-oligarch-under-u-s-sanctions-files-suit-against -nordic-banks-idUSKCN1MW1AJ.

9. "Treasury Sanctions Russian Officials, Members of the Russian Leadership's Inner Circle, and an Entity for Involvement in the Situation in Ukraine," U.S. Treasury, March 20, 2014, https://www.treasury.gov/press-center/press-releases/Pages/jl23331 .aspx.

10. "Shanghai Cooperation Organisation to Introduce 'Mutual Settlement in National Currencies' and Ditch US Dollar," Silk Road Briefing, March 18, 2020, https://www .silkroadbriefing.com/news/2020/03/18/shanghai-cooperation-organisation-introduce -mutual-settlement-national-currencies-ditch-us-dollar.

11. Dimitri Simes, "China and Russia Ditch Dollar in Move Towards 'Financial Alliance,'" *Financial Times*, August 16, 2020, https://www.ft.com/content/8421b6a2-1dc6 -4747-b2e9-1bbfb7277747.

12. Anna Andrianova and Andrey Biryukov, "U.S. 'Shooting Itself' with Steps That Harm Dollar, Putin Says," Bloomberg, November 28, 2018, https://www.bloomberg .com/news/articles/2018-11-28/u-s-shooting-itself-with-steps-that-harm-dollar-putin -says.

13. Olesya Astakhova, Elena Fabrichnaya, and Andrey Ostroukh, "Rosneft Switches Contracts to Euros from Dollars Due to U.S. Sanctions," Reuters, October 24, 2019, https:// www.reuters.com/article/us-rosneft-contracts-euro/rosneft-switches-contracts-to -euros-from-dollars-due-to-u-s-sanctions-idUSKBN1X31JT.

14. Ortenca Aliaj and Nastassia Astrasheuskaya, "Russia's Rosneft Switches All Export Contracts to Euros," *Financial Times*, October 24, 2019, https://www.ft.com/content /f886658c-f65c-11e9-a79c-bc9acae3b654.

15. Edoardo Saravalle, "How U.S. Sanctions Depend on the Federal Reserve," Center for a New American Security, July 29, 2020, https://www.cnas.org/publications/commentary /how-u-s-sanctions-depend-on-the-federal-reserve.

16. Benn Steil, "Central Bank Currency Swaps Tracker," Council on Foreign Relations, accessed August 9, 2020, https://www.cfr.org/article/central-bank-currency-swaps-tracker.

17. "India, Japan Sign $75 Billion Currency Swap Agreement," *Economic Times*, October 30, 2018, https://economictimes.indiatimes.com/markets/forex/india-japan-sign-75-billion -currency-swap-agreement/articleshow/66415790.cms.

18. Franz-Stefan Gady, "India Makes $800 Million Advance Payment for Russian S-400 Air Defense Systems," *Diplomat*, November 2019, https://thediplomat.com/2019/11/india -makes-800-million-advance-payment-for-russian-s-400-air-defense-systems.

19. Dinakar Peri, "Payment Issues over S-400 Deal Resolved: Russian Officials," *Hindu*, August 29, 2019, https://www.thehindu.com/news/national/payment-issues-over-s-400 -deal-resolved-russian-officials/article29281658.ece.

20. "SWIFT IN FIGURES, YTD June 2020," Swift, accessed August 15, 2020, https://www .swift.com/sites/default/files/files/SIF_202006.pdf.

21. Kazuhiro Kida, Masayuki Kubota, and Yusho Cho, "Rise of the Yuan: China-Based Payment Settlements Jump 80 Percent," *Nikkei Asia*, May 20, 2019, https://asia.nikkei.com /Business/Markets/Rise-of-the-yuan-China-based-payment-settlements-jump-80.

22. "Dethroning the Dollar: America's Aggressive Use of Sanctions Endangers the Dollar's Reign," *Economist*, January 18, 2020, https://www.economist.com/briefing/2020/01/18 /americas-aggressive-use-of-sanctions-endangers-the-dollars-reign.

23. "China's Global Payment System for Yuan Sees Limited Launch," *South China Morning Post*, October 9, 2015, https://www.scmp.com/business/banking-finance/article /1865370/chinas-global-payment-system-yuan-sees-limited-launch.

24. "CIPS to Break Chinese Banks' Global Monopoly over Yuan Clearing," *South China Morning Post*, September 11, 2015, https://www.scmp.com/business/banking-finance /article/1857121/cips-break-chinese-banks-global-monopoly-over-yuan-clearing.

25. Saikat Chatterjee, "Exclusive—China's Payments System Scaled Back; Trade Deals Only: Sources," Reuters, July 13, 2015, https://uk.reuters.com/article/uk-china-yuan -payments/exclusive-chinas-payments-system-scaled-back-trade-deals-only-sources -idUKKCN0PN0P020150713.

26. Kida, Kubota, and Cho, "Rise of the yuan."

27. Peter Harrell and Elizabeth Rosenberg, "Economic Dominance, Financial Technology, and the Future of U.S. Economic Coercion," Center for a New American Security, April 29, 2019, https://www.cnas.org/publications/reports/economic-dominance-financial -technology-and-the-future-of-u-s-economic-coercion.

28. Cheng Leng, Zhang Yan, and Ryan Woo, "Chinese Banks Urged to Switch Away from SWIFT as U.S. Sanctions Loom," Reuters, July 29, 2020, https://www.reuters.com/article /us-china-banks-usa-sanctions/chinese-banks-urged-to-switch-away-from-swift-as -u-s-sanctions-loom-idUSKCN24U0SN.

29. "Factbox: What Is China's Onshore Yuan Clearing and Settlement System CIPS?" Reuters, February 28, 2022, https://www.reuters.com/markets/europe/what-is-chinas -onshore-yuan-clearing-settlement-system-cips-2022-02-28.

30. "Announcement of Additional Treasury Sanctions on Russian Financial Institutions and on a Defense Technology Entity," U.S. Treasury, July 29, 2014, https://www.treasury.gov/press-center/press-releases/pages/jl2590.aspx.

31. "VTB Bank Connects to CIPS," Finextra, March 10, 2016, https://www.finextra.com/pressarticle/63508/vtb-bank-connects-to-cips.

32. "FACTBOX—China's Onshore Yuan Clearing and Settlement System CIPS," Reuters, July 30, 2020, https://www.reuters.com/article/china-banks-clearing-idUSL3N2F115E.

33. Jonathan Hillman, "China and Russia: Economic Unequals," Center for Strategic & International Studies, July 15, 2020, https://www.csis.org/analysis/china-and-russia-economic-unequals.

34. "The Financial World's Nervous System Is Being Rewired," Economist, May 9, 2020, https://www.economist.com/special-report/2020/05/07/the-financial-worlds-nervous-system-is-being-rewired.

35. "Report to Congress of the U.S.-China Economic and Security Review Commission," U.S. Congress, November 2019, https://www.uscc.gov/sites/default/files/2019-11/2019%20Annual%20Report%20to%20Congress.pdf.

36. Author's calculations using Economist Intelligence Unit data, January 2022.

37. "UPI Product Statistics," National Payments Corporation of India, accessed January 23, 2022, https://www.npci.org.in/product-statistics/upi-product-statistics.

38. "Poverty and Equity Brief: India," World Bank, October 2020, https://databank.worldbank.org/data/download/poverty/987B9C90-CB9F-4D93-AE8C-750588BF00QA/AM2020/Global_POVEQ_IND.pdf.

39. Andrey Ostroukh and Elena Fabrichnaya, "Russia Backs Global Use of Its Alternative SWIFT System," Reuters, March 19, 2019, https://uk.reuters.com/article/russia-banks-swift/russia-backs-global-use-of-its-alternative-swift-system-idUKL8N2163BU.

40. "The Financial World's Nervous System Is Being Rewired," Economist.

41. Natasha Turak, "Russia's Central Bank Governor Touts Moscow Alternative to SWIFT Transfer System as Protection from US Sanctions," CNBC, May 23, 2018, https://www.cnbc.com/2018/05/23/russias-central-bank-governor-touts-moscow-alternative-to-swift-transfer-system-as-protection-from-us-sanctions.html.

42. Andrey Ostroukh, "Russia Says BRICS Nations Favour Idea of Common Payment System," Reuters, November 14, 2019, https://www.reuters.com/article/uk-brics-summit-russia-fx/russia-says-brics-nations-favour-idea-of-common-payment-system-idUSKBN1XO1KQ.

43. Virginie Robert, "Pierre Vimont: 'Il faut que l'Europe soit capable de montrer qu'on peut mordre face aux sanctions extraterritoriales,'" Les Echos, March 22, 2021, https://www.lesechos.fr/monde/enjeux-internationaux/pierre-vimont-il-faut-que-leurope-soit-capable-de-montrer-quon-peut-mordre-face-aux-sanctions-extraterritoriales-1300265.

44. Simond de Galbert, "Transatlantic Economic Statecraft," Center for a New American Security, June 21, 2016, https://www.cnas.org/publications/reports/transatlantic-economic-statecraft-the-challenge-to-building-a-balanced-transatlantic-sanctions-policy-between-the-united-states-and-the-european-union.

45. Tom Keatinge, Emil Dall, Aniseh Bassiri Tabrizi, and Sarah Lain, "Transatlantic (Mis) alignment: Challenges to US-EU Sanctions Design and Implementation," Royal United Services Institute, July 7, 2017, https://rusi.org/sites/default/files/20170707_transatlantic _misalignment_keatinge.dall_.tabrizi.lain_final.pdf.

46. Ellie Geranmayeh and Manuel Lafont Rapnouil, "Meeting the Challenge of Secondary Sanctions," European Council on Foreign Relations, June 2019, https://www.ecfr.eu /page/-/4_Meeting_the_challenge_of_secondary_sanctions.pdf.

47. Keatinge, Dall, Bassiri Tabrizi, and Lain, "Transatlantic (Mis)alignment."

48. Marcin Szczepański, "Economic Impact on the EU of Sanctions over Ukraine Conflict," European Parliament, October 2015, https://www.europarl.europa.eu/RegData /etudes/BRIE/2015/569020/EPRS_BRI(2015)569020_EN.pdf.

49. David Enrich, Gabriele Steinhauser, and Matthew Dalton, "Loopholes Blunt Impact of U.S., EU Sanctions over Ukraine," Wall Street Journal, July 30, 2014, https://www.wsj .com/articles/eu-units-of-russian-banks-exempt-from-sanctions-1406714101.

50. Rick Gladstone, "U.S. Says Greek Executive Evaded Sanctions on Iran," New York Times, March 14, 2013, https://www.nytimes.com/2013/03/15/world/middleeast/us-says -a-greek-helped-iran-evade-sanctions.html.

51. Geranmayeh and Rapnouil, "Meeting the Challenge of Secondary Sanctions."

52. Niklas Helwig and Juha Jokela, "Future Prospects: Adapting to the Geo-economic Environment," in Sharpening EU Sanctions Policy for a Geopolitical Era, ed. Niklas Helwig, Juha Jokela, and Clara Portela (Helsinki: Publications of the Government's Analysis, Assessment and Research Activities, 2020), https://www.fiia.fi/wp-content /uploads/2020/05/vnteas_report_sharpening-eu-sanctions-policy-for-a-geopolitical -era.pdf.

53. Jonathan Hackenbroich, "Defending Europe's Economic Sovereignty: New Ways to Resist Economic Coercion," European Council on Foreign Relations, October 20, 2020, https://ecfr.eu/publication/defending_europe_economic_sovereignty_new_ways _to_resist_economic_coercion.

54. "Joint Statement on the Creation of INSTEX, the Special Purpose Vehicle Aimed at Facilitating Legitimate Trade with Iran in the Framework of the Efforts to Preserve the Joint Comprehensive Plan of Action (JCPOA)," E3 Foreign Ministers, January 31, 2019, https://www.diplomatie.gouv.fr/en/country-files/iran/news/article/joint-statement -on-the-creation-of-instex-the-special-purpose-vehicle-aimed-at.

55. "European Union, Trade in Goods with Iran," European Commission, May 8, 2020, https://webgate.ec.europa.eu/isdb_results/factsheets/country/details_iran_en.pdf.

56. Jim Brunsden, Sam Fleming, and Philip Stafford, "EU Sets Out Plans to Curb Reliance on Dollar in Post-Trump Era," Financial Times, January 16, 2021, https://www.ft.com /content/20f39e33-e360-479e-82e2-5441d24f0e0b.

57. "Communication from the Commission to the European Parliament, the Council, the European Central Bank, the European Economic and Social Committee and the Committee of the Regions, the European Economic and Financial System: Fostering Openness, Strength and Resilience," European Commission, January 19, 2021, https://eur-lex .europa.eu/legal-content/EN/TXT/HTML/?uri=CELEX:52021DC0032&from=EN.

58. Kit Rees and Viktoria Dendrinou, "EU Sets Out Plans to Limit U.S. Dollar Reli-
     ance, Boost Euro," Bloomberg, January 16, 2021, https://www.bloomberg.com/news
     /articles/2021-01-16/eu-draft-sets-out-plans-to-limit-u-s-dollar-reliance-ft.
59. Geranmayeh and Rapnouil, "Meeting the Challenge of Secondary Sanctions."
60. "The International Role of the Euro," European Central Bank, accessed March 18, 2021,
     https://www.ecb.europa.eu/pub/ire/html/ecb.ire202006~81495c263a.en.html.
61. "Dethroning the Dollar," *Economist*.
62. Geranmayeh and Rapnouil, "Meeting the Challenge of Secondary Sanctions."
63. Kate Duguid, "Iran Oil Sanctions Could Advance China's 'Petro-yuan,'" Reuters, May 10,
     2018, https://uk.reuters.com/article/uk-iran-nuclear-china-oil/iran-oil-sanctions-could
     -advance-chinas-petro-yuan-idUKKBN1IB32H.
64. Max Seddon and Henry Foy, "Russia Looks at Alternatives to Dollar for Energy Trans-
     actions," *Financial Times*, October 13, 2019, https://www.ft.com/content/704cde6c-eb53
     -11e9-a240-3b065ef5fc55.

9. DOING DOWN THE DOLLAR

1.   Nikhilesh De, "In Wargaming Exercise, a Digital Renminbi Neuters US Sanctions and
     North Korea Buys Nukes," MIT Media Lab, November 20, 2019, https://www.media
     .mit.edu/articles/in-wargaming-exercise-a-digital-yuan-neuters-us-sanctions-and
     -north-korea-buys-nukes.
2.   Natasha Bright, "Sanctioned Nations Explore Bypassing Swift," Association of Certified
     Sanctions Specialists, February 6, 2020, https://sanctionsassociation.org/sanctioned
     -nations-explore-bypassing-swift.
3.   Clea Simon, "Cryptocurrency and National Insecurity," *Harvard Gazette*, November 20,
     2019, https://news.harvard.edu/gazette/story/2019/11/crisis-simulation-maps-national
     -security-risks-of-digital-currency.
4.   Raju Gopalakrishnan and Manuel Mogato, "Bangladesh Bank Official's Computer Was
     Hacked to Carry Out $81 Million Heist: Diplomat," Reuters, May 19, 2016, https://www
     .reuters.com/article/us-cyber-heist-philippines-idUSKCN0YA0CH.
5.   James Areddy, "China Creates Its Own Digital Currency, a First for Major Economy,"
     Wall Street Journal, April 5, 2021, https://www.wsj.com/articles/china-creates-its-own
     -digital-currency-a-first-for-major-economy-11617634118.
6.   "Top 100 Cryptocurrencies by Market Capitalization," CoinMarketCap, accessed May
     13, 2022, https://coinmarketcap.com.
7.   Ruchir Sharma, "Will Bitcoin End the Dollar's Reign?," *Financial Times*, December 9,
     2020, https://www.ft.com/content/ea33b688-12e0-459c-80c5-2efba58e6f1a.
8.   "Bitcoin at 'Tipping Point,' Citi Says as Price Surges," Reuters, March 1, 2021, https://
     www.reuters.com/article/us-crypto-currency-bitcoin-citi-idUSKCN2AT23H.
9.   Peter Harrell and Elizabeth Rosenberg, "Economic Dominance, Financial Technology,
     and the Future of U.S. Economic Coercion," Center for a New American Security,
     April 29, 2019, https://www.cnas.org/publications/reports/economic-dominance-financial
     -technology-and-the-future-of-u-s-economic-coercion.

10. Thomas Erdbrink, "How Bitcoin Could Help Iran Undermine U.S. Sanctions," *New York Times*, January 29, 2019, https://www.nytimes.com/2019/01/29/world/middleeast/bitcoin-iran-sanctions.html.

11. Ellen Nakashima, "U.S. Accuses Three North Koreans of Conspiring to Steal More than $1.3 Billion in Cash and Cryptocurrency," *Washington Post*, February 18, 2021, https://www.washingtonpost.com/national-security/north-korea-hackers-banks-theft/2021/02/17/3dccfodc-7129-11eb-93be-c10813e358a2_story.html.

12. "The Financial World's Nervous System Is Being Rewired," *Economist*, May 9, 2020, https://www.economist.com/special-report/2020/05/07/the-financial-worlds-nervous-system-is-being-rewired.

13. Natasha Bright, "Do Cryptocurrencies Pose a Sanctions Risk?," Association of Certified Sanctions Specialists, October 4, 2019, https://sanctionsassociation.org/do-cryptocurrencies-pose-a-sanctions-risk.

14. Tanvi Ratna, "Iran Has a Bitcoin Strategy to Beat Trump," *Foreign Policy*, January 24, 2020, https://foreignpolicy.com/2020/01/24/iran-bitcoin-strategy-cryptocurrency-blockchain-sanctions.

15. "Sanctions Compliance for Banks in the Age of Crypto-assets," LexisNexis, June 5, 2020, https://blogs.lexisnexis.com/financial-crime-in-focus/sanctions-compliance-for-banks-in-the-age-of-crypto-assets.

16. Author's calculations using Swift, CHIPS, and Fedwire data.

17. Justin Scheck and Shane Shifflett, "How Dirty Money Disappears into the Black Hole of Cryptocurrency," *Wall Street Journal*, September 28, 2018, https://www.wsj.com/articles/how-dirty-money-disappears-into-the-black-hole-of-cryptocurrency-1538149743.

18. Ratna, "Iran Has a Bitcoin Strategy to Beat Trump."

19. Wei Chew, "The Future of China's Blockchain Industry," Medium, May 22, 2018, https://medium.com/hackernoon/the-future-of-chinas-blockchain-industry-7a1c37abcef.

20. Harrell and Rosenberg, "Economic Dominance, Financial Technology."

21. "China Needs First Mover Advantage in Digital Currency Race: PBOC Magazine," Reuters, September 21, 2020, https://www.reuters.com/article/china-pboc-renminnbi-digital/refile-china-needs-first-mover-advantage-in-digital-currency-race-pboc-magazine-idUSL3N2GI11F.

22. Chew, "The Future of China's Blockchain Industry."

23. Tanzeel Akhtar, "People's Bank of China Official Says Fully Anonymous Digital Yuan 'Not Feasible,'" Coindesk, March 22, 2021, https://www.coindesk.com/peoples-bank-of-china-official-says-fully-anonymous-digital-yuan-not-feasible.

24. Evelyn Cheng, "China's Digital Yuan Notches $8.3 Billion in Transactions in 6 Months, Taking a Tiny Share of Payments," CNBC, January 18, 2022, https://www.cnbc.com/2022/01/18/chinas-digital-yuan-notches-8point3-billion-transactions-in-half-a-year.html.

25. Arjun Kharpal, "China Launches App for Its Own Digital Currency as It Looks to Expand Usage," CNBC, January 4, 2022, https://www.cnbc.com/2022/01/04/china-launches-digital-currency-app-to-expand-usage.html.

26. Narayanan Somasundaram, "China Sets Trial Run for Digital Renminbi in Top City Hubs," *Nikkei Asia*, August 14, 2020, https://asia.nikkei.com/Business/China-tech/China-sets-trial-run-for-digital-yuan-in-top-city-hubs.

27. "The Financial World's Nervous System Is Being Rewired," *Economist.*

28. James Kynge and Sun Yu, "Virtual Control: The Agenda Behind China's New Digital Currency," *Financial Times*, February 17, 2021, https://www.ft.com/content/7511809e -827e-4526-81ad-ae83f405f623.

29. David Pan, "How Ant's Suspended IPO Is Related to China's Digital Yuan," Coindesk, November 12, 2020, https://www.coindesk.com/how-ants-suspended-ipo-is-related-to -chinas-digital-yuan.

30. Issaku Harada, "China Aims to Launch Digital Yuan by 2022 Winter Olympics," *Nikkei Asia*, May 27, 2020, https://asia.nikkei.com/Spotlight/Cryptocurrencies/China-aims -to-launch-digital-yuan-by-2022-Winter-Olympics.

31. Cissy Zhou, "China's Digital Currency Edges Closer with Large-Scale Test by Four State-Owned Banks," *South China Morning Post*, August 6, 2020, https://www.scmp .com/economy/china-economy/article/3096296/chinas-digital-currency-edges-closer -large-scale-test-four.

32. Veta Chan, "'An Absolute Necessity': Why This Expert Says China Desperately Needs a Digital Currency," *Fortune*, July 30, 2020, https://fortune.com/2020/07/30 /china-digital-currency-renminnbi-cbdc.

33. David Pan, "Goldman Sachs Expects Digital Yuan to Reach 1B Users Within 10 Years," Coindesk, November 19, 2020, https://www.coindesk.com/goldman-sachs-digital-yuan -report.

34. Qian Chen, "The Good, the Bad and the Ugly of a Chinese State-Backed Digital Currency," CNBC, November 22, 2019, https://www.cnbc.com/2019/11/22/chinese-crypto -beijing-sees-opportunity-but-concerns-linger.html.

35. Jason Brett, "Trend Continues for Countries Looking to Evade U.S. Sanctions Using Crypto," *Forbes*, January 29, 2020, https://www.forbes.com/sites/jasonbrett/2020/01/29 /trend-continues-for-countries-looking-to-evade-us-sanctions-using-crypto.

36. Mercedes Ruehl and James Kynge, "The US's Big Plan to Cut Supply Chain Reliance on China," *Financial Times*, February 24, 2021, https://www.ft.com/content /6bc86e88-81d6-4f3b-8e30-337ca640c760.

37. Author's calculations using Economist Intelligence Unit data, January 2022.

38. Gillian Tett, "Central Bankers' Crypto Experiments Should Put Investors on Alert," *Financial Times*, March 25, 2021, https://www.ft.com/content/8356521a-0bb1-4a80-973b -a9c6d60a0f19.

39. "China Needs First Mover Advantage," Reuters.

40. Stewart Paterson, "The Digital Renminbi and China's Potential Financial Revolution: A Primer on Central Bank Digital Currencies," Hinrich Foundation, July 2020, https:// www.hinrichfoundation.com/media/2kybhumm/hinrich-foundation-white-paper -digitual-yuan-and-china-s-potential-financial-revolution-july-2020.pdf.

41. Gideon Rachmann, "A New Cold War: Trump, Xi and the Escalating US-China Confrontation," *Financial Times*, October 5, 2020, https://www.ft.com/content/7b809c6a -f733-46f5-a312-9152aed28172.

42. Author's calculations using Economist Intelligence Unit data, January 2022.

43. Author's calculations using Economist Intelligence Unit data, January 2022.

44. Author's calculations using Economist Intelligence Unit data, January 2022.

45. "As China Goes Global, Its Banks Are Coming Out, Too," *Economist*, May 9, 2020, https://www.economist.com/special-report/2020/05/07/as-china-goes-global-its -banks-are-coming-out-too.

46. "China Now Has the World's Second Largest Bond Market After the US," Bank of Finland Institute for Emerging Economies (BOFIT), July 30, 2021, https://www.bofit.fi/en /monitoring/weekly/2021/vw202130_2.

47. "China Wants to Make the Renminbi a Central-Bank Favourite," *Economist*, May 9, 2020, https://www.economist.com/special-report/2020/05/07/china-wants-to-make-the -renminnbi-a-central-bank-favourite.

48. "China Wants to Make the Renminbi a Central-Bank Favourite," *Economist*.

49. "China Wants to Make the Renminbi a Central-Bank Favourite," *Economist*.

50. "The International Role of the Euro," European Central Bank, accessed March 18, 2021, https://www.ecb.europa.eu/pub/ire/html/ecb.ire202006~81495c263a.en.html.

51. "International Trade in Goods," Eurostat, accessed March 2, 2021, https://ec.europa.eu /eurostat/statistics-explained/index.php/International_trade_in_goods.

52. Edoardo Saravalle, "How U.S. Sanctions Depend on the Federal Reserve," Center for a New American Security, July 29, 2020, https://www.cnas.org/publications/commentary /how-u-s-sanctions-depend-on-the-federal-reserve.

53. Tommy Stubbington, "EU Enjoys 'Outrageous Demand' for First Covid-Related Bond," *Financial Times*, October 20, 2020, https://www.ft.com/content/e3553b68-22c8 -487c-a7c0-7e1c6dc0ec4b.

54. Sam Fleming, Mehreen Khan, and Jim Brunsden, "EU Leaders Strike Deal on €750bn Recovery Fund After Marathon Summit," *Financial Times*, July 21, 2020, https://www .ft.com/content/713be467-ed19-4663-95ff-66f775af55cc.

55. "We Must Be Prepared to Issue a Digital Euro," European Central Bank, October 2, 2020, https://www.ecb.europa.eu/press/blog/date/2020/html/ecb.blog201002~12ab1c06b5 .en.html.

56. Ferdinando Giugliano, "Europe Is Planning Its Very Own E-Currency," Bloomberg, November 16, 2020, https://www.bloomberg.com/opinion/articles/2020-11-16/christine -lagarde-s-ecb-is-planning-its-very-own-e-currency.

57. "Report on a Digital Euro," European Central Bank, October 2020, https://www.ecb .europa.eu/pub/pdf/other/Report_on_a_digital_euro~4d7268b458.en.pdf.

58. William Schomberg, "World Needs to End Risky Reliance on U.S. Dollar: BoE's Carney," Reuters, August 23, 2019, https://www.reuters.com/article/us-usa-fed -jacksonhole-carney-idUSKCN1VD28C.

59. Michael Greenwald, "The Future of the Dollar in a Post-Iran Deal World," Atlantic Council, October 29, 2018, https://www.atlanticcouncil.org/blogs/new-atlanticist/the -future-of-the-dollar-in-a-post-iran-deal-world.

60. Miriam Campanella, "Far-reaching Consequences of U.S. Financial Sanctions," Robert Triffin International, June 2019, http://triffininternational.eu/publications/articles -papers/1285-far-reaching-consequences-of-u-s-financial-sanctions-the-dollar-shortage -and-the-triffin-moment.

61. Author's calculations using Economist Intelligence Unit data, January 2022.

62. Author's calculations using Economist Intelligence Unit data, January 2022.

63. "United States of America: Staff Concluding Statement of the 2020 Article IV Mission," IMF, July 17, 2020, https://www.imf.org/en/News/Articles/2020/07/17/mcs-071720-united -states-of-america-staff-concluding-statement-of-the-2020-article-iv-mission.

64. Sharma, "Will Bitcoin End the Dollar's Reign?"

65. "The Pandemic's True Death Toll," *Economist*, accessed January 23, 2022, https://www .economist.com/graphic-detail/coronavirus-excess-deaths-estimates.

66. Colby Smith, Eva Szalay, and Katie Martin, "Dollar Blues: Why the Pandemic Is Testing Confidence in the US Currency," *Financial Times*, July 31, 2020, https://www.ft.com /content/7c963379-10df-4314-9bd0-351ddcdc699e.

67. "Down but Not Out? Globalisation and the Threat of Covid-19," Economist Intelli- gence Unit, July 2020, https://www.eiu.com/public/topical_report.aspx?campaignid =globalisation-covid.

68. Barry Eichengreen, Arnaud Mehl, and Livia Chiţu, *How Global Currencies Work: Past, Present, and Future* (Princeton, NJ: Princeton University Press, 2018).

69. "Currency Composition of Official Foreign Exchange Reserves (COFER)," IMF, accessed January 22, 2022, https://data.imf.org/?sk=E6A5F467-C14B-4AA8-9F6D -5A09EC4E62A4.

70. Alina Iancu, "Reserve Currencies in an Evolving International Monetary System," IMF Departmental Papers (Washington, DC: International Monetary Fund, November 2020), https://www.imf.org/en/Publications/Departmental-Papers-Policy-Papers/Issues /2020/11/17/Reserve-Currencies-in-an-Evolving-International-Monetary-System-49864.

71. Evelyn Cheng, "China's Renminbi Could Become the World's Third Largest Reserve Currency in 10 Years, Morgan Stanley Predicts," CNBC, September 4, 2020, https:// www.cnbc.com/2020/09/04/chinas-renminnbi-rmb-to-become-third-largest-reserve -currency-by-2030-morgan-stanley.html.

72. "IMF Adds Chinese Renminbi to Special Drawing Rights Basket," IMF, September 30, 2016, https://www.imf.org/en/News/Articles/2016/09/29/AM16-NA093016IMF-Adds -Chinese-Renminbi-to-Special-Drawing-Rights-Basket.

73. Richard Nephew, "China and Economic Sanctions: Where Does Washington Have Leverage?," Brookings, September 2019, https://www.brookings.edu/research/china-and -economic-sanctions-where-does-washington-have-leverage.

74. Anna Yukhananov and Warren Strobel, "After Success on Iran, U.S. Treasury's Sanc- tions Team Faces New Challenges," Reuters, April 15, 2014, https://www.reuters.com /article/us-usa-sanctions-insight/after-success-on-iran-u-s-treasurys-sanctions-team -faces-new-challenges-idUSBREA3D1O820140415.

75. Darren Lim, "Chinese Economic Coercion During the THAAD Dispute," The Asan Forum, December 28, 2019, www.theasanforum.org/chinese-economic-coercion-during -the-thaad-dispute.

76. Lim, "Chinese Economic Coercion During the THAAD Dispute."

10. HIGH-TECH FUTURE

1. "Interior Department Grounds Drone Fleet Amid Concerns of Chinese Spying," Cnet.com, January 29, 2020, https://www.cnet.com/news/interior-department-officially-grounds -drones-made-in-china.

2. Elizabeth Rosenberg, Peter Harrell, and Ashley Feng, "A New Arsenal for Competition, Coercive Economic Measures in the U.S.-China Relationship," Center for a New American Security, April 24, 2020, https://www.cnas.org/publications/reports/a-new-arsenal-for -competition.

3. Kiran Stacey, "US to Ground Civilian Drone Programme on Concerns over China Tech," *Financial Times*, January 12, 2020, https://www.ft.com/content/a50088de-33f6 -11ea-9703-eeaocae3fode.

4. Lisa Friedman and David McCabe, "Interior Dept. Grounds Its Drones over Chinese Spying Fears," *New York Times*, January 29, 2020, https://www.nytimes.com/2020/01/29 /technology/interior-chinese-drones.html.

5. Kiran Stacey, "Trump Ban on Chinese Drone Parts Risks Worsening Wildfires," *Financial Times*, August 31, 2020, https://www.ft.com/content/387d2270-eded-4b8d-80e9 -b23dd7ff694a.

6. "Department of the Interior Recognizes IGNIS Technology," Ignis, January 17, 2019, https://droneamplified.com/department-of-the-interior-recognizes-ignis-technology.

7. Stacey, "US to Ground Civilian Drone Programme."

8. Mark Magnier, "In the Crosshairs: Chinese Drones a Target for US Ban as Security Risk," *South China Morning Post*, December 10, 2019, https://www.scmp.com/news/china /article/3041073/crosshairs-chinese-drones-target-us-ban-security-risk.

9. "Current Year Statistics," Cal Fire, accessed October 12, 2020, https://www.fire.ca.gov /stats-events.

10. Karen Sutter, "U.S.-China Trade and Economic Relations: Overview," Congressional Research Service, accessed October 13, 2020, https://fas.org/sgp/crs/row/IF11284.pdf.

11. "Findings of the Investigation into China's Acts, Policies, and Practices Related to Tech-nology Transfer, Intellectual Property, and Innovation Under Section 301 of the Trade Act of 1974," U.S. Trade Representative, March 22, 2018, https://ustr.gov/sites/default /files/Section%20301%20FINAL.PDF.

12. "Foreign Spies Stealing US Economic Secrets in Cyberspace, Report to Congress on Foreign Economic Collection and Industrial Espionage, 2009–2011," U.S. Office of the National Counterintelligence Executive, October 2011, https://www.dni.gov/files /documents/Newsroom/Reports%20and%20Pubs/20111103_report_fecie.pdf.

13. James Lewis, "Tech Crisis with China," Center for Strategic & International Studies, August 7, 2020, https://www.csis.org/analysis/tech-crisis-china.

14. Kathrin Hille, "The Great Uncoupling: One Supply Chain for China, One for Every-where Else," *Financial Times*, October 6, 2020, https://www.ft.com/content/40ebd786 -a576-4dc2-ad38-b97f796b72a0.

15. Raphael Satter, "Exclusive-Suspected Chinese Hackers Stole Camera Footage from African Union—Memo," Reuters, December 16, 2020, https://in.mobile.reuters.com /article/amp/idINKBN28Q1DB.

16. Joan Tilouine and Ghalia Kadiri, "A Addis-Abeba, le siège de l'Union africaine espionné par Pékin," *Le Monde*, January 26, 2018, https://www.lemonde.fr/afrique/article/2018/01/26 /a-addis-abeba-le-siege-de-l-union-africaine-espionne-par-les-chinois_5247521_3212.html.

17. Rosenberg, Harrell, and Feng, "A New Arsenal for Competition."

18. Gideon Rachmann, "A New Cold War: Trump, Xi and the Escalating US-China Confrontation," *Financial Times*, October 5, 2020, https://www.ft.com/content/7b809c6a -f733-46f5-a312-9152aed28172.

19. Rosenberg, Harrell, and Feng, "A New Arsenal for Competition."

20. "Notes from a CSIS Virtual Event: Strategic Competition and the U.S. Semiconductor Industry," Center for Strategic and International Studies, July 23, 2020, https://csis-website -prod.s3.amazonaws.com/s3fs-public/event/200724_Semiconductor_Industry.pdf.

21. Bob Davis and Yuka Hayashi, "New Trade Representative Says U.S. Isn't Ready to Lift China Tariffs," *Wall Street Journal*, March 28, 2021, https://www.wsj.com/articles /new-trade-representative-says-u-s-isnt-ready-to-lift-china-tariffs-11616929200.

22. Pete Schroder, "U.S. Lawmakers Seek to Ban Federal Pension Fund from Investing in China," Reuters, November 6, 2019, https://www.reuters.com/article/us-usa-trade -rubio-tsp-idUSKBN1XG2QO.

23. "America Files a New Financial Salvo at Beijing," *Economist*, May 16, 2020, https:// www.economist.com/finance-and-economics/2020/05/14/america-files-a-new -financial-salvo-at-beijing.

24. Author's calculations using Economist Intelligence Unit data, January 2022.

25. Mary Amiti, Stephen J. Redding, and David Weinstein, "The Impact of the 2018 Trade War on U.S. Prices and Welfare," Centre for Economic Performance, March 2019, http://cep.lse.ac.uk/pubs/download/dp1603.pdf.

26. "How America Might Wield Its Ultimate Weapon of Mass Disruption," *Economist*, August 15, 2020, https://www.economist.com/business/2020/08/13/how-america-might -wield-its-ultimate-weapon-of-mass-disruption.

27. "American National-Security Maximalism Can Be Self-Defeating," *Economist*, August 22, 2020, https://www.economist.com/united-states/2020/08/20/american-national -security-maximalism-can-be-self-defeating.

28. "America's Latest Salvo Against Huawei Is Aimed at Chipmaking in China," *Economist*, May 23, 2020, https://www.economist.com/business/2020/05/23/americas-latest -salvo-against-huawei-is-aimed-at-chipmaking-in-china.

29. "Measuring Distortions in International Markets: The Semiconductor Value Chain," Organization for Economic Cooperation and Development, December 12, 2019, https://doi.org/10.1787/8fe4491d-en.

30. Antonio Varas and Raj Varadarajan, "How Restrictions to Trade with China Could End US Leadership in Semiconductors," Boston Consulting Group, March 2020, https:// image-src.bcg.com/Images/BCG-How-Restricting-Trade-with-China-Could-End -US-Semiconductor-Mar-2020_tcm9-240526.pdf.

31. Ian Fergusson and Karen Sutter, "U.S. Export Control Reforms and China: Issues for Congress," Congressional Research Service, accessed October 13, 2020, https://crsreports .congress.gov/product/pdf/IF/IF11627.

32. "Global Semiconductor Sales Increase 24 Percent Year-to-Year in October; Annual Sales Projected to Increase 26 Percent in 2021, Exceed $600 Billion in 2022," Semiconductor Industry Association, December 3, 2021, https://www.semiconductors.org /global-semiconductor-sales-increase-24-year-to-year-in-october-annual-sales-projected -to-increase-26-in-2021-exceed-600-billion-in-2022.

33. Chris Miller, "America Is Going to Decapitate Huawei," *New York Times*, September 15, 2020, https://www.nytimes.com/2020/09/15/opinion/united-states-huawei.html.

34. Aurélien Duthoit, "China: Riding the Silicon Ox?," Euler Hermes, February 9, 2021, https://www.eulerhermes.com/en_global/news-insights/economic-insights/China -Riding-the-silicon-ox.html.

35. Lauly Li, Cheng Ting-Fang, and Yifan Yu, "How a Handful of US Companies Can Cripple Huawei's Supply Chain," *Nikkei Asia*, August 19, 2020, https://asia.nikkei .com/Spotlight/Huawei-crackdown/How-a-handful-of-US-companies-can-cripple -Huawei-s-supply-chain.

36. Varas and Varadarajan, "How Restrictions to Trade with China Could End US Leadership in Semiconductors."

37. "The 2020 SIA Factbook: Your Source for Semiconductor Industry Data," Semiconductor Industry Association, accessed October 13, 2020, https://www.semiconductors.org /the-2020-sia-factbook-your-source-for-semiconductor-industry-data.

38. "Notes from a CSIS Virtual Event," Center for Strategic and International Studies.

39. Chad Bown, "The US Is Trying to Use Export Controls to Restrict Huawei's Access to Semiconductors," Peterson Institute for International Economics, October 13, 2020, https://www.piie.com/research/piie-charts/us-trying-use-export-controls-restrict -huaweis-access-semiconductors.

40. Chad Bown, "How Trump's Export Curbs on Semiconductors and Equipment Hurt the US Technology Sector," Peterson Institute for International Economics, September 28, 2020, https://www.piie.com/blogs/trade-and-investment-policy-watch/how-trumps -export-curbs-semiconductors-and-equipment-hurt-us.

41. Li, Ting-Fang, and Yu, "How a Handful of US Companies Can Cripple Huawei's Supply Chain."

42. Li, Ting-Fang, and Yu, "How a Handful of US Companies Can Cripple Huawei's Supply Chain."

43. "Semiconductor Design and Manufacturing: Achieving Leading-Edge Capabilities," McKinsey & Company, August 20, 2020, https://www.mckinsey.com/industries /advanced-electronics/our-insights/semiconductor-design-and-manufacturing -achieving-leading-edge-capabilities.

44. Cheng Ting-Fang and Lauly Li, "China's SMIC Stockpiles Chip Equipment to Counter US Restrictions," *Nikkei Asia*, September 30, 2020, https://asia.nikkei.com /Politics/International-relations/US-China-tensions/China-s-SMIC-stockpiles-chip -equipment-to-counter-US-restrictions.

45. Alex Webb, "The $150 Million Machine with $200 Billion at Stake for China," Bloomberg, January 16, 2020, https://www.bloomberg.com/opinion/articles/2020-01-16/dutch-ban-raises-stakes-in-u-s-china-technology-war.

46. Ting-Fang and Li, "China's SMIC Stockpiles Chip Equipment."

47. "Measuring Distortions in International Markets," Organization for Economic Cooperation and Development.

48. "Measuring Distortions in International Markets," Organization for Economic Cooperation and Development.

49. "Semiconductor Design and Manufacturing," McKinsey & Company.

50. Chad Bown, "Export Controls: America's Other National Security Threat," Peterson Institute for International Economics, May 2020, https://www.piie.com/system/files/documents/wp20-8.pdf.

51. "H.R.5040—Export Control Reform Act of 2018," U.S. Congress, April 17, 2018, https://www.congress.gov/bill/115th-congress/house-bill/5040/text.

52. Chad Bown, "Export Controls."

53. Rosenberg, Harrell, and Feng, "A New Arsenal for Competition."

54. "H.R.5841—Foreign Investment Risk Review Modernization Act of 2018," U.S. Congress, June 27, 2018, https://www.congress.gov/bill/115th-congress/house-bill/5040/text.

55. Stewart Paterson, "US-China Decoupling: How Far Could It Go?," Hinrich Foundation, September 2, 2020, https://www.hinrichfoundation.com/research/wp/us-china/us-china-decoupling.

56. Uptin Saiidi, "China's Foreign Direct Investment into the US Dropped Precipitously in 2018, Data Show," CNBC, January 15, 2019, https://www.cnbc.com/2019/01/15/chinese-foreign-direct-investment-to-the-us-falls-in-2018-data.html.

57. Rosenberg, Harrell, and Feng, "A New Arsenal for Competition."

58. "Addition of Entities to the Entity List," *Federal Register*, May 21, 2019, https://www.federalregister.gov/documents/2019/05/21/2019-10616/addition-of-entities-to-the-entity-list.

59. "Huawei Entity List and Temporary General License Frequently Asked Questions," U.S. Department of Commerce, accessed October 13, 2020, https://www.bis.doc.gov/index.php/documents/pdfs/2447-huawei-entity-listing-faqs/file.

60. Scott Kennedy, "America's Huawei Challenges," Center for Strategic and International Studies, July 31, 2020, https://www.csis.org/blogs/trustee-china-hand/americas-huawei-challenges.

61. Sutter, "U.S.-China Trade and Economic Relations: Overview."

62. David Shepardson, "U.S. Tightening Restrictions on Huawei Access to Technology, Chips," Reuters, August 17, 2020, https://www.reuters.com/article/us-usa-huawei-tech-exclusive/exclusive-u-s-to-tighten-restrictions-on-huawei-access-to-technology-chips-sources-say-idUSKCN25D1CC.

63. David Shepardson, Karen Freifeld, and Alexandra Alper, "U.S. Moves to Cut Huawei Off from Global Chip Suppliers as China Eyes Retaliation," Reuters, May 15, 2020, https://www.reuters.com/article/us-usa-huawei-tech-exclusive/exclusive-us-moves-to-cut-huawei-off-from-global-chip-suppliers-idUSKBN22R1KC.

64. Frank Bajak, "US Adds New Sanction on Chinese Tech Giant Huawei," Associated Press, May 16, 2020, https://apnews.com/article/22e139b05c8f6b8a9c910eebea8c295e.

65. Cheng Ting-Fang and Lauly Li, "Asia Suppliers Hit After US Cuts Huawei's Access to Foreign Chips," *Nikkei Asia*, August 18, 2020, https://asia.nikkei.com/Spotlight /Huawei-crackdown/Asia-suppliers-hit-after-US-cuts-Huawei-s-access-to-foreign-chips.

66. James Politi, Demetri Sevastopulo, and Hudson Locke, "US Adds China's Largest Chipmaker to Export Blacklist," *Financial Times*, December 18, 2020, https://www .ft.com/content/7dcc105e-986b-4768-9239-9f8fa9073b53https://www.ft.com/content /7dcc105e-986b-4768-9239-9f8fa9073b53.

67. Joe McDonald, "Huawei: Smartphone Chips Running Out Under US Sanctions," Associated Press, August 8, 2020, https://apnews.com/article/smartphones-technology-business -ap-top-news-china-270e93e985733a4d086c06a01375ceao.

68. Cheng Ting-Fang, Lauly Li, and Kenji Kawase, "China's Top Chipmaker SMIC Cuts Spending Due to US Export Curbs," *Nikkei Asia*, November 12, 2020, https://asia .nikkei.com/Economy/Trade-war/China-s-top-chipmaker-SMIC-cuts-spending-due -to-US-export-curbs.

69. Alexandra Alper, Toby Sterling, and Stephen Nellis, "Trump Administration Pressed Dutch Hard to Cancel China Chip-Equipment Sale: Sources," Reuters, January 6, 2020, https:// www.reuters.com/article/us-asml-holding-usa-china-insight-idUSKBN1Z50HN.

70. Ellen Proper, "ASML Stays Positive Despite Being Caught by U.S., China Rift," Bloomberg, October 14, 2020, https://www.bloomberg.com/news/articles/2020-10-14 /asml-expects-low-double-digit-growth-next-year-resumes-buybacks.

71. "Measuring Distortions in International Markets," Organization for Economic Cooperation and Development.

72. "Edited Transcript of ASML.AS Earnings Conference Call or Presentation 14-Oct-20 1:00pm GMT," Yahoo News, October 14, 2020, https://www.yahoo.com/amphtml/now /edited-transcript-asml-earnings-conference-130000661.html.

73. Jeanne Whalen, "Huawei Helped Bring Internet to Small-Town America. Now Its Equipment Has to Go," *Washington Post*, October 10, 2019, https://www.washingtonpost .com/business/2019/10/10/huawei-helped-bring-internet-small-town-america-now- its-equipment-has-go.

74. Kathrin Hille, Edward White, and Kana Inagaki, "US Allows Sales of Chips to Huawei's Non-5G Businesses," *Financial Times*, October 29, 2020, https://www.ft.com /content/508b0828-bcd5-46a6-84f8-d05cb2887e0a.

75. Akinori Kahata, "Semiconductors as Natural Resources—Exploring the National Security Dimensions of U.S.-China Technology Competition," Center for Strategic and International Studies, February 17, 2021, https://www.csis.org/blogs/technology-policy-blog /semiconductors-natural-resources---exploring-national-security.

76. Matt Sheehan, "China Technology 2025: Fragile Tech Superpower," Macro Polo, Paulson Institute, October 26, 2020, https://macropolo.org/analysis/china-technology-forecast -2025-fragile-tech-superpower.

77. Duthoit, "China: Riding the Silicon Ox?"

78. Taisei Hoyama and Yu Nakamura, "US and Allies to Build 'China-Free' Tech Supply Chain," *Nikkei Asia*, February 24, 2021, https://asia.nikkei.com/Politics/International-relations /Biden-s-Asia-policy/US-and-allies-to-build-China-free-tech-supply-chain.

79. Jeong-Ho Lee and Sohee Kim, "Biden Finds a Key Ally Wary of His Bid to Outpace China on Chips," Bloomberg, March 25, 2021, https://www.bloomberg.com/news /articles/2021-03-25/south-korea-s-chip-industry-is-trapped-between-the-u-s-and -china.

80. "Why Tiny Magnets Could Be China's Destructive New Trade-War Weapon," Bloomberg, June 5, 2019, https://www.bloomberg.com/news/articles/2019-06-05/why -tiny-magnets-could-be-china-s-destructive-new-trade-weapon.

81. Lucy Hornby and Henry Sanderson, "Rare Earths: Beijing Threatens a New Front in the Trade War," Financial Times, June 4, 2019, https://www.ft.com/content/3cd18372 -85e0-11e9-a028-86cea8523dc2.

82. "Rare Earths Give China Leverage in the Trade War, at a Cost," Economist, June 15, 2019, https://www.economist.com/china/2019/06/15/rare-earths-give-china-leverage-in -the-trade-war-at-a-cost.

83. Marc Humphries, "Critical Minerals and U.S. Public Policy," Congressional Research Service, accessed March 6, 2021, https://crsreports.congress.gov/product/pdf/R /R45810.

84. June Teufel Dreyer, "China's Monopoly on Rare Earth Elements—and Why We Should Care," Foreign Policy Research Institute, October 7, 2020, https://www.fpri .org/article/2020/10/chinas-monopoly-on-rare-earth-elements-and-why-we-should -care.

85. Teufel Dreyer, "China's Monopoly on Rare Earth Elements."

86. Yoichi Funabashi, "The Mideast Has Oil, China Has Rare Earths," Japan Times, August 9, 2019, https://www.japantimes.co.jp/opinion/2019/08/09/commentary/japan -commentary/mideast-oil-china-rare-earths.

87. Martijn Rasser and Ashley Feng, "This Is How to Solve America's Rare-Earths Dilemma," National Interest, June 28, 2019, https://nationalinterest.org/feature/how -solve-americas-rare-earths-dilemma-64751.

88. "Explainer: U.S. Dependence on China's Rare Earth—Trade War Vulnerability," Reuters, June 3, 2019, https://www.reuters.com/article/us-usa-trade-china-rareearth -explainer/explainer-u-s-dependence-on-chinas-rare-earth-trade-war-vulnerability -idUSKCN1T42RP.

89. David Lynch, "China Hints It Will Choke off U.S. 'Rare Earths' Access. But It's Not That Easy," Washington Post, June 10, 2019, https://www.washingtonpost.com/business /economy/2019/06/07/80a06794-8649-11e9-a491-25df61c78dc4_story.html.

90. "Does China Pose a Threat to Global Rare Earth Supply Chains?," Center for Strategic and International Studies, accessed October 14, 2020, https://chinapower.csis.org /china-rare-earths.

91. Nicholas Crawford, "Defending Against Economic Statecraft: China, the US and the Rest," International Institute for Strategic Studies, October 2020, https://www.iiss.org /blogs/analysis/2020/10/economic-statecraft-china-us.

92. Sun Yu and Demetri Sevastopulo, "China Targets Rare Earth Export Curbs to Hobble US Defence Industry," Financial Times, February 16, 2021, https://www.ft.com/content /d3ed83f4-19bc-4d16-b510-415749c032c1.

93. "China Passes New Law Restricting Sensitive Exports," Associated Press, October 18, 2020, https://apnews.com/article/technology-beijing-global-trade-china-national-security-396e42dbf147c9b55863fb90099303cb.

94. Ernest Scheyder, "EXCLUSIVE U.S. Bill Would Block Defense Contractors from Using Chinese Rare Earths," Reuters, January 14, 2022, https://www.reuters.com/business/energy/exclusive-us-bill-would-block-defense-contractors-using-chinese-rare-earths-2022-01-14.

95. "To Combat China's Hold on Rare Earth Minerals, Pentagon Looks to Australia," Defense-News.com, August 27, 2019, https://www.defensenews.com/pen-tagon/2019/08/27/to-combat-chinas-hold-on-rare-earth-minerals-pentagon-looks-to-australia.

96. Ernest Scheyder, "Miners Praise U.S. Spending Bill That Funds Rare Earths Programs," Reuters, December 30, 2020, https://www.reuters.com/article/us-usa-mining-congress-idUSKBN29424R.

97. Jamie Smyth, "US-China: Washington Revives Plans for Its Rare Earths Industry," *Financial Times*, September 14, 2020, https://www.ft.com/content/5104d84d-a78f-4648-b695-bd7e14c135d6.

98. Melanie Burton, Yuka Obayashi, and Aaron Sheldrick, "How Rare Earth Shocks Lifted an Upstart Australian Mining Company," Reuters, December 17, 2019, https://www.reuters.com/article/us-rareearths-lynas-focus-idUSKBN1YL0R0.

99. James Lewis, "Semiconductors and Modern Defense Spending," Center for Strategic and International Studies, September 8, 2020, https://www.csis.org/analysis/semiconductors-and-modern-defense-spending.

11. WHEN SANCTIONS WORK TOO WELL

1. Peter Harrell, "Export Controls Are Bigger and Broader. But Are We Safer?," Center for a New American Security, August 13, 2020, https://www.cnas.org/publications/commentary/export-controls-are-bigger-and-broader-but-are-we-safer.

2. "U.S. Space Industry 'Deep Dive' Assessment: Impact of the U.S. Export Controls on the Space Industrial Base," U.S. Department of Commerce, February 2014, https://www.bis.doc.gov/index.php/documents/technology-evaluation/898-space-export-control-report/file.

3. "U.S. Space Industry 'Deep Dive' Assessment," U.S. Department of Commerce.

4. Jeff Foust, "Federal Government Tweaks Space Export Control Rules," SpaceNews.com, January 12, 2017, https://spacenews.com/federal-government-tweaks-space-export-control-rules.

5. Chad Bown, "How Trump's Export Curbs on Semiconductors and Equipment Hurt the US Technology Sector," Peterson Institute for International Economics, September 28, 2020, https://www.piie.com/blogs/trade-and-investment-policy-watch/how-trumps-export-curbs-semiconductors-and-equipment-hurt-us.

6. Kathrin Hille, "The Great Uncoupling: One Supply Chain for China, One for Everywhere Else," *Financial Times*, October 6, 2020, https://www.ft.com/content/40ebd786-a576-4dc2-ad38-b97f796b72a0.

7. David Ignatius, " 'Decoupling' the U.S. from China Would Backfire," *Washington Post*, September 8, 2020, https://www.washingtonpost.com/opinions/global-opinions/decoupling-the-us-from-china-would-backfire/2020/09/08/46880cfe-f1fc-11ea-999c-67ff7b-f6a9d2_story.html.

8. Gideon Rachmann, "A New Cold War: Trump, Xi and the Escalating US-China Confrontation," *Financial Times*, October 5, 2020, https://www.ft.com/content/7b809c6a-f733-46f5-a312-9152aed28172.

9. "A Confident China Seeks to Insulate Itself from the World," *Economist*, March 13, 2021, https://www.economist.com/china/2021/03/13/a-confident-china-seeks-to-insulate-itself-from-the-world.

10. Karen Sutter, "U.S.-China Trade and Economic Relations: Overview," Congressional Research Service, accessed January 22, 2022, https://fas.org/sgp/crs/row/IF11284.pdf.

11. Richard Nephew, "The Impact of Covid-19 on Global Supply Chains and Sanctions," Columbia/SIPA Center on Global Energy Policy, May 2020, https://www.energypolicy.columbia.edu/sites/default/files/file-uploads/SupplyChains+Sanctions_CGEP_Commentary_050720-2.pdf.

12. Hille, "The Great Uncoupling."

13. "The Cost of Remaking Supply Chains: Significant but Not Prohibitive," Bank of America, July 23, 2020, https://www.bofaml.com/content/dam/boamlimages/documents/articles/ID20_0734/cost_of_remaking_supply_chains.pdf.

14. "SIA Urges U.S. Government Action to Strengthen America's Semiconductor Supply Chain," Semiconductor Industry Association, April 5, 2021, https://www.semiconductors.org/sia-urges-u-s-government-action-to-strengthen-americas-semiconductor-supply-chain.

15. Scott Kennedy, "Washington's China Policy Has Lost Its Wei," Center for Strategic and International Studies, July 2020, https://csis-website-prod.s3.amazonaws.com/s3fs-public/publication/200727_Kennedy_USChinaPolicyLost-Brief_v3.pdf.

16. Antonio Varas and Raj Varadarajan, "How Restrictions to Trade with China Could End US Leadership in Semiconductors," Boston Consulting Group, March 2020, https://image-src.bcg.com/Images/BCG-How-Restricting-Trade-with-China-Could-End-US-Semiconductor-Mar-2020_tcm9-240526.pdf.

17. "America's Latest Salvo Against Huawei Is Aimed at Chipmaking in China," *Economist*, May 23, 2020, https://www.economist.com/business/2020/05/23/americas-latest-salvo-against-huawei-is-aimed-at-chipmaking-in-china.

18. Kennedy, "Washington's China Policy Has Lost Its Wei."

19. "America's Latest Salvo Against Huawei," *Economist*.

20. Sherisse Pham, "Losing Huawei as a Customer Could Cost US Tech Companies $11 Billion," CNN, May 17, 2019, https://www.cnn.com/2019/05/17/tech/hua-wei-us-ban-suppliers/index.html.

21. Varas and Varadarajan, "How Restrictions to Trade with China Could End US Leadership."

22. Varas and Varadarajan, "How Restrictions to Trade with China Could End US Leadership."

23. Varas and Varadarajan, "How Restrictions to Trade with China Could End US Leadership."

24. "Measuring Distortions in International Markets: The Semiconductor Value Chain," Organization for Economic Cooperation and Development, December 12, 2019, https://doi.org/10.1787/8fe4491d-en.

25. Varas and Varadarajan, "How Restrictions to Trade with China Could End US Leadership."

26. James Kynge and Nian Liu, "From AI to Facial Recognition: How China Is Setting the Rules in New Tech," *Financial Times*, October 7, 2020, https://www.ft.com /content/188d86df-6e82-47eb-a134-2e1e45c777b6.

27. John Seaman, "China and the New Geopolitics of Technical Standardization," Institut Français des Relations Internationales, January 2020, https://www.ifri.org/sites /default/files/atoms/files/seaman_china_standardization_2020.pdf.

28. Seaman, "China and the New Geopolitics of Technical Standardization."

29. Ping Gao, "WAPI: A Chinese Attempt to Establish Wireless Standards and the International Coalition That Resisted," *Communications of the Association for Information Systems* 23 (2018), https://doi.org/10.17705/1CAIS.02308.

30. "Assessing China's Digital Silk Road Initiative," Council on Foreign Relations, accessed March 13, 2021, https://www.cfr.org/china-digital-silk-road.

31. "China's Smart Cities Development," U.S. Congress, January 2020, https://www.uscc .gov/sites/default/files/2020-04/China_Smart_Cities_Development.pdf.

32. "Assessing China's Digital Silk Road Initiative," Council on Foreign Relations.

33. Rebecca Arcesati, "The Digital Silk Road Is a Development Issue," Mercator Institute for China Studies, April 28, 2020, https://merics.org/en/analysis/digital-silk-road -development-issue.

34. "Feature: Huawei Auxiliary Systems Help Detect COVID-19 in Ecuador," Xinhua, April 30, 2020, www.xinhuanet.com/english/2020-04/30/c_139020269.htm.

35. Toru Tsunashima, "In 165 Countries, China's Beidou Eclipses American GPS," *Nikkei Asia*, November 25, 2020, https://asia.nikkei.com/Politics/International-relations /In-165-countries-China-s-Beidou-eclipses-American-GPS.

36. Cheng Ting-Fang and Lauly Li, "China's SMIC Stockpiles Chip Equipment to Counter US Restrictions," *Nikkei Asia*, September 30, 2020, https://asia.nikkei.com /Politics/International-relations/US-China-tensions/China-s-SMIC-stockpiles-chip -equipment-to-counter-US-restrictions.

37. Aurélien Duthoit, "China: Riding the Silicon Ox?," Euler Hermes, February 9, 2021, https://www.eulerhermes.com/en_global/news-insights/economic-insights/China -Riding-the-silicon-ox.html.

38. Kathrin Hille and Sun Yu, "Chinese Groups Go from Fish to Chips in New 'Great Leap Forward,'" *Financial Times*, October 13, 2020, https://www.ft.com/content/46edd2b2 -1734-47da-8e77-21854ca5b212.

39. Salvatore Babones, "China's Drive to Make Semiconductor Chips Is Failing," *Foreign Policy*, December 14, 2020, https://foreignpolicy.com/2020/12/14/china-technology -sanctions-huawei-chips-semiconductors.

40. Graham Kendall, "Apollo 11 Anniversary: Could an iPhone Fly Me to the Moon?," *Independent*, July 9, 2019, https://www.independent.co.uk/news/science/apollo-11-moon -landing-mobile-phones-smartphone-iphone-a8988351.html.

41. Chris Miller, "America Is Going to Decapitate Huawei," *New York Times*, September 15, 2020, https://www.nytimes.com/2020/09/15/opinion/united-states-huawei.html.

42. Bown, "How Trump's Export Curbs on Semiconductors and Equipment Hurt the US."

43. Varas and Varadarajan, "How Restrictions to Trade with China Could End US Leadership."

44. James Kynge, "Huawei Records Biggest Jump in Patent Ownership in 2020," *Financial Times*, March 17, 2021, https://www.ft.com/content/614c6149-2f6e-482f-b64a-97aa2496ac7f.

45. Ting-Fang and Li, "China's SMIC Stockpiles Chip Equipment."

46. Kathrin Hille, Yuan Yang, and Qianer Liu, "Huawei Develops Plan for Chip Plant to Help Beat US Sanctions," *Financial Times*, November 1, 2020, https://www.ft.com /content/84eb666e-0af3-48eb-8b60-3f53b19435cb.

47. Karen Sutter, "'Made in China 2025' Industrial Policies: Issues for Congress," Congressional Research Service, accessed October 14, 2020, https://crsreports.congress.gov /product/pdf/IF/IF10964.

48. Varas and Varadarajan, "How Restrictions to Trade with China Could End US Leadership."

49. James Kynge and Mercedes Ruehl, "China Snaps Up Chip Talent from US Firms," *Financial Times*, November 25, 2020, https://www.ft.com/content/9f5e4e53-7f7c-4206 -a929-9a0d5baa9bf5.

50. Ian Fergusson and Karen Sutter, "U.S. Export Control Reforms and China: Issues for Congress," Congressional Research Service, accessed October 13, 2020, https://crsreports .congress.gov/product/pdf/IF/IF11627.

51. Varas and Varadarajan, "How Restrictions to Trade with China Could End US Leadership."

52. James Lewis, "Semiconductors and Modern Defense Spending," Center for Strategic and International Studies, September 8, 2020, https://www.csis.org/analysis/semiconductors -and-modern-defense-spending.

53. Yue Yue, Wang Liwei, and Han Wei, "Four Things to Know About the State's Role in China's Private Investment Market," Caixin Global, October 14, 2020, https://www .caixinglobal.com/2020-10-14/four-things-to-know-about-the-states-role-in-chinas -private-investment-market-101614377.html.

54. "America's Latest Salvo Against Huawei," *Economist*.

55. Yoko Kubota, "China Sets Up New $29 Billion Semiconductor Fund," *Wall Street Journal*, October 25, 2019, https://www.wsj.com/articles/china-sets-up-new-29-billion -semiconductor-fund-11572034480.

56. Samuel Shen and Josh Horwitz, "China Tech Veterans to Launch 'Domestic Replacement' Fund Amid U.S. Sanctions," Reuters, September 15, 2020, https://www.reuters .com/article/china-tech-fund-idUSKBN25Z1R9.

57. Frank Tang, "China's Five-Year Plan to Focus on Independence as US Decoupling Threat Grows," *South China Morning Post*, May 24, 2020, https://www.scmp.com/economy /china-economy/article/3085683/coronavirus-china-five-year-plan-focus-independence-us.

58. Lewis, "Semiconductors and Modern Defense Spending."

59. "Notes from a CSIS Virtual Event: American Leadership in Semiconductor Manufacturing," Center for Strategic and International Studies, October 13, 2020, https://csis-website

-prod.s3.amazonaws.com/s3fs-public/event/201014_Leadership_Semiconductor
_Manufacturing.pdf.

60. Zeyi Yang, "Chinese Companies Are Making Their Own Semiconductors," Protocol, March
13, 2021, https://www.protocol.com/china/chinese-companies-make-own-semiconductors.

61. Hille and Yu, "Chinese Groups Go from Fish to Chips."

62. Sidney Leng, "US Semiconductor Giant Shuts China Factory Hailed as 'a Miracle,'
in Blow to Beijing's Chip Plans," South China Morning Post, May 20, 2020, https://
www.scmp.com/economy/china-economy/article/3085230/us-semiconductor-giant
-shuts-china-factory-hailed-miracle.

63. Sidney Leng and Orange Wang, "China's Semiconductor Drive Stalls in Wuhan,
Exposing Gap in Hi-Tech Production Capabilities," South China Morning Post, August
28, 2020, https://www.scmp.com/economy/china-economy/article/3099100/chinas
-semiconductor-drive-stalls-wuhan-exposing-gap-hi-tech.

64. Hille and Yu, "Chinese Groups Go from Fish to Chips."

65. Hille, Yang, and Liu, "Huawei Develops Plan for Chip Plant."

66. Duthoit, "China: Riding the Silicon Ox?"

67. Ting-Fang and Li, "China's SMIC Stockpiles Chip Equipment."

68. Babones, "China's Drive to Make Semiconductor Chips Is Failing."

69. Eliza Gkritsi, "A Chinese Firm Made a Memory Chip That Can Compete with Samsung. What's Next?," Technode.com, April 23, 2020, https://technode.com/2020/04/23
/ymtc-memory-chip.

70. Cheng Ting-Fang, "China's Top Maker of Memory Chips Plans to Double Output
in 2021," Nikkei Asia, January 12, 2021, https://asia.nikkei.com/Business/China-tech
/China-s-top-maker-of-memory-chips-plans-to-double-output-in-2021.

71. Varas and Varadarajan, "How Restrictions to Trade with China Could End US
Leadership."

72. "SIA Urges U.S. Government Action," Semiconductor Industry Association.

73. "China's "Dual-Circulation" Strategy Means Relying Less on Foreigners," Economist,
November 7, 2020, https://www.economist.com/china/2020/11/07/chinas-dual-circulation
-strategy-means-relying-less-on-foreigners.

74. Duthoit, "China: Riding the Silicon Ox?"

75. "The Meaning of RCEP, the World's Biggest Trade Agreement," Economist, November 15,
2020, https://www.economist.com/finance-and-economics/2020/11/15/the-meaning-of
-rcep-the-worlds-biggest-trade-agreement.

76. Steven Erlanger, "Europe Struggles to Defend Itself Against a Weaponized Dollar,"
New York Times, March 12, 2021, https://www.nytimes.com/2021/03/12/world/europe
/europe-us-sanctions.html.

77. Kennedy, "Washington's China Policy Has Lost Its Wei."

78. Demetri Sevastopulo and Kathrin Hille, "US Fears China Is Flirting with Seizing
Control of Taiwan," Financial Times, March 27, 2021, https://www.ft.com/content
/3ed169b8-3f47-4f66-a914-58b6e2215f7d.

79. Robert Blackwill and Philip Zelikow, "The United States, China, and Taiwan: A Strategy to Prevent War," Council on Foreign Relations, February 9, 2021, https://www.cfr
.org/report/united-states-china-and-taiwan-strategy-prevent-war.

BIBLIOGRAPHY

Aizhu, Chen. "CNPC Suspends Investment in Iran's South Pars After U.S. Pressure: Sources." Reuters, December 12, 2018. https://www.reuters.com/article/us-china-iran-gas-sanctions /cnpc-suspends-investment-in-irans-south-pars-after-u-s-pressure-sources-idUSKBN1OB0RU.

Akhtar, Tanzeel. "People's Bank of China Official Says Fully Anonymous Digital Yuan 'Not Feasible.'" Coindesk. March 22, 2021. https://www.coindesk.com/peoples-bank-of-china-official -says-fully-anonymous-digital-yuan-not-feasible.

Albert, Eleanor. "What to Know About Sanctions on North Korea." Council on Foreign Relations. Last updated July 16, 2019. https://www.cfr.org/backgrounder/what-know-about-sanctions -north-korea.

Aliaj, Ortenca, and Nastassia Astrasheuskaya. "Russia's Rosneft Switches All Export Contracts to Euros." *Financial Times*, October 24, 2019. https://www.ft.com/content/f886658c-f65c -11e9-a79c-bc9acae3b654.

AllSeas. "Allseas Suspends Nord Stream 2 Pipelay Activities." December 21, 2019. https://allseas .com/wp-content/uploads/2019/12/2019-1221-Media-statement-Allseas-discontinues -Nord-Stream-2-pipelay.pdf.

Alper, Alexandra, Toby Sterling, and Stephen Nellis. "Trump Administration Pressed Dutch Hard to Cancel China Chip-Equipment Sale: Sources." Reuters, January 6, 2020. https:// www.reuters.com/article/us-asml-holding-usa-china-insight-idUSKBN1Z50HN.

Amiti, Mary, Stephen J. Redding, and David Weinstein. "The Impact of the 2018 Trade War on U.S. Prices and Welfare." Centre for Economic Performance. March 2019. http://cep.lse .ac.uk/pubs/download/dp1603.pdf.

Anderson, Lisa. "Rogue Libya's Long Road." *Middle East Report*, no. 241 (2006): 42–47. https:// doi.org/10.2307/25164764.

Andrianova, Anna, and Andrey Biryukov. "U.S. 'Shooting Itself' with Steps That Harm Dollar, Putin Says." Bloomberg, November 28, 2018. https://www.bloomberg.com/news/articles /2018-11-28/u-s-shooting-itself-with-steps-that-harm-dollar-putin-says.

Arachnys. "Providing Frictionless AML for a Global Bank's 3,000 Analysts." September 15, 2019. https://www.arachnys.com/providing-frictionless-aml-for-a-global-banks-3000-analysts.

Araud, Gérard. *Passeport Diplomatique, Quarante Ans au Quai d'Orsay.* Paris: Grasset, 2019.

Arcesati, Rebecca. "The Digital Silk Road Is a Development Issue." Mercator Institute for China Studies. April 28, 2020. https://merics.org/en/analysis/digital-silk-road-development -issue.

Areddy, James. "China Creates Its Own Digital Currency, a First for Major Economy." *Wall Street Journal,* April 5, 2021. https://www.wsj.com/articles/china-creates-its-own-digital -currency-a-first-for-major-economy-11617634118.

Argus Media. "US Treasury Extends Block on Takeover of Citgo." Accessed December 1, 2020. https://www.argusmedia.com/en/news/2123539-us-treasury-extends-block-on-takeover -of-citgo.

Associated Press. "China Passes New Law Restricting Sensitive Exports." October 18, 2020. https://apnews.com/article/technology-beijing-global-trade-china-national-security -396e42dbf147c9b55863fb90099303cb.

Astakhova, Olesya, Elena Fabrichnaya, and Andrey Ostroukh. "Rosneft Switches Contracts to Euros from Dollars Due to U.S. Sanctions." Reuters, October 24, 2019. https://www .reuters.com/article/us-rosneft-contracts-euro/rosneft-switches-contracts-to-euros-from -dollars-due-to-u-s-sanctions-idUSKBN1X31JT.

Aubouin, Marc. "Use of Currencies in International Trade: Any Changes in the Picture?" World Trade Organization. May 2012. https://www.wto.org/english/res_e/reser_e/ersd201210 _e.pdf.

Austrian Federal Ministry for European and International Affairs. "Foreign Ministry Ceases Investigations Against BAWAG Bank." June 21, 2007. https://www.bmeia.gv.at/en/the-ministry /press/announcements/2007/foreign-ministry-ceases-investigations-against-bawag-bank.

Babones, Salvatore. "China's Drive to Make Semiconductor Chips Is Failing." *Foreign Policy,* December 14, 2020. https://foreignpolicy.com/2020/12/14/china-technology-sanctions -huawei-chips-semiconductors.

Bahar, Dany, Sebastian Bustos, Jose R. Morales, and Miguel A. Santos. "Impact of the 2017 Sanctions on Venezuela, Revisiting the Evidence." Brookings. May 2019. https://www.brookings .edu/wp-content/uploads/2019/05/impact-of-the-2017-sanctions-on-venezuela_final.pdf.

Bajak, Frank. "US Adds New Sanction on Chinese Tech Giant Huawei." Associated Press, May 16, 2020. https://apnews.com/article/22e139b05c8f6b8a9c910eebea8c295e.

Baker, Stephanie. "U.S. Senator Asks Treasury for Sanctions Briefing on Deripaska." Bloomberg, December 23, 2020. https://www.bloomberg.com/news/articles/2020-12-23/u-s-senator-asks -treasury-for-sanctions-briefing-on-deripaska.

Banco, Erin. "Treasury Department Chaos Leads to Exodus of Key Staffers." Daily Beast, January 9, 2019. https://www.thedailybeast.com/treasury-department-chaos-leads-to-exodus -of-key-staffers.

Bank of America. "The Cost of Remaking Supply Chains: Significant but Not Prohibitive." July 23, 2020. https://www.bofaml.com/content/dam/boamlimages/documents/articles/ID20 _0734/cost_of_remaking_supply_chains.pdf.

Bank of Finland Institute for Emerging Economies (BOFIT). "China Now Has the World's Second Largest Bond Market After the US." July 30, 2021. https://www.bofit.fi/en/monitoring /weekly/2021/vw202130_2.

Bartlett, Jason, and Megan Ophel. "Sanctions by the Numbers: U.S. Secondary Sanctions." Center for a New American Security. August 26, 2021. https://www.cnas.org/publications /reports/sanctions-by-the-numbers-u-s-secondary-sanctions.

Batmanghelidj, Esfandyar. "Resistance Is Simple, Resilience Is Complex: Sanctions and the Composition of Iranian Trade." Johns Hopkins University. Accessed December 10, 2020. https:// static1.squarespace.com/static/5f0f5b1018e89f351b8b3ef8/t/5fd0e4a906d21916ed79ba75 /1607525546925/IranUnderSanctions_Batmanghelidj.pdf.

Batmanghelidj, Esfandyar, and Abbas Kebriaeezadeh. "As Coronavirus Spreads, Iranian Doctors Fear the Worst." *Foreign Policy*, March 3, 2020. https://foreignpolicy.com/2020/03/03 /iran-coronavirus-spreads-sanctions-covid19-iranian-doctors-fear-worst.

Batmanghelidj, Esfandyar, and Ellie Geranmayeh. "America's Latest Wave of Iran Sanctions." European Council on Foreign Relations. November 6, 2018. https://www.ecfr.eu/article /commentary_americas_latest_wave_of_iran_sanctions.

Batmanghelidj, Esfandyar, and Sahil Shah. "As Iran Faces Virus, Trump Admin Fails to Use Swiss Channel to Ease Medical Exports." European Leadership Network. May 6, 2020. https://www.europeanleadershipnetwork.org/commentary/as-iran-faces-virus-trump -admin-fails-to-use-touted-swiss-channel-to-ease-medical-exports.

BBC News. "Coronavirus: Iran and the US Trade Blame Over Sanctions." April 17, 2020. https://www.bbc.com/news/world-middle-east-52218656.

BBC News. "Iran Nuclear Deal: US Rejects EU Plea for Sanctions Exemption." July 16, 2018. https://www.bbc.co.uk/news/world-us-canada-44842723.

Beesley, Arthur. "US Sanctions Puts Future of Aughinish Plant in Doubt." *Irish Times*, April 23, 2018. https://www.irishtimes.com/business/energy-and-resources/us-sanctions-puts -future-of-aughinish-plant-in-doubt-1.3470888.

Belkin, Paul, Michael Ratner, and Cory Welt. "Russia's Nord Stream 2 Pipeline: A Push for the Finish Line." Congressional Research Service. Accessed March 18, 2021. https://fas.org /sgp/crs/row/IF11138.pdf.

Bershidsky, Leonid. "The U.S. List of Russian Oligarchs Is a Disgrace." Bloomberg, January 30, 2018. https://www.bloomberg.com/opinion/articles/2018-01-30/the-u-s-list-of-russian -oligarchs-is-a-disgrace.

Birnbaum, Michael. "Putin's Approval Ratings Hit 89 Percent, the Highest They've Ever Been." *Washington Post*, June 24, 2015. https://www.washingtonpost.com/news/worldviews/wp /2015/06/24/putins-approval-ratings-hit-89-percent-the-highest-theyve-ever-been.

Blackwill, Robert, and Philip Zelikow. "The United States, China, and Taiwan: A Strategy to Prevent War." Council on Foreign Relations. February 9, 2021. https://www.cfr.org/report /united-states-china-and-taiwan-strategy-prevent-war.

Blake, Aaron. "Trump Echoes Putin on Venezuela—and Contradicts His Own Secretary of State." *Washington Post*, May 3, 2019. https://www.washingtonpost.com/politics/2019/05/03 /trump-echoes-putin-venezuela-contradicts-his-own-secretary-state.

Blinken, Antony. *Ally Versus Ally: America, Europe, and the Siberian Pipeline Crisis*. Westport, CT: Praeger Publishers, 1987.

Bloem, Jeffrey. "The Unintended Consequences of Regulating 'Conflict Minerals' in Africa's Great Lakes Region." World Bank Blogs. November 25, 2019. https://blogs.worldbank .org/impactevaluations/unintended-consequences-regulating-conflict-minerals-africas -great-lakes-region.

Bloomberg. "Why Tiny Magnets Could Be China's Destructive New Trade-War Weapon." June 5, 2019. https://www.bloomberg.com/news/articles/2019-06-05/why-tiny-magnets-could-be -china-s-destructive-new-trade-weapon.

Bosilkovski, Igor. "Treasury Department's Russia Oligarchs List Is Copied from Forbes." *Forbes*, January 30, 2018. https://www.forbes.com/sites/igorbosilkovski/2018/01/30/treasury -departments-russias-oligarchs-list-is-copied-from-forbes.

Bousso, Ron, and Bate Felix. "France's Total Opens Washington Office as Iran Risks Loom." Reuters, November 3, 2017. https://www.reuters.com/article/us-total-usa/frances-total-opens -washington-office-as-iran-risks-loom-idINKBN1D31H2.

Bowley, Graham. "Senate Report: Opaque Art Market Helped Oligarchs Evade Sanctions." *New York Times*, July 29, 2020. https://www.nytimes.com/2020/07/29/arts/design/senate -report-art-market-russia-oligarchs-sanctions.html.

Bown, Chad. "Export Controls: America's Other National Security Threat." Peterson Institute for International Economics. May 2020. https://www.piie.com/system/files/documents /wp20-8.pdf.

Bown, Chad. "How Trump's Export Curbs on Semiconductors and Equipment Hurt the US Technology Sector." Peterson Institute for International Economics. September 28, 2020. https://www.piie.com/blogs/trade-and-investment-policy-watch/how-trumps-export -curbs-semiconductors-and-equipment-hurt-us.

Bown, Chad. "Russia's War on Ukraine: A Sanctions Timeline." Peterson Institute for International Economics. March 14, 2022, updated May 10, 2022. https://www.piie.com/blogs /realtime-economic-issues-watch/russias-war-ukraine-sanctions-timeline.

Bown, Chad. "The US Is Trying to Use Export Controls to Restrict Huawei's Access to Semiconductors." Peterson Institute for International Economics. October 13, 2020. https://www.piie.com/research/piie-charts/us-trying-use-export-controls-restrict-huaweis -access-semiconductors.

BP. "Statistical Review of World Energy 2019." Accessed May 8, 2020. https://www.bp.com /content/dam/bp/business-sites/en/global/corporate/pdfs/energy-economics/statistical -review/bp-stats-review-2019-full-report.pdf.

Brett, Jason. "Trend Continues for Countries Looking to Evade U.S. Sanctions Using Crypto." *Forbes*, January 29, 2020. https://www.forbes.com/sites/jasonbrett/2020/01/29/trend-continues -for-countries-looking-to-evade-us-sanctions-using-crypto.

Breuninger, Kevin. "Putin Ally Oleg Deripaska Sues Treasury and Steven Mnuchin to Lift Sanctions, Claiming 'Utter Devastation' of His Wealth." CNBC, March 15, 2019. https:// www.cnbc.com/2019/03/15/putin-ally-deripaska-sues-treasury-to-block-sanctions-says -hes-lost-billions.html.

Bright, Natasha. "Do Cryptocurrencies Pose a Sanctions Risk?" Association of Certified Sanctions Specialists. October 4, 2019. https://sanctionsassociation.org/do-cryptocurrencies-pose-a-sanctions-risk.

Bright, Natasha. "Sanctioned Nations Explore Bypassing Swift." Association of Certified Sanctions Specialists. February 6, 2020. https://sanctionsassociation.org/sanctioned-nations-explore-bypassing-swift.

Britannica, The Editors of Encyclopaedia. "Napoleonic Wars." Encyclopaedia Britannica. https://www.britannica.com/event/Napoleonic-Wars.

British Parliament Archives. "European Council." Accessed July 28, 2020. https://api.parliament.uk/historic-hansard/commons/1982/jul/01/european-council#S6CV0026P0_19820701_HOC_153.

Brunnstrom, David. "Tillerson: Evidence Sanctions 'Really Starting to Hurt' North Korea." Reuters, January 17, 2018. https://www.reuters.com/article/us-northkorea-missiles-tillerson/tillerson-evidence-sanctions-really-starting-to-hurt-north-korea-idUSKBN1F62UV.

Brunsden, Jim, Sam Fleming, and Philip Stafford. "EU Sets Out Plans to Curb Reliance on Dollar in Post-Trump Era." *Financial Times*, January 16, 2021. https://www.ft.com/content/20f39e33-e360-479e-82e2-5441d24f0e0b.

Burton, Melanie. "Rio Tinto Stands to Win from Rusal Sanctions; U.S. Consumers to Lose." Reuters, April 9, 2018, https://www.reuters.com/article/us-rusal-sanctions-aluminium/rio-tinto-stands-to-win-from-rusal-sanctions-u-s-consumers-to-lose-idUSKBN1HG1NL.

Burton, Melanie, Yuka Obayashi, and Aaron Sheldrick. "How Rare Earth Shocks Lifted an Upstart Australian Mining Company." Reuters, December 17, 2019. https://www.reuters.com/article/us-rareearths-lynas-focus-idUSKBN1YL0R0.

Butler, Declan. "How US Sanctions Are Crippling Science in Iran." *Nature* 574 (October 2019): 13–14, https://media.nature.com/original/magazine-assets/d41586-019-02795-y/d41586-019-02795-y.pdf.

Cal Fire. "Current Year Statistics." Accessed October 12, 2020. https://www.fire.ca.gov/stats-events.

Campanella, Miriam. "Far-reaching Consequences of U.S. Financial Sanctions." Robert Triffin International. June 2019. http://triffininternational.eu/publications/articles-papers/1285-far-reaching-consequences-of-u-s-financial-sanctions-the-dollar-shortage-and-the-triffin-moment.

Caryl, Christian. "Why Treasury's 'Oligarch List' Is Driving Russian Tycoons Crazy." *Forbes*, January 30, 2018. https://www.washingtonpost.com/news/democracy-post/wp/2018/01/30/why-the-treasurys-oligarch-list-is-driving-russian-tycoons-crazy.

Center for Constitutional Rights. "Filártiga v. Peña-Irala." Accessed March 27, 2021. https://ccrjustice.org/home/what-we-do/our-cases/fil-rtiga-v-pe-irala.

Center for Strategic and International Studies. "Does China Pose a Threat to Global Rare Earth Supply Chains?" Accessed October 14, 2020. https://chinapower.csis.org/china-rare-earths.

Center for Strategic and International Studies. "Notes from a CSIS Virtual Event: American Leadership in Semiconductor Manufacturing." October 13, 2020. https://csis-website-prod.s3.amazonaws.com/s3fs-public/event/201014_Leadership_Semiconductor_Manufacturing.pdf.

Center for Strategic and International Studies. "Notes from a CSIS Virtual Event: Strategic Competition and the U.S. Semiconductor Industry." July 23, 2020. https://csis-website-prod.s3.amazonaws.com/s3fs-public/event/200724_Semiconductor_Industry.pdf.

Center for Systems Science and Engineering (CSSE) at Johns Hopkins University (JHU). "COVID-19 Dashboard." Accessed April 18, 2022. https://coronavirus.jhu.edu/map.html.

Chabrol, Denis. "Oldendorff Closing Bauxite Transshipment Operations in Guyana Due to US Sanctions Against RUSAL." Demerara Waves. April 19, 2018. https://demerarawaves.com/2018/04/19/oldendorff-closing-bauxite-transshipment-operations-in-guyana-due-to-us-sanctions-against-rusal.

Chan, Veta. "'An Absolute Necessity': Why This Expert Says China Desperately Needs a Digital Currency." Fortune, July 30, 2020. https://fortune.com/2020/07/30/china-digital-currency-renminnbi-cbdc.

Chatterjee, Saikat. "Exclusive—China's Payments System Scaled Back; Trade Deals Only: Sources." Reuters, July 13, 2015. https://uk.reuters.com/article/uk-china-yuan-payments/exclusive-chinas-payments-system-scaled-back-trade-deals-only-sources-idUKKCN-0PN0P020150713.

Chen, Qian. "The Good, the Bad and the Ugly of a Chinese State-Backed Digital Currency." CNBC, November 22, 2019. https://www.cnbc.com/2019/11/22/chinese-crypto-beijing-sees-opportunity-but-concerns-linger.html.

Cheng, Evelyn. "China's Digital Yuan Notches $8.3 Billion in Transactions in 6 Months, Taking a Tiny Share of Payments." CNBC, January 18, 2022. https://www.cnbc.com/2022/01/18/chinas-digital-yuan-notches-8point3-billion-transactions-in-half-a-year.html.

Cheng, Evelyn. "China's Renminbi Could Become the World's Third Largest Reserve Currency in 10 Years, Morgan Stanley Predicts." CNBC, September 4, 2020. https://www.cnbc.com/2020/09/04/chinas-renminnbi-rmb-to-become-third-largest-reserve-currency-by-2030-morgan-stanley.html.

Chew, Wei. "The Future of China's Blockchain Industry." Medium. May 22, 2018. https://medium.com/hackernoon/the-future-of-chinas-blockchain-industry-7a1c37abcef.

Cnet.com. "Interior Department Grounds Drone Fleet Amid Concerns of Chinese Spying." January 29, 2020. https://www.cnet.com/news/interior-department-officially-grounds-drones-made-in-china.

Cohen, Luc, and Carina Pons. "New Venezuela Sanctions Protect Citgo, Encourage Debt Talks: Opposition." Reuters, August 6, 2019. https://www.reuters.com/article/us-venezuela-politics-usa-citgo/new-venezuela-sanctions-protect-citgo-encourage-debt-talks-opposition-idUSKCN1UW1YK.

CoinMarketCap. "Top 100 Cryptocurrencies by Market Capitalization." Accessed May 13, 2022. https://coinmarketcap.com.

Coll, Steve. Ghost Wars: The Secret History of the CIA, Afghanistan and Bin Laden, from the Soviet Invasion to September 10, 2001. London: Penguin, 2004.

Congressman Jared Huffman. "House & Senate Members Call on President Trump to End Sanctions Against Iran During Covid-19." Accessed May 13, 2020. https://huffman.house.gov/media-center/press-releases/house-and-senate-members-call-on-president-trump-to-end-sanctions-against-iran-during-covid-19.

Council on Foreign Relations. "Assessing China's Digital Silk Road Initiative." Accessed March 13, 2021. https://www.cfr.org/china-digital-silk-road.

Crawford, Nicholas. "Defending Against Economic Statecraft: China, the US and the Rest." International Institute for Strategic Studies. October 2020. https://www.iiss.org/blogs /analysis/2020/10/economic-statecraft-china-us.

Crooks, Ed, and Jack Farchy. "Exxon Considers Its Course After Sanctions Hit Russian Ambitions." *Financial Times*, September 30, 2014. https://www.ft.com/content/586ae5c0 -487c-11e4-ad19-00144feab7de.

Crow, Kelly. "How Two Sanctioned Russian Billionaire Brothers Bought Art Anyway." *Wall Street Journal*, July 29, 2020. https://www.wsj.com/articles/how-two-sanctioned-russian -billionaire-brothers-bought-art-anyway-11596035186.

Cunningham, Erin. "As Coronavirus Cases Explode in Iran, U.S. Sanctions Hinder Its Access to Drugs and Medical Equipment." *Washington Post*, March 29, 2020. https://www .washingtonpost.com/world/middle_east/as-coronavirus-cases-explode-in-iran-us-sanctions -hinder-its-access-to-drugs-and-medical-equipment/2020/03/28/0656a196-6aba-11ea -b199-3a9799c54512_story.html.

Cunningham, Erin. "Fresh Sanctions on Iran Are Already Choking Off Medicine Imports, Economists Say." *Washington Post*, November 17, 2018. https://www.washingtonpost.com /world/middle_east/fresh-sanctions-on-iran-are-already-choking-off-medicine-imports -economists-say/2018/11/17/c94ce574-e763-11e8-8449-1ff263609a31_story.html.

Dallas, Rita. "Britain Orders Firms to Defy Pipeline Ban." *Washington Post*, August 3, 1982.

Davari, Mohammad. "Iran's Rowhani Takes Office with Vow to Rescue Economy." Agence France Presse, August 3, 2013. https://sg.news.yahoo.com/rowhani-set-become-irans-7th -president-073501208.html.

Davis, Bob, and Yuka Hayashi. "New Trade Representative Says U.S. Isn't Ready to Lift China Tariffs." *Wall Street Journal*, March 28, 2021. https://www.wsj.com/articles/new-trade -representative-says-u-s-isnt-ready-to-lift-china-tariffs-11616929200.

De, Nikhilesh. "In Wargaming Exercise, a Digital Renminbi Neuters US Sanctions and North Korea Buys Nukes." MIT Media Lab. November 20, 2019. https://www.media.mit.edu /articles/in-wargaming-exercise-a-digital-yuan-neuters-us-sanctions-and-north-korea -buys-nukes.

DefenseNews.com. "To Combat China's Hold on Rare Earth Minerals, Pentagon Looks to Aus-tralia." August 27, 2019. https://www.defensenews.com/pen-tagon/2019/08/27/to-combat -chinas-hold-on-rare-earth-minerals-pentagon-looks-to-australia.

Dehghanpisheh, Babak. "Foreign Funds for Iran's Oil Sector a Top Priority: Oil Minister." Reuters, August 20, 2017. https://www.reuters.com/article/us-iran-oil-zanganeh-idUSKCN1B00T0.

Delcas, Marie. "Venezuela: quelles seront les conséquences des sanctions américaines contre Maduro." *Le Monde*, January 29, 2019. https://www.lemonde.fr/international/article/2019 /01/29/venezuela-les-etats-unis-durcissent-les-sanctions-contre-maduro_5416029_3210 .html.

De Luce, Dan, Abigail Williams, and Andrea Mitchell. "U.S. Refuses European Requests for Exemp-tions from Its New Sanctions on Iran." NBC News, July 14, 2018. https://www.nbcnews.com /news/world/u-s-refuses-european-requests-exemptions-its-new-sanctions-iran-n891371.

DeSouza, Patrick. "The Soviet Gas Pipeline Incident: Extension of Collective Security Responsibilities to Peacetime Commercial Trade." Yale University Law School. Accessed July 28, 2020. http://digitalcommons.law.yale.edu/cgi/viewcontent.cgi?article=1317&context=yjil.

Deutsche Welle. "US Senators Threaten Germany's Port Town of Sassnitz over Nord Stream 2 Gas Project." August 14, 2020. https://www.dw.com/en/us-sanctions-nord-stream-2-gas/a-54565504.

Devitt, Polina. "Russia's Rusal Lands First U.S. Investment Since Sanctions Lifted." Reuters, April 15, 2019. https://www.reuters.com/article/us-russia-rusal-usa/russias-rusal-lands-first-u-s-investment-since-sanctions-lifted-idUSKCN1RR09V.

Devitt, Polina, and Arshad Mohammed. "Questions Linger Over Deripaska's Rusal Influence After U.S. Deal." Reuters, February 4, 2019. https://www.reuters.com/article/us-usa-russia-sanctions-rusal-analysis-idUSKCN1PT0K9.

Dizard, John. "Russia Sanctions—Easy to Announce, Hard to Implement." *Financial Times*, March 25, 2021. https://www.ft.com/content/0d16212a-2d52-49f1-af5d-80e43d1be5b7.

Dizolele, Mvemba Phezo. "Dodd-Frank 1502 and the Congo Crisis." Center for Strategic and International Studies. August 22, 2017. https://www.csis.org/analysis/dodd-frank-1502-and-congo-crisis.

Dubowitz, Mark, and Annie Fixler. " 'SWIFT' Warfare: Power, Blowback, and Hardening American Defenses." Foundation for Defense of Democracies. July 2015. https://s3.us-east-2.amazonaws.com/defenddemocracy/uploads/publications/Cyber_Enabled_Swift.pdf.

Duguid, Kate. "Iran Oil Sanctions Could Advance China's 'Petro-yuan.' " Reuters, May 10, 2018. https://uk.reuters.com/article/uk-iran-nuclear-china-oil/iran-oil-sanctions-could-advance-chinas-petro-yuan-idUKKBN1IB32H.

Duthoit, Aurélien. "China: Riding the Silicon Ox?" Euler Hermes. February 9, 2021. https://www.eulerhermes.com/en_global/news-insights/economic-insights/China-Riding-the-silicon-ox.html.

Dyson, Tim, and Valeria Cetorelli. "Changing Views on Child Mortality and Economic Sanctions in Iraq: A History Of Lies, Damned Lies and Statistics." *BMJ Global Health* (July 2017). https://dx.doi.org/10.1136/bmjgh-2017-000311.

Dziggel, Oliver. "The Reagan Pipeline Sanctions: Implications for U.S. Domestic Policy and the Future of International Law." *Towson University Journal of International Affairs* L, no. 1 (2016). https://cpb-us-w2.wpmucdn.com/wp.towson.edu/dist/b/55/files/2017/11/REAGAN-PIPELINE-SANCTIONS-19q4sd1.pdf.

E3 Foreign Ministers. "Joint Statement on the Creation of INSTEX, the Special Purpose Vehicle Aimed at Facilitating Legitimate Trade with Iran in the Framework of the Efforts to Preserve the Joint Comprehensive Plan of Action (JCPOA)." January 31, 2019. https://www.diplomatie.gouv.fr/en/country-files/iran/news/article/joint-statement-on-the-creation-of-instex-the-special-purpose-vehicle-aimed-at.

Early, Bryan, and Keith Preble. "Trends in U.S. Sanctions Enforcement During the Trump Administration." New York University School of Law Program on Corporate Compliance and Enforcement. Accessed August 7, 2020. https://wp.nyu.edu/compliance_enforcement/2019/01/30/trends-in-u-s-sanctions-enforcement-during-the-trump-administration.

Eaton, Collin, and Luc Cohen. "Explainer: U.S. Sanctions and Venezuela's Trade and Oil Industry Partners." Reuters, August 14, 2019. https://www.reuters.com/article/us-venezuela -politics-crude-sanctions-ex/explainer-u-s-sanctions-and-venezuelas-trade-and-oil -industry-partners-idUSKCN1V420P.

Economic Times. "India, Japan Sign $75 Billion Currency Swap Agreement." October 30, 2018. https://economictimes.indiatimes.com/markets/forex/india-japan-sign-75-billion-currency -swap-agreement/articleshow/66415790.cms.

Economist. "A Confident China Seeks to Insulate Itself from the World." March 13, 2021. https://www.economist.com/china/2021/03/13/a-confident-china-seeks-to-insulate-itself -from-the-world.

Economist. "America Files a New Financial Salvo at Beijing." May 16, 2020. https://www .economist.com/finance-and-economics/2020/05/14/america-files-a-new-financial-salvo-at -beijing.

Economist. "America's Latest Salvo Against Huawei Is Aimed at Chipmaking in China." May 23, 2020. https://www.economist.com/business/2020/05/23/americas-latest-salvo -against-huawei-is-aimed-at-chipmaking-in-china.

Economist. "American National-Security Maximalism Can Be Self-Defeating." August 22, 2020. https://www.economist.com/united-states/2020/08/20/american-national-security -maximalism-can-be-self-defeating.

Economist. "As China Goes Global, Its Banks Are Coming Out, Too." May 9, 2020. https:// www.economist.com/special-report/2020/05/07/as-china-goes-global-its-banks-are -coming-out-too.

Economist. "China Wants to Make the Renminbi a Central-Bank Favourite." May 9, 2020. https://www.economist.com/special-report/2020/05/07/china-wants-to-make-the -renminnbi-a-central-bank-favourite.

Economist. "China's "Dual-Circulation" Strategy Means Relying Less on Foreigners." November 7, 2020. https://www.economist.com/china/2020/11/07/chinas-dual-circulation-strategy-means -relying-less-on-foreigners.

Economist. "Dethroning the Dollar: America's Aggressive Use of Sanctions Endangers the Dollar's Reign." January 18, 2020. https://www.economist.com/briefing/2020/01/18 /americas-aggressive-use-of-sanctions-endangers-the-dollars-reign.

Economist. "Donald Trump Uses Sanctions More Keenly than Any of His Predecessors." November 24, 2019. https://www.economist.com/united-states/2019/11/24/donald-trump -uses-sanctions-more-keenly-than-any-of-his-predecessors.

Economist. "How America Might Wield Its Ultimate Weapon of Mass Disruption." August 15, 2020. https://www.economist.com/business/2020/08/13/how-america-might-wield-its -ultimate-weapon-of-mass-disruption.

Economist. "Rare Earths Give China Leverage in the Trade War, at a Cost." June 15, 2019. https://www.economist.com/china/2019/06/15/rare-earths-give-china-leverage-in-the -trade-war-at-a-cost.

Economist. "The Financial World's Nervous System Is Being Rewired." May 9, 2020. https:// www.economist.com/special-report/2020/05/07/the-financial-worlds-nervous-system -is-being-rewired.

Economist. "The Meaning of RCEP, the World's Biggest Trade Agreement." November 15, 2020. https://www.economist.com/finance-and-economics/2020/11/15/the-meaning-of-rcep -the-worlds-biggest-trade-agreement.

Economist. "The Pandemic's True Death Toll." Accessed January 23, 2022. https://www.economist .com/graphic-detail/coronavirus-excess-deaths-estimates.

Economist. "The Past Decade Has Brought a Compliance Boom in Banking." May 4, 2019. https://www.economist.com/finance-and-economics/2019/05/02/the-past-decade-has -brought-a-compliance-boom-in-banking.

Economist. "Why It's Hard for Congo's Coltan Miners to Abide by the Law." January 23, 2021. https://www.economist.com/middle-east-and-africa/2021/01/23/why-its-hard-for-congos -coltan-miners-to-abide-by-the-law.

Economist Intelligence Unit. "A Closer Look at US Oil Sanctions." February 21, 2019. http://country .eiu.com/article.aspx?articleid=1017682885&Country=Venezuela&topic=Economy_1.

Economist Intelligence Unit. "Cuba Country Forecast." 2020.

Economist Intelligence Unit. "Democratic Republic of Congo Country Report." 2021.

Economist Intelligence Unit. "Down but Not Out? Globalisation and the Threat of Covid-19." July 2020. https://www.eiu.com/public/topical_report.aspx?campaignid=globalisation-covid.

Economist Intelligence Unit. "Iran Country Report." 2021.

Economist Intelligence Unit. "Major Drop in OPEC+ Supplies." Accessed December 1, 2020. http://industry.eiu.com/handlers/filehandler.ashx?mode=pdf&issue_id=1059705889.

Economist Intelligence Unit. "Russia Country Report." 2021.

Economist Intelligence Unit. "US Sanctions Rosneft Subsidiary Over Venezuela." February 24, 2020. https://country.eiu.com/article.aspx?articleid=79103591&Country=Venezuela&topic =Economy.

Economist Intelligence Unit. "Venezuela Country Report." 2020.

Eddy, Melissa, and Steven Erlanger. "German Town Fears Ruin by U.S. Effort to Stop Russian Pipeline." *New York Times,* August 25, 2020. https://www.nytimes.com/2020/08/25/world /europe/nord-stream-2-germany-us-russia.html.

Editorial Board of the New York Times. "This Coronavirus Crisis Is the Time to Ease Sanc- tions on Iran." *New York Times,* March 25, 2020. https://www.nytimes.com/2020/03/25 /opinion/iran-sanctions-covid.html.

Eichengreen, Barry, Arnaud Mehl, and Livia Chiţu. *How Global Currencies Work: Past, Pres- ent, and Future.* Princeton, NJ: Princeton University Press, 2018.

Eineman, Abigail. "Sanctions by the Numbers, Spotlight on Iran." Center for a New American Security. September 15, 2020. https://www.cnas.org/publications/reports/sanctions-by-the -numbers-spotlight-on-iran.

Eineman, Abigail. "Sanctions by the Numbers, the Geographic Distribution of U.S. Sanctions." Center for a New American Security. June 15 2020. https://www.cnas.org/publications /reports/sanctions-by-the-numbers-1.

Elliott, Kimberly Ann. "Evidence on the Costs and Benefits of Economic Sanctions." Subcom- mittee on Trade, Committee on Ways and Means, U.S. House of Representatives. October 23, 1997. https://www.piie.com/commentary/testimonies/evidence-costs-and-benefits-economic -sanctions.

Elliott, Stuart. "European Parliament Reiterates Call for Nord Stream 2 Gas Link To Be Halted." S&P Global Platts. January 21, 2021. https://www.spglobal.com/platts/en/market-insights /latest-news/natural-gas/012121-european-parliament-reiterates-call-for-nord-stream-2 -gas-link-to-be-halted.

Ellsworth, Brian. "Trump Says U.S. Military Intervention in Venezuela 'an Option'; Russia Objects." Reuters, February 3, 2019. https://www.reuters.com/article/us-venezuela-politics -idUSKCN1PS0DK.

Enrich, David, Gabriele Steinhauser, and Matthew Dalton. "Loopholes Blunt Impact of U.S., EU Sanctions over Ukraine." *Wall Street Journal*, July 30, 2014. https://www.wsj.com /articles/eu-units-of-russian-banks-exempt-from-sanctions-1406714101.

Erdbrink, Thomas. "How Bitcoin Could Help Iran Undermine U.S. Sanctions." *New York Times*, January 29, 2019. https://www.nytimes.com/2019/01/29/world/middleeast/bitcoin -iran-sanctions.html.

Erlanger, Steven. "Europe Struggles to Defend Itself Against a Weaponized Dollar." *New York Times*, March 12, 2021. https://www.nytimes.com/2021/03/12/world/europe/europe-us -sanctions.html.

Erlanger, Steven, and Melissa Eddy. "Navalny Poisoning Raises Pressure on Merkel to Cancel Russian Pipeline." *New York Times*, September 3, 2020. https://www.nytimes.com /2020/09/03/world/europe/navalny-poisoning-merkel-nord-stream.html.

Euractiv. "'Freedom Gas': US Opens LNG Floodgates to Europe." Updated August 28, 2019. https://www.euractiv.com/section/energy/news/freedom-gas-us-opens-lng-floodgates -to-europe.

European Central Bank. "Report on a Digital Euro." October 2020. https://www.ecb.europa .eu/pub/pdf/other/Report_on_a_digital_euro~4d7268b458.en.pdf.

European Central Bank. "The International Role of the Euro." Accessed March 18, 2021. https:// www.ecb.europa.eu/pub/ire/html/ecb.ire202006~81495c263a.en.html.

European Central Bank. "We Must Be Prepared to Issue a Digital Euro." October 2, 2020. https://www.ecb.europa.eu/press/blog/date/2020/html/ecb.blog201002~12ab1c06b5.en .html.

European Commission. "Communication from the Commission to the European Parliament, the Council, the European Central Bank, the European Economic and Social Committee and the Committee of the Regions, the European Economic and Financial System: Fostering Openness, Strength and Resilience." January 19, 2021. https://eur-lex.europa.eu /legal-content/EN/TXT/HTML/?uri=CELEX:52021DC0032&from=EN.

European Commission. "European Union, Trade in Goods with Iran." May 8, 2020. https:// webgate.ec.europa.eu/isdb_results/factsheets/country/details_iran_en.pdf.

Eurostat. "EU Imports of Energy Products—Recent Developments." Accessed May 8, 2020. https://ec.europa.eu/eurostat/statistics-explained/index.php/EU_imports_of_energy _products_-_recent_developments#Overview.

Eurostat. "From Where Do We Import Energy and How Dependent Are We?" Accessed February 15, 2021. https://ec.europa.eu/eurostat/cache/infographs/energy/bloc-2c.html.

Eurostat. "International Trade in Goods." Accessed March 2, 2021. https://ec.europa.eu /eurostat/statistics-explained/index.php/International_trade_in_goods.

ExxonMobil. "Financial Statements and Supplemental Information." Accessed May 8, 2020. https://corporate.exxonmobil.com/-/media/Global/Files/investor-relations/annual-meeting-materials/financial-statements/2014-financial-statements.pdf.

Federal Register. "Addition of Entities to the Entity List." May 21, 2019. https://www.federalregister.gov/documents/2019/05/21/2019-10616/addition-of-entities-to-the-entity-list.

Federal Register. "Financial Crimes Enforcement Network; Repeal of Special Measure Involving Banco Delta Asia (BDA)." October 8, 2020. https://www.federalregister.gov/documents/2020/08/10/2020-17143/financial-crimes-enforcement-network-repeal-of-special-measure-involving-banco-delta-asia-bda.

Feliciano, Joseph. "The Economic Instrument of Power and Globalization." U.S. Army War College. March 24, 2011. https://apps.dtic.mil/dtic/tr/fulltext/u2/a560021.pdf.

Felix, Bate. "Oil Major Total Says Final Iran Project Investment Decision Depends on Renewal of U.S. Waivers." Reuters, February 9, 2017. https://www.reuters.com/article/iran-total-sanctions-idUSL5N1FU1VT.

Fergusson, Ian, and Karen Sutter. "U.S. Export Control Reforms and China: Issues for Congress." Congressional Research Service. Accessed October 13, 2020. https://crsreports.congress.gov/product/pdf/IF/IF11627.

Feron, James. "Mrs Thatcher Faults U.S. on Siberia Pipeline." *New York Times*, July 2, 1982. https://www.nytimes.com/1982/07/02/world/mrs-thatcher-faults-us-on-siberia-pipeline.html.

Finextra. "VTB Bank Connects to CIPS." March 10, 2016. https://www.finextra.com/pressarticle/63508/vtb-bank-connects-to-cips.

Fleming, Sam, Mehreen Khan, and Jim Brunsden. "EU Leaders Strike Deal on €750bn Recovery Fund After Marathon Summit." *Financial Times*, July 21, 2020. https://www.ft.com/content/713be467-ed19-4663-95ff-66f775af55cc.

Flicker, Scott, Lauren Kelly Greenbacker, Talya Hutchison, and Holly Flynn. "Humanitarian Aid to Iran Under Existing Sanctions—An Important Reminder in a Time of Pandemic." Paul Hastings. April 21, 2020. https://www.paulhastings.com/publications-items/details/?id=84f02f6f-2334-6428-811c-ff00004cbded.

Forbes. "Real Time Net Worth, No. 1548, Arkady Rotenberg." Accessed April 17, 2022. https://www.forbes.com/profile/arkady-rotenberg.

Forbes. "Real Time Net Worth, No. 1050, Oleg Deripaska." Accessed April 17, 2022. https://www.forbes.com/profile/oleg-deripaska.

Forbes. "Real Time Net Worth, No. 2526, Boris Rotenberg." Accessed April 17, 2022. https://www.forbes.com/profile/boris-rotenberg.

Foust, Jeff. "Federal Government Tweaks Space Export Control Rules." SpaceNews.com. January 12, 2017. https://spacenews.com/federal-government-tweaks-space-export-control-rules.

Foy, Henry. "Nord Stream 2 Pipeline Targeted in US Sanctions Broadside." *Financial Times*, June 15, 2017. https://www.ft.com/content/03a9fd6a-51d8-11e7-bfb8-997009366969.

Foy, Henry, and Erika Solomon. "Gazprom to Restart Nord Stream 2 Construction." *Financial Times*, January 10, 2021. https://www.ft.com/content/d3f86ba6-95ce-496a-b323-62109775364d.

Francis, Diane. "US Expands Sanctions Against Putin's Pipeline." Atlantic Council. October 22, 2020. https://www.atlanticcouncil.org/blogs/ukrainealert/us-expands-sanctions-against-putins-pipeline.

Fried, Daniel, and Brian O'Toole. "The New Russia Sanctions Law, What It Does and How to Make It Work." Atlantic Council. September 29, 2017. https://www.atlanticcouncil.org /wp-content/uploads/2017/09/The_New_Russia_Sanctions_Law_web_0929.pdf.

Fried, Daniel, Richard Morningstar, and Daniel Stein. "Reconciling Transatlantic Differences over Nord Stream 2." Atlantic Council. February 2, 2021. https://www.atlanticcouncil.org /blogs/energysource/reconciling-transatlantic-differences-over-nord-stream-2.

Friedman, Lisa, and David McCabe. "Interior Dept. Grounds Its Drones over Chinese Spying Fears." New York Times, January 29, 2020. https://www.nytimes.com/2020/01/29/technology /interior-chinese-drones.html.

Friedman, Thomas. "Biden Made Sure 'Trump Is Not Going to Be President for Four More Years.'" New York Times, December 2, 2020. https://www.nytimes.com/2020/12/02/opinion /biden-interview-mcconnell-china-iran.html.

Funabashi, Yoichi. "The Mideast Has Oil, China Has Rare Earths." Japan Times, August 9, 2019. https://www.japantimes.co.jp/opinion/2019/08/09/commentary/japan-commentary /mideast-oil-china-rare-earths.

G7 Summit. "Declaration of the Seven Heads of State and Government and Representatives of the European Communities." Versailles, June 6, 1982. http://www.g8.utoronto.ca/summit /1982versailles/communique.html.

Gady, Franz-Stefan. "India Makes $800 Million Advance Payment for Russian S-400 Air Defense Systems." Diplomat, November 2019. https://thediplomat.com/2019/11/india-makes-800 -million-advance-payment-for-russian-s-400-air-defense-systems.

Galbert, Simond de. "Transatlantic Economic Statecraft." Center for a New American Security. June 21, 2016. https://www.cnas.org/publications/reports/transatlantic-economic-statecraft -the-challenge-to-building-a-balanced-transatlantic-sanctions-policy-between-the-united -states-and-the-european-union.

Gambrell, Jon. "Iran Leader Refuses US Help, Citing Virus Conspiracy Theory." Associated Press, March 22, 2020. https://apnews.com/2cffa4c49cbf085562a71cd36a4e4378.

Gao, Ping. "WAPI: A Chinese Attempt to Establish Wireless Standards and the International Coalition That Resisted." Communications of the Association for Information Systems 23 (2018). https://doi.org/10.17705/1CAIS.02308.

Gaylord, Mark. "The Banco Delta Asia Affair: The USA PATRIOT Act and Allegations of Money Laundering in Macau." Crime Law and Social Change 50 (2008): 293–305. https:// doi.org/10.1007/s10611-008-9127-3.

Geranmayeh, Ellie. "Reviving the Revolutionaries: Trump's Maximum Pressure Is Shifting Iran's Domestic Politics." European Council on Foreign Relations. June 2020. https://www.ecfr.eu /page/-/reviving_the_revolutionaries_how_trumps_maximum_pressure_is_shifting_irans.pdf.

Geranmayeh, Ellie, and Manuel Lafont Rapnouil. "Meeting the Challenge of Secondary Sanc- tions." European Council on Foreign Relations. June 2019. https://www.ecfr.eu/page/-/4 _Meeting_the_challenge_of_secondary_sanctions.pdf.

Gianella, Christian, Magali Cesana, Audrey Cezard-Assouad, et al. "Economic Sanctions: What Have We Learned from the Recent and Not so Recent Past?" Trésor-Economics, no. 150 (2015). https://www.tresor.economie.gouv.fr/Articles/2015/07/29/tresor-economics -no-150-economic-sanctions-what-have-we-learned-from-the-recent-and-not-so-recent-past.

Gibney, James. "Trump's Sanctions Are Losing Their Bite." Bloomberg, April 2, 2020. https:// www.bloomberg.com/opinion/articles/2020-04-02/trump-s-overuse-of-sanctions-is -weakening-their-effectiveness.

Giugliano, Ferdinando. "Europe Is Planning Its Very Own E-Currency." Bloomberg, November 16, 2020. https://www.bloomberg.com/opinion/articles/2020-11-16/christine-lagarde-s-ecb-is -planning-its-very-own-e-currency.

Gkritsi, Eliza. "A Chinese Firm Made a Memory Chip That Can Compete with Samsung. What's Next?" Technode.com. April 23, 2020. https://technode.com/2020/04/23/ymtc -memory-chip.

Gladstone, Rick. "U.S. Says Greek Executive Evaded Sanctions on Iran." *New York Times*, March 14, 2013. https://www.nytimes.com/2013/03/15/world/middleeast/us-says-a-greek -helped-iran-evade-sanctions.html.

Gopalakrishnan, Raju, and Manuel Mogato. "Bangladesh Bank Official's Computer Was Hacked to Carry Out $81 Million Heist: Diplomat." Reuters, May 19, 2016. https://www .reuters.com/article/us-cyber-heist-philippines-idUSKCN0YA0CH.

Gordon, Joy. *Invisible War: The United States and the Iraq Sanctions*. Cambridge, MA: Harvard University Press, 2010.

Gordon, Meghan. "US Steps Up Sanctions Pressure on Nord Stream 2 Gas Pipeline Contrac- tors." S&P Global Platts. October 20, 2020. https://www.spglobal.com/platts/en/market -insights/latest-news/natural-gas/102020-us-steps-up-sanctions-pressure-on-nord -stream-2-gas-pipeline-contractors.

Gould-Davies, Nigel. "Russia, the West and Sanctions." *Survival: Global Politics and Strategy* 62 (February–March 2020): 7–28. https://doi.org/10.1080/00396338.2020.1715060.

Grabar, Maria. "Russian Pipe-Laying Vessel Moors at Nord Stream 2 Hub in Germany: Data." Reuters, May 18, 2020. https://www.reuters.com/article/us-germany-gas-nord-stream-2 /russian-pipe-laying-vessel-moors-at-nord-stream-2-hub-in-germany-data-idUSKBN22U1TZ.

Grabar, Maria. "Russia's Rotenberg Denies Buying Gazprom Stake." Reuters, August 7, 2019. https://uk.reuters.com/article/us-russia-gazprom-rotenberg/russias-rotenberg-denies -buying-gazprom-stake-idUKKCN1UX1VP.

Greenwald, Michael. "The Future of the Dollar in a Post-Iran Deal World." Atlantic Council. October 29, 2018. https://www.atlanticcouncil.org/blogs/new-atlanticist/the-future-of-the -dollar-in-a-post-iran-deal-world.

Grigas, Agnia, and Lukas Trakimavičius. "Nord Stream 2 Is a Bad Deal for Europe." Atlantic Council. July 10, 2018. https://www.atlanticcouncil.org/blogs/new-atlanticist/nord-stream -2-is-a-bad-deal-for-europe.

Guardian. "Sixty Years of US Aid to Pakistan." July 11, 2011. https://www.theguardian.com /global-development/poverty-matters/2011/jul/11/us-aid-to-pakistan.

Gwertzman, Bernard. "Lifting of U.S. Sanctions." *New York Times*, November 15, 1982. https:// www.nytimes.com/1982/11/15/world/lifting-of-us-sanctions-news-analysis.html.

Gwertzman, Bernard. "Reagan Lifts Sanctions on Sales for Soviet Pipeline; Reports Accord with Allies." *New York Times*, November 14, 1982. https://www.nytimes.com/1982/11/14 /world/reagan-lifts-sanctions-on-sales-for-soviet-pipeline-reports-accord-with-allies .html.

Haass, Richard. "Economic Sanctions: Too Much of a Bad Thing." Brookings. June 1, 1998. https://www.brookings.edu/research/economic-sanctions-too-much-of-a-bad-thing.

Hackenbroich, Jonathan. "Defending Europe's Economic Sovereignty: New Ways to Resist Economic Coercion." European Council on Foreign Relations. October 20, 2020. https://ecfr.eu/publication/defending_europe_economic_sovereignty_new_ways_to_resist_economic_coercion.

Harada, Issaku. "China Aims to Launch Digital Yuan by 2022 Winter Olympics." *Nikkei Asia*, May 27, 2020. https://asia.nikkei.com/Spotlight/Cryptocurrencies/China-aims-to-launch-digital-yuan-by-2022-Winter-Olympics.

Hardt, John. "Energy Equipment Sales to U.S.S.R." Congressional Research Service. October 22, 1982. https://www.everycrsreport.com/files/19821022_IP0219S_d8bc44c63e6d2816a3fc8cbe261e4338ac65de49.pdf.

Harrell, Peter. "Cuba: U.S. Sanctions Policy After the Embargo." Columbia University Center on Global Energy Policy. November 2016. https://energypolicy.columbia.edu/sites/default/files/Cuba%3A%20US%20Sanctions%20Policy%20After%20the%20Embargo.pdf.

Harrell, Peter. "Export Controls Are Bigger and Broader. But Are We Safer?" Center for a New American Security. August 13, 2020. https://www.cnas.org/publications/commentary/export-controls-are-bigger-and-broader-but-are-we-safer.

Harrell, Peter. "Is the U.S. Using Sanctions Too Aggressively? The Steps Washington Can Take to Guard Against Overuse." *Foreign Affairs*, September 11, 2018. https://www.foreignaffairs.com/articles/2018-09-11/us-using-sanctions-too-aggressively.

Harrell, Peter, and Elizabeth Rosenberg. "Economic Dominance, Financial Technology, and the Future of U.S. Economic Coercion." Center for a New American Security. April 29, 2019. https://www.cnas.org/publications/reports/economic-dominance-financial-technology-and-the-future-of-u-s-economic-coercion.

Harris, Andrew, David Voreacos, and Stephanie Baker. "Deripaska Sues Over U.S. Sanctions, Claims $7.5 Billion Loss." Bloomberg, March 15, 2019. https://www.bloomberg.com/news/articles/2019-03-15/deripaska-sues-u-s-treasury-to-block-sanctions-against-him.

Helms, Jesse. "What Sanctions Epidemic? U.S. Business' Curious Crusade." *Foreign Affairs*, January/February 1999. https://www.foreignaffairs.com/articles/1999-01-01/what-sanctions-epidemic-us-business-curious-crusade.

Helwig, Niklas, and Juha Jokela. "Future Prospects: Adapting to the Geo-economic Environment." In *Sharpening EU Sanctions Policy for a Geopolitical Era*, ed. Niklas Helwig, Juha Jokela, and Clara Portela. Helsinki: Publications of the Government's Analysis, Assessment and Research Activities, 2020. https://www.fiia.fi/wp-content/uploads/2020/05/vnteas_report_sharpening-eu-sanctions-policy-for-a-geopolitical-era.pdf.

Herb, Jeremy, and Ted Barrett. "Senate Democrats' Effort to Block Trump Move on Russia Sanctions Fails." CNN, January 16, 2019. https://edition.cnn.com/2019/01/16/politics/senate-democrats-sanctions-russia/index.html.

Hernández, Igor, and Francisco Monaldi. "Weathering Collapse: An Assessment of the Financial and Operational Situation of the Venezuelan Oil Industry." Center for International Development at Harvard University. November 2016. https://growthlab.cid.harvard.edu/files/growthlab/files/venezuela_oil_cidwp_327.pdf.

Hille, Kathrin. "The Great Uncoupling: One Supply Chain for China, One for Everywhere Else." *Financial Times*, October 6, 2020. https://www.ft.com/content/40ebd786-a576-4dc2 -ad38-b97f796b72a0.

Hille, Kathrin, Edward White, and Kana Inagaki. "US Allows Sales of Chips to Huawei's Non-5G Businesses." *Financial Times*, October 29, 2020. https://www.ft.com/content /508b0828-bcd5-46a6-84f8-d05cb2887e0a.

Hille, Kathrin, and Sun Yu. "Chinese Groups Go from Fish to Chips in New 'Great Leap Forward.'" *Financial Times*, October 13, 2020. https://www.ft.com/content/46edd2b2-1734 -47da-8e77-21854ca5b212.

Hille, Kathrin, Yuan Yang, and Qianer Liu. "Huawei Develops Plan for Chip Plant to Help Beat US Sanctions." *Financial Times*, November 1, 2020. https://www.ft.com/content /84eb666e-0af3-48eb-8b60-3f53b19435cb.

Hillman, Jonathan. "China and Russia: Economic Unequals." Center for Strategic & International Studies. July 15, 2020. https://www.csis.org/analysis/china-and-russia-economic-unequals.

Hornby, Lucy, and Henry Sanderson. "Rare Earths: Beijing Threatens a New Front In the Trade War." *Financial Times*, June 4, 2019. https://www.ft.com/content/3cd18372-85e0-11e9 -a028-86cea8523dc2.

House of Lords. "Economic Affairs—Second Report." April 24, 2007. https://publications .parliament.uk/pa/ld200607/ldselect/ldeconaf/96/9606.htm#a8.

Hoyama, Taisei, and Yu Nakamura. "US and Allies to Build 'China-Free' Tech Supply Chain." *Nikkei Asia*, February 24, 2021. https://asia.nikkei.com/Politics/International-relations /Biden-s-Asia-policy/US-and-allies-to-build-China-free-tech-supply-chain.

Hufbauer, Gary. "Sanctions-Happy USA." *Washington Post*, July 12, 1998.

Hufbauer, Gary, and Barbara Oegg. "New Frontier in the Sanctions Debate." Peterson Institute for International Economics. May 2002. https://www.piie.com/publications/policy-briefs /capital-market-access-new-frontier-sanctions-debate.

Hufbauer, Gary, Jeffrey Schott, Kimberly Ann Elliott, and Barbara Oegg. *Economic Sanctions Reconsidered*, 3rd ed. Washington, DC: Peterson Institute for International Economics, 2009.

Hufbauer, Gary, Kimberly Ann Elliott, Tess Cyrus, and Elizabeth Ann Winston. "US Economic Sanctions: Their Impact on Trade, Jobs, and Wages." Peterson Institute for International Economics Working Paper, Peterson Institute for International Economics, Washington, DC, April 1997. https://www.piie.com/publications/working-papers/us-economic-sanctions -their-impact-trade-jobs-and-wages.

Human Rights Watch. "Crackdown on Dissent: Brutality, Torture, and Political Persecution in Venezuela." November 2017. https://www.hrw.org/sites/default/files/report_pdf/venezuela1117web _0.pdf.

Human Rights Watch. "Iran: Sanctions Threatening Health." October 29, 2019. https://www .hrw.org/news/2019/10/29/iran-sanctions-threatening-health.

Human Rights Watch. "Iran: Threats to Free, Fair Elections." May 24, 2013. https://www.hrw .org/news/2013/05/24/iran-threats-free-fair-elections.

Hume, Neil, and David Sheppard. "Supply Deals with Rusal's Irish Plant to Restart as Sanctions Ease." *Financial Times*, April 24, 2018. https://www.ft.com/content/c4ace960-479f -11e8-8ee8-cae73aab7ccb.

Hume, Neil, Henry Sanderson, and Arthur Beesley. "Rio Tinto Declares Force Majeure on Rusal Deals." *Financial Times*, April 13, 2018. https://www.ft.com/content/6a56584e-3f38-11e8-b9f9-de94fa33a81e.

Humphries, Marc. "Critical Minerals and U.S. Public Policy." Congressional Research Service. Accessed March 6, 2021. https://crsreports.congress.gov/product/pdf/R/R45810.

Humud, Carla. "Lebanese Hezbollah." Congressional Research Service. Accessed March 18, 2021. https://crsreports.congress.gov/product/pdf/IF/IF10703.

IAEA Report to the Board of Governors. "Implementation of the NPT Safeguards Agreement in the Islamic Republic of Iran." June 6, 2003. https://www.iaea.org/sites/default/files/gov2003-40.pdf.

Iancu, Alina. "Reserve Currencies in an Evolving International Monetary System." IMF Departmental Papers. Washington, DC: International Monetary Fund, November 2020. https://www.imf.org/en/Publications/Departmental-Papers-Policy-Papers/Issues/2020/11/17/Reserve-Currencies-in-an-Evolving-International-Monetary-System-49864.

Ignatius, David. "'Decoupling' the U.S. from China Would Backfire." *Washington Post*, September 8, 2020. https://www.washingtonpost.com/opinions/global-opinions/decoupling-the-us-from-china-would-backfire/2020/09/08/46880cfe-f1fc-11ea-999c-67ff7bf6a9d2_story.html.

Ignis. "Department of the Interior Recognizes IGNIS Technology." January 17, 2019. https://droneamplified.com/department-of-the-interior-recognizes-ignis-technology.

IMF. "Currency Composition of Official Foreign Exchange Reserves (COFER)." Accessed January 22, 2022. https://data.imf.org/?sk=E6A5F467-C14B-4AA8-9F6D-5A09EC4E62A4.

IMF. "IMF Adds Chinese Renminbi to Special Drawing Rights Basket." September 30, 2016. https://www.imf.org/en/News/Articles/2016/09/29/AM16-NA093016IMF-Adds-Chinese-Renminbi-to-Special-Drawing-Rights-Basket.

IMF. "United States of America: Staff Concluding Statement of the 2020 Article IV Mission." July 17, 2020. https://www.imf.org/en/News/Articles/2020/07/17/mcs-071720-united-states-of-america-staff-concluding-statement-of-the-2020-article-iv-mission.

Irish Times. "Aughinish Alumina Supply Contract Hit by Russian Parent's US Sanctions." April 13, 2018. https://www.irishtimes.com/business/energy-and-resources/aughinish-alumina-supply-contract-hit-by-russian-parent-s-us-sanctions-1.3460988.

Jaeger, Jaclyn. "Exxon Wins Legal Battle with OFAC over Sanctions Violation." Compliance Week. January 3, 2020. https://www.complianceweek.com/sanctions/exxon-wins-legal-battle-with-ofac-over-sanctions-violation/28258.article.

Jalilvand, David. "Progress, Challenges, Uncertainty: Ambivalent Times for Iran's Energy Sector." Oxford University Institute for Energy Studies. April 2018. https://www.oxfordenergy.org/publications/progress-challenges-uncertainty-ambivalent-times-irans-energy-sector.

Jalilvand, David. "The US Exit from the JCPOA: What Consequences for Iranian Energy?" Oxford University Institute for Energy Studies. June 2018. https://www.oxfordenergy.org/publications/us-exit-jcpoa-consequences-iranian-energy.

Jordans, Frank. "US Senators Take Aim at German Port over Russia Pipeline." Associated Press, August 6, 2020. https://apnews.com/93f980822fdc4ed8f53d6dfef380746f.

Коммерсантъ. "Труба пришла в движение." October 14, 2020. https://www.kommersant.ru/doc/4530356.

Kahata, Akinori. "Semiconductors as Natural Resources—Exploring the National Security Dimensions of U.S.-China Technology Competition." Center for Strategic and International Studies. February 17, 2021. https://www.csis.org/blogs/technology-policy-blog/semiconductors-natural-resources---exploring-national-security.

Kar-Gupta, Sudip, and John Irish. "France's Total to Quit Iran Gas Project if No Sanctions Waiver." Reuters, May 16, 2018. https://www.reuters.com/article/us-iran-nuclear-france-total-idUSKCN1IH1XK.

Karnitschnig, Matthew. "Germany Blames Trump in Pursuit of Nord Stream 2 Pipeline." Politico, August 10, 2020. https://www.politico.eu/article/germany-plays-trump-card-in-pursuit-of-russian-nord-stream-2-pipeline-dream.

Katz, Alan, Kitty Donaldson, and Stephanie Baker. "Oleg Deripaska's Rusal Role Spurred Europe Sanctions Warning to U.S." BNN Bloomberg, December 17, 2020. https://www.bnnbloomberg.ca/oleg-deripaska-s-rusal-role-spurred-europe-sanctions-warning-to-u-s-1.1537929.

Katzman, Kenneth. "Iran Sanctions." Congressional Research Service. Accessed April 25, 2020. https://fas.org/sgp/crs/mideast/RS20871.pdf.

Kauranen, Anne, and Jussi Rosendahl. "Russian Oligarch Under U.S. Sanctions Files Suit Against Nordic Banks." Reuters, October 22, 2018. https://www.reuters.com/article/us-finland-russia-sanctions/russian-oligarch-under-u-s-sanctions-files-suit-against-nordic-banks-idUSKCN1MW1AJ.

Keatinge, Tom, Emil Dall, Aniseh Bassiri Tabrizi, and Sarah Lain. "Transatlantic (Mis)alignment: Challenges to US-EU Sanctions Design and Implementation." Royal United Services Institute. July 7, 2017. https://rusi.org/sites/default/files/20170707_transatlantic_misalignment_keatinge.dall_.tabrizi.lain_final.pdf.

Kendall, Graham. "Apollo 11 Anniversary: Could an iPhone Fly Me to the Moon?" *Independent*, July 9, 2019. https://www.independent.co.uk/news/science/apollo-11-moon-landing-mobile-phones-smartphone-iphone-a8988351.html.

Kennedy, Scott. "America's Huawei Challenges." Center for Strategic and International Studies. July 31, 2020. https://www.csis.org/blogs/trustee-china-hand/americas-huawei-challenges.

Kennedy, Scott. "Washington's China Policy Has Lost Its Wei." Center for Strategic and International Studies. July 2020. https://csis-website-prod.s3.amazonaws.com/s3fs-public/publication/200727_Kennedy_USChinaPolicyLost-Brief_v3.pdf.

Keohane, David. "Total Vows Iran Pullout Over Trump Sanctions Threat." *Financial Times*, May 16, 2018. https://www.ft.com/content/cf9a7ef8-5912-11e8-bdb7-f6677d2e1ce8.

Keohane, David, and Andrew Ward. "Total Chief Told Trump to Stick with Iran Nuclear Deal." *Financial Times*, February 11, 2018. https://www.ft.com/content/f3c2d084-0e83-11e8-8cb6-b9ccc4c4dbbb.

Keohane, David, and Najmeh Bozorgmehr. "Threat of US Sanctions Pushes France's Total Out of Iran." *Financial Times*, August 20, 2018. https://www.ft.com/content/6baba178-a459-11e8-926a-7342fe5e173f.

Kharpal, Arjun. "China Launches App for Its Own Digital Currency as It Looks to Expand Usage." CNBC, January 4, 2022. https://www.cnbc.com/2022/01/04/china-launches-digital-currency-app-to-expand-usage.html.

Khrennikova, Dina, and Anna Andrianova. "Trump's Oil Sanctions Leave Russian Exporters $1 Billion Richer." Bloomberg, August 16, 2019. https://www.bloomberg.com/news /articles/2019-08-16/trump-s-oil-sanctions-leave-russian-exporters-1-billion-richer.

Kida, Kazuhiro, Masayuki Kubota, and Yusho Cho. "Rise of the Yuan: China-Based Payment Settlements Jump 80 Percent." *Nikkei Asia*, May 20, 2019. https://asia.nikkei.com/Business /Markets/Rise-of-the-yuan-China-based-payment-settlements-jump-80.

King, Iain. "Not Contributing Enough? A Summary of European Military and Development Assistance to Ukraine Since 2014." Center for Strategic & International Studies. September 26, 2019. https://www.csis.org/analysis/not-contributing-enough-summary-european -military-and-development-assistance-ukraine-2014.

Klapper, Bradley. "Trump's Choice for Top Diplomat Is no Fan of Sanctions." Associated Press, December 15, 2016. https://apnews.com/ba5a55b4956846b5af90962c290679ac/trumps-choice -top-diplomat-no-fan-sanctions.

Kolbe, Paul. "With Hacking, the United States Needs to Stop Playing the Victim." *New York Times*, December 23, 2020. https://www.nytimes.com/2020/12/23/opinion/russia-united -states-hack.html.

Kramer, Andrew. "Exxon Reaches Arctic Oil Deal with Russians." *New York Times*, August 31, 2011. https://www.nytimes.com/2011/08/31/business/global/exxon-and-rosneft-partner-in -russian-oil-deal.html.

Krauss, Clifford. "Exxon Mobil Seeks U.S. Sanctions Waiver for Oil Project in Russia." *New York Times*, April 19, 2017. https://www.nytimes.com/2017/04/19/business/energy-environment /exxon-mobil-russia-sanctions-waiver-oil.html.

Krauss, Clifford. " 'It's the Only Way to Get Paid': A Struggle for Citgo, Venezuela's U.S. Oil Company." *New York Times*, October 17, 2019. https://www.nytimes.com/2019/10/17/business /energy-environment/citgo-venezuela-creditors.html.

Krauss, Clifford. "White House Raises Pressure on Venezuela with New Financial Sanctions." *New York Times*, August 25, 2017. https://www.nytimes.com/2017/08/25/world/americas /venezuela-sanctions-maduro-trump.html.

Kreisel, Wilfrid. "Health Situation in Iraq." World Health Organization. February 26, 2001. https://apps.who.int/disasters/repo/6386.doc.

Kubota, Yoko. "China Sets Up New $29 Billion Semiconductor Fund." *Wall Street Journal*, October 25, 2019. https://www.wsj.com/articles/china-sets-up-new-29-billion-semiconductor -fund-11572034480.

Kulikov, Dmitry, and Natalia Porokhova. "US Residents Hold 8 Percent of Russian Sovereign Debt." Analytical Credit Rating Agency. August 17, 2018. https://www.acra-ratings.com /research/868.

Kumar Sen, Ashish. "Trump Administration Targets Russian Oligarchs." Atlantic Council. April 6, 2018. https://www.atlanticcouncil.org/blogs/new-atlanticist/trump-administration -targets-russian-oligarchs.

Kynge, James. "Huawei Records Biggest Jump in Patent Ownership in 2020." *Financial Times*, March 17, 2021. https://www.ft.com/content/614c6149-2f6e-482f-b64a-97aa2496ac7f.

Kynge, James, and Mercedes Ruehl. "China Snaps Up Chip Talent from US Firms." *Financial Times*, November 25, 2020. https://www.ft.com/content/9f5e4e53-7f7c-4206-a929-9a0d5baa9bf5.

Kynge, James, and Nian Liu. "From AI to Facial Recognition: How China Is Setting the Rules in New Tech." *Financial Times*, October 7, 2020. https://www.ft.com/content/188d86df-6e82-47eb-a134-2e1e45c777b6.

Kynge, James, and Sun Yu. "Virtual Control: The Agenda Behind China's New Digital Currency." *Financial Times*, February 17, 2021. https://www.ft.com/content/7511809e-827e-4526-81ad-ae83f405f623.

Latham & Watkins. "Top 10 Things to Know About Expanded US Sanctions on Iran." November 6, 2018. https://www.lw.com/thoughtLeadership/lw-top-10-things-to-know-expanded-us-sanctions-iran.

Lederer, Edith. "Russia, China Block UN from Saying North Korea Violated Sanctions." Associated Press, June 19, 2019. https://apnews.com/article/cb6be1337d2a48ecbde14dac590be083.

Lee, Jeong-Ho, and Sohee Kim. "Biden Finds a Key Ally Wary of His Bid to Outpace China on Chips." Bloomberg, March 25, 2021. https://www.bloomberg.com/news/articles/2021-03-25/south-korea-s-chip-industry-is-trapped-between-the-u-s-and-china.

Leng, Cheng, Zhang Yan, and Ryan Woo. "Chinese Banks Urged to Switch Away from SWIFT as U.S. Sanctions Loom." Reuters, July 29, 2020. https://www.reuters.com/article/us-china-banks-usa-sanctions/chinese-banks-urged-to-switch-away-from-swift-as-u-s-sanctions-loom-idUSKCN24U0SN.

Leng, Sidney. "US Semiconductor Giant Shuts China Factory Hailed as 'a Miracle,' in Blow to Beijing's Chip Plans." *South China Morning Post*, May 20, 2020. https://www.scmp.com/economy/china-economy/article/3085230/us-semiconductor-giant-shuts-china-factory-hailed-miracle.

Leng, Sidney, and Orange Wang. "China's Semiconductor Drive Stalls in Wuhan, Exposing Gap in Hi-Tech Production Capabilities." *South China Morning Post*, August 28, 2020. https://www.scmp.com/economy/china-economy/article/3099100/chinas-semiconductor-drive-stalls-wuhan-exposing-gap-hi-tech.

Levitt, Matthew. "Hezbollah: A Case Study of Global Reach, Remarks to a Conference on Post-Modern Terrorism: Trends, Scenarios, and Future Threats." American Civil Liberties Union. September 8, 2003. https://www.aclu.org/sites/default/files/field_document/ACLURM001616.pdf.

Lewis, James. "Semiconductors and Modern Defense Spending." Center for Strategic and International Studies. September 8, 2020. https://www.csis.org/analysis/semiconductors-and-modern-defense-spending.

Lewis, James. "Tech Crisis with China." Center for Strategic & International Studies. August 7, 2020. https://www.csis.org/analysis/tech-crisis-china.

Lewis, Paul. "A Soviet Project Tempts Europe." *New York Times*, May 30, 1982. https://timesmachine.nytimes.com/timesmachine/1982/05/30/173299.html?pageNumber=156.

LexisNexis. "Sanctions Compliance for Banks in the Age of Crypto-assets." June 5, 2020. https://blogs.lexisnexis.com/financial-crime-in-focus/sanctions-compliance-for-banks-in-the-age-of-crypto-assets.

Li, Lauly, Cheng Ting-Fang, and Yifan Yu. "How a Handful of US Companies Can Cripple Huawei's Supply Chain." *Nikkei Asia*, August 19, 2020. https://asia.nikkei.com/Spotlight/Huawei-crackdown/How-a-handful-of-US-companies-can-cripple-Huawei-s-supply-chain.

Liik, Kadri. "Into the Jungle." *Berlin Policy Journal* (January/February 2019). https://berlinpolicy journal.com/into-the-jungle.

Lim, Darren. "Chinese Economic Coercion During the THAAD Dispute." The Asan Forum. December 28, 2019. www.theasanforum.org/chinese-economic-coercion-during-the-thaad -dispute.

Lohmann, Sascha. "Extraterritorial U.S. Sanctions, Only Domestic Courts Could Effectively Curb the Enforcement of U.S. Law Abroad." Stiftung Wissenschaft und Politik. February 2019. https://www.swp-berlin.org/fileadmin/contents/products/comments/2019C05_lom.pdf.

Lynch, David. "China Hints It Will Choke Off U.S. 'Rare Earths' Access. But It's Not That Easy." *Washington Post*, June 10, 2019. https://www.washingtonpost.com/business/economy/2019 /06/07/80a06794-8649-11e9-a491-25df61c78dc4_story.html.

Macdonald, Alastair. "U.S. Envoy Warns Sanctions Still an Option Against Nord Stream 2." Reuters, November 13, 2018. https://www.reuters.com/article/us-eu-gazprom-nordstream -usa-idUSKCN1NI1FY.

Magnier, Mark. "In the Crosshairs: Chinese Drones a Target for US Ban as Security Risk." *South China Morning Post*, December 10, 2019. https://www.scmp.com/news/china/article /3041073/crosshairs-chinese-drones-target-us-ban-security-risk.

Malik, Nazia. "Economic Sanctions Imposed on Pakistan and Their Impact (1979–2001)." Lee Kuan Yew School of Public Policy, National University Singapore. Accessed May 20, 2020. http://www.ipedr.com/vol39/028-ICITE2012-K00006.pdf.

Maritime Executive. "Sanctions on UC Rusal Hit Shipping." April 20, 2018. https://www .maritime-executive.com/article/sanctions-on-uc-rusal-hit-shipping.

Marquardt, Paul, and Sameer Jaywant. "OFAC Reporting Still Required for Transactions with EN+, Rusal, and EuroSibEnergo." Cleary Gottlieb. January 31, 2019. https://www.clearytradewatch .com/2019/01/ofac-reporting-still-required-transactions-en-rusal-eurosibenergo.

Marson, James. "Russian Natural-Gas Project Gets Funding from China." *Wall Street Journal*, April 29, 2016. https://www.wsj.com/articles/russian-natural-gas-project-gets-funding-from -china-1461934776.

Martin, Lisa. *Coercive Cooperation, Explaining Multilateral Sanctions*. Princeton, NJ: Princeton University Press, 1992.

McDonald, Joe. "Huawei: Smartphone Chips Running Out Under US Sanctions." Associated Press, August 8, 2020. https://apnews.com/article/smartphones-technology-business -ap-top-news-china-270e93e985733a4d086c06a01375ceao.

McElroy, Damien. "Hassan Rouhani Vows to Lift Sanctions on Iran." *Telegraph*, August 3, 2013. https://www.telegraph.co.uk/news/worldnews/middleeast/iran/10220564/Hassan-Rouhani -vows-to-lift-sanctions-on-Iran.html.

McKinney, Byron. "COSCO Shipping & OFAC Sanctions—The Nightmare in the Haystack." IHS Markit. October 8, 2019. https://ihsmarkit.com/research-analysis/cosco-shipping-ofac -sanctions.html.

McKinsey & Company. "Semiconductor Design and Manufacturing: Achieving Leading-Edge Capabilities." August 20, 2020. https://www.mckinsey.com/industries/advanced -electronics/our-insights/semiconductor-design-and-manufacturing-achieving-leading -edge-capabilities.

Meredith, Sam, and Natasha Turak. "Putin Ally Oleg Deripaska Denies Kremlin Encouraged His Lawsuit Against US Treasury Sanctions." CNBC, March 18, 2019. https://www.cnbc .com/2019/03/18/putin-ally-deripaska-explains-why-hes-suing-us-treasury-department.html.

Michael, Maggie. "Doctors and Nurses Suffered as Iran Ignored Virus Concerns." Associated Press, May 12, 2020. https://apnews.com/6c7715f300797502329f6117e1141503.

Middlekauff, Robert. *Benjamin Franklin and His Enemies*. Oakland: University of California Press, 1998.

Miller, Chris. "America Is Going to Decapitate Huawei." *New York Times*, September 15, 2020. https://www.nytimes.com/2020/09/15/opinion/united-states-huawei.html.

Miller, Greg. "Sanctions Are Cleaving the Global Shipping Fleet in Two." American Shipper. September 30, 2019. https://www.freightwaves.com/news/sanctions-are-cleaving-the-global -shipping-fleet-in-two.

Moehr, Ole. "A Breakdown of the Sanctions Deal Between the United States and Oleg Deripaska." Atlantic Council. February 6, 2019. https://www.atlanticcouncil.org/blogs/econographics /us-sanctions-lifted-coles-2.

Moehr, Ole. "US Sanctions' Global Impact—A Case Study of RUSAL's Supply Chain." Atlantic Council. May 18, 2018. https://www.atlanticcouncil.org/blogs/econographics/us-sanctions -global-impact.

Mordant, Nicole. "Rio Tinto Reviewing Rusal Ties, Mum on Queensland Venture." Reuters, April 10, 2018. https://www.reuters.com/article/us-rio-tinto-rusal/rio-tinto-reviewing-rusal -ties-mum-on-queensland-venture-idUSKBN1HH2C7.

Moret, Erica. "Humanitarian Impacts of Economic Sanctions on Iran and Syria." *European Security* 24, no. 1 (2015). https://doi.org/10.1080/09662839.2014.893427.

Morris, Frank. "Farmers Swept Up in Trade Wars Remember '80s Grain Embargo." National Public Radio, August 16, 2018. https://www.npr.org/2018/08/16/639149657/farmers-caught -up-in-u-s-trade-war-s-remember-80-s-grain-embargo.

Mossberg, Hilary. "Beyond Carrots, Better Sticks." The Sentry. October 2019. https://cdn .thesentry.org/wp-content/uploads/2019/10/SanctionsEffectiveness_TheSentry_Oct2019 -web.pdf.

Motamedi, Maziar. "Parsian Bank CEO: US Treasury Made 'Mistake' in Iran Sanctions Designation." Bourse and Bazaar. October 21, 2018. https://www.bourseandbazaar.com /articles/2018/10/21/parsian-bank-ceo-us-treasury-made-mistake-in-iran-sanctions -designation.

Mourlon-Druol, Emmanuel, and Angela Romano. "The Iran Nuclear Deal Crisis: Lessons from the 1982 Transatlantic Dispute over the Siberian Gas Pipeline." Bruegel. May 2018. https://www.bruegel.org/2018/05/the-iran-nuclear-deal-crisis-lessons-from-the-1982 -transatlantic-dispute-over-the-siberian-gas-pipeline.

Mustian, Jim. "Report: Oligarchs Skirt US Sanctions Through Shady Art Sales," Associated Press, July 29, 2020. https://apnews.com/85e77f9b520cefc1f536bc417d9099cc.

Nakashima, Ellen. "U.S. Accuses Three North Koreans of Conspiring to Steal More than $1.3 Billion in Cash and Cryptocurrency." *Washington Post*, February 18, 2021. https://www .washingtonpost.com/national-security/north-korea-hackers-banks-theft/2021/02/17 /3dccfodc-7129-11eb-93be-c10813e358a2_story.html.

Namazi, Siamak. "Sanctions and Medical Supply Shortages in Iran." Woodrow Wilson Center. February 2013. https://www.wilsoncenter.org/sites/default/files/media/documents/publication/sanctions_medical_supply_shortages_in_iran.pdf.

National Payments Corporation of India. "UPI Product Statistics." Accessed January 23, 2022. https://www.npci.org.in/product-statistics/upi-product-statistics.

Nephew, Richard. "China and Economic Sanctions: Where Does Washington Have Leverage?" Brookings. September 2019. https://www.brookings.edu/research/china-and-economic-sanctions-where-does-washington-have-leverage.

Nephew, Richard. "Collateral Damage: The Impact on Pakistan from U.S. Sanctions Against Iran." Columbia/SIPA Center on Global Energy Policy. August 2017. https://energypolicy.columbia.edu/sites/default/files/CGEPSanctionsandtheRisk%20ofCollateralDamage TheImpactofUSIranSanctionsonPakistan0717.pdf.

Nephew, Richard. "Decertification of the JCPOA and the Risk of European Union 'Blocking Regulation.'" Columbia/SIPA Center on Global Energy Policy. October 31, 2017. https://energypolicy.columbia.edu/research/commentary/decertification-jcpoa-and-risk-european-union-blocking-regulations.

Nephew, Richard. "Evaluating the Trump's Administration's Approach to Sanctions, Case: Iran." Columbia/SIPA Center on Global Energy Policy. November 8, 2019. https://www.energypolicy.columbia.edu/research/commentary/evaluating-trump-administration-s-approach-sanctions-iran.

Nephew, Richard. "Evaluating the Trump Administration's Approach to Sanctions, Case: Venezuela." Columbia/SIPA Center on Global Energy Policy. June 17, 2020. https://energypolicy.columbia.edu/research/commentary/evaluating-trump-administration-s-approach-sanctions-venezuela.

Nephew, Richard. "Issue Brief: The Future of Economic Sanctions in a Global Economy." Columbia/SIPA Center on Global Energy Policy. May 21, 2015. https://www.energypolicy.columbia.edu/research/report/future-economic-sanctions-global-economy.

Nephew, Richard. "Libya: Sanctions Removal Done Right? A Review of the Libyan Sanctions Experience." Columbia/SIPA Center on Global Energy Policy. March 2018. https://energypolicy.columbia.edu/sites/default/files/pictures/Libya%20Sanctions%20Removal_CGEP_Report_031918.pdf.

Nephew, Richard. "Reconsidering US Sanctions Policy Amid the Coronavirus Crisis and the Oil Market Crash." Columbia/SIPA Center on Global Energy Policy. March 2020. https://energypolicy.columbia.edu/sites/default/files/file-uploads/Sanctions_CGEP_Commentary_033120-2.pdf.

Nephew, Richard. The Art of Sanctions, a View from the Field. New York: Columbia University Press, 2018.

Nephew, Richard. "The Humanitarian Impact of Sanctions." Columbia/SIPA Center on Global Energy Policy. April 29, 2015. https://energypolicy.columbia.edu/sanctions-blog-columbia-s-center-global-energy-policy-post-six.

Nephew, Richard. "The Impact of Covid-19 on Global Supply Chains and Sanctions." Columbia/SIPA Center on Global Energy Policy. May 2020. https://www.energypolicy.columbia.edu/sites/default/files/file-uploads/SupplyChains+Sanctions_CGEP_Commentary_050720-2.pdf.

Nephew, Richard. "Transatlantic Sanctions Policy: From the 1982 Soviet Gas Pipeline Episode to Today." Columbia/SIPA Center on Global Energy Policy. March 22, 2019. https://energypolicy.columbia.edu/research/report/transatlantic-sanctions-policy-1982-soviet-gas-pipeline-episode-today.

Nephew, Richard. "Understanding and Assessing the New US Sanctions Legislation Against Russia." Columbia/SIPA Center on Global Energy Policy. February 15, 2019. https://energypolicy.columbia.edu/research/commentary/understanding-and-assessing-new-us-sanctions-legislation-against-russia.

Nephew, Richard. "U.S. Sanctions Relief: Good for Russian Companies but Bad for Policy?" Columbia/SIPA Center on Global Energy Policy. January 11, 2019. https://energypolicy.columbia.edu/research/commentary/us-sanctions-relief-good-russian-companies-bad-policy.

Nephew, Richard, and Colin Rowat. "ExxonMobil Just Challenged Trump to Get Serious with Russia Policy." *Fortune*, April 30, 2017. https://fortune.com/2017/04/30/sanctions-waivers-donald-trump-russia-exxonmobil.

New York Times. "Bombings in Beirut." October 25, 1983. https://www.nytimes.com/1983/10/25/nyregion/tuesday-october-25-1983-bombings-in-beirut.html.

New York Times. "Bonn Needs the Business Even More than the Gas." August 16, 1981. https://www.nytimes.com/1981/08/16/weekinreview/bonn-needs-the-business-even-more-than-the-gas.html.

New York Times. "Caterpillar Gets Export License." December 10, 1981. https://www.nytimes.com/1981/12/10/business/caterpillar-gets-export-license.html.

Nord Stream 2. "Background Story: Pipeline Construction—Nord Stream 2." Accessed February 7, 2021. https://www.nord-stream2.com/media/documents/pdf/en/2018/10/background-story-pipeline-construction-en.pdf.

Nossal, Kim. "Liberal-Democratic Regimes, International Sanctions, and Global Governance." In *Globalization and Global Governance*, ed. Raimo Väyrynen, 127–49. Lanham, MD: Rowman & Littlefield, 1999.

O'Dwyer, Peter. "State Vows to Fight for Alumina Plant." *Sunday Times* (London, UK), January 29, 2019. https://www.thetimes.co.uk/article/state-vows-to-fight-for-alumina-plant-qzv89rf6g.

O'Halloran, Barry. "Deal to Lift Sanctions Against Aughinish Alumina Refinery at Shannon in the Balance." *Irish Times*, November 12, 2018. https://www.irishtimes.com/business/manufacturing/deal-to-lift-sanctions-against-aughinish-alumina-refinery-at-shannon-in-the-balance-1.3694140.

Organization for Economic Cooperation and Development. "Measuring Distortions in International Markets: The Semiconductor Value Chain." December 12, 2019. https://doi.org/10.1787/8fe4491d-en.

Ostroukh, Andrey. "Russia Says BRICS Nations Favour Idea of Common Payment System." Reuters, November 14, 2019. https://www.reuters.com/article/uk-brics-summit-russia-fx/russia-says-brics-nations-favour-idea-of-common-payment-system-idUSKBN1XO1KQ.

Ostroukh, Andrey, and Elena Fabrichnaya. "Russia Backs Global Use of Its Alternative SWIFT System." Reuters, March 19, 2019. https://uk.reuters.com/article/russia-banks-swift/russia-backs-global-use-of-its-alternative-swift-system-idUKL8N2163BU.

Oswald, Rachel. "Calls Grow for Trump to Relax Humanitarian Sanctions on Iran." *CQ Roll Call*, April 9, 2020. https://www.rollcall.com/2020/04/09/calls-grow-for-trump-to-relax -humanitarian-sanctions-on-iran.

O'Toole, Brian, and Daniel Fried. "US Opens Door to Nord Stream II Sanctions and Transatlantic Tensions." Atlantic Council. July 15, 2020. https://www.atlanticcouncil.org /blogs/new-atlanticist/us-opens-door-to-nord-stream-ii-sanctions-and-transatlantic -tensions.

O'Toole, Brian, and Samantha Sultoon. "Memo to Congress: Treasury's Plan to Lift Sanctions on Russian Oligarch's Companies Is a Good One." Atlantic Council. January 11, 2019. https://www.atlanticcouncil.org/blogs/new-atlanticist/memo-to-congress-treasury-s -plan-to-lift-sanctions-on-russian-oligarch-s-companies-is-a-good-one.

Oxford Analytica. "Western Use of Targeted Sanctions Is Intensifying." March 30, 2021. https://dailybrief.oxan.com/Analysis/GA260544/Western-use-of-targeted-sanctions-is -intensifying.

Pallardy, Diane. "US Threatens Nord Stream 2 Gas Pipe Investors with Sanctions." Independent Commodity Intelligence Services. July 16, 2020. https://www.icis.com/explore/resources /news/2020/07/16/10530894/us-threatens-nord-stream-2-gas-pipe-investors-with-sanctions.

Pamuk, Humeyra, and Timothy Gardner. "U.S. Lifts Iran Sanctions on One Unit of Chinese Shipping Giant COSCO." Reuters, January 31, 2020. https://www.reuters.com/article/us -iran-nuclear-usa-cosco/u-s-lifts-iran-sanctions-on-one-unit-of-chinese-shipping-giant -cosco-idUSKBN1ZU04I.

Pan, David. "Goldman Sachs Expects Digital Yuan to Reach 1B Users Within 10 Years." Coindesk. November 19, 2020. https://www.coindesk.com/goldman-sachs-digital-yuan-report.

Pan, David. "How Ant's Suspended IPO Is Related to China's Digital Yuan." Coindesk. November 12, 2020. https://www.coindesk.com/how-ants-suspended-ipo-is-related-to-chinas -digital-yuan.

Parker, Dominic, Jeremy Foltz, and David Elsea. "Unintended Consequences of Sanctions for Human Rights. Conflict Minerals and Infant Mortality." *Journal of Law and Economics* 59, no. 4 (November 2016): 731–74, https://doi.org/10.1086/691793.

Parraga, Marianna. "Exclusive: As Citgo Profit Rises, Pressure to Restore Dividend Grows—Sources." Reuters, December 4, 2019. https://www.reuters.com/article/us-citgo-dividends -exclusive/exclusive-as-citgo-profit-rises-pressure-to-restore-dividend-grows-sources -idUSKBN1Y82SQ.

Parraga, Marianna, Rinat Sagdiev, and Parisa Hafezi. "Special Report: Phantom Oil Buyers in Russia, Advice from Iran Help Venezuela Skirt Sanctions." Reuters, November 10, 2020. https://www.reuters.com/article/venezuela-oil-exports-special-report/special -report-phantom-buyers-in-russia-advice-from-iran-help-venezuela-skirt-sanctions -idUSKBN27Q2CB.

Parry, Angharad. "Rusal Sanctions: Market Turmoil and Legal Fall-out." Essex Street. April 2018. https://twentyessex.com/wp-content/uploads/2019/06/Rusal-sanctions.pdf.

Partington, Richard. "14m Bolivars for a Chicken: Venezuela Hyperinflation Explained." *Guardian*, August 20, 2018. https://www.theguardian.com/world/2018/aug/20/venezuela -bolivars-hyperinflation-banknotes.

Paterson, Stewart. "The Digital Renminbi and China's Potential Financial Revolution: A Primer on Central Bank Digital Currencies." Hinrich Foundation. July 2020. https://www .hinrichfoundation.com/media/2kybhumm/hinrich-foundation-white-paper-digitual -yuan-and-china-s-potential-financial-revolution-july-2020.pdf.

Paterson, Stewart. "US-China Decoupling: How Far Could It Go?" Hinrich Foundation. September 2, 2020. https://www.hinrichfoundation.com/research/wp/us-china/us-china-decoupling.

Peksen, Dursun. "Better or Worse? The Effect of Economic Sanctions on Human Rights." *Journal of Peace Research* 46, no. 1 (January 2009): 59–77. https://doi.org/10.1177/0022343308098404.

Peri, Dinakar. "Payment Issues over S-400 Deal Resolved: Russian Officials." *Hindu*, August 29, 2019. https://www.thehindu.com/news/national/payment-issues-over-s-400-deal-resolved -russian-officials/article29281658.ece.

Perl, Raphael. "Drug Trafficking and North Korea: Issues for U.S. Policy." Congressional Research Service. January 25, 2007. https://fas.org/sgp/crs/row/RL32167.pdf.

Perlow, Gary. "Taking Peacetime Trade Sanctions to the Limit: The Soviet Pipeline Embargo." *Case Western Reserve Journal of International Law* 15, no. 253 (1983). https://scholarlycommons .law.case.edu/jil/vol15/iss2/4.

Pham, Sherisse. "Losing Huawei as a Customer Could Cost US Tech Companies $11 Billion." CNN, May 17, 2019. https://www.cnn.com/2019/05/17/tech/hua-wei-us-ban-suppliers/index.html.

Politi, James, Demetri Sevastopulo, and Hudson Locke. "US Adds China's Largest Chipmaker to Export Blacklist." *Financial Times*, December 18, 2020. https://www.ft.com/content/7dcc105e -986b-4768-9239-9f8fa9073b53https://www.ft.com/content/7dcc105e-986b-4768-9239 -9f8fa9073b53.

Proper, Ellen. "ASML Stays Positive Despite Being Caught by U.S., China Rift." Bloomberg, October 14, 2020. https://www.bloomberg.com/news/articles/2020-10-14/asml-expects-low -double-digit-growth-next-year-resumes-buybacks.

Public Papers of the Presidents of the United States. "Presidential Documents—January 1 to June 30." No. 01 (1998): 998. https://www.govinfo.gov/content/pkg/PPP-1998-book1/pdf /PPP-1998-book1.pdf.

Quenelle, Benjamin. "Sanctions: le 'roi de l'aluminium' russe accuse Washington." *Les Echos*, February 14, 2020. https://www.lesechos.fr/finance-marches/marches-financiers/sanctions -loligarque-de-laluminium-accuse-washington-1171891.

Rachmann, Gideon. "A New Cold War: Trump, Xi and the Escalating US-China Confrontation." *Financial Times*, October 5, 2020. https://www.ft.com/content/7b809c6a-f733-46f5-a312 -9152aed28172.

Rappeport, Alan. "Exxon Mobil Fined for Violating Sanctions on Russia." *New York Times*, July 20, 2017. https://www.nytimes.com/2017/07/20/us/politics/exxon-mobil-fined-russia -tillerson-sanctions.html.

Rasser, Martijn, and Ashley Feng. "This Is How to Solve America's Rare-Earths Dilemma." National Interest. June 28, 2019. https://nationalinterest.org/feature/how-solve-americas -rare-earths-dilemma-64751.

Ratna, Tanvi. "Iran Has a Bitcoin Strategy to Beat Trump." *Foreign Policy*, January 24, 2020. https:// foreignpolicy.com/2020/01/24/iran-bitcoin-strategy-cryptocurrency-blockchain-sanctions.

Reed, Stanley. "Total Signs Deal with Iran, Exposing It to Big Risks and Rewards." *New York Times*, July 3, 2017. https://www.nytimes.com/2017/07/03/business/energy-environment /iran-total-france-gas-energy.html.

Reed, Stanley, and Lara Jakes. "A Russian Gas Pipeline Increases Tension Between the U.S. and Europe." *New York Times*, July 24, 2020. https://www.nytimes.com/2020/07/24/business /nord-stream-pipeline-russia.html.

Rees, Kit, and Viktoria Dendrinou. "EU Sets Out Plans to Limit U.S. Dollar Reliance, Boost Euro." Bloomberg, January 16, 2021. https://www.bloomberg.com/news/articles/2021-01-16 /eu-draft-sets-out-plans-to-limit-u-s-dollar-reliance-ft.

Rennack, Dianne. "North Korea: Economic Sanctions." Congressional Research Service. October 17, 2006. https://fas.org/sgp/crs/row/RL31696.pdf.

Reuters. "Austria Charges Bank After Cuban Accounts Cancelled." April 27, 2007. https:// www.reuters.com/article/austria-bawag/austria-charges-bank-after-cuban-accounts -cancelled-idUSL2711446820070427.

Reuters. "BAWAG Restores Cuban Accounts After Public Uproar." May 4, 2007. https://www .reuters.com/article/austria-bawag-cuba-idUSL0450488520070504.

Reuters. "Bitcoin at 'Tipping Point,' Citi Says as Price Surges." March 1, 2021. https://www .reuters.com/article/us-crypto-currency-bitcoin-citi-idUSKCN2AT23H.

Reuters. "China Needs First Mover Advantage in Digital Currency Race: PBOC Magazine." September 21, 2020. https://www.reuters.com/article/china-pboc-renminnbi-digital /refile-china-needs-first-mover-advantage-in-digital-currency-race-pboc-magazine -idUSL3N2GI11F.

Reuters. "Explainer: U.S. Dependence on China's Rare Earth—Trade War Vulnerability." June 3, 2019. https://www.reuters.com/article/us-usa-trade-china-rareearth-explainer/explainer -u-s-dependence-on-chinas-rare-earth-trade-war-vulnerability-idUSKCN1T42RP.

Reuters. "FACTBOX—China's Onshore Yuan Clearing and Settlement System CIPS." July 30, 2020. https://www.reuters.com/article/china-banks-clearing-idUSL3N2F115E.

Reuters. "Factbox: Oil, Loans, Military—Russia's Exposure to Venezuela." January 24, 2019. https://www.reuters.com/article/us-venezuela-politics-russia-factbox/factbox-oil-loans -military-russias-exposure-to-venezuela-idUSKCN1PI1T4.

Reuters. "Factbox: What Is China's Onshore Yuan Clearing and Settlement System CIPS?" February 28, 2022. https://www.reuters.com/markets/europe/what-is-chinas-onshore-yuan -clearing-settlement-system-cips-2022-02-28.

Reuters. "Iran Says China's CNPC Replacing France's Total in Gas Project." November 25, 2018. https://www.reuters.com/article/us-oil-iran-cnpc/iran-says-chinas-cnpc-replacing -frances-total-in-gas-project-idUSKCN1NU0FP.

Reuters. "Putin Says Nord Stream 2 Link Ready to Calm Gas Prices." December 29, 2021. https://www.reuters.com/markets/commodities/putin-declares-nord-stream-2-ready -gas-exports-2021-12-29.

Reuters. "Russia's Gazprom Expects Nord Stream 2 Launch in 2021: RIA." February 11, 2021. https://www.reuters.com/article/us-gazprom-nordstream2/russias-gazprom-expects -nord-stream-2-launch-in-2021-ria-idUSKBN2AB1JL.

Reuters. "Russia Says 'Nothing Catastrophic' About U.S. Sanctions on Nord Stream 2." December 23, 2019. https://www.reuters.com/article/us-usa-russia-nord-stream-medvedev/russia-says-nothing-catastrophic-about-u-s-sanctions-on-nord-stream-2-idUSKBN1YR1Q8.

Reuters. "U.S. Judge Rules PDVSA's 2020 Bonds Are Valid, Citgo Still Protected." October 16, 2020. https://uk.reuters.com/article/us-venezuela-debt/u-s-judge-rules-pdvsas-2020-bonds-are-valid-citgo-still-protected-idUKKBN2712DG.

Reuters. "U.S. Trade Embargo Has Cost Cuba $130 Billion, U.N. Says." May 9, 2018. https://www.reuters.com/article/us-cuba-economy-un-idUSKBN1IA00T.

Ribando Seelke, Clare. "Venezuela: Overview of U.S. Sanctions." Congressional Research Service. Accessed April 23, 2020. https://fas.org/sgp/crs/row/IF10715.pdf.

Rieff, David. "Were Sanctions Right?" *New York Times*, July 27, 2003. https://www.nytimes.com/2003/07/27/magazine/were-sanctions-right.html.

Riley, Alan. "Nord Stream 2: Understanding the Potential Consequences." Atlantic Council. June 2018. https://www.atlanticcouncil.org/wp-content/uploads/2018/06/Nord_Stream_2_interactive.pdf.

Rio Tinto. "Rio Tinto Reviews Arrangements with Rusal." April 13, 2018. https://www.riotinto.com/news/releases/Rusal-arrangements-reviewed.

Risen, James, and Mark Mazzetti. "U.S. Agencies See No Move by Iran to Build a Bomb." *New York Times*, February 24, 2012. https://www.nytimes.com/2012/02/25/world/middleeast/us-agencies-see-no-move-by-iran-to-build-a-bomb.html.

Robert, Virginie. "Pierre Vimont: 'Il faut que l'Europe soit capable de montrer qu'on peut mordre face aux sanctions extraterritoriales.'" *Les Echos*, March 22, 2021. https://www.lesechos.fr/monde/enjeux-internationaux/pierre-vimont-il-faut-que-leurope-soit-capable-de-montrer-quon-peut-mordre-face-aux-sanctions-extraterritoriales-1300265.

Rodríguez, Francisco. "Why More Sanctions Won't Help Venezuela." *Foreign Policy*, January 12, 2018. https://foreignpolicy.com/2018/01/12/why-more-sanctions-wont-help-venezuela.

Rosenberg, Elizabeth, and Neil Bhatiya. "Busting North Korea's Sanctions Evasion." Center for a New American Security. March 4, 2020. https://www.cnas.org/publications/commentary/busting-north-koreas-sanctions-evasion.

Rosenberg, Elizabeth, Peter Harrell, and Ashley Feng. "A New Arsenal for Competition, Coercive Economic Measures in the U.S.-China Relationship." Center for a New American Security. April 24, 2020. https://www.cnas.org/publications/reports/a-new-arsenal-for-competition.

Roth, Andrew, and Carol Morello. "Kremlin Reacts with Anger and Ridicule to Treasury List of Influential Russians." *Washington Post*, January 30, 2018. https://www.washingtonpost.com/world/kremlin-reacts-with-anger-and-ridicule-to-treasury-list-of-influential-russians/2018/01/30/f5405586-05c7-11e8-8777-2a059f168dd2_story.html.

Roth, John, Douglas Greenburg, and Serena Wille. "Monograph on Terrorist Financing." National Commission on Terrorist Attacks Upon the United States. 2004. Accessed June 17, 2020. https://govinfo.library.unt.edu/911/staff_statements/911_TerrFin_Monograph.pdf.

Rubenfeld, Samuel. "U.S. Sanctions Listing Could Hurt Humanitarian Trade with Iran." *Wall Street Journal*, October 19, 2018. https://www.wsj.com/articles/u-s-sanctions-listing-could-hurt-humanitarian-trade-with-iran-1539941400.

Ruehl, Mercedes, and James Kynge. "The US's Big Plan to Cut Supply Chain Reliance on China." *Financial Times*, February 24, 2021. https://www.ft.com/content/6bc86e88-81d6-4f3b-8e30-337ca640c760.

Sadjapour, Karim. "How to Win the Cold War with Iran." *Atlantic*, March 25, 2021. https://www.theatlantic.com/ideas/archive/2021/03/how-win-cold-war-iran/618388.

Sadjapour, Karim. "Iranian Supreme Leader Ali Khamenei Is One Despot Trump Might Not Win Over." *Time*, October 3, 2019. https://time.com/5691642/iran-supreme-leader-ali-khamenei-trump.

Saiidi, Uptin. "China's Foreign Direct Investment into the US Dropped Precipitously in 2018, Data Show." CNBC, January 15, 2019. https://www.cnbc.com/2019/01/15/chinese-foreign-direct-investment-to-the-us-falls-in-2018-data.html.

Salehi-Isfahani, Djavad. "Impact of Sanctions on Household Welfare and Employment." Johns Hopkins University. Accessed December 10, 2020. https://static1.squarespace.com/static/5f0f5b1018e89f351b8b3ef8/t/5fd0e13ca4b4ef2db6b17e06/1607524670688/Iran UnderSanctions_Salehi-Isfahani.pdf.

Saravalle, Edoardo. "How U.S. Sanctions Depend on the Federal Reserve." Center for a New American Security. July 29, 2020. https://www.cnas.org/publications/commentary/how-u-s-sanctions-depend-on-the-federal-reserve.

Satter, Raphael. "Exclusive-Suspected Chinese Hackers Stole Camera Footage from African Union—Memo." Reuters, December 16, 2020. https://in.mobile.reuters.com/article/amp/idINKBN28Q1DB.

Saul, Jonathan. "Ship Firm Oldendorff Halting Guyana Operation Due to Rusal Crisis." Reuters, April 20, 2018. https://www.reuters.com/article/us-usa-sanctions-oldendorff/ship-firm-oldendorff-halting-guyana-operation-due-to-rusal-crisis-idUSKBN1HR2AD.

Saul, Jonathan, and Chen Aizhu. "Unipec Replaces Ship Charters After U.S. Sanctions COSCO Tanker Units: Sources." Reuters, September 26, 2019. https://www.reuters.com/article/us-iran-nuclear-usa-china/unipec-replaces-ship-charters-after-u-s-sanctions-cosco-tanker-units-sources-idUSKBN1WB1XY.

Scheck, Justin, and Shane Shifflett. "How Dirty Money Disappears into the Black Hole of Cryptocurrency." *Wall Street Journal*, September 28, 2018. https://www.wsj.com/articles/how-dirty-money-disappears-into-the-black-hole-of-cryptocurrency-1538149743.

Scheid, Brian. "Chevron's Venezuela Sanctions Waiver Extended to April: US Treasury." S&P Global Platts. January 18, 2020. https://www.spglobal.com/platts/en/market-insights/latest-news/oil/011820-chevrons-venezuela-sanctions-waiver-extended-to-april-us-treasury.

Scheid, Brian. "End of Cosco Sanctions Shows US Reluctance for Penalizing Key Oil Market Players: Analysts." S&P Global Platts. February 3, 2020. https://www.spglobal.com/platts/en/market-insights/latest-news/oil/020320-end-of-cosco-sanctions-shows-us-reluctance-for-penalizing-key-oil-market-players-analysts.

Scheid, Brian. "US Set to Sanction Rosneft Oil, Fuel Trade with PDVSA: Senior Trump Administration Official." S&P Global Platts. August 15, 2019. https://www.spglobal.com/platts/es/market-insights/latest-news/oil/081519-us-set-to-sanction-rosneft-oil-fuel-trade-with-pdvsa-senior-trump-administration-official.

Scheyder, Ernest. "EXCLUSIVE U.S. Bill Would Block Defense Contractors from Using Chinese Rare Earths." Reuters, January 14, 2022. https://www.reuters.com/business/energy/exclusive-us-bill-would-block-defense-contractors-using-chinese-rare-earths-2022-01-14.

Scheyder, Ernest. "Miners Praise U.S. Spending Bill That Funds Rare Earths Programs." Reuters, December 30, 2020. https://www.reuters.com/article/us-usa-mining-congress -idUSKBN29424R.

Schmitt, Benjamin. "Hot Issue—They're Gonna Need a Bigger Boat: The Curious Voyage of the Akademik Cherskiy." Jamestown Foundation. March 31, 2020. https://jamestown.org /program/hot-issue-theyre-gonna-need-a-bigger-boat-the-curious-voyage-of-the-akademik -cherskiy.

Schomberg, William. "World Needs to End Risky Reliance on U.S. Dollar: BoE's Carney." Reuters, August 23, 2019. https://www.reuters.com/article/us-usa-fed-jacksonhole-carney -idUSKCN1VD28C.

Schroder, Pete. "U.S. Lawmakers Seek to Ban Federal Pension Fund from Investing in China." Reuters, November 6, 2019. https://www.reuters.com/article/us-usa-trade-rubio -tsp-idUSKBN1XG2QO.

Schroders. "Banks: A New Approach to Risk? Governance, Culture and Risk in a Revamped Banking Industry." January 2015. https://www.schroders.com/en/sysglobalassets/digital /insights/pdfs/banks-a-new-approach-to-risk.pdf.

Schwirtz, Michael, and Melissa Eddy. "Aleksei Navalny Was Poisoned with Novichok, Germany Says." New York Times, September 2, 2020. https://www.nytimes.com/2020/09/02 /world/europe/navalny-poison-novichok.html.

Seaman, John. "China and the New Geopolitics of Technical Standardization." Institut Français des Relations Internationales. January 2020. https://www.ifri.org/sites/default/files/atoms /files/seaman_china_standardization_2020.pdf.

Seddon, Max, and Henry Foy. "Russia Looks at Alternatives to Dollar for Energy Transactions." Financial Times, October 13, 2019. https://www.ft.com/content/704cde6c-eb53-11e9-a240 -3b065ef5fc55.

Semiconductor Industry Association. "Global Semiconductor Sales Increase 24 Percent Year-to-Year in October; Annual Sales Projected to Increase 26 Percent in 2021, Exceed $600 Billion in 2022." December 3, 2021. https://www.semiconductors.org/global-semiconductor -sales-increase-24-year-to-year-in-october-annual-sales-projected-to-increase-26-in -2021-exceed-600-billion-in-2022.

Semiconductor Industry Association. "SIA Urges U.S. Government Action to Strengthen America's Semiconductor Supply Chain." April 5, 2021. https://www.semiconductors .org/sia-urges-u-s-government-action-to-strengthen-americas-semiconductor-supply -chain.

Semiconductor Industry Association. "The 2020 SIA Factbook: Your Source for Semiconductor Industry Data." Accessed October 13, 2020. https://www.semiconductors.org /the-2020-sia-factbook-your-source-for-semiconductor-industry-data.

Senator Ted Cruz. "Sen. Cruz: 'The Administration Needs to Immediately Begin Implementing These Sanctions' on Nord Stream 2 Pipe-Laying Vessels." December 12, 2019. https:// www.cruz.senate.gov/?p=press_release&id=4818.

Sevastopulo, Demetri, and Kathrin Hille. "US Fears China Is Flirting with Seizing Control of Taiwan." Financial Times, March 27, 2021. https://www.ft.com/content/3ed169b8 -3f47-4f66-a914-58b6e2215f7d.

Sevastopulo, Demetri, Henry Foy, and David Sheppard. "US Steps Up Threats over Nord Stream 2 Pipeline." *Financial Times*, July 15, 2020. https://www.ft.com/content/ff3edd61 -a404-48b0-adb8-65b91bc90486.

Shagina, Maria. "A Tale of Two Pipelines." Riddle Russia. January 13, 2021, https://www.ridl.io /en/a-tale-of-two-pipelines.

Sharma, Ruchir. "Will Bitcoin End the Dollar's Reign?" *Financial Times*, December 9, 2020. https://www.ft.com/content/ea33b688-12e0-459c-80c5-2efba58e6f1a.

Sheehan, Matt. "China Technology 2025: Fragile Tech Superpower." Macro Polo, Paulson Institute. October 26, 2020. https://macropolo.org/analysis/china-technology-forecast-2025 -fragile-tech-superpower.

Shen, Samuel, and Josh Horwitz. "China Tech Veterans to Launch 'Domestic Replacement' Fund Amid U.S. Sanctions." Reuters, September 15, 2020. https://www.reuters.com/article /china-tech-fund-idUSKBN25Z1R9.

Shepardson, David. "U.S. Tightening Restrictions on Huawei Access to Technology, Chips." Reuters, August 17, 2020. https://www.reuters.com/article/us-usa-huawei-tech-exclusive /exclusive-u-s-to-tighten-restrictions-on-huawei-access-to-technology-chips-sources -say-idUSKCN25D1CC.

Shepardson, David, Karen Freifeld, and Alexandra Alper. "U.S. Moves to Cut Huawei Off from Global Chip Suppliers as China Eyes Retaliation." Reuters, May 15, 2020. https://www .reuters.com/article/us-usa-huawei-tech-exclusive/exclusive-us-moves-to-cut-huawei -off-from-global-chip-suppliers-idUSKBN22R1KC.

Silk Road Briefing. "Shanghai Cooperation Organisation to Introduce 'Mutual Settlement in National Currencies' and Ditch US Dollar." March 18, 2020. https://www.silkroadbriefing .com/news/2020/03/18/shanghai-cooperation-organisation-introduce-mutual-settlement -national-currencies-ditch-us-dollar.

Simes, Dimitri. "China and Russia Ditch Dollar in Move Towards 'Financial Alliance.'" *Financial Times*, August 16, 2020. https://www.ft.com/content/8421b6a2-1dc6-4747-b2e9-1bbfb7277747.

Simon, Clea. "Cryptocurrency and National Insecurity." *Harvard Gazette*, November 20, 2019. https://news.harvard.edu/gazette/story/2019/11/crisis-simulation-maps-national-security -risks-of-digital-currency.

Smets, Marteen. "Can Economic Sanctions Be Effective?" WTO Staff Working Paper, No. 2018/03. Geneva: World Trade Organization, 2018. https://dx.doi.org/10.30875/0b967ac6-en.

Smis, Stefaan, and Kim Van Der Borght. "The EU-U.S. Compromise on the Helms-Burton and D'Amato Acts." *American Journal of International Law* 93, no. 1 (1999): 227–36. https://doi .org/10.2307/2997968.

Smith, Colby, Eva Szalay, and Katie Martin. "Dollar Blues: Why the Pandemic Is Testing Confidence in the US Currency." *Financial Times*, July 31, 2020. https://www.ft.com /content/7c963379-10df-4314-9bd0-351ddcdc699e.

Smyth, Jamie. "US-China: Washington Revives Plans for Its Rare Earths Industry." *Financial Times*, September 14, 2020. https://www.ft.com/content/5104d84d-a78f-4648-b695-bd7e14c135d6.

Soldatkin, Vladimir. "Exxon Pursues Cost Cuts at Russia's Sakhalin-1 Project." Reuters, May 8, 2020. https://uk.reuters.com/article/health-coronavirus-russia-exxon/update-1-exxon-pursues -cost-cuts-at-russias-sakhalin-1-project-idUKL8N2CQ1TR.

Soldatkin, Vladimir, and Natalia Chumakova. "Russian Vessel Able to Complete Nord Stream 2 Pipeline Departs from German Port." Reuters, July 8, 2020. https://www.reuters.com /article/us-nordstream-vessel/russian-vessel-able-to-complete-nord-stream-2-pipeline -departs-from-german-port-idUSKBN2491WE.

Solomon, Erika, and Katrina Manson. "US Senators' Letter on Nord Stream 2 Sparks Outrage in Germany." Financial Times, August 19, 2020. https://www.ft.com/content/f43fa079-bf7f -4efa-8f72-ae9fd4a5368f.

Solsvik, Terje. "Russia, Brazil Woes Could Lead to Aluminum Supply Shortage: Hydro CEO." Reuters, April 16, 2018, https://www.reuters.com/article/us-norsk-hydro-aluminium/russia -brazil-woes-could-lead-to-aluminum-supply-shortage-hydro-ceo-idUSKBN1HN18G.

Somasundaram, Narayanan. "China Sets Trial Run for Digital Renminbi in Top City Hubs." Nikkei Asia, August 14, 2020. https://asia.nikkei.com/Business/China-tech/China-sets-trial -run-for-digital-yuan-in-top-city-hubs.

South China Morning Post. "China's Global Payment System for Yuan Sees Limited Launch." October 9, 2015. https://www.scmp.com/business/banking-finance/article/1865370/chinas -global-payment-system-yuan-sees-limited-launch.

South China Morning Post. "CIPS to Break Chinese Banks' Global Monopoly over Yuan Clearing." September 11, 2015. https://www.scmp.com/business/banking-finance/article/1857121 /cips-break-chinese-banks-global-monopoly-over-yuan-clearing.

Spiegel. "US-Botschafter Grenell schreibt Drohbriefe an deutsche Firmen." Accessed July 30, 2020. https://www.spiegel.de/politik/deutschland/richard-grenell-us-botschafter-schreibt -drohbriefe-an-deutsche-firmen-a-1247785.html.

Staalesen, Atle. "These Are Rex Tillerson's Assets in Arctic Russia." Barents Observer, December 2016. https://thebarentsobserver.com/en/arctic-industry-and-energy/2016/12 /these-are-rex-tillersons-assets-arctic-russia.

Staalesen, Atle. "They Found One of Russia's Biggest Arctic Oil Fields, but Now Abandon It." Barents Observer, March 2018. https://thebarentsobserver.com/en/industry-and-energy/2018/03/ they-found-one-russias-biggest-offshore-arctic-oil-field-now-abandon-it.

Stacey, Kiran. "Trump Ban on Chinese Drone Parts Risks Worsening Wildfires." Financial Times, August 31, 2020. https://www.ft.com/content/387d2270-eded-4b8d-80e9-b23dd7ff694a.

Stacey, Kiran. "US to Ground Civilian Drone Programme on Concerns over China Tech." Financial Times, January 12, 2020. https://www.ft.com/content/a50088de-33f6-11ea-9703-eea0cae3f0de.

Steil, Benn. "Central Bank Currency Swaps Tracker." Council on Foreign Relations. Accessed August 9, 2020. https://www.cfr.org/article/central-bank-currency-swaps-tracker.

Stephens, Philip. "Sanctions Are Donald Trump's New Way of War." Financial Times, October 17, 2019. https://www.ft.com/content/86eb2db4-f016-11e9-ad1e-4367d8281195.

Stoop, Nik, Marijke Verpoorten, and Peter van der Windt. "More Legislation, More Violence? The Impact of Dodd-Frank in the DRC." PloS ONE 13, no. 8 (August 2018), https://doi .org/10.1371/journal.pone.0201783.

Stoop, Nik, Marijke Verpoorten, and Peter van der Windt. "Trump Threatened to Suspend the 'Conflict Minerals' Provision of Dodd-Frank. That Might Actually Be Good for Congo." Washington Post, September 27, 2018. https://www.washingtonpost.com/news /monkey-cage/wp/2018/09/27/trump-canceled-the-conflict-minerals-provision-of-dodd -frank-thats-probably-good-for-the-congo.

Stroobants, Jean-Pierre, Faustine Vincent, Benoît Vitkine, et al. "Nord Stream 2, le gazoduc russe qui sème la zizanie en Europe." *Le Monde*, February 26, 2021. https://www.lemonde .fr/international/article/2021/02/26/nord-stream-2-le-gazoduc-russe-qui-seme-la-zizanie -en-europe_6071337_3210.html.

Stubbington, Tommy. "EU Enjoys 'Outrageous Demand' for First Covid-Related Bond." *Financial Times*, October 20, 2020. https://www.ft.com/content/e3553b68-22c8-487c-a7c0 -7e1c6dcoec4b.

Sultoon, Samantha, and Justine Walker. "Secondary Sanctions' Implications and the Transatlantic Relationship." Atlantic Council. September 2019. https://www.atlanticcouncil.org/wp -content/uploads/2019/09/SecondarySanctions_Final.pdf.

Sutter, Karen. "'Made in China 2025' Industrial Policies: Issues for Congress." Congressional Research Service. Accessed October 14, 2020. https://crsreports.congress.gov/product /pdf/IF/IF10964.

Sutter, Karen. "U.S.-China Trade and Economic Relations: Overview." Congressional Research Service. Accessed January 22, 2022. https://fas.org/sgp/crs/row/IF11284.pdf.

Swift. "SWIFT IN FIGURES, YTD June 2020." Accessed August 15, 2020. https://www.swift .com/sites/default/files/files/SIF_202006.pdf.

Szczepański, Marcin. "Economic Impact on the EU of Sanctions over Ukraine Conflict." European Parliament. October 2015. https://www.europarl.europa.eu/RegData/etudes/BRIE /2015/569020/EPRS_BRI(2015)569020_EN.pdf.

Ткачёв, Иван. "Танкеры с пропиской в России подключились к перевозке венесуэльской нефти." *РБК*. December 14, 2020. https://www.rbc.ru/economics/14/12/2020/5fce9d879a 79471c1e8cb6b4.

Tagliabue, John. "Europeans in Pact on Soviet Gas." *New York Times*, September 30, 1981. https://www.nytimes.com/1981/09/30/business/europeans-in-pact-on-soviet-gas.html.

Tang, Frank. "China's Five-Year Plan to Focus on Independence as US Decoupling Threat Grows." *South China Morning Post*, May 24, 2020. https://www.scmp.com/economy/china-economy /article/3085683/coronavirus-china-five-year-plan-focus-independence-us.

Tétrault-Farber, Gabrielle, and Olesya Astakhova. "Rosneft Sells Venezuelan Assets to Russia After U.S. Sanctions Ramp Up." Reuters, March 28, 2020. https://www.reuters.com/article /us-russia-rosneft-venezuela/rosneft-sells-venezuelan-assets-to-russia-after-u-s-sanctions -ramp-up-idUSKBN21F0W2.

Tett, Gillian. "Central Bankers' Crypto Experiments Should Put Investors on Alert." *Financial Times*, March 25, 2021. https://www.ft.com/content/8356521a-0bb1-4a80-973b-a9c6d60a0f19.

Teufel Dreyer, June. "China's Monopoly on Rare Earth Elements—and Why We Should Care." Foreign Policy Research Institute. October 7, 2020. https://www.fpri.org/article/2020/10 /chinas-monopoly-on-rare-earth-elements-and-why-we-should-care.

Thomson Reuters. "Regulatory Intelligence Desktop." Accessed June 13, 2020. https://legal .thomsonreuters.com/content/dam/ewp-m/documents/legal/en/pdf/brochures/tr _regulatory_intelligence_desktop_digital_us.pdf.

Tilouine, Joan, and Ghalia Kadiri. "A Addis-Abeba, le siège de l'Union africaine espionné par Pékin." *Le Monde*, January 26, 2018. https://www.lemonde.fr/afrique/article/2018/01/26 /a-addis-abeba-le-siege-de-l-union-africaine-espionne-par-les-chinois_5247521_3212 .html.

Ting-Fang, Cheng. "China's Top Maker of Memory Chips Plans to Double Output in 2021." *Nikkei Asia*, January 12, 2021. https://asia.nikkei.com/Business/China-tech/China-s-top -maker-of-memory-chips-plans-to-double-output-in-2021.

Ting-Fang, Cheng, and Lauly Li. "Asia Suppliers Hit After US Cuts Huawei's Access to Foreign Chips." *Nikkei Asia*, August 18, 2020. https://asia.nikkei.com/Spotlight/Huawei-crackdown /Asia-suppliers-hit-after-US-cuts-Huawei-s-access-to-foreign-chips.

Ting-Fang, Cheng, and Lauly Li. "China's SMIC Stockpiles Chip Equipment to Counter US Restrictions." *Nikkei Asia*, September 30, 2020. https://asia.nikkei.com/Politics /International-relations/US-China-tensions/China-s-SMIC-stockpiles-chip-equipment -to-counter-US-restrictions.

Ting-Fang, Cheng, Lauly Li, and Kenji Kawase. "China's Top Chipmaker SMIC Cuts Spending Due to US Export Curbs." *Nikkei Asia*, November 12, 2020. https://asia.nikkei.com/Economy /Trade-war/China-s-top-chipmaker-SMIC-cuts-spending-due-to-US-export-curbs.

Torbati, Yeganeh, and Ernest Scheyder. "Exxon Sues U.S. Over Fine Levied for Russia Deal Under Tillerson." Reuters, July 20, 2017. https://www.reuters.com/article/us-exxon-mobil -usa-ukraine-idUSKBN1A51UH.

Total. "2017 Factbook." Accessed June 20, 2020. https://www.total.com/sites/g/files/nytnzq111 /files/atoms/files/factbook-2017_web_0.pdf.

Total. "U.S.: Total, Borealis and NOVA Chemicals Sign Definitive Agreements to Form a Joint Venture in Petrochemicals." February 19, 2018. https://www.total.com/media/news /press-releases/us-total-borealis-and-nova-chemicals-sign-definitive-agreements-form -joint-venture-petrochemicals.

Total. "US Withdrawal from the JCPOA: Total's Position Related to the South Pars 11 Project in Iran." May 16, 2018. https://www.total.com/media/news/press-releases/us-withdrawal -jcpoa-totals-position-related-south-pars-11-project-iran.

Tsunashima, Toru. "In 165 Countries, China's Beidou Eclipses American GPS." *Nikkei Asia*, November 25, 2020. https://asia.nikkei.com/Politics/International-relations/In-165-countries -China-s-Beidou-eclipses-American-GPS.

Turak, Natasha. "Russia's Central Bank Governor Touts Moscow Alternative to SWIFT Trans- fer System as Protection from US Sanctions." CNBC, May 23, 2018. https://www.cnbc .com/2018/05/23/russias-central-bank-governor-touts-moscow-alternative-to-swift -transfer-system-as-protection-from-us-sanctions.html.

UN. "Bachelet Calls for Easing of Sanctions to Enable Medical Systems to Fight COVID-19 and Limit Global Contagion." Accessed May 12, 2020. https://ohchr.org/EN/NewsEvents /Pages/DisplayNews.aspx?NewsID=25744&LangID=E.

UN. "Report of the Panel of Experts Established Pursuant to Resolution 1874." March 5, 2019. https://www.undocs.org/S/2019/171.

UN. "Review of Maritime Transport 2019." October 30, 2019. https://unctad.org/en/Publications Library/rmt2019_en.pdf.

U.S. Central Intelligence Agency. "The Soviet Gas Pipeline in Perspective." September 21, 1982. https://www.cia.gov/library/readingroom/docs/19820921.pdf.

U.S. Congress. "China's Smart Cities Development." January 2020. https://www.uscc.gov/sites /default/files/2020-04/China_Smart_Cities_Development.pdf.

U.S. Congress. "H.R.5040—Export Control Reform Act of 2018." April 17, 2018. https://www .congress.gov/bill/115th-congress/house-bill/5040/text.

U.S. Congress. "H.R.5841—Foreign Investment Risk Review Modernization Act of 2018." June 27, 2018. https://www.congress.gov/bill/115th-congress/house-bill/5040/text.

U.S. Congress. "Report to Congress of the U.S.-China Economic and Security Review Commission." November 2019. https://www.uscc.gov/sites/default/files/2019-11/2019%20Annual% 20Report%20to%20Congress.pdf.

U.S. Congress. "The Art Industry and U.S. Policies That Undermine Sanctions." July 29, 2020. https://www.hsgac.senate.gov/imo/media/doc/2020-07-29%20PSI%20Staff%20Report%20 -%20The%20Art%20Industry%20and%20U.S.%20Policies%20that%20Undermine%20 Sanctions.pdf.

U.S. Department of Commerce. "Huawei Entity List and Temporary General License Frequently Asked Questions." Accessed October 13, 2020. https://www.bis.doc.gov/index.php /documents/pdfs/2447-huawei-entity-listing-faqs/file.

U.S. Department of Commerce. "Section 232 Investigation on the Effect of Imports of Steel on U.S. National Security." Accessed March 26, 2021. https://www.commerce.gov/section -232-investigation-effect-imports-steel-us-national-security.

U.S. Department of Commerce. "U.S. Space Industry 'Deep Dive' Assessment: Impact of the U.S. Export Controls on the Space Industrial Base." February 2014. https://www.bis .doc.gov/index.php/documents/technology-evaluation/898-space-export-control-report /file.

U.S. Department of Justice. "BNP Paribas Agrees to Plead Guilty and to Pay $8.9 Billion for Illegally Processing Financial Transactions for Countries Subject to U.S. Economic Sanctions." Accessed April 20, 2020. https://www.justice.gov/opa/pr/bnp-paribas-agrees-plead -guilty-and-pay-89-billion-illegally-processing-financial.

U.S. Department of State. "CAATSA/CRIEEA Section 232 Public Guidance." Accessed July 28, 2020. https://www.state.gov/caatsa-crieea-section-232-public-guidance.

U.S. Department of State. "Iran's Sanctions Relief Scam." Accessed January 6, 2021. https:// www.state.gov/irans-sanctions-relief-scam.

U.S. Department of State. "Section 231 of the Countering America's Adversaries Through Sanctions Act of 2017: Public Guidance/Frequently Asked Questions." Accessed March 27, 2021. https://www.state.gov/countering-americas-adversaries-through-sanctions-act/public -guidance-frequently-asked-questions.

U.S. Government Accountability Office. "Economic Sanctions: Agencies Assess Impacts on Targets, and Studies Suggest Several Factors Contribute to Sanctions' Effectiveness." October 2019. https://www.gao.gov/assets/710/701891.pdf.

U.S. Government Accountability Office. "Economic Sanctions: Treasury and State Have Received Increased Resources for Sanctions Implementation but Face Hiring Challenges." Accessed May 10, 2020. https://www.gao.gov/assets/710/701891.pdf.

U.S. Office of the National Counterintelligence Executive. "Foreign Spies Stealing US Economic Secrets in Cyberspace, Report to Congress on Foreign Economic Collection and Industrial Espionage, 2009–2011." October 2011. https://www.dni.gov/files/documents /Newsroom/Reports%20and%20Pubs/20111103_report_fecie.pdf.

U.S. Trade Representative. "Findings of the Investigation into China's Acts, Policies, and Practices Related to Technology Transfer, Intellectual Property, and Innovation Under Section 301 of the Trade Act of 1974." March 22, 2018. https://ustr.gov/sites/default/files/Section%20301%20 FINAL.PDF.

U.S. Treasury. "Announcement of Additional Treasury Sanctions on Russian Financial Institutions and on a Defense Technology Entity." July 29, 2014. https://www.treasury.gov /press-center/press-releases/pages/jl2590.aspx.

U.S. Treasury. "Civil Penalties and Enforcement Information." Accessed May 7, 2020. https:// www.treasury.gov/resource-center/sanctions/CivPen/Pages/civpen-index2.aspx.

U.S. Treasury. "Countering America's Adversaries Through Sanctions Act." Accessed April 26, 2020. https://www.treasury.gov/resource-center/sanctions/Programs/Pages/caatsa .aspx.

U.S. Treasury. "Fact Sheet: Designation of Iranian Entities and Individuals for Proliferation Activities and Support for Terrorism." October 25, 2007. https://www.treasury.gov /press-center/press-releases/Pages/hp644.aspx.

U.S. Treasury. "Finding That Banco Delta Asia SARL Is a Financial Institution of Primary Money Laundering Concern; Notice Financial Crimes Enforcement Network; Amendment to the Bank Secrecy Act Regulations—Imposition of Special Measure Against Banco Delta Asia SARL; Proposed Rule." September 20, 2005. https://www.fincen.gov/sites/default /files/shared/finding_banco.pdf.

U.S. Treasury. "Iran-Related Designations and Updates; Counter Terrorism Designations and Updates; Administrative Removals from Executive Order 13599 List." Accessed May 10, 2020. https://www.treasury.gov/resource-center/sanctions/OFAC-Enforcement/Pages/20181016 .aspx.

U.S. Treasury. "Issuance of Executive Order 'Blocking Property with Respect to the Situation in Burma,' Burma-Related Designations and Designations Updates." February 11, 2021. https://home.treasury.gov/policy-issues/financial-sanctions/recent-actions/20210211.

U.S. Treasury. "Treasury Cuts Iran's Bank Saderat Off from U.S. Financial System." September 8, 2006. https://www.treasury.gov/press-center/press-releases/Pages/hp87.aspx.

U.S. Treasury. "Treasury Designates Russian Oligarchs, Officials, and Entities in Response to Worldwide Malign Activity." April 6, 2018. https://home.treasury.gov/news/press-releases /sm0338.

U.S. Treasury. "Treasury Targets Additional Russian Oil Brokerage Firm for Continued Support of Maduro Regime." March 12, 2020. https://home.treasury.gov/news/press-releases/sm937.

U.S. Treasury. "Treasury Sanctions Russian Officials, Members of the Russian Leadership's Inner Circle, and an Entity for Involvement in the Situation in Ukraine." March 20, 2014. https://www.treasury.gov/press-center/press-releases/Pages/jl23331.aspx.

U.S. Treasury. "Treasury Targets Sanctions Evasion Network Supporting Corrupt Venezuelan Actors." June 18, 2020. https://home.treasury.gov/news/press-releases/sm1038.

Varas, Antonio, and Raj Varadarajan. "How Restrictions to Trade with China Could End US Leadership in Semiconductors." Boston Consulting Group. March 2020. https://image-src .bcg.com/Images/BCG-How-Restricting-Trade-with-China-Could-End-US-Semiconductor -Mar-2020_tcm9-240526.pdf.

Vogel, Kenneth. "Lewandowski's Firm Quietly Inked Deal with Venezuela-Owned Company." Politico, March 5, 2017. https://www.politico.com/story/2017/05/03/corey-lewandowski-citgo-deal-237960.

Wadhams, Nick, and Saleha Mohsin. "Trump Set Record Sanctions Use That Biden Is Likely to Keep." Bloomberg, December 10, 2020. https://www.bloombergquint.com/business/trump-set-record-sanctions-use-that-biden-is-likely-to-maintain.

Weaver, Courtney, Katrina Manson, and Max Seddon. "Trump and Putin: Inside the Muddled American Policy on Russia." Financial Times, July 10, 2018. https://www.ft.com/content/31bccode-8102-11e8-bc55-50daf11b720d.

Webb, Alex. "The $150 Million Machine with $200 Billion at Stake for China." Bloomberg, January 16, 2020. https://www.bloomberg.com/opinion/articles/2020-01-16/dutch-ban-raises-stakes-in-u-s-china-technology-war.

Weintraub, Richard. "President Lifts Sanctions on Soviet Pipeline." Washington Post, November 14, 1982. https://www.washingtonpost.com/archive/politics/1982/11/14/president-lifts-sanctions-on-soviet-pipeline/f04df97a-bbb9-4ef6-acae-4484effd0282.

Whalen, Jeanne. "Huawei Helped Bring Internet to Small-Town America. Now Its Equipment Has to Go." Washington Post, October 10, 2019. https://www.washingtonpost.com/business/2019/10/10/huawei-helped-bring-internet-small-town-america-now-its-equipment-has-go.

Whang, Taehee. "Playing to the Home Crowd? Symbolic Use of Economic Sanctions in the United States." International Studies Quarterly 55, no. 3 (2011): 787–801. https://doi.org/10.1111/j.1468-2478.2011.00668.x.

White, Sarah. "Head of France's Total Urged Trump to Stick with Iran Nuclear Deal: FT." Reuters, February 12, 2018. https://www.reuters.com/article/us-total-iran-trump/head-of-frances-total-urged-trump-to-stick-with-iran-nuclear-deal-ft-idUSKBN1FW0NL.

Wieder, Thomas. "En Allemagne, la peur d'un abandon du gazoduc Nord Stream 2." Le Monde, January 28, 2021. https://www.lemonde.fr/international/article/2021/01/28/en-allemagne-la-peur-d-un-abandon-de-nord-stream-2_6067944_3210.html.

Williams, Aime. "US Congress Passes $738bn Defence Spending Bill." Financial Times, December 17, 2019. https://www.ft.com/content/d144c6ec-20e8-11ea-b8a1-584213ee7b2b.

Windsor, Duane. "Alien Tort Claims Act." Encyclopaedia Britannica. Accessed April 9, 2022. https://www.britannica.com/topic/Alien-Tort-Claims-Act.

Wolfe, Lauren. "How Dodd-Frank Is Failing Congo." Foreign Policy, February 2, 2015. https://foreignpolicy.com/2015/02/02/how-dodd-frank-is-failing-congo-mining-conflict-minerals.

World Bank. "Poverty and Equity Brief: India." October 2020. https://databank.worldbank.org/data/download/poverty/987B9C90-CB9F-4D93-AE8C-750588BF00QA/AM2020/Global_POVEQ_IND.pdf.

Xinhua. "Feature: Huawei Auxiliary Systems Help Detect COVID-19 in Ecuador." April 30, 2020. www.xinhuanet.com/english/2020-04/30/c_139020269.htm.

Yaffa, Joshua. "Putin's Shadow Cabinet and the Bridge to Crimea." New Yorker, May 29, 2017. https://www.newyorker.com/magazine/2017/05/29/putins-shadow-cabinet-and-the-bridge-to-crimea.

Yahoo News. "Edited Transcript of ASML.AS Earnings Conference Call or Presentation 14-Oct-20 1:00pm GMT." October 14, 2020. https://www.yahoo.com/amphtml/now/edited-transcript-asml-earnings-conference-130000661.html.

Yang, Zeyi. "Chinese Companies Are Making Their Own Semiconductors." Protocol. March 13, 2021. https://www.protocol.com/china/chinese-companies-make-own-semiconductors.

Yu, Sun, and Demetri Sevastopulo. "China Targets Rare Earth Export Curbs to Hobble US Defence Industry." *Financial Times*, February 16, 2021. https://www.ft.com/content/d3ed83f4-19bc-4d16-b510-415749c032c1.

Yue, Yue, Wang Liwei, and Han Wei. "Four Things to Know About the State's Role in China's Private Investment Market." Caixin Global. October 14, 2020. https://www.caixinglobal.com/2020-10-14/four-things-to-know-about-the-states-role-in-chinas-private-investment-market-101614377.html.

Yukhananov, Anna, and Warren Strobel. "After Success on Iran, U.S. Treasury's Sanctions Team Faces New Challenges." Reuters, April 15, 2014. https://www.reuters.com/article/us-usa-sanctions-insight/after-success-on-iran-u-s-treasurys-sanctions-team-faces-new-challenges-idUSBREA3D1O820140415.

Zaidi, Sarah, and Mary Smith Fawzi. "Health of Baghdad's Children." *Lancet* 346, no. 8988 (1995): 1485. https://doi.org/10.1016/s0140-6736(95)92499-x.

Zarate, Juan. *Treasury's War*. New York: Public Affairs, 2013.

Zeimetz, Kathryn. "USSR Agricultural Trade, August 1991." *Statistical Bulletin* 808 (August 1991): 13–19. https://ageconsearch.umn.edu/record/154704/files/sb808.pdf.

Zhou, Cissy. "China's Digital Currency Edges Closer with Large-Scale Test by Four State-Owned Banks." *South China Morning Post*, August 6, 2020. https://www.scmp.com/economy/china-economy/article/3096296/chinas-digital-currency-edges-closer-large-scale-test-four.

Zulauf, Carl, Jonathan Coppess, Nick Paulson, and Gary Schnitkey. "U.S. Corn, Soybean, Wheat Exports and USSR Grain Embargo: Contemporary Implications." *farmdoc daily* 8, no. 129 (July 2018). https://farmdocdaily.illinois.edu/2018/07/us-corn-soybean-wheat-exports-and-ussr-grain-embargo-contemporary-implications.html.

INDEX

Specially Designated Nationals (SDN). *See*
Office of Foreign Assets Control, and
Specially Designated Nationals
standards. *See* technical standards
State Department, 38; and Iran, 58–59,
79; and Nord Stream 2, 107, 110, 115;
political appointees at, 98–99; staff
shortages at, 41
Sudan, ix–x, 63
supply chains, 152–53, 167, 172
Suzuki, Zenko, 100
swap. *See* bilateral currency swap
Swift, 129–32, 136, 139–40, 146; and Iran,
18–20; and Russia, 26–27, 130
Swiss channel, 59–60, 63

Taiwan, 161, 166–67, 170, 188, 192, 194–96
targeters, 12–13, 15
tariff. *See* trade tariff
technical standards, 26, 178, 183–86,
188, 193
Tehran hostage crisis (1979), 17
Thatcher, Margaret, 104, 106
Thomson CSF, 101
Tillerson, Rex, 83
Total, 24, 75–82
trade embargo, 5, 17, 46–47, 54; and Cuba,
7–8, 70–71, 76, 86; and North Korea,
9–12
trade tariff, 90, 95–96, 162–63
Trump, Donald: and China, 158, 162, 169–70;
and decoupling, 177; election of, 78–79;
and Iran, 40, 75, 79–82, 133; sanctions
designations from, 4; and Venezuela,
28, 49
TSMC, 167, 170, 172
Turkey, x, 17, 73–74, 127, 139; sanctions on, 39,
41–42, 73–74

Ukraine, 22–27, 107, 116–17, 124, 133–34,
197–99
UN. *See* United Nations
Unified Payments Interface (UPI), 131
United Kingdom, 5, 45, 81, 104–106,
136, 150

United Nations (UN): and Cuba, 7; and
Iran, 58; and Iraq, 53; and Libya, 36–37;
and North Korea, 9–12; sanctions from,
3, 42–43, 199–200; Security Council of
(UNSC), 22, 43, 163
United Nations Security Council (UNSC).
See United Nations, Security Council of
UNSC. *See* United Nations, Security
Council of
UPI. *See* Unified Payments Interface
U.S.-China: and conflict, 153, 159, 162–64,
173–75, 186, 194–98; and decoupling,
175, 177–83, 186, 192–96; and ties,
169, 179
U.S. dollar, 70–71, 125; and global
dominance, 124–29, 136–39, 140–43,
146, 149–57; as global reserve currency
152–153
U.S. economy, 18, 71, 150–51, 161, 179, 190
USSR. *See* Soviet Union
U.S. Treasury, 38, 149; and banks, 126; bonds
of, 149; and Iran, 18–19, 59–60, 63, 79;
and Russia, 26, 84, 87–88, 93–94, 97;
and Venezuela, 33, 83. *See also* Office of
Foreign Assets Control

Venezuela, 27–34, 45, 48–49, 54, 83, 145
von Siemens, Werner, 183
VTB, 25, 96, 130

waiver, 48, 58, 74, 83–84, 86, 134
WAPI, 184–85
WHO. *See* World Health Organization
WiFi, 184–85
Wilson, Woodrow, 37
World Health Organization (WHO), 56, 58
World Trade Organization (WTO), 71,
76–77, 162
WTO. *See* World Trade Organization

Xiaoping, Deng, 173
Xinjiang, 162

Yangtze Memory Technologies, 191–92
Yuk-Tung, 10–11